MA   MAY 1985

Washington County Library
WITHDRAWN
Minnesota

The New York Times
GUIDE TO BUYING OR BUILDING A HOME

The New York Times
GUIDE TO BUYING OR BUILDING A HOME

WILLIAM G. CONNOLLY

Times BOOKS

8504621

Published by TIMES BOOKS
The New York Times Book Co., Inc.
130 Fifth Avenue, New York, N.Y. 10011

Published simultaneously in Canada by
Fitzhenry & Whiteside, Ltd., Toronto

Copyright © 1978, 1984 by William G. Connolly

All rights reserved. No part of this book may
be reproduced in any form or by any electronic
or mechanical means including information storage
and retrieval systems without permission in writing
from the publisher, except by a reviewer who may
quote brief passages in a review.

Library of Congress Cataloging in Publication Data

Connolly, William G.
The New York Times guide to buying or building a home.

Includes index.
1. House buying. 2. House construction. 3. Real estate business. I. New York Times. II. Title.
HD1379.C58   1984   643'.12   84-40111
ISBN 0-8129-1119-9

Manufactured in the United States of America

84 85 86 87 88   5 4 3 2 1

To Clair, Bill, Kathy, and Hal,
who lived through it all — and patiently

Contents

INTRODUCTION	xiii
PART ONE: MAKING THE DECISION	1
1. Should you own a house or apartment?	3
Financial advantages of ownership	4
Other advantages of ownership	6
Disadvantages of ownership	6
2. How soon must you decide whether to take the plunge?	9
Meeting a deadline	10
The best times to look	10
3. How much can you afford to spend?	13
Rules of thumb	13
The monthly payments	15
The down payment	16
The mortgage	18
PART TWO: BUILDING OR FINDING THE RIGHT PLACE	23
4. How should you own a home?	25
Fee-simple homes	25
Homeowners' associations	26
Condominiums	26
Cooperatives	28

5. What type of home should you own? 30
    Detached houses 30
    Attached houses 31
    Apartments 31
    Mobile homes 32
    New towns and PUD's 32

6. How much home do you need? 35
    Setting your priorities 35

7. What style and design do you want? 38
    One-story houses and apartments 38
    One-and-a-half-story houses 39
    Two-story and three-story houses and apartments 40
    Split-level houses 41
    Split-entry houses 41

8. What area should it be in? 43
    Commuting 43
    Your living habits 44
    Taxes in general 44
    Social chic 45
    The future 45

9. Within the area you've chosen, what towns or sections should you look in? 48
    The school district 49
    Medical services 50
    Local government 51
    Local taxes 52
    Narrowing the search 54

10. Which neighborhood should you choose? 55
    The environment 55
    Convenience 56
    The local school 56
    Public services 56
    The neighbors 57
    The future 57

CONTENTS

11.	**Should you buy a new home or an old one?**	59
	New homes	59
	Older homes	60
	Antique homes	60
	Rundown homes	61
	New and old apartments	63
12.	**If it's new, should it be custom-built or a developer's home?**	64
	The custom home	64
	The development home	66
	The speculative home	68
	Industrialized building	68
13.	**If you decide on a new custom house, how do you find the land?**	73
	Growth restrictions	73
	Environmental restrictions	74
	Financial advice	75
	Technical advice	77
	Looking at the land	77
14.	**How should you get a custom home designed?**	79
	Stock plans	80
	Architects and designers	81
	Dealing with an architect	83
15.	**How should you find the right contractor to build your home?**	87
	Getting advice	87
	Interviewing the candidates	90
16.	**How should you deal with the contractor?**	92
	What the contractor expects	92
	Negotiating the agreement	93
	The contract	95
	Supervising construction	97
	Settling disputes	98
	Special arrangements	99

CONTENTS

17. **If it's a new development home, how do you find it?** 101
    - Advertising — 101
    - Brokers — 103
    - Visiting model homes — 103
    - Choosing the lot — 105
    - Dealing with the salesmen — 107
    - Inspecting the home site — 108
    - Checking on the developer — 109

18. **If it's an older home, how do you find it?** 112
    - The broker — 112
    - Dealing with a broker — 115
    - Other sources — 116
    - Taking a tour — 118

19. **How do you tell whether the place is worth considering?** 119
    - The neighborhood — 119
    - The exterior — 120
    - The interior — 120
    - Economic considerations — 121
    - Narrowing the choices — 122

20. **How do you inspect a home, new or old?** 123
    - Preparing for the chore — 124
    - Getting started — 125
    - The exterior — 126
    - The basement or crawl space — 131
    - The living areas — 138
    - The attic — 144

21. **How should you evaluate what you've seen?** 148
    - Questions for the seller — 148
    - What the plans say — 149
    - Matters of opinion — 152

22. **How do you estimate what it will cost you to keep the place?** 156
    - Insurance — 157
    - Commuting costs — 161
    - Other extra costs — 162
    - Income taxes — 163

PART THREE: CLOSING THE DEAL — 167

23. What professional help do you need? — 169
- The lawyer — 169
- The accountant — 173
- The engineer — 174
- Other experts — 178

24. How should you handle the preliminary negotiations? — 181
- The basic rules — 182
- Haggling over price — 183
- Stand-in negotiators — 184
- The pressure to sign — 185
- Making an offer — 187
- The binder — 190

25. How should you negotiate the contract? — 196
- What you're buying — 197
- What you'll pay and how — 203
- When you'll get it — 205
- How you can back out — 206
- Contracts for land — 209
- Contracts with developers — 210
- Legal niceties — 213
- How to take title — 214

26. How should you finance it? — 217
- The advantages of financing — 217
- Sources of mortgages — 218
- Purchase-money mortgages and assumptions — 221
- The company and the government — 224
- The VA and FHA — 226
- Conventional mortgages — 230
- Varieties of mortgages — 231
- Second mortgages — 236
- Construction financing — 237
- Package mortgages — 239
- Land contracts and trust deeds — 239
- Mortgage shopping — 241
- Twisting the bank's arm — 247
- Comparing the offers — 248
- Applying for a loan — 249

27. How should you prepare for the closing and what
   happens there? 251
   Closing costs 252
   Title insurance 254
   Getting ready 255
   The meeting 256

PART FOUR: SPECIAL KINDS OF HOMES 259

28. What should you look for in a condominium or
   co-op? 261
   Inspecting the place 263
   Condominium documents 270
   Cooperative documents 275

29. What should you look for in a mobile home? 279
   Finding a parking place 282
   Finding a dealer 285
   Finding a home 286
   Negotiating the purchase 287
   Financing 290
   The title 291
   Moving your home 292

INDEX 293

Introduction

The purpose of this book is to tell you all you need to know to buy shelter — anything from a cooperative studio apartment to a 27-acre estate with a heated swimming pool and six outbuildings. The estate buyers will find all of this less useful than will the folks interested in studio apartments or the families in search of three bedrooms with a bath and a half, but that's fair enough; there are plenty of professionals more than ready to help anyone who has $250,000 in loose change to sink into a little real estate. It's the rest of us who really have a problem when we set out to buy something that'll keep the wind and the rain at bay.

While you will undoubtedly find between these covers more than you need to know, the theory underlying this book is that you can find what you require and skip the rest. Now, this approach may produce a bit of repetition here and there, but the repetition of sound advice hasn't hurt anyone yet.

This book tries to assume nothing on the reader's part beyond a neophyte's interest in the subject, basic intelligence, and a modicum of common sense. Because it represents an attempt to tell you "everything," it has assumed the point of view of the first-time home or apartment buyer who is starting from scratch — who is looking for a home or apartment in a large, complex, unfamiliar metropolitan area. It assumes that the buyer is looking in a place like the New York metropolitan area, where he may choose a home in any of three states, perhaps 22 counties, and literally hundreds of cities, towns, villages, boroughs, and hamlets beyond the city itself. It assumes that the buyer is not sure at the outset what sort of home or apartment he really wants and that he knows virtually nothing about the conventions of the real estate industry or about such exotic matters as deeds, financing, sewage, and taxation.

This book attempts to explain everything such a buyer would have to know to find and purchase — or to have built — a house or apartment that reflects his fondest dreams.

Perhaps the first thing such a buyer should know is that he will sooner or later need professional advice, the advice of a lawyer, broker, architect, engineer, appraiser, or some other specialist. This book does not attempt to replace such professionals. Any book must deal with more-or-less typical situations if it is not to become a 25-volume study in boredom. Moreover, typical guidelines don't always apply to particular transactions. The lawyer, broker, architect, or other professional you retain will know the customs and regulations in your locale as well as the peculiarities of your transaction. The most this book can hope to do is demonstrate what sort of professional you should consult and how to question him efficiently and intelligently.

Neither the professionals nor this book will attempt to make decisions for you. The book can only point out the decisions that have to be made, the order in which they have to be made (more or less), the major factors that have to be considered in making them, and the biggest pitfalls that lie ahead. The professionals will do pretty much the same thing, but more specifically. It will ultimately be up to you to weigh the advantages and disadvantages and make the final decision. There will always be risks. But since you will be the one assuming those risks, you must be the one to decide whether they're worth it. It's your money and your life.

This book will not attempt to deal in detail with such special situations as vacation homes or adult communities, though the process it describes can be applied to them, too, with a bit of thought and good judgment.

The book will not attempt to tell you, once you've bought a home or apartment, how to maintain, repair, or remodel it. There are plenty of do-it-yourself handbooks and a great many lumber and hardware merchants — not to mention all-knowing neighbors — who will be happy to shoulder that burden.

What this book will attempt to do is present something of use to the sophisticated shopper as well as the neophyte. In theory, at least, even a mortgage broker with degrees in architecture and law can find something of value here — some pointers on how to examine a house or apartment, a logical method for narrowing the choice to a few potential purchases, a way to decide whether a neighborhood is the right one.

Perhaps the core of this book is a logical system for narrowing the choices from thousands to a manageable few. It is logical enough, but it is hardly the only way to find a home, and it is offered with the caution that no reasonable shopper would follow it slavishly. The young couple who vow to take every precaution suggested here, to check every facet of every decision, may ultimately find themselves wondering whether to buy a home or cemetery plots. There is no perfect home, even if you design it and build it yourself without regard to cost.

Another thing this book does is define a few terms with no thought for anything but literary convenience. It assumes, for instance, that "he" and "him" signify humankind, not men to the exclusion of women. There are probably more female than male real estate agents, and — all things considered — the females may well be better at that business than their male counterparts. There are increasing numbers of female lawyers, engineers, and architects, and there's no reason to believe that they are any less competent than males in the same professions. There are also increasing numbers of female buyers and sellers of homes. This book will not assume that every buyer or seller is necessarily married and a parent, but for reasons of brevity, not sexual chauvinism, everybody will be known as "he" or "him."

For equally arbitrary reasons, the term "home" will encompass all sorts of human shelter from lean-to to palace, though the extreme examples will be eliminated here in favor of a broad middle ground that includes mobile homes, apartments that are owned rather than rented, and attached and detached houses. From here on, they're all "homes," even if they don't have quarter-acre lots and white picket fences.

Given all those caveats, what will you have learned when you finish this book that you didn't know before you plunked down good money for it? Well, you'll know where you stand in relation to a lot of people with whom you may not be accustomed to dealing. You'll know just how treacherous is the area into which you're thinking of venturing. And if you've been attentive and perceptive, you'll know that the wise home buyer is neither fanatic nor slipshod — that he will be careful but reasonable, willing to forego absolute certainty in the knowledge that it is unattainable, but intent upon understanding the risks he faces in what is, after all, a rather basic process: deciding where, and therefore how, he will live.

When you boil it all down, there are really only three maxims for the potential homeowner:

- The law of averages is with you; most homes turn out to be good investments
- Nothing is forever; you can almost always sell the place.
- Whatever happens, maintain your sense of humor; it's only money, right?

PART ONE
Making the Decision

1
Should You Own a House or Apartment?

The first things to remember in buying a home are these: Everything you do will affect everything else you do — buying a home is not a purely financial decision; and there is no "free lunch" — everything you get costs something.

Let's say you're single and you like the social life of the city and the 10-minute commute to work, but you're sick of throwing rent money away every month. From a purely economic point of view, you should no doubt buy a home. But your point of view cannot be purely economic. There are social considerations, too; you can get pretty lonely out there in suburbia. Despite what you may read, suburbia has its high side, but it is still not Nirvana for the unattached. And, whatever the rest of the world says, social values can outweigh financial ones.

Suppose you're married and have young children. One more reason to buy your own home — you can fix up a nursery or have a family room; there will probably be space for backyard play; the kids can ride bikes on the streets or wander off to visit friends without your becoming a nervous wreck. You should buy a home, right? Well, maybe — but not if the longer commute will drive you to drink and have you snarling at the kids every night. Not if you have so little cash for a down payment that the place will be unfurnished for seven or eight years. Not if the payments on this home will mean that you can't pay the rent for your aged and dependent parents.

You can't, in other words, make these decisions in a vacuum. And there's no free lunch — everything you get costs something, whether you're buying a studio apartment or a mansion. If you don't pay in money, then you'll pay in space, convenience, aesthetics, social appeal, or something else. Homes tend to be cheaper in towns that have inferior schools because most home buyers want good schools. Homes are more expensive in towns that have low tax rates because everybody wants low taxes. Co-op apartments seem outrageously expensive when the monthly carrying charges are low, and alarmingly cheap when the carrying charges are astronomical, which they often are. Old houses mean fine craftsmanship, high ceilings, large rooms — lots of charm. But they may also mean inadequate insulation, dangerous wiring, and no air conditioning. New houses mean central air, more insulation, and a built-in dishwasher as well as air conditioning — lots of convenience. But they may also mean low ceilings, small rooms, and shoddy workmanship.

Moreover, new houses tend to be in one kind of neighborhood and old houses in another. Cooperative and condominium apartments are generally found in still another kind of neighborhood. And the kind of neighborhood you live in will affect the way you live — the kinds of friends you make, and the kinds of friends your children make. There's no free lunch. In fact, there's not even a free breakfast.

FINANCIAL ADVANTAGES OF OWNERSHIP

But given all these reasons to be wary, buying a home is still, traditionally, a sound investment, perhaps the best one available to an average citizen who can't afford to hire investment counselors and accountants.

Homes have almost always appreciated in recent times, though there is no assurance that they will do so. Soaring interest rates can depress the value of all real estate. There are thousands of inner-city homeowners whose property values went sour when their neighborhoods began to decline. There are others whose homes were reduced in value when highways were built nearby or sewage plants appeared next door. A home is an investment, and, like any investment, it involves an element of risk.

But unexpected highway construction is relatively rare, there are only so many sewage plants, and most neighborhoods are stable. So the average American homeowner has done quite well, thank you. A significant part of his financial good fortune has resulted from his ability to use "leverage," a device much admired by astute money men but rarely available to the average Joe except through the purchase of a home. In the financial context, leverage is the effective use of money, the ability to maximize the return on an investment. It's available to the home purchaser because he usually puts in relatively little of his own money — the down payment — and relies on other people's money — the mortgage loan — to make up the difference. The buyer may put down only 10 percent of the purchase price, while the lender — a savings and loan association, bank, or insurance company — supplies the rest.

To begin with, the buyer pays the lender over a long term with dollars that, because of inflation, grow steadily less valuable than the dollars he borrowed. In the meantime, the property is probably growing more valuable, and in the traditional form of mortgage, all of the increase in value belongs to the owner, not the lender; at the outset, there is a ceiling on the lender's share of ownership. And each monthly payment on the mortgage usually reduces the lender's share a bit. The buyer's share of ownership — his equity — increases with every monthly payment. In that sense, home ownership is a form of enforced savings. Part of every monthly payment remains your own; it doesn't disappear into a landlord's pocket.

Moreover, federal tax laws have traditionally provided some extra advantages for those who own their homes. A large part of the monthly payment — the interest and the real estate taxes — is deductible from federal income taxes. That can reduce your effective monthly payment substantially, and it is an advantage not available to the renter, whose payments to cover the landlord's interest and tax bills have not traditionally been deductible.

Other tax breaks are available when the home is sold. The profit realized on the sale is taxed as a capital gain rather than as ordinary income, and tax rates are sharply lower on capital gains. The capital gain can be reduced if permanent improvements have been made in the home while you owned it, even though you enjoyed the improvements while you lived there, and they will probably add to the value of the home, which means you'll be able to recover at least some of their cost when you sell. There are even more tax breaks if you work at home or have to maintain an office there, or if you rent out part of the place. And the whole ball of wax — all the capital gains taxes — can be deferred under some circumstances.

There is one more financial advantage to ownership: The owner's housing costs are less likely to rise over the years than the renter's, though they will probably be higher initially. That's because the landlord usually makes a two-year or three-year agreement with the tenant (the lease), and rents usually rise when a new agreement is made. The lender, on the other hand, usually makes a 20-year or 30-year agreement with the buyer (the mortgage), and there is a limit on increases in principal and interest payments during that term. The lender is, in that sense, stuck with the buyer once a mortgage is made. Of course, there is no restriction on the degree to which the other costs of ownership — taxes and maintenance, for instance — can rise. But one big factor in the owner's monthly housing costs is under some control.

The widespread adoption of some relatively new-fangled types of mortgage in which the monthly payment rises over time or the interest rate fluctuates with the financial market has eroded that advantage. So has the spread of "balloon" rather than self-liquidating mortgages. A balloon mortgage doesn't pay itself off. At the end of the term — after five or ten or twenty years — some of the principal remains, and what remains comes due in one big payment. The payment is usually so big that it requires another, smaller mortgage. Theoretically, that process can go on forever. In the past, such mortgages were most common in cooperatives, and co-op owners who have been on the scene when the mortgage had to be renewed can tell you some ulcer-producing stories about what happened to their monthly carrying charges.

OTHER ADVANTAGES OF OWNERSHIP

In addition to the financial advantages of ownership, there are some advantages in comfort and efficiency. The owner usually enjoys better housing than the renter — more living space and storage space, more labor-saving conveniences, better insulation and sound-proofing, perhaps a garage, a yard, and privacy. It is the conventional wisdom in the building business that in multiple-family housing built for sale — cooperative and condominium apartments — a unit must be more spacious and luxurious than a unit built to rent, even if the potential renters and buyers are the same group. People will, in other words, rent a place that they wouldn't buy. If the builders accept that principle, it must be reflected in the housing they build. Beyond the housing itself, the areas devoted primarily to privately owned homes are usually less congested, noisy, dirty, and crime-ridden than areas devoted to rental housing — even very expensive rental housing. In part, this is a reflection of the tradition that privately owned homes are single-family detached dwellings on quarter-acre lots. But it is also a reflection of the builders' conviction that ownership housing, if it is to sell, must be more attractive. And it is a reflection as well of the strength of the owner's ties to the community in which he lives.

The owner is much more likely than the renter to put down roots where he lives, to consider himself a permanent resident with an interest in the affairs of the community. That tends to influence the way he maintains his property, the way he treats his neighbors, and what he will allow City Hall or some other outside force to do to his neighborhood. Owners tend to be more stable people, in the broadest sense, if for no other reason than that a 30-year mortgage produces a certain degree of stability. Life necessarily becomes more ordered and predictable, more in your own control, when you own your home.

One way in which the owner is in greater control of his life can be seen in the degree to which he can alter his environment to suit his own tastes and inclinations. He can, for instance, turn the fourth bedroom into an office, build bookcases in the living room, or install a lavish bar in the family room. Such things can be done by renters, too, of course, but only with the terrible suspicion that all of it may have to be ripped out when the lease expires. Despite what you've heard about suburban neighbors, the owner is better able than the renter to live exactly as he pleases (in most neighborhoods, provided he pays his bills). This may be another factor that contributes to the stability and permanence of owners.

DISADVANTAGES OF OWNERSHIP

But ownership is not just one pleasure heaped upon another, especially for those to whom stability and permanence are not particularly attractive. If you're an owner rather than a renter, you can't break a lease or buy your way out of a lease when someone offers you a better job a thousand miles away. You've got to keep the thing — and pay the taxes and maintenance costs on it — until you can sell it. You are tied down, for being tied down is the other side of the coin called stability and permanence.

And being tied down isn't half of it. To start with, the owner has to make a down payment. That's a large chunk of money that can't be invested elsewhere in what might be more profitable ways. In recent years, few better investments have been available to average wage earners — but imagine how you'd feel if you had refused to back young Henry Ford with $500 because you needed the money for the down payment on a house. Somewhere there are better deals. If you can find them, you'll eventually be able to buy all the homes you want.

Moreover, while you live in the home you've bought, you'll have to make sure that it doesn't fall apart. There will be no "super" to fix or replace the things that inevitably break or wear out, no automatic repainting when a new lease is signed. When you own it, you are the landlord and the super. The owner has to perform himself or arrange to have someone else perform. He must either suffer the frustration of bent nails and smashed thumbs, not to mention the surliness that seems to breed in every lumberyard and plumbing-supply house, or suffer the frustration of dealing with unreliable and obscenely expensive tradesmen who always seem to be on vacation in Tahiti when the sink backs up or the roof springs a leak.

Let us agree instantly that not all mechanics and repairmen are unreliable and obscenely expensive. Most of them are honest, many of them are skillful in ways that would never occur to the rest of us, and some are as reliable as the phases of the moon. But you may own a home for quite a while before you meet a craftsman who has all those qualities. In the meantime, you are likely to learn a great deal.

Ownership also means that you pay directly, rather than as a hidden factor in the rent, not only for maintenance but also for fuel, electricity, and taxes. Paying directly is always harder psychologically, and fuel and electricity have been among the heaviest contributors to inflation in recent times. The tenant who cannot understand the hue and cry over increases in such costs will begin to understand very soon after he becomes an owner. Pain is a great teacher.

If you live in a large metropolitan area as a renter, becoming an owner will probably mean becoming a commuter as well. If you commute as a renter, you'll probably have to commute farther as an owner. Commuting is expensive, and not just in money. It consumes vast amounts of time and can do incredible psychological damage after a while; trains don't have bar cars for nothing. While the money may be less important in the long run than the time lost or the psychological wear and tear, money can nevertheless be a considerable factor. Commuting can, for example, mean an extra car (requiring extra license fees, insurance premiums, gas bills, repair charges, and parking costs) as well as a monthly railroad or bus ticket. Not to mention the bar bill.

And let's not forget the suburbia of Levittown legend. The legend doesn't really exist and probably never did, but it is nonetheless true that areas where ownership housing is more likely to be found — suburban areas, if you will, though many of them are technically in the city — tend to be more conservative and homogeneous than areas where renters are more likely to live — urban and downtown areas. There are some advantages to the suburban milieu, but there are disadvantages, too. If an all-night deli or tavern, neighbors who speak 11 languages, and restaurants that serve everything from terrapin soup to teriyaki are essential to your survival, be wary of buying a home, especially if you're not looking for a high-rise cooperative or condominium apartment. Such social niceties appeal to relatively fewer people than the A&P and McDonald's. Their operators therefore depend for survival upon a concentration of people to provide the customers they need. Concentration means congestion, and people trying to sell housing try to avoid areas of congestion.

In suburbia's defense, however, it must be said that the boondocks are not usually the bland middle-class places that legend has made them out to be. Migration from urban centers has been going on a long time now, and all sorts of people have made the trek. As time passes, that trend will probably become more pronounced. The courts, and to a lesser extent the legislatures, have been edging toward policies that would speed the process, so you can probably count on its continuing.

Finally, whether the home you're thinking about is suburban, urban, or otherwise, there is an intangible but nonetheless real psychological barrier to buying. The purchase represents a financial commitment that is no doubt larger than any investment the first-time buyer has ever made before. The mortgage represents a debt of thousands of dollars that will extend over decades — not a matter to be taken lightly.

But a mortgage is not just another credit-card balance. Look at it the way the professional real estate men do. To them, a debt is not so much an obligation as a tool — an opportunity to use money that happens to be borrowed to make much more money by investing it wisely. If the investment is a sound one and the loan is carefully negotiated, the whole transaction is simply good business. The lender is happy with the profit he makes on his interest, and the borrower is happy with the profit he earns from the investment made possible by the loan. Buying a home is making an investment. The object is not to get rich but to have the best obtainable housing, given financial reality, and with luck to make a bit of a profit in the long run. In that sense, the debt involved represents not a crushing burden but an opportunity to live better on someone else's money. If the lender makes a profit along the way, that will merely encourage him to extend the same opportunity to the next borrower who comes by. If your home appreciates, as it probably will if you've bought wisely, you'll make a profit, too.

2
How Soon Must You Decide Whether to Take the Plunge?

The simplest way to say when you should make up your mind is, "the sooner the better." It's really never too early. Anything you learn by idly driving around and looking at available houses or apartments will be useful later on, when you really get serious about buying or deciding not to buy. The more you know, the better equipped you will be to make that decision. A keen sense of the market will help you to negotiate a better deal. You'll know what the competition is, and you'll be better able to evaluate grand claims about schools, taxes, and other esoteric matters. You'll also feel a bit calmer and more confident, and that's no small advantage when you're embarking upon a venture so great.

So don't hesitate, as you think larger thoughts, to read the classified ads, visit the builders' models, and call a few real estate agents. As your tastes become more refined — as you narrow your choices of areas, towns, housing styles, and so forth — you can focus such efforts. There's little point, after all, in reading classified ads for areas in which you know you don't want to or can't afford to live. And it is always possible that in such idle wandering around you will stumble across just what you're looking for. If you find it sooner than you expected, there's no harm done. In fact, that's an advantage: You're in no hurry, and the seller probably is. He may be an owner who has committed himself to a new home for which he can't pay without selling the old one. He may be a builder for whom carrying costs — maintenance, taxes, and interest on the mortgage — are becoming a crushing burden. Whatever the reason, if the seller is in a hurry and the buyer is not, the buyer is in the driver's seat during the sale negotiations.

There are some factors that will tend to shorten your search time. One is a familiarity with the general area in which you're looking. A native who has at one time or another prowled every section of the city or town will not have to wait for answers to many of the questions that a reasonably cautious newcomer might be expected to ask. And more money is an advantage, too — as always. The more you have to spend, the easier your search is likely to be because you can reasonably afford to buy a greater proportion of all the homes available. (On the other hand, you'll have a devil of a time getting some real estate agents to show you homes that they consider to be beneath your means. You may also be more fussy than most — you probably ought to be, if you can afford it — and that may reduce the number of available homes that appeal to you. Suffice it to say that if money isn't your principal worry in this enterprise, you can count yourself among the lucky few.)

MEETING A DEADLINE

Many buyers will face a firm deadline — the starting date for a new job in a new city, perhaps, or the opening day of school in the new neighborhood. The best course for them is to start looking as far in advance as possible. For renters who merely want to find a suitable place with a minimum of trouble, the expiration date of the lease provides a handy target, though it is hardly inflexible.

A year is not an unreasonable time to spend looking for and buying a home in a large and complex area, though many people do it in much less time. A year before the expiration of your lease would be a good time to start the process. That doesn't mean, however, that if your lease has several years to run you should sprawl on the balcony twiddling your thumbs until the right moment arrives. If you discover a home you want at a price you like, and you're otherwise ready to move, you can find a way out of your lease. It may, for example, contain a clause that allows you to sublease the apartment. Even if it prohibits such goings-on, the landlord may be willing to excuse you from the balance of the lease. He may know that he can rent the place quickly for much more than you've been paying. And if the landlord won't excuse you, he may be willing to let you buy your way out of the lease by paying him a lump sum for its cancellation. Such an extra payment may be more than worthwhile if you've found exactly what you want at a good price. If you wait until the end of your lease, the increase in the price of the place may be far greater than the landlord's extra payment would have been.

THE BEST TIMES TO LOOK

All else being equal — which it rarely is — the seasons when it's easiest to find homes for sale are spring and early summer. That's partly because most sellers have children, and most of them want to be able to close a deal and move into a new home before fall, so the kids can start the new year in a new school. It can take several months to find a buyer and weeks or months more to arrange all the details and actually transfer the property. So spring, from the seller's point of view, is a good time to start. It's also a good time for the seller because he knows that his home and neighborhood will look best in the spring. The lawns will be fertilized and thriving (but crabgrass will not yet have appeared), and sunshine will be streaming in through all the windows. The weather will be mild enough so that the average potential buyer will not put the heating system to the ultimate test — turning it on to see if it works. He probably won't try the air conditioning, either, or look for storm windows. Moreover, the seller knows that spring will tempt all those apartment dwellers from downtown to spend a pleasant Sunday driving in "the country" just to see the flowers and trees. He knows that many people who set out merely to look at trees wind up buying them, with yards and houses attached.

For all of these reasons, it will probably be easier to find a home that suits you in the spring or early summer. But for precisely the same reasons, that's when its price is likely to be highest. Resale houses and apartments — those that have been lived in — usually go on the market at the highest price the seller thinks he can get. The longer the place remains unsold, the more pressure there is on the seller. And what can he do to stir up interest where there is none? Just one thing: cut the price. So if most homes go on the market in the spring, most will be at their highest prices in the spring. The ones that are available then at depressed prices are likely to have been available for some time, and it is likely — though hardly certain — that something is wrong. What is wrong may be nothing but the old price, or it may be some small detail that turns a lot of potential buyers off but doesn't bother you a bit. It may also have nothing to do with the home. A bitter divorce or a sudden death, for example, can cause an owner to put a home on the market at a price that is designed to move it quickly. Pure ignorance can have the same effect; maybe the seller simply doesn't realize what his home is worth. All of which is to say that such situations should be approached warily, but with common sense. It does not necessarily follow, by the way, that any home on the market in the fall or winter has festered there for months waiting to visit a terrible financial cancer upon the unwary buyer. Some perfectly good homes go on the market in the winter because people get transferred to new jobs, get divorced, retire, or die in the winter. And sometimes, they simply decide during the winter that they'd like to sell the old family homestead and move to a bigger, smaller, newer, older, or different home. Nothing wrong with that. Things happen. That's life.

In any case, value is a personal thing. If you're willing to pay $50,000 for a lean-to with a dirt floor — knowing what $50,000 will buy elsewhere — then that's what it's worth to you. It may not be worth so much to the neighbors or the bank's appraisers or the real estate mavin down on the corner, but if it's worth that to you, so be it. Even if you decide later that you made a mistake and paid too much, the chances are that a little patience on your part will be accompanied by enough inflation to justify your decision.

So when should you start looking for a home? Whatever the season and whatever the lifespan of your lease, when you're ready. Presuming, of course, that your finances can stand the assault.

3
How Much Can You Afford to Spend?

Perhaps the only sure thing about your finances is that they won't be sufficient to buy what you'd really like to have in the way of housing. That's a fact of life. It's been that way since the invention of the roof, and it will no doubt continue to be that way. All you can do is accept the fact and plunge ahead.

RULES OF THUMB

While finances are, like so many things, very personal matters that have to be decided on an individual basis, there are some rules of thumb that bankers and brokers (not to mention authors) have for years been fond of quoting to buyers. The rules are not graven in stone, but they are handy reference points.

The first rule is that the price of your home should not exceed two-and-a-half times your gross annual income. If you earn $30,000, by this measure, you can theoretically afford a $75,000 house or apartment. Because in past years the average owner's income has tended to rise faster than the monthly payments for the purchase and upkeep of a home, the use of this formula usually produced a few years of absolute penury at first, then a gradual easing of the burden. In times when interest rates are high, of course, or when inflation is rampant, the rule simply may not apply. Lenders have been known, for example, to consider deals involving three times gross income. And from the lender's point of view, your income may not be all it seems to be. Until recently, for instance, lenders were reluctant in many cases to consider fully the income of a working wife in calculating what a couple could afford. They are now required to mend their chauvinistic ways, considering all steady income of both spouses, including alimony and child support that are likely to be paid consistently, but a bit of caution may still be wise. As the lenders have been so quick to point out, an unforeseen pregnancy can play havoc with family income — and outgo. By the same token, lenders have been wary of giving full weight to such things as freelance income, bonuses, or overtime. That sort of income has a nasty way of evaporating without warning. You should probably share the lenders' suspicion of any income that seems assured but is not yet in hand. Next year's Christmas bonus or the promotion you know you're in line for may simply never materialize. If it doesn't, but you've already made a decision on the assumption that it will, you may be in real trouble. Before you take the big step, you should examine your own income and prospects realistically and give some thought to what the future may hold for your employer. A good job is of little value if it's with a company that's about to go under.

The second rule of thumb that has been bandied about in the real estate industry since your Uncle Irv was in short pants is that the monthly payments for principal and interest on the mortgage, taxes, and insurance should about equal your gross weekly income. A variation on this rule is that those payments should equal your gross annual income, divided by 60. If you earn $30,000, in other words, your payments should be about $575 under the first version of the formula and about $500 under the second. All of the cautions about conservatism in considering second income and expected income that apply to the first rule apply to the second one, too. But so does a certain flexibility borne of high interest rates and unbridled inflation. Lenders who traditionally wanted to limit monthly payments to about 25 percent of income are now often willing to consider purchases that will require a monthly outlay that totals 33 percent of income. Indeed the National Association of Realtors estimated in 1981 that the average buyer was forking over a rousing 35 to 40 percent of income to keep a roof over his head.

Nonetheless, conservatism, much maligned as bankers are for embracing it, may be the soundest principle to follow in making a decision on how much home you can afford. Conservatism — mellowed with a large measure of realism. It's probably wise not to exceed the rules of thumb by much. They were devised by lenders whose aim is to insure that their loans are repaid. But it's in your interest, too, to see that your mortgage loan is repaid; if it isn't, you'll lose your home. Since you have only so much for a down payment and must depend upon a mortgage for the rest, you will sooner or later — barring a very rich uncle or very generous in-laws — be at the mercy of the lenders. If they are reluctant to lend you the amount you want for the home you want, find out why. It may be that they simply don't have the money to lend (it happens) or that the financial markets are such that they can make much better investments than mortgages. But it also may be that the bank knows something you don't, either about the condition of your finances or about the value of the home you'd like to buy. The banks have been through this a million times, and their conservatism is not always bad. Honest.

On the other hand, Congress has not enacted the lenders' rules of thumb into law. These rules are guidelines, not mandates. If you have an unusually healthy savings account or extensive investments that can be turned into a down payment, if you have a rich and doting uncle or father-in-law, or if you have a big equity in a home you're going to sell before you buy the new one, you may be able to spend substantially more than the guidelines suggest. If you have aged parents to support or huge medical bills or 11 kids in college, perhaps you should spend less. And if you are young and poor but struggling, hopeful, and absolutely determined to own your own home at the cost of all else, perhaps you should do whatever you must. If you feel that strongly, it will probably have been worth the hardship.

In the final analysis, everyone allocates his resources differently. Single people have different spending patterns than married people. Parents have different spending patterns than childless couples. Men have different spending patterns than women. Some people, whatever their state in life, exist only for their homes, spending all available funds there. Others are fond of books or concerts, fast cars or expensive booze, flashy clothes or exotic vacations, loose women or loose men. How much you can spend for a home — given all your other interests — is a unique and personal decision. Only you can decide whether (or to what extent) you're a reader, a boozer, a dresser, or a homer.

THE MONTHLY PAYMENTS

To make your decision on how much you can spend, study your past expenses and figure out what you're willing to allocate to home owning and the obligations that come with it. Get out your old checkbooks and add up what shelter and location have cost you — everything you have spent in the last year that would cost more or less if you were to move. If you're a renter now, some of the obvious components of the total are these: rent; utilities; carfare or other commuting expense; extra parking expense, if any; laundry expenses if you can't have a washer and dryer in your apartment; taxes (sales and income), if they're higher in the urban, rental area than in most suburban, ownership areas; private-school tuition if the children would be able to attend a public school in suburbia; tips for doormen, maintenance men, and other service personnel at Christmastime; dues for the tenants' association, if any; and personal property and liability insurance premiums. There are no doubt other components that you'll find if you make an honest search.

While you're adding things up, remember that sending off a check every month for a mortgage payment and taxes will not be the end of your obligations as a homeowner. You'll have to pay for all of the utilities — heat, water, electricity, telephone, and perhaps even sewer service and trash collection. You'll have to pay for insurance on the property as well as on your furnishings and possessions, and you'll have to maintain the place — fix the roof when it leaks, replace the hot-water heater when it goes, fertilize the lawn every year. You will probably face higher commutation expenses, perhaps including an extra car and all the outlays that go with it. But also remember that this is an investment as well as the purchase of shelter; with any luck, the value of your property will grow while you own it. And there are those built-in tax breaks and the knowledge that, while your costs may be higher originally, they probably will not rise as fast as rents.

If you're already a homeowner, the list of ownership costs is a familiar litany, but you will still probably learn something if you tote up all your expenditures in the areas of ownership, maintenance, and commutation for the last year. It can come as a shock.

Once you've added up what you have been spending to live where you live, you're halfway to knowing what you can spend to live somewhere else. Take your average monthly total for the last year and add $10 to it. What would that do to your life? What would you have to give up? If that seems painless, add $20 or $50 or $100 a month. How many nights out with the boys or girls would you have to give up to provide $50 a month extra for housing? How many weekly hair-dos or ties that light up in the dark? What would happen to next year's vacation? To next year's Christmas presents? To dinners at posh restaurants or evenings at the theater? When the gradual additions to your housing costs really begin to hurt, back off a step or two and you have probably arrived at the place you want to be — the point where you can pay for the most home without doing things to the rest of your life that will make you regret you ever saw the thing. Be careful in all of this to preserve a cushion, a little bit left at the end of every month to cover unanticipated expenses (suppose the water heater goes during the first month you own it?) and to finance an occasional evening away from it all. The most lavish home in the world can turn into a prison if you can't afford to leave it.

THE DOWN PAYMENT

Now you've got an estimate of what you can shell out every month to stay out of the rain and get yourself to work in the morning. The next step is to figure out what kind of down payment you have. The size of your down payment will determine the size of the mortgage you'll need for a given house or apartment, and the size of the mortgage will be a major factor in the size of your monthly payments — so it all fits together. The size of your down payment will also influence a lender's reaction to your mortgage application. The bigger the down payment, relative to the price of the home, the safer the loan looks to the lender. If you don't keep paying, you have more to lose; the lender has less to lose. And the bigger your down payment, relative to your income, the more responsible and trustworthy you look to the lender. A

HOW MUCH CAN YOU AFFORD TO SPEND?   17

$30,000-a-year applicant with $40,000 in cash has probably been budgeting his money wisely. A good man to lend to.

On the other hand, a larger down payment means a larger equity, or share of ownership in the home, and the larger your equity the harder the home may be to sell if potential buyers are hard put to find mortgages. And it makes no sense to hold down the amount of the mortgage, which has a relatively low interest rate, then borrow extra money for a car, home improvements, new furniture, or the family's Christmas presents. All of those loans will probably bear higher interest rates than the mortgage, so if the whole project is going to require borrowing, the place to do it is on the mortgage. Whatever the amount of the mortgage, though, don't put your last reserves into the down payment; the price of the home will not be your only initial expense. There will be settlement or closing costs, moving expenses, and perhaps some redecorating. You may have to buy a good deal of furniture for a home that is bigger than the place you're leaving. If you've been an apartment dweller and are moving into a house, you may have to ante up for appliances, a lawn mower, a rake, trash cans, a hammer, and a screwdriver.

Bear in mind that if the place you decide upon is just right "except" that it needs new plumbing and wiring or an extra bedroom and bath, the cost of those improvements must be considered part of the cost of the home — and the cost of the improvements will include financing charges of some sort, in a larger mortgage or elsewhere.

How much you can afford to spend for a down payment and the other initial costs of buying a home often depends upon what you're willing to give up. Theoretically, you can turn everything you own into cash and use the cash as a down payment. Obviously, that's impractical, but you'll have to make a list of the things you are willing to turn into housing. For instance:

- Balances in checking and savings accounts and credit unions, and the cash you have stuffed in the mattress.
- The market value now (not when you bought them) of stocks, bonds, and other securities.
- Your equity in the home you live in now, if you own it.
- The value of any car, boat, airplane, motorcycle, velocipede, or other contraption that you would be willing to sell to swing a deal on a home.
- The value of your collections of art, jewelry, furs, stamps, coins, antiques, books, or Mickey Mouse watches, if you would be willing to sell them.

In every case, it's the value when you sell that counts, not what you have invested. And there's no point in kidding yourself. Don't imagine grand receipts that you won't realize. If, when the time comes, the stamp collection brings $50, not $500, you'll be $450 short of a down payment, and the last minute is no time to discover that. If you're planning to turn the stamp collection into a home, get an expert appraisal of it (or actually sell it and bank the money) before you commit yourself to a deal you can't afford.

Having totaled all the ready cash you have, consider the extra expenses you're likely to run into. If you're looking for a four-bedroom home and you now live in a two-bedroom place, you will probably want to buy two sets of bedroom furniture, right? Figure out what they will cost you, and subtract it from the total. Do the same for a lawn mower, the extra car you'll need for commuting, the new washer and dryer, a decent living room rug, and anything else you can think of. Then subtract a nice round number for decorating — let's say $500 if you're planning on moving into a three-bedroom, two-bath place that will need draperies, curtains, and some paint here and there. Closing or settlement costs can run from virtually nothing (if you're buying a new home from a large builder) to astronomical sums. They vary from place to place and from one lender to another in the same place. Check with a lender or real estate broker to get a rough estimate. Now subtract moving expenses, which can also vary greatly, depending upon how much you have, how far you're planning to move and how much of the work you're willing or able to do yourself. A mover can tell you about what it's likely to cost. What's left is what you can put down on a home. Maybe you'd better sell the stamp collection after all, huh?

Understand that all of these estimates are just that, estimates, and very rough ones. As your search progresses and you get a better idea of what's available and what you want, you'll be able to make some more accurate calculations.

THE MORTGAGE

For the moment, you have a rough idea of the kind of down payment you can make and the monthly payments you can stand. Now call a few lenders — savings and loan associations, savings banks, or commercial banks — and ask what kind of mortgages they're making. The facts you're interested in are (1) the required down payment, (2) the interest rate now and how much it can vary during the life of the loan, (3) the maximum term, or number of years you have to repay, and (4) the ceiling (the maximum amount the institution will lend on a mortgage). You will probably be told that the bank is making, say, 75 percent loans at 13 percent initially with a three-point cap for 30 years with a ceiling of $100,000. In English, this means that you can borrow as much as 75 percent of the appraised value of the house, but no more than $100,000. You'll have to pay 13 percent a year on the outstanding balance at first, and that may rise as high as 16 percent. You'll have no more than 30 years to pay off the loan.

If the lending institutions in your area are limiting their mortgages to 75 percent of value, you'll have to make a down payment of 25 percent. So you can afford a home that costs roughly four times the down payment you have. If the banks are making 80 percent mortgages, you'll only have to have a 20 percent down payment, so you'll be able to spend five times your down payment. That's one way of figuring it.

Another way — and you'd better try this one, too — is on the basis of the monthly payments. The table at the end of this chapter tells you what the monthly payments will be on a typical mortgage of a given size at a given interest rate, and you've already calculated what you can spend each month over-all. Subtract from the total sum available monthly such things as payments on the extra car and other commuting expenses, then throw in, say, one 120th of your down payment (the payment divided by 120) for maintenance. You'll have to ask a lawyer or broker for estimates of monthly tax and insurance costs. Subtract them, and you'll be pretty close to what you can pay on the mortgage. Given that sum, use your calculator or a sharp pencil and the table to figure how much mortgage you can stand. If the mortgage has a variable interest rate, you'll have to repeat the calculation a time or two. Yes, these are very rough figures. Better ones will be available by and by, but you have to start somewhere.

The number you've arrived at — the size mortgage you can afford, given your monthly payments — should be added to the down payment you have, and the result will be an indication of what you can afford in a home. An indication. If the number is $70,000, don't refuse to look at homes on the market for $75,000 or $67,500, but be a little wary of places that are available for $88,000. They're probably out of your range, even if you give up bowling and smoking. Remember, too, that virtually no resale home sells for the advertised price. Almost every owner sets his price in the expectation that he'll accept less. Real estate is one of the few areas left in the United States in which the fine old art of haggling is alive and well.

Approximate Monthly Payment to Amortize $1,000

TERM IN YEARS

RATE	1	3	5	10	15	20	25	30	35	40
5%	85.61	29.98	18.88	10.61	7.91	6.60	5.85	5.37	5.05	4.83
5½%	85.84	30.20	19.11	10.86	8.18	6.88	6.15	5.68	5.38	5.16
6%	86.07	30.43	19.34	11.11	8.44	7.17	6.45	6.00	5.71	5.51
6½%	86.30	30.65	19.57	11.36	8.72	7.46	6.76	6.33	6.05	5.86
7%	86.53	30.88	19.81	11.62	8.99	7.76	7.07	6.66	6.39	6.22
7½%	86.76	31.11	20.04	11.88	9.28	8.06	7.39	7.00	6.75	6.59
8%	86.99	31.34	20.28	12.14	9.56	8.37	7.72	7.34	7.11	6.96
8½%	87.22	31.57	20.52	12.40	9.85	8.68	8.06	7.69	7.47	7.34
9%	87.46	31.80	20.76	12.67	10.15	9.00	8.40	8.05	7.84	7.72
9½%	87.69	32.04	21.01	12.94	10.45	9.33	8.74	8.41	8.22	8.11
10%	87.92	32.27	21.25	13.22	10.75	9.66	9.09	8.78	8.60	8.50

10½%	88.15	32.51	21.50	13.50	11.06	9.99	9.45	9.15	8.99	8.89
11%	88.39	32.51	21.75	13.78	11.37	10.33	9.81	9.53	9.37	9.29
11½%	88.62	32.74	22.00	14.06	11.69	10.67	10.17	9.91	9.77	9.69
12%	88.85	32.98	22.25	14.35	12.01	11.02	10.54	10.29	10.16	10.09
12½%	89.09	33.22	22.50	14.64	12.33	11.37	10.91	10.68	10.56	10.49
13%	89.32	33.46	22.76	14.94	12.66	11.72	11.28	11.07	10.96	10.90
13½%	89.56	33.70	23.01	15.23	12.99	12.08	11.66	11.46	11.36	11.31
14%	89.79	33.94	23.27	15.53	13.32	12.44	12.04	11.85	11.76	11.72
14½%	90.03	34.18	23.53	15.83	13.66	12.80	12.43	12.25	12.17	12.13
15%	90.26	34.43	23.79	16.14	14.00	13.17	12.81	12.65	12.57	12.54
15½%	90.50	34.67	24.06	16.45	14.34	13.54	13.20	13.05	12.98	12.95
16%	90.74	34.92	24.32	16.76	14.69	13.92	13.59	13.45	13.39	13.36
16½%	90.97	35.16	24.59	17.07	15.04	14.29	13.99	13.86	13.80	13.77
17%	91.21	35.41	24.86	17.38	15.40	14.67	14.38	14.26	14.21	14.19

17½%	91.45	35.91	25.13	17.70	15.75	15.05	14.78	14.67	14.62	14.60
18%	91.68	36.16	25.40	18.02	16.11	15.44	15.18	15.08	15.03	15.02
18½%	91.92	36.41	25.67	18.35	16.47	15.82	15.58	15.48	15.45	15.43
19%	92.16	36.66	25.95	18.67	16.83	16.21	15.98	15.89	15.86	15.85
19½%	92.40	36.91	26.22	19.00	17.20	16.60	16.39	16.30	16.27	16.26
20%	92.64	37.17	26.50	19.33	17.57	16.99	16.79	16.72	16.69	16.68
20½%	92.88	37.42	26.78	19.66	17.94	17.39	17.20	17.13	17.10	17.09
21%	93.12	37.68	27.06	20.00	18.31	17.78	17.60	17.54	17.52	17.51
21½%	93.36	37.94	27.34	20.34	18.69	18.18	18.01	17.95	17.93	17.93
22%	93.60	38.20	27.62	20.67	19.06	18.58	18.42	18.36	18.35	18.34
22½%	93.84	38.45	27.91	21.02	19.44	18.97	18.83	18.78	18.76	18.76
23%	94.08	38.71	28.20	21.36	19.82	19.38	19.24	19.19	19.18	19.17
23½%	94.32	38.98	28.48	21.71	20.20	19.78	19.65	19.61	19.59	19.59
24%	94.56	39.24	28.77	22.05	20.59	20.18	20.06	20.02	20.01	20.01

To find roughly what a fixed-rate mortgage will cost you, multiply the monthly payment given above by the number of thousands you're borrowing. If the amount you want is $34,500, for example, multiply by 34.5. The result will be approximate because all fractions of cents in the table have been rounded up to the next highest penny. Remember that the figure you come up with will account for principal and interest payments only, not for taxes, insurance, or other costs. To estimate the cost of a variable-rate or graduated-payment loan, repeat the calculation at different interest levels.

PART TWO

Building or Finding the Right Place

4
How Should You Own a Home?

Nothing is simple these days. You can't just figure out, the way your father did, how much you can afford to spend and go out and buy a house. Now you have to decide whether you want a house or an apartment, and what kind — not only physically what kind, but legally what kind. You have to decide, in other words, not just what you want to own but how you want to own it. In general, there are four ways to own residential real estate: (1) in fee simple, (2) with a homeowners' association, (3) in a condominium, or (4) in a cooperative. Each has advantages and disadvantages.

FEE-SIMPLE HOMES

Fee-simple ownership is the grand old American dream, the clapboard house with the white picket fence, an apple tree in the front yard and a see-saw in the back. It is the traditional form of ownership in the United States: You own the lot and the building, and your neighbors have nothing to do with it. This form of ownership is most common in single-family detached homes, though it is also found in single-family attached (townhouses and brownstones) and mobile homes. For obvious reasons, it is not found in multiple-family housing — everybody in a 50-family building can't be the sole owner of the land.

Fee simple is the most expensive form of ownership. In part, that's because every owner has his exclusive lot, and in part it's because most fee-simple homes are detached buildings. Every owner has his own land and his own complete, self-sustaining structure. It's the most expensive, but it's also the most private — it usually has that buffer of land around it — and the most psychologically secure form of ownership. Nobody else messes around with your home. Beyond that, because of its long history in this country and the relatively short histories of other forms of ownership, fee simple is the system most familiar to builders, lawyers, zoners, inspectors, and the courts. It is therefore likely, all else being equal, to produce fewer technical problems. And finally, fee-simple ownership of a detached single-family house is what most people say they want. It may be expensive and ecologically wasteful because of the land it eats up, but it's still the American dream.

HOMEOWNERS' ASSOCIATIONS

A variation of the traditional arrangement is fee-simple ownership with a homeowners' association. In this form, you own the lot and the building, and you and your neighbors own jointly, through an association, some common areas or recreation facilities. This is a relatively rare form of ownership in the United States, but it's been around for a long time, especially in resort areas, where a lake may belong to an association of all the owners of homes along its shore. It is a form of ownership applicable to attached and detached single-family houses and to mobile homes. Its great advantage is that it will probably offer more extensive recreational or other public facilities than a traditional fee-simple home. If there isn't a lake, there may be an association playground or swimming pool or tennis court. There has to be some jointly owned property or there wouldn't be an association. Whatever the amenity is, it will probably come to the individual homeowner more cheaply through an association than it would if he built a modest version of it himself. There is economy in numbers. But there's also a lack of privacy in numbers, and it can become impossible to escape your neighbors. The homeowner in an association neighborhood will probably be required to join and pay dues to the association. At least part of his life, the part that has to do with operating, enjoying, or paying for the association facilities, will be subject to the will of the neighborhood majority. Even what he doesn't want or use he will have to pay for if the association wills it. The association may provide great tennis courts, but one way or another you'll have to pay for them.

CONDOMINIUMS

One step beyond the homeowners' association is the condominium, the latest rage in American housing. In this arrangement, you own your home outright and you own jointly with your neighbors the land and such common facilities as lawns, walks, recreation areas, and, in high-rise or other large developments, the elevators, stairways, hallways, laundry rooms, and so forth. Your interest in the common facilities (everything outside your four walls) is legally part of your home and is bought and sold with it. The condominium form of ownership is most commonly found in single-family attached and multiple-family housing, though it is also applicable to mobile homes and single-family detached homes. Because it is likely to be attached or high-rise housing, which consumes less land and allows for some construction economies, the condominium is usually cheaper than the fee-simple home. And, like the home in the homeowners' association development, it usually offers superior amenities, most often recreation facilities, at a price the buyer of a traditional house simply couldn't match. But, because the potential market for it is narrower, a condominium unit probably won't appreciate as fast as a fee-simple home. And the owner of a condominium unit is a member of the condominium — he must pay monthly charges that cover his share of the cost of operating and maintaining the common facilities, whether or not he uses them. As all the condominium ads are quick to point out, he will not have to face exterior maintenance chores, at least not to the same extent as his brethren in fee-simple homes, but the cost of maintaining the exterior will be included in his monthly fees, and he will still have to keep up the interior. No matter what the building looks like, the condominium unit owner is not a tenant. When his sink drain is stopped up, he will probably have to arrange — and pay — for a plumber to clear it if he is not willing or able to clear it himself. When the living room needs repainting, he will have to assume the burden. There is no landlord in a condominium, even if it's a 50-story building containing hundreds of apartments. Everybody is the landlord.

Since everybody is the landlord, everybody has a say in how the joint is run. That can be psychologically taxing, to say the least. It can produce some bitter neighborhood fights, fights that become especially bitter because the neighborhood is so compact. In a condominium, your life is thrown in with that of your neighbors. Understand what that may mean before you decide. There are also some serious financial problems in condominiums, which have often been at loggerheads with their own members over reserve funds. When money is scarce, there is a great temptation to vote to reduce the monthly payment by cutting out the part that goes into a contingency fund to pay for a new roof or a new swimming pool, which will be needed sooner or later. If the vote carries, some morning after a good thunderstorm everybody's monthly fees may suddenly double so the top-floor residents can stay out of the weather. Next year, still higher fees may disappear into that crack in the swimming pool. In some areas — notably, but not exclusively, Florida — condominiums have had financial problems resulting from exploitation by unscrupulous developers. The favorite schemes have been long-term management contracts — the developer gets an unconscionable annual fee to manage the place for 25 years or so — and hidden recreation leases — the developer retains ownership of the recreation facilities (that's in the fine print) and leases them to the unit owners for, say, 99 years, though they'll obviously never last 40 years.

This is not to say that condominiums are no good. They have many advantages, some of which are those of fee-simple homes. A condominium unit, for example, can be mortgaged like a fee-simple home, and it is taxed the same way; each owner gets his own tax bill every year. That means the condominium owner is not a slave to his neighbor's solvency. If the guy down the hall or down the street doesn't pay his taxes, the municipality will foreclose on his unit, not on the whole development. If the same fellow doesn't pay his mortgage, the lender can move against his unit, but not any of the others. And, in theory anyway, if the lender or the town takes a unit, the lender or the town becomes a member of the condominium and has to pay the same monthly fees for operations and maintenance as any other unit owner. In theory. The failure of the fellow down the street to pay his monthly maintenance charges will leave the condominium somewhat strapped for cash, of course, and may mean an increase in your fees. But only in the most extreme cases — say, if half the owners are thrown out of work at the same time — will you have to worry about the financial survival of the project. You won't have to worry about your neighbors' psychological health, either, since in most cases your fellow condominium owners will not be able to judge the acceptability of the potential buyer if you decide to sell your unit. You can usually sell it to anyone you please, though the condominium may reserve the right of first refusal, the right to match another buyer's offer.

COOPERATIVES

In a cooperative, you own shares in a corporation that owns your home and all the common facilities around it. As a stockholder, you get a lease on your unit that lasts as long as you own the stock. When you sell, you're technically selling just the stock, not the real estate, and the board of directors of the corporation can usually vote on whether to accept your buyer as a stockholder. They can be amazingly arbitrary. Some of the country's most famous and wealthiest entertainers have been turned down because they're black or Jewish or simply because they're entertainers; diplomats have been turned down because they're diplomats; any number of women have been turned down because they're divorced; and hordes of people of every profession, hue, and persuasion have been rejected because they would have to borrow money to buy. It's a swell set-up if you happen to be a bigot. You can theoretically exclude everybody but your relatives.

But not all co-op owners — not even most co-op owners — are bigots. There are lots of co-ops whose residents are as polyglot as any city, and most are probably more varied in their residency than all but a handful of suburban neighborhoods. Though one of the reasons for the popularity of the cooperative after World War II was its opportunity for exclusivity, that's not the only reason people moved into them. Condominiums were then virtually unheard-of in the mainland United States, and those who wanted to own their own homes but remain in an urban setting often had no choice but the cooperative. In some big cities — most obviously, New York, but also Chicago and Miami, among others — there are still lots of co-ops, though condominiums have pretty much overtaken cooperatives almost everywhere. While a smart lawyer may be able to apply the cooperative ownership concept to any form of housing, it has been largely limited to multiple-family buildings and a few attached single-family structures.

Cooperative units are usually cheaper to buy than their condominium counterparts because the purchase price normally does not cover the full cost of the unit. The cooperative corporation — the corporation in which the purchaser is buying shares — typically has a mortgage on the whole complex. So the purchase price need only supply the difference between that unit's share of the mortgage and its full value. In a condominium, there is no such underlying "master" mortgage. While that distinction is an advantage for the cooperative owner at first, he will have to make monthly payments that include not just the cost of maintaining the common areas but also the monthly mortgage payments. Moreover, most such master mortgages are of the "balloon" type — when the end of the term is reached one huge payment is due. That means negotiating a new mortgage to cover the balance due, and if interest rates have risen since the old mortgage was made, the result can be a tooth-rattling increase in monthly carrying charges. The same sort of increase can be produced by unexpected emergency repairs — a new roof or an elevator overhaul — though that is a danger common to both cooperatives and condominiums. Because of the need to renew mortgages at sharply higher interest rates and because of the rising cost of repairs and maintenance, the monthly carrying charges for some co-op units have shot up, and when that happens a unit's resale value is reduced. At times there have been lavish New York City co-op apartments that one would pick up for a song — if one could manage to meet the monthly payments.

Price aside, a co-op unit may be harder to sell than a comparable condominium home because the corporation's board of directors usually has veto power over a sale. That is one of the reasons banks have been relatively reluctant to make loans for the purchase of co-ops. If the buyer fails to pay his debt, the bank's collateral is stock, not real estate, and the bankers are not anxious to get into a hassle with the board of directors when they try to sell the stock to collect their money. New York State probably has the co-op lending system that is most active and most comparable to conventional mortgage lending, but even there, a loan on a co-op is likely to cost more than the same loan on a condominium or a fee-simple property.

Cooperative units are generally smaller than fee-simple homes and, at least initially, cheaper. But monthly costs tend to rise more, and the monthly fee includes the cost of maintaining all the facilities, even those the unit owner doesn't use. And while cooperative living relieves the owner of many maintenance responsibilities, in this form of ownership more than any other he is dependent upon the good will and common sense of his neighbors. The majority will decide not only how his home is maintained, but when and to whom he can sell it. Moreover, if one of the cooperative shareholders defaults on his monthly payments, everyone else will have to chip in enough to cover his share of the mortgage and tax bills. That's a whole heap of togetherness.

5
What Type of Home Should You Own?

In many ways, the type of home you buy will be determined by the location you choose. Single-family houses on two-acre lots are not normally constructed near the central city, and high-rise condominium apartments are rarely found in the hinterlands. Nonetheless, it's a useful exercise to decide what you would like to have if you could have it anyplace and, conversely, what you will be giving up if you accept second-best in housing type to get the right location.

DETACHED HOUSES

What most Americans live in and what most of the rest say they would like to live in is the single-family detached house — the traditional house on its own lot. This is the form of housing that generally provides the greatest privacy, the most room, and the greatest number of extra comforts and amenities. It is also — you can hardly be surprised — the most expensive, both to buy and to maintain, and the most demanding in the sense that it requires both outside and inside maintenance and a lot of landscaping, gardening, and that sort of thing. It can be like having another child. From an ecological point of view, detached housing is the most wasteful. It uses up a lot of land, and because it spreads a few people over a relatively large area it makes public transportation less efficient and requires much more use of the automobile. Each building must be heated in cold weather and cooled in warm weather, and 50 small heaters are less efficient than one big one. Moreover, each unit is open to the weather on all sides, so it is poorly insulated compared to the average unit in attached or multiple-family housing, which is surrounded, at least partially, by other units that are being heated or cooled. For all that, owning a single-family detached home is probably as close as you'll get to being master or mistress of all you survey. It is your castle, your turf in a much more complete way than any other type of home. There is (except in rare cases) no committee to tell you how to maintain it, no neighbor upstairs to drop his shoes every night just as you're drifting off to sleep, no concern that the people next door will complain about the stereo. It is yours in every way.

ATTACHED HOUSES

A single-family attached home — a townhouse, rowhouse, brownstone, or quadruplex, among other names, depending on where it is — can be yours in every way, too, but perhaps not so privately. By definition, it involves one or more common walls that you share with a neighbor. The chances are that sharing a wall will mean sharing a little of your life as well. Yards, if there are any, tend to be very small. And they are close together, of course, so making them private means building between them something akin to the Great Wall of China, and then they're hardly yards anymore. But attached single-family housing has some advantages. It costs less than detached housing, for one thing. It's cheaper to buy because it requires less land and offers some opportunities for construction economy. It costs less to maintain because one or more of the exterior walls is hidden — and therefore doesn't need painting — and because those adjoining homes offer the best imaginable insulation. It may also offer better recreational facilities such as tennis courts or swimming pool, especially if it's in a condominium. And attached housing has become fairly universal. Some of it — brownstones, rowhouses, and townhouses — is right downtown, in the most urban of neighborhoods. And some of it — townhouses or quadruplexes (four attached units, usually in a block rather than a row) — is in suburbia or even exurbia. Wherever it is, it offers a more urban lifestyle than the detached house, and usually at lower cost than such a house in the same place.

APARTMENTS

The most urban of lifestyles and the lowest costs are generally to be found in multiple-family housing, which can take several forms. In outer suburbia, it's usually garden apartments, apartments in one-story or two-story buildings. The closer you get to the center of things, the taller the building is likely to grow because land gets more expensive, and a taller building can put more units on every valuable acre. While there are condominium and cooperative apartments that sell for hundreds of thousands of dollars, multiple-family housing units are generally cheaper, unit for unit, than single-family attached or detached homes. But they generally offer less privacy — one neighbor may be dropping his shoes upstairs while another listens to your stereo through the wall. They are, however, ecologically sounder, they require less maintenance, and they are usually much more convenient to work or whatever else interests you — unless you're interested in wilderness.

MOBILE HOMES

Finally, there are mobile homes — not the house trailers of yore but 60-foot or 70-foot contraptions designed to be moved only rarely, if at all, once they've been put in place. Though they are prohibited in many municipalities, they are probably the cheapest form of ownership housing you can readily find. However, financing costs are comparable to those for automobiles, much higher than mortgage rates; mobile homes tend to depreciate rather than grow in value, and if you don't own your own land the price of keeping your home in a mobile-home park can be alarmingly high, all things considered. Moreover, there are severe safety problems with such homes, and, flashy as they have become, they are hardly the answer to anyone's aesthetic dreams.

NEW TOWNS AND PUD'S

Many of the housing types — all except mobile homes — may be combined in a large development called a "new town" or "planned unit development" (PUD, for short). Though many developers have latched onto these trendy new names, a true new town or PUD should combine various types of housing with commercial and industrial buildings. It's supposed to be just what its name suggests — a whole new town, complete with homes, stores, offices, and industries. It's supposed to be more or less self-sufficient, at least from a tax point of view. The commercial and industrial development is supposed to generate enough tax to finance the public services required by the new homes — police and fire protection, sewers, schools, and so forth. If it doesn't have all those things, it isn't really a PUD, whatever the developer tells you, though it may be a "planned residential development" or PRD — a PUD without the commerce and industry.

Many builders have adopted these new designations on the theory that buyers are interested in being in the most up-to-date, chic sort of community, and this must be it. Like everything else, they have advantages and disadvantages. Their greatest problem is that people don't seem to conform to a developer's idea of how they should live. The developer's theory is that if he builds a variety of housing, good recreational facilities, plenty of shopping, and lots of office and industrial space as well, everybody can do without a second — or maybe even a first — car. All the residents can walk to the offices or factories as well as to the stores, theaters, schools, and so forth. A more economical, carefree, pollution-free life for all. Well, maybe. Some of the people who work for the companies that move into the industrial space in the PUD choose for some reason to live elsewhere. They drive to work. Some of the people who live in the PUD work downtown. They drive to work. Some of the employees and residents are not fond of the PUD's supermarket. They drive to a place down the road. And some people who live down the road like the PUD's supermarket, so they drive there. In the end, there's usually little difference between the traffic density in the PUD and that in any other neighborhood.

Another theory behind PUD's is that if all types of housing are built, all kinds of people will move in. Rental apartments will attract those who can't afford or don't want ownership — the poor, the young, and the elderly. There will be low-rise, mid-rise and high-rise condominiums for the well-off singles, the childless high-livers, and the families on the way up. The middle-level family men can buy townhouses, and those who have "made it" can pay an arm and a leg for detached homes. But everybody, from the bottom of the social scale to the top, will theoretically be living in the same place. That's integration — voluntary and painless.

The problem is that real estate, like water, has a way of reaching its own level. A buyer who can afford $150,000 is reluctant to invest it next to a $60,000 home, and the $60,000 buyer looks warily at a $35,000 place next door. Ultimately, the bottom price starts to creep up and the top one begins to dwindle. Everything heads toward a common level, producing the very homogeneity the PUD was designed to avoid.

Still, you're likely to find a wider mix of people in a PUD than in an average suburban neighborhood. There will be high-rise people and low-rise people, rental and ownership people, apartment, townhouse, and single-family house people. The single-family detached homes are likely to be few and on very small lots, relative to those in the conventional neighborhood. The bulk of the ownership housing may be single-family attached — townhouses. The prices will probably be competitive with, perhaps a little better than, those in nearby conventional developments. That's because the PUD developer is doing things — buying land and materials, letting contracts, hiring labor — on a grand scale. But the very size of his project controls where it can be built. PUD's tend to be on the fringes of suburbia, where there's more open land. That makes commuting more difficult and expensive if you work in the center of a metropolitan area. Their nature also dictates that PUD's take a long time to build. The developer must pace himself or go broke; he must build some units and get sales going, then build some more and wait for sales before he goes on. That means early buyers had better come equipped with a pioneer spirit. You may live a long time with a sea of mud or a construction site in your backyard. And it may take a while before public services catch up with the townhouse set. The railroad is not likely to add extra commuter trains until it considers the passenger traffic worth the extra expense. You may consider it worthwhile long before the railroad does. The town fathers, who, when the proposal was made, heard only that this development would pay for itself in taxes, may have a much different idea of adequate education than those "city slickers" who bought condominiums and now want open classrooms and advanced courses. Moreover, the financial experience of PUD's and new towns has not thus far been overly happy. If there's financial trouble, it invariably takes longer than anticipated to complete a development. In the meantime, the amenities that will probably be delayed are the things that tempted you in the first place — the golf course, tennis courts, swimming pool, teen-age recreation center. And if things really get tight during that long wait for a sell-out, there may be a great temptation for the developer to cut a few corners where you can't see them.

But don't overestimate the problems of PUD's. To a large extent, they are the problems of all developments, magnified by sheer size. The developer who sets out to build a PUD rather than 600 ticky-tacky houses is taking a chance, and he's probably taking it because he has more vision and conscience than his competitors. Sooner or later, most developments — after severe growing pains — tend to work out. When a PUD matures, it'll make a fantastic place to live.

6

How Much Home Do You Need?

Asking how much home you need may be just another way of asking how much you can afford, for a shopper's desires almost always seem to exceed his means. The trick is to distinguish between what you need and what you'd like to have. It would be nice, all else being equal, to have a stable, a greenhouse, and maid's quarters. But then you'd have to buy horses for the stable, supply feed to the horses, and hire grooms, exercise boys, and stable hands. You'd have to buy exotic plants for the greenhouse and hire a gardener to make sure that such delicate and expensive things didn't die. And what good are maid's quarters if you don't have a maid? Beyond all that, homes with such embellishments tend to be rather large places that attract rather large tax and utility bills. They are expensive places to keep. So the question ultimately becomes not what you'd like to have but what you really need.

How much home you really need will depend upon how you want — and can reasonably afford — to live, stable boys, gardeners, and maids aside. It's possible to turn one bedroom into a dormitory that will house a dozen children and to eat all your meals in the living room. It's also possible to have a bedroom for each of the dozen kids and a dining room that will comfortably seat all of them plus a guest for each one. Somewhere in between is probably where you're at, childwise, moneywise, and otherwise. Think carefully about where that is.

SETTING YOUR PRIORITIES

Before you start looking seriously, make some lists — a list of what is absolutely essential, a list of what would be useful every day or every week, and a list of what would simply be nice to have. Don't try to knock the job off in an hour or so. Let it sit overnight and come back to it; revise it; throw it away and make new lists. Encourage your spouse or roommate, if you have one who will be in on the purchase, to make separate lists. Compare them. Be critical of both sets. Force yourself to be realistic.

Take, for example, the subject of bedrooms, one common measure of a home's size and comfort. How many bedrooms are really necessary, how many do you need simply to live comfortably tomorrow? That does not include bedrooms for children you expect to have. It does not include a bedroom to be used as an office if you use it twice a month and can get by quite well with a corner of the family room. It doesn't include a guest room if your only regular guests are in-laws who drop in like clockwork every St. Swithin's Day. The only bedrooms that are really essential in most families are one for parents, one for male children, and one for female children. Everything else is in the realm of luxury, more or less. And if the male and female children haven't started school yet and you suspect that the company will be transferring you to Guam within a few years, you can probably get by with two bedrooms in the meantime.

All of this is not to say that a third or even a fourth bedroom would not be both desirable and a wise investment. But it is not literally essential. If your list of the bare minimum essentials includes two bedrooms, the compilation of useful extras might include a third one, and the list reserved for things that would be nice to have could include a fourth. If you find a four-bedroom home at the right price with all the other essentials, so much the better. But don't walk around believing that you can't live decently without the extras when in fact you can, and many people do.

Once you've got the bedroom question out of the way, do the same number on everything else. How many bathrooms do you really need? Picture the morning rush hour, when all hands are anxious to get off to school or work. If two bathrooms will handle that demand, you certainly don't need more than two. A powder room near the living room may be handy, of course, but it's not essential. Is a dining room essential or just desirable? Does your business require that you give frequent dinner parties? If so, it may be essential. Do you simply like to throw big, formal bashes? Well, it may be useful in that case, but you can probably survive without it; there are other ways to throw parties. How necessary is a family room? It may be very necessary if you have a big family, especially if it's a young family that will have nowhere else to go in inclement weather. It may be useful but not essential if your family is older or smaller. And it may be an utter waste if you're childless and not the entertaining sort.

How important is a two-car garage? A screened porch? A workshop? Space for a darkroom, a pool table, or Aunt Charlotte's collection of crystal cuspidors? To some people, they may make all the difference between a good home and a bad one; others would be ill-advised to make the extra investment they represent. What about a fireplace and a swimming pool? Do you insist upon a basement because that's where you conduct your business in secondhand mining machinery, or simply because you've always thought that every good house should have one? What about land? Do you really need an acre and a half? Will it be worth what it costs in time as well as money to maintain it?

If you're reasonably sure that you'll live in this home for a while, and some of the space you're thinking about as essential is for future use, could you get along with a home that has a floor plan suitable for later expansion, or an unfinished attic or basement that could someday be turned into a family room or an extra bedroom and bath? That may offer an opportunity to get the initial financial shock of the purchase out of the way before you undertake the expense of building the addition, not to mention maintaining and paying the taxes on it.

Once you've thrown six sets of lists away in exasperation and have finally — and coolly — delineated what's essential from what's useful and merely desirable, you ought to consider what styles and designs interest you most.

7
What Style and Design Do You Want?

There are many things about housing that fall into the category of personal taste. At the head of the list is style. Whether your home is Victorian or contemporary, Spanish or Tudor, Georgian, Italianate, or a log cabin is purely up to you. The chances are, in any case, that the place will, like most household pets, be of mixed or undetermined origin. It will probably contain many details that looked good to the builder or were selling well at the time the home was constructed but that do not necessarily reflect a single architectural school. What passes these days for colonial design can be a far cry from the structures built when this country was a British possession. Unless you're a student of such things, it probably makes little difference, anyway. How the place will work for you and the degree to which it appeals to you are, after all, more important than the purity and unity of its detailing, though if you are lucky enough to find — and can pay for — those qualities as well as the more practical ones, you should have an enviable and very valuable home.

Unlike style, design in the broader sense — the general configuration or layout of the home and how its elements fit together — does lend itself to a modicum of objective discussion. And that discussion is made considerably more convenient by the arbitrary division of housing into a few categories: one-story houses and apartments; one-and-a-half-story houses; two-story and three-story houses and apartments; split-levels, and split-entry or raised-ranch houses.

ONE-STORY HOUSES AND APARTMENTS

One-story houses and single-level apartments offer a unique measure of convenience in that they require no stair-climbing. That is an asset particularly valuable to the elderly and to families with very young children. But the absence of stairs has its shortcomings, too. The one-level layout increases the need for interior zoning — for the placement of some physical buffer between the living and working areas (typically, the living room, dining room, kitchen, and family room) and the sleeping area. The need for such a buffer — like the need for no stair-climbing — may be greater than average in a family that includes very young or very old members who may retire earlier or arise later than the rest of the fun-loving gang.

Single-level apartments are called simply — and one might say, logically — apartments. They tend to be cheaper than their multiple-level counterparts, partly because they tend to be smaller over-all, partly because they're easier (and therefore cheaper) to design and build, and partly because they're less exotic and therefore — at least in the builder's mind — have less sales appeal.

Single-level houses are called ranches or Western houses or, if they're small, bungalows. They tend to look best when they're constructed on level land and hug the ground. They are easier and cheaper to maintain than houses with two or three floors because you don't have to rent the local hook-and-ladder to reach the roof. But heating and cooling costs may be higher, square foot for square foot, because all of the ceilings and floors are, in effect, exterior surfaces, while some of them are interior surfaces in a multiple-level house. Exterior surfaces allow heat to leak out during the winter and in during the summer. Single-story houses will also be more expensive to build, square foot for square foot. That's because the roof and foundation are bigger in proportion to the interior space than they are in a house with two to three floors, and roofs and foundations are expensive. Finally, expanding a one-story house can be more expensive because the house is already spread out on the lot and zoning regulations may prohibit building any closer to the line. On the other hand, if the house is built in such a way that you can go up rather than out, a ranch or Western house may have great expansion possibilities. But don't plan on expansion unless you're sure that conditions are right — that the foundation and load-bearing walls will take the extra weight and that the local zoning board will approve the project.

ONE-AND-A-HALF-STORY HOUSES

One-and-a-half-story houses (apartments of this configuration are rare or nonexistent) are sometimes called bungalows but more often termed Cape Cods. The Cape Cod may have a so-called expansion attic, one designed to be finished later, creating an extra bedroom or two and, perhaps, an extra bath. The Cape Cod usually has a very steep roof to allow the extra attic headroom that will be needed when the new rooms are built. The big advantage of the expansion house is the low initial price. It was very popular with young married couples in the years after World War II because they could afford the basic house and worry about the cost of expansion later, when they were better able to afford it and when their families had grown to the point where they really needed it. The disadvantage of the expansion attic is that the added rooms tend to be small, with low ceilings and less-than-adequate windows. They also tend, try as you might, to be hot in summer and cold in winter.

The buyer of a Cape Cod who has later expansion in mind should be sure that the attic floor, the load-bearing partitions below, and the foundation are adequate for the load he's about to build, and that the heating plant can handle the extra space. If the house is new, the buyer should also insist upon extra ventilation and heating in the attic, and have the ducts, pipes, and wiring run up to the attic level and closed off. Much cheaper to do it during construction than to break into walls later. It is also wise to build attic dormers when the house is being constructed so you won't have to break through the roof when you want to expand. By this time, of course, the purchase price is edging up toward the point where you might as well build a two-story house that already has the extra bedrooms and bath. Such is life.

TWO-STORY AND THREE-STORY HOUSES AND APARTMENTS

Two-story and three-story houses and apartments have a degree of natural interior zoning that is not available in single-story construction. Some things — usually the sleeping areas — are upstairs, and the floor serves as a buffer between them and the rest of the raucous goings-on. Such homes do, however, require some stair-climbing if you can't afford an elevator, and stairs can be hazardous for the elderly and the young. Stairs also occupy space, in some cases enough space to have provided another room at virtually no extra cost. And to some extent, stairs limit design flexibility.

Two-story apartments are called duplexes, and those of three stories are called triplexes. They are relatively rare and expensive because it's hard to design a building around them and they tend to be on the large side as apartments go — say, three or four bedrooms.

Most attached single-family homes — townhouses, rowhouses, brownstones, or whatever — have two or more floors, and probably the majority of single-family detached homes — "houses" — are of this design. In some areas, almost any house with two or three floors will be called a colonial, though the styling may be closer to the Korean war than the Revolution. Some developers fancy that two-story houses are more attractive when called bi-levels, apparently because that sounds more chic and mod.

Whatever the joint is called, though, two floors are two floors, and two-floor houses are generally adaptable to small lots. They usually provide relatively more space for the money than single-story houses because of the lower ratio of roof and foundation to interior space. The square-foot costs of construction, heating, and cooling will probably be lower, but getting the thing painted may cost you an arm, a leg, and four toes.

SPLIT-LEVEL HOUSES

Split-level houses — apartments of this design are rare — have a main level that is halfway between the upper and lower levels. This design can play havoc with interior traffic flow and planning. If the house is small, every room may be on its own level, which means that you have to go up or down stairs to get anywhere at all. And because the stairways are usually more open than those in two-story houses, split-levels can be very difficult to heat. The heat rises through those stairways, making the top level much too hot and rendering the lowest level suitable for ice skating. In a sense, the split-level design produces almost automatic interior zoning — the sleeping area is on one level and the working and living areas are on others — but those open stairways reduce the effect of the zoning because they allow odors, noise, and whatever else you have floating around to move right along with the heat. On the other hand, the split-level house uses its floor area completely, having brought the basement halfway out of the ground and made it respectable.

Split-levels — also called bi-levels (two levels off the main one), tri-levels (three other levels), and multi-levels — lend themselves to sloping land. Ideally, a split looks like a ranch, hugging a sloping lot as it descends. Unfortunately, developers have discovered a market for split-levels that has nothing to do with aesthetics, and they are often built on lots more suited to other designs. On land that doesn't slope, a split-level tends to look like some derelict vehicle that ran out of fuel before it got where it was going. Splits built in the wrong places are one of the major reasons suburbia has a bad aesthetic name.

SPLIT-ENTRY HOUSES

The split-entry house is a variation on the split-level. In it, the entry is halfway between the two floors, with the lower level sunk halfway into the ground. Apartments are rarely built this way. The split-entry is also called a raised ranch, a high-rise ranch, or a raised-entry house. The split-entry's foundation is cheaper to construct than that of a conventional two-story house, and the levels that contain the living areas are easier to build than those of a true split-level. In addition, the design offers easy entry from outside to either interior level. But split-entry houses are, almost without exception, aesthetic disasters. If suburbia didn't have a bad name before they came along, it would have one now.

If even the split-entry design has an advantage or two, it should be obvious that there are advantages to any design. But there are disadvantages to any design as well. Homes are uniquely personal things. It is probably a mistake to set out specifically in search of "a two-bedroom duplex condominium in a high-rise building," or "a two-story center-hall colonial house with four bedrooms and two baths." Shop for something that will work for you. You may discover that you can learn to love a ranch or a split or a duplex, despite your earlier convictions, because it has just what you want in a home. All designs have pluses and minuses. Look for one that has the pluses you want and avoids the minuses you're trying to flee. For you, that's a good home.

8
What Area Should It Be In?

There's an old adage in the real estate business to the effect that the three most important factors in the choice of any property are location, location, and location. Which proves that, while real estate men may not be terribly witty, they often know what they're talking about. By all means the most important factor in your choice of a home is its location. If the place is held together with baling wire and chewing gum, is painted an obnoxious color and is barely large enough for a family of midgets, but it's in the right neighborhood, it'll probably sell. And all the extra features and loving care in the world will fail to impress buyer after buyer if it's in an inconvenient, unattractive area. Consider location more carefully than anything else as you set out to look for a home.

COMMUTING

If you're looking in a large metropolitan area, start by trying to isolate a few sections — perhaps a whole suburban county or the west end of the city — that appeal to you. Analyze the relative advantages of such sections by applying what you know about the way you'll be living when you move to the new place. First of all, you or someone in your family will probably work and will have to get from home to office or plant every day. Consider transportation from the viewpoints of both cost and convenience. Look for large areas that offer relatively good commuting to your plant or office, not just the best commuting to downtown. Before you get too serious about an area, grit your teeth, buy a ticket and try to commute. Be sure to do it during the hours when you'll actually be traveling. The fact that the trip takes only 25 minutes at 3 P.M. on Sunday is immaterial if you want to be at work at 9 A.M. on

Monday. It may take an hour and a half then. Once you've tried a few commutes, you'll have an idea of what you're up against. Then decide how much you're willing to spend — in hours, dollars, and nervous frustration — getting to work and back. A few timetables from the bus lines and commuter railroads that serve your area will allow you to translate the maximum time and money into maximum miles. If you set the limit at an hour and a 20-mile commute takes an hour in your area, you don't want to live farther out than 20 miles. You can use that distance as a radius and work at the center and draw a circle on a map. You want a home inside that circle.

YOUR LIVING HABITS

But not just any home within the circle. Some will be much too expensive, others may be too urban or too rural for your taste. In general, the closer you get to the center of the metropolitan area, the more expensive a given home will be. Neighborhoods close to the center are likely to offer less land and living space, too. High-rise condominiums in the suburbs or exurbs may have rolling lawns and tennis courts, while those downtown may have no exterior amenities at all. In single-family residential areas right in the city, lots 20 feet wide may be the norm, while a couple of acres may be common out at the edge of your circle.

On the other hand, the closer you are to the center of town, the easier and cheaper your commuting is likely to be. And all the urban amenities — theater, concerts, museums, professional sports, and shopping — will probably be more plentiful and convenient than they are in the hinterlands. But of course crime, dirt, and noise are likely to be more plentiful, too, as you get closer to downtown. There is, in other words, no free lunch. Everything is a trade-off for something else, and what you choose to trade off must depend upon your own preferences and living habits.

Think about your living habits and try to imagine how a change in homes may affect them. If you are a beach freak, give extra thought to the areas closer to the lake or the shore. If you move in that direction, you won't have to drive through the heart of town every summer weekend. If theater is your bag and your favorite repertory company is 25 miles to the east, be aware of how you'll suffer if you move 15 miles to the west. If all of your relatives live on the north side and you visit one another daily, don't move to the south side unless you're prepared to find new friends.

TAXES IN GENERAL

If the metropolitan area in which you're looking crosses the borders of several municipalities, counties, or even states, consider their relative tax situations.

Is there an income tax in one state but not in another? Is the sales tax higher in one state, county, or city than another? Does one area have a personal property tax or some other levy that neighboring politicians have not yet discovered? Are there tax breaks for which you might qualify — for veterans, say, or senior citizens? The various systems will undoubtedly be difficult to compare. One jurisdiction may have a higher income tax, for example, but a lower sales tax than another. You'll never be able to figure out to the dime where you stand, but it's worth taking the trouble to get a rough idea. A competent real estate agent will be able to answer questions about the general tax situation in the area he handles, and if you want more detailed information you can call the municipal, county, or state tax office. Through it all, keep in mind the fact that most local taxes are deductible from federal income taxes, so the bite ultimately may not be as large as it first seems. And keep in mind the relationship between taxes and public services. Good education and professional police and fire protection cost money. The better they are, the more they're likely to cost and the higher taxes are likely to be. Look at both sides of the coin before you make an irrevocable decision.

SOCIAL CHIC

Within the circle on your map, there will no doubt be some neighborhoods or towns that are "in" — the places populated by folks whose names litter the local society pages — and other areas that are just as attractive physically but lack social chic. Unless the social value of your address is important to you, consider avoiding the "in" places because you will probably have to pay a premium for them. In the New York metropolitan area, for example, a New Jersey home will probably cost less than the same home in Westchester County or Connecticut. One major reason is that New Yorkers tend to think of New Jersey as an infinite string of refineries, garbage dumps, and pig farms, presided over by the world's most corrupt politicians. New Yorkers have over the years therefore created a greater demand for housing in other suburban areas, and New Jersey land prices have not risen as quickly as those in more sought-after places. There is many a millionaire in New Jersey who chuckles all the way to Wall Street every morning.

THE FUTURE

The "in" place can change from year to year, of course, and so can everything else. If you can't predict where "the beautiful people" will want to live five years from now, you may be able to predict what the future holds in other ways. Read a metropolitan newspaper for a while with that in mind. Where are major facilities — offices, factories, stores, government buildings —

being constructed or planned? Where is transportation being improved? Where are utilities being extended and upgraded? Where are businesses moving? Where are developers aggressively advertising new homes? What you should be looking for is some indication of a balanced, healthy local economy — one that is not dependent on a single hair-oil factory for its survival and one that is strong enough to encourage local businessmen to invest in expansion and modernization. That kind of growing economy is the best assurance of rising real estate values. And growth is most likely to occur in the direction in which public transportation and utilities — sewers, water lines, and so forth — are being extended into previously unserved areas.

Municipal, county, and state or regional planning departments will have some ideas about where change will take place and what form it is likely to take. They may have some publications that would prove interesting, and if they don't, some of their staff members may be flattered to be asked for advice. Planners sometimes think of themselves — not without justification — as crying in the wilderness. Census data may be helpful in telling you what an area is like now and how it has changed in the past, which could give you a clue to what's likely to happen in the future. Try the reference room at the best local library. Be wary of census data in one regard, however. The most detailed and interesting statistics — for example, housing values and family characteristics, block by block — are gathered only once every 10 years. They will probably be old if you can find them, and a lot of things may have changed since they were compiled. The reference librarian may be able to steer you to other data of value, and the League of Women Voters, the Chamber of Commerce, and municipal or county economic-development agencies may have publications that will be enlightening.

Such research will tell you in general terms where growth or renewal, which is a form of growth, are likely to take place. The next trick is to apply that information to your own situation. How does what you've learned affect your potential home? Here are some rules of thumb:

- Property values are most likely to rise in the path of growth.
- Values are most likely to fall in areas that are losing population and employment to the growing sectors.
- Areas that are attracting manufacturing facilities and similar industry are more likely than others to have housing planned or available in the lower price categories.
- Areas that are attracting corporate headquarters or research facilities are more likely to have housing planned and priced with executives or professionals in mind.
- Local taxes are likely to be lowest in stable areas, higher in areas of intense development, and highest in areas that are losing population and employment.

Having pondered all the imponderables — your living habits, relative tax situations, commuting efficiency and the future — you are ready to complete the first step in the search for your home. Within that big circle you drew on your map, mark off some large sections that seem to fill your bill better than others. Don't try to be too precise. Whack off a whole county or a large group of towns or a big section of the city. Remember that you're still working in broad strokes. Remember, too, that nothing's perfect.

9

Within the Area You've Chosen, What Towns or Sections Should You Look In?

The search process will vary a bit, depending upon whether you're searching for an apartment in the city or a house in the suburbs or the country, but the principles are about the same. Whatever the kind of area, read a local newspaper for a while — a neighborhood weekly if you're looking in the city and whatever's available locally if you're concentrating on the suburbs or the exurbs. If you're not familiar with the area, get a local telephone book. Then look around for yourself, on foot if it's a city area, by car if it's in the boondocks. Try to get an appreciation for the "flavor" of the place. Does the local newspaper report a dozen muggings every day? Are the hardware stores advertising specials on deadbolt locks and burglar alarms rather than paint and wheelbarrows? Both the news articles and the ads in the local paper will give you clues as to what people are concerned with and how they live. Do you get the impression reading the local paper and looking around for yourself that all of the residents are Protestant and rich? Or Catholic and poor? Or all Scandinavian sailmakers? Or Nepalese herdsmen? Would you feel comfortable as the only outsider in such a place? Conversely, if you're a Nepalese herdsman, is everybody in the area likely to be so much like you that you'd soon begin to hanker for a little variety?

Does the area have a church or synagogue of your denomination? Does it offer the kind of cultural and recreational facilities that appeal to you — theater or art, boating or golf? Are the stores and restaurants the kind you would probably patronize, even if there were others available? Would you feel comfortable with them when there's nothing else? If you're looking in a city neighborhood, alternatives may be available without too much hassle, but outside of town you may be limited to what's on the premises except for an infrequent expedition into the city.

THE SCHOOL DISTRICT

If you have children or expect to have them, look into the schools. The school administration can provide some helpful information about such indicators of quality as these:

- Annual expenditure per pupil; the higher the better.
- Average class size; the lower the better.
- Pupil-teacher ratio; the more teachers per pupil, the more education each pupil is likely to get.
- Availability of special programs — facilities for the handicapped, say, or remedial courses — if your children need them.
- Average achievement test scores; the higher the better.
- Percentage of high school graduates who go to college, and the colleges to which they go. If your child is more interested in auto mechanics than sociology and probably will not — maybe even should not — go to college, don't get too enthusiastic about a system that is likely to prod him into doing something unwise.
- Age of the physical plant. Is it out-of-date or too small and in need of expansion or replacement?
- Are any students on double sessions? Have there been double sessions in recent years? Does it look as though there will be double sessions in the near future? Although double sessions — in effect, two student bodies using the same school building, one in the morning and one in the afternoon — are utilized and discontinued as populations shift, the district using them is usually a good one to avoid.
- Is the school administration expecting and planning for growth? If the school staff is not expecting growth but the planners and business people in the area are, the district is likely to be in serious trouble within a few years.
- What has been the district's history with school-bond proposals? Are they usually passed or defeated? A district that has a large proportion of elderly voters is likely to defeat school-bond proposals time after time. That's the district most likely to be on double sessions sooner or later and most likely to cut any corner it can find.
- Finally, what is the administration's educational philosophy? Is it traditional and restrictive, emphasizing The Three R's and enforcing rigid discipline, or is it progressive and liberal, experimenting with new kinds of equipment and programs? Does its approach match or complement your own? Will you be fuming and calling the principal

every time your child comes home from school with another tale of what we did today?

The League of Women Voters may have some informative publications about the local schools or may be able to refer you to sources other than the school administration. The local newspaper, if you read it for several weeks or months, may also be helpful here. It can provide information on public controversies about school policy and such financial matters as bond issues and tax increases. It can also offer informative little tidbits in the spring about students or graduates who have won scholarships or other awards. And it can give you an impression about whether the local leaders see football as more important than geometry or vice versa — perhaps a better impression than you will get from talking to school officials, who sometimes talk one way and act another.

Remember that all of these measures of a school system are relative. A school that your cousin thinks is the best in the world may be simply the wrong place for your child. And public schools, by definition, must try to be all things to all taxpayers. Some may be a little better than others in one area, but they'll probably fall short somewhere else. There's no such thing as a perfect school. What you want is one that comes reasonably close to meeting your own needs. Remember, too, that children grow with remarkable speed. Choose a school district for the future, not just this year. The problems of the elementary school will be moot when your kids are all in high school. And the place that's on double sessions now but has two schools under construction may be a virtually ideal school district next year.

If you do not have or expect to have children, or if your progeny have grown and gone, you might do well to avoid the place that has a reputation for good schools. That reputation can add substantially to the price of a home because good schools are a major factor in the decisions of most buyers. And later on, good schools, being very expensive, can mean higher real estate taxes.

MEDICAL SERVICES

If you're satisfied that your child's head will be treated properly in the schools, you ought to try to make sure that the rest of him — and you — can be properly served by the local medical establishment. That may take a bit of trying, but it's important, so have a shot at it. If you require a specialist to treat the numb feeling between your ears, at least have a glance at the telephone book to be sure there's one within a reasonable distance. You might even call his office to see if he deigns to accept new patients. If you don't know precisely what specialized medical treatment or equipment to look for, consult the doctor who's been treating you in your old neighborhood before you start narrowing your search for a home. In any case, try to be sure that there are some doctors of the sort you need in the area that interests you, that there is a reasonably modern hospital fairly close at hand, and that there is some kind of ambulance service. The best ambulance service is probably that provided by the full-time professional staff of a hospital or a fire or police department. In suburban or rural areas, the service is likely to be provided by a volunteer rescue squad, and many of them are well-equipped, highly trained, and very reliable. The ambulance service to avoid is that provided by undertakers or independent commercial operators in areas where no other emergency service is available. In some instances, the free enterprise system makes them more interested in dead bodies than in live patients.

LOCAL GOVERNMENT

What about local government? How efficient is it? How corrupt? How responsive to the people? The local paper can tell you a great deal. If three-quarters of the town council is under indictment and two former mayors are in jail, it might be best to find another town unless you have a reform political career in mind. Reading the paper for a while can give you a picture of what's been going on in the area. The League of Women Voters, in the meantime, may be able to supply you with some publications that describe the organization and function of the local government. And it may be worthwhile, especially if you're considering a small town, to attend a meeting of the local legislature — the city council, township committee, or board of aldermen. Much of the business at hand will be of an arcane local nature that will render it incomprehensible to a stranger, but attitudes and impressions can count for a good deal here. Do the members of the council or board seem intelligent and attentive? Do they appear to understand what's going on? Is there citizen participation? Do you get the feeling that all the decisions were made yesterday in the back room, or are the speeches being made from the floor actually influencing the proceedings? It may be too much to ask whether you would like to be governed by this group of people, but could you stand to be governed by them? If the citizenry seems unduly wrought up, it may be that you have accidentally chosen a meeting at which some particularly sensitive issue is being considered. If, however, that local paper you've been reading takes no notice in its next issue of the chairs that flew through the air at the council meeting, it may be a safe assumption that chairs always fly through the air. In which case, it may be a safe assumption that you want to live somewhere else. If you're really in doubt, attend another meeting. If the chairs are still flying, buy elsewhere.

One thing to look for — again in the local paper — is a flourishing two-party system. It's harder to cheat when the other side is on its toes, and a political machine — whatever party runs it and however large or small the town — is a political machine. If you're on the inside, it may strike you as the greatest government in the world. If you're on the outside, it won't.

Notice the obvious public services and compare them with those available elsewhere. Are the streets paved and in good repair? Do the policemen look like oafish bumpkins or like trained, responsible professionals? Drop into the police station or precinct house and ask for directions to someplace or other. Are you treated courteously? Are the directions correct? Are there fire hydrants along the streets? Is the fire department paid or volunteer? Is it well equipped, given the nature of the area it must protect? If the department doesn't have a big ladder truck, don't move into a high-rise building in the town. Does the municipal government provide trash collection and sewer service, or are there additional charges for such things? Are there parks and playgrounds? Are they well equipped and maintained? Does there appear to be an organized, supervised recreation program, or do the children simply fend for themselves? Does the parking seem adequate in shopping areas and at such places as the railroad station? Is there a charge for commuter parking where it is needed? Is there a zoning ordinance? A master plan? Are they adhered to? City Hall can tell you whether they exist. A local lawyer can tell you how rigidly they're enforced.

LOCAL TAXES

Now get back to taxes, but on a narrower basis. Are there local income, sales, or personal property taxes? Ask at City Hall. What about real estate taxes? Ask the tax assessor:

- At what percentage of market value is residential property assessed? The assessment — the value upon which the tax is based — needn't be anything like the home's true value. It can be almost any fraction of that value, and it's still more or less fair if the same fraction is applied to all property.
- How often is property reassessed? When was it last reassessed? The more frequently the property in a town is revalued, the fairer the taxation is likely to be. Between reassessments, or revaluations, the newcomer will probably pay more than his share of the over-all burden. Ideally, property should be revalued every year, though many jurisdictions have not computerized their tax rolls to the point where they are able to accomplish this feat.
- Are homes automatically reassessed when they're sold? In many places, what you pay for a house becomes its assessment until the next revaluation. In a town that hasn't had a reassessment for 10 years, you're being taxed at today's value, but the guy next door, if

he's owned the place long enough, is being taxed at the value of a decade ago. Unfair! But the older residents like it, naturally, and they're the ones who voted for the town fathers last time around. Moreover, the longer you live there, the more you'll benefit from it, relative to later arrivals, and the better you'll like it.

- What is the tax rate? The assessment by itself is meaningless; the assessment and tax rate have to be considered together. The rate is usually given in dollars and cents. The rate of $3.89 means that a homeowner pays $3.89 in taxes each year for every $100 of his assessment. The owner of a home valued at $20,000 — and perhaps really worth $30,000, $50,000, or $100,000 — would therefore pay $778 a year in real estate taxes. You will no doubt hear of places where the tax rate is enough to curl your hair. Keep in mind that the rate means nothing until you know how property is assessed. A rate of $2 in a jurisdiction that maintains 100 percent valuation is the same as a rate of $8 in a place that assesses at 25 percent.

- How stable has the tax rate been in the last five years? Here's an area where you'll have to use your own intuition and observation as well as some expert advice. Tax rates tend to shoot up in areas that are growing quickly; all of a sudden, they have to pay for new schools and sewers, more policemen and firemen, and a host of other services. They also tend to shoot up in places where politicians have done some fancy bookkeeping during an election year, trying to postpone the day of reckoning until everybody's safely back in office. Sooner or later, the day of reckoning comes, however, and when it does it can be a shock. There's nothing gained by buying a home on the basis of this year's tax bills and then learning that the bill will double or triple next year. So it's wise to look at history in an effort to find a pattern if there is one.

Bear in mind through all of this that high taxes do not necessarily produce a bad place to live. Taxes support schools, police and fire departments, and libraries; they provide parks, streets, and sewers. Education is by all odds the most expensive service provided by most localities. If you're interested in good schools — and most buyers say they are — you'll have to be ready to pay for them. There are, from time to time, intense efforts to find new ways of financing education, of divorcing schools from the real estate tax. But the magic formula seems elusive, so you'll probably just have to grin and bear it. In that connection, it's wise to appreciate the service performed by large industrial and commercial facilities. Nobody wants to live next to a factory, especially in a suburban or rural setting. But factories pay more taxes than homes do, and factories don't send kids to school. A few factories, shopping centers, or apartment houses in a small town can work wonders on everyone else's tax bill.

NARROWING THE SEARCH

Having compared schools, taxes, medical services, and other public facilities in a few towns or sections within the large area you previously marked on your map, you are now prepared to narrow the search further. This is the step that's going to hurt. Mark off on your map the towns or sections that please you the most, then pour yourself a good, stiff drink, get out the classified real estate ads, and look for listings in those places. Look particularly at the prices.

If you're like most potential home buyers, you will now have another stiff drink. The best course to follow then is to go out to dinner and forget the whole thing. After a good night's sleep — or even two good nights of sleep — check the classified listings for the towns or sections that seemed almost as good as your first choices. If that requires two more drinks and another restaurant dinner, wait a week and start again, one notch lower. Eventually, you'll find the place that fits. It won't be quite as lavish or exotic as you might have hoped, but it will probably keep the rain out, and it will fatten your wallet a lot more readily than rent receipts do. Almost nobody can afford the home he'd really like to have, but millions of people have found homes in which they're quite happy. There's no reason why you can't do the same. Once you've come to terms with that fact, you can start looking realistically at neighborhoods and specific houses or apartments.

10
Which Neighborhood Should You Choose?

Now you've picked out a town or a section of the city that you know generally suits your needs. It's time to get down to the nitty-gritty. You want to zero in on one or more neighborhoods and look at them very carefully. The neighborhood, after all, is going to have a considerable impact on the way you live. Your examination of the neighborhood will have to be pretty much a do-it-yourself effort. There are very few experts to question when you get down to such a small area. You'll just have to look and listen and judge for yourself.

THE ENVIRONMENT

Start with the environment. Is the air relatively clean? Is there industrial or highway noise, even if the factory or the highway isn't visible? Check it on a weekday as well as a Sunday, during the day as well as the evening. Is the neighborhood under the flight path of an airport? Is there a junkyard or other blight nearby? Blight, whether it's the social blight of slums or the commercial blight of dumps and slaughter houses, has a way of spreading. Be careful. Are there such hazards as pipelines or oil or gas tanks? Are there railroad tracks nearby? Get a street map of the town or the area and look for highways, railroad tracks, oil depots, and other potential hazards and annoyances that may not be obvious when you're driving or walking around. What about the general topography? Is the neighborhood down in a valley and likely to be foggy half the time — and flooded the other half? Where is the nearest lake, river, or other potential source of floodwaters? Is the neighborhood sure to stay high and dry? Is it so high up on a hill that it will be constantly buffeted by winds, that it will be a nightmare for pedestrians and drivers in winter?

CONVENIENCE

How convenient would the neighborhood be, given the way you like to live? Is there adequate public transportation — subways, buses, streetcars, cable cars, taxis, or rickshaws? Look in the telephone book and call the local transit authority or bus company for schedules. Are the church and school reasonably close? Check the distances in minutes, not miles. Would your children take a school bus or would they have to walk? Ask the school administration. If they would have to walk, are there potential hazards between home and school? The only way to find out is to walk — not drive — the route yourself. Is there shopping — the kind you will use — close enough to be handy, but not so close as to intrude? Take an old shopping list and do a dry run: see how difficult it would be to fill it in the neighborhood you're thinking about. Suppose the car breaks down; how easy would it be to survive for a few days?

THE LOCAL SCHOOL

Does the local school live up to the district's reputation? There must be at least one "foul-ball" principal in every good school district, and a weak or incompetent principal can produce a bad school, no matter what the administration has in mind. Visit the principal and ask him the sort of things you asked the school administration earlier. Ask about average class sizes, pupil-teacher ratio, the availability of special programs, average achievement test scores, and the age of the plant and equipment. Ask if you can look around the school and visit a class. You may not be able to take a professional's measure of the place, but you can notice how well the building is maintained, whether the equipment seems to be adequate, whether the teachers and staff look bright, helpful, and glad to be there or whether they seem to be serving indeterminate sentences. Try to figure out, in other words, whether this is a dungeon for small offenders or whether it's a place where children learn how interesting the world is and how much fun it is to do new things. If you find the latter, you've discovered a precious commodity. Hang onto it.

PUBLIC SERVICES

Look over the public services in the neighborhood. Are the streets paved and the sidewalks and curbs installed? If not, you may find yourself paying a special assessment for the improvements later. Are the storm and sanitary sewers in place? Are gas, city water, and electric service available? Call the local utilities and ask. If the sewers are not in, you face the headache of septic tanks. If water service is not available, you'll have to take your chances with a well. Both can be expensive. If you're looking in a city neighborhood where the sewers and water lines are certainly in, find out whether you have to pay sewer taxes or water fees, or whether those services are included in your real estate taxes. If you're buying in the suburbs or the country, be sure to find out whether trash collection is provided by the municipality or whether you have to hire a private contractor.

THE NEIGHBORS

Does the neighborhood look like a congenial place? Are the properties well maintained? Are they maintained so well that you'd soon have an inferiority complex? Do the people seem to be so much alike that you'd soon be bored? Or are they a mixed bag of the sort of riff-raff you don't care to associate with? Would you be happy to have your friends or relatives walk or drive through this neighborhood on the way to your home? Are the activities you see going on — on weekdays as well as weekends, during the day as well as the evening — the sort of things you could join in and enjoy? If you have children, are there others in the neighborhood about the same age? Does it look as though you'd be the richest or the poorest man in town? Neither one is an especially comfortable position. The common wisdom is that you should buy in the best neighborhood you can afford, but not buy the most expensive place in the neighborhood.

THE FUTURE

How much is the neighborhood likely to change in the next few years? Look around and study your map. Are there big undeveloped tracts of land nearby? Find out from City Hall or the local planning agency how they're zoned; today's pasture can be tomorrow's junkyard, and this year's golf course can be next year's townhouses. If you're looking in a city neighborhood, are there nearby rundown areas? Ask the planners whether renewal is in the works or on the horizon. If not, the blight may be moving your way. If it's a neighborhood of single-family homes, is multiple-family residential development beginning to encroach upon it? Is the neighborhood in the path of spreading commercial or industrial development? Does the state highway department have plans to run a freeway through the neighborhood? One look at a map may tell you whether such a possibility is logical. Is the neighborhood, for example, midway between the airport and downtown, with only outmoded, overcrowded roads connecting the two? If you're thinking of moving into a renewal area in a city, you know you're taking a chance, so you'd better measure the risks carefully. How much renewal has taken place and how much is merely planned or expected? Has the neighborhood "tipped" back toward respectability yet? Visit the local police precinct and ask about the street or block you have in mind. Have the police seen a gradual but steady improvement there in recent years, or are you going to be the pioneer? How many "problem" properties — abandoned buildings, single-room-occupancy hotels or rooming houses, ill-maintained or unmaintained apartment houses — remain? If they're in the majority, the risk you're taking is very high. You may be able to buy a restorable home for a song, but you're in for years of effort, expense, and anguish.

Whatever the neighborhood — city, suburban, or rural — visit the local planning commission or zoning board and ask to see two maps: a zoning map of the neighborhood that interests you and a map reflecting the provisions of the master plan. The first possibility is that there may not be a master plan. Be wary in that case, for you're thinking about buying in a place that doesn't know where it's going or wants to go. There are still a lot of places like that. The second possibility is that the master plan is in the process of completion, but its details are still being ironed out. If that's the case, pay close attention to the differences between the master plan and the existing zoning in the neighborhood you have in mind. The trick is to figure out which will give way to the other — will the zoning be changed to conform to the master plan or vice versa? Ideally, master plans should take precedence and the zoning should be made to conform. But master plans are often — perhaps usually — politically unpopular documents. All sorts of people are likely to object to proposed changes in their neighborhoods, and when they do politicians are inclined to make exceptions — sometimes to the point where the whole master plan is simply an aggregation of exceptions. The question of which version of intended use will ultimately prevail is most pressing in places where the master plan is still in preparation; it's easier to change then. In the case of the third possibility — the master plan is complete and in force — it's wise to find out which came first, the plan or the zoning. If they differ, the zoning may represent a pre-existing exception that will gradually be brought into conformance with the plan. But it may also represent a second thought, a change with which the plan will ultimately be made to conform. Whatever the case in the neighborhood you have in mind, it will be worth your effort to try to find out what the local establishment has as its goal and whether that jibes with your own plans. And don't assume that it's all inflexible. Zoning is constantly changing, and master plans are constantly updated to take account of new factors. That's fair enough. If you and the municipality have the same thing in mind when you buy, at least you'll be a voter and a taxpayer when they decide to change directions, and you'll be able to hustle down to City Hall and register your complaint. Finally, don't leave the planning office without asking whether they have any hints about changes in the offing for your neighborhood. Planners tend to have very good sources for such information.

11
Should You Buy a New Home or an Old One?

Should you marry a tall girl or a short one? A fat man or a thin one? Should you eat steak or lobster? Should you buy an old home or a new one? Suit yourself. There are, as you may have heard somewhere before, advantages and disadvantages. Just be sure you know what they are.

NEW HOMES

A new home is not likely to require radical updating the minute you buy it. It will probably have such modern conveniences as central air-conditioning — or at least that's likely to be an available option — and its mechanical systems will probably be up-to-date and efficient. But along with modern technology, a new home will probably have modern workmanship, which in most cases is no match for the stuff that old-fashioned craftsmen used to turn out.

While a new home can be expected to make use of easily maintained materials, it will be subject to a shakedown period as it settles and dries out, expands and contracts. Its new systems — the electricity, plumbing, heating — will have to be broken in. Some of them may contain components that are relatively new and untested, in which there remain some "bugs." "Bugs" is the manufacturers' term for their own disasters. But "bugs" usually get corrected, one way or another, and there's something to be said for a dishwasher and central air-conditioning, even if it takes them a while to start working properly The one-piece plastic tub and shower enclosure may give under your weight when you step into it, making you fear that you are about to land, stark naked, in the middle of the bridge club's luncheon at the dining room table below. Good old ceramic tile doesn't bend like that. But even after years of showers you probably won't go through the new-fangled gadget, and it's markedly cheaper and infinitely easier to clean than good old ceramic tile. You give some and you get some.

A new home will undoubtedly lack the charm of an older one with the high ceilings, plaster walls, lavish woodwork, and careful detailing that have become prohibitively expensive in recent years. But the new home may require a lower down payment than an older one, and financing may be easier to arrange. Moreover, it may appreciate more, as a percentage of its original cost, than an older one.

OLDER HOMES

An older, or resale, home — any one that's been lived in by somebody else, if only for six months — is a different financial deal entirely. When you buy from an individual seller, you'll have to go into the financial market as an individual consumer and find a mortgage. The chances are that if you buy a new home from a big builder he will have gone into the market — the wholesale market — to find financing for you and all your neighbors-to-be. Obviously, when he goes looking for a hundred mortgages, he has more clout than you do looking for one. He can usually get you better terms than you can get for yourself.

Not that you have to throw up your hands and forget about older houses. They're what most people buy, partly because there are more of them and partly because they have a certain appeal. They are the kind of place where most people grew up or wish they grew up — roomy and warm and comfortable, in a creaky sort of way. Not too chic, perhaps, but home. Most of them may not have central air conditioning or garbage disposers, but they are more likely than new homes to have soundproof walls, hardwood floors, and such niceties as basements and trees. They will have that solid old construction and a patina of age and charm. All the "bugs" will have long since been worked out; the place will have been lived in and made to work as a machine for living. It is also less likely than a new home to look just like the place next door or across the street. It may have been built before assembly-line construction became popular. Or it may simply have been added onto and modified over the years until it looks nothing like its fellows.

ANTIQUE HOMES

One sort of older house, the genuine antique — say, an authentic colonial — deserves special mention because it has joys and problems all its own. More than the run-of-the-mill resale house, the very old one may need radical updating, and the process may be extremely difficult, particularly if you're a purist who wants to be sure that every detail is as authentic as possible. The colonials, unfortunately, didn't build walls with a thought for electrical conduit or air-conditioning ducts. Concealing such things — not to mention plumbing and heating — can be difficult in a house that was built before anyone dreamed they would exist. Even fixing or restoring simple things like windows and doors may be difficult. The parts and fittings may be of odd designs and sizes that are no longer manufactured. They may, in fact, have been hand-made on the spot in the first place and have to be hand-made now. If you don't have the sort of hands that can make them, you'd better have a big bank account and a lot of patience. Even if you can find all the components, however, and the home is restored to its original splendor, it may be full of disappointing surprises. Living standards were different in those days, and not just because of the lack of color television and garbage disposers. Heating systems were inefficient. That meant rooms had to be small, and since people had to build a fireplace for every room, they built as few rooms as they could get away with. Moreover, colonial craftsmen — geniuses that they were — did not come equipped with table saws and routers. They had tools that are fairly crude by today's standards, and the results sometimes show. In many old homes — really old ones — there's not a single surface that's level or plumb, not a single joint that's really snug. These were houses built simply to keep out the elements, not to supply a comfy spot for a stereo turntable. You may find that floors dip and walls weave to the point where you get dizzy on your way to the dining room even without your customary six martinis. Nonetheless, if you have the psychological and financial equipment to complete a restoration, or the extra financial equipment to buy a place that's already in top shape, you will have a truly enviable home, one that may be worth all the sacrifice it required and much, much more.

RUNDOWN HOMES

Even though the home you're thinking about is only 25, not 200, years old, if what you have in mind is fixing up a rundown or outdated place that can be purchased at a ridiculously low price, analyze your own skills and frame of mind very carefully. And don't underestimate the costs you face. It's almost always more expensive to add something later than it is to build it in the first place. To add it, you've got to cut into or remove something else, then fit it into a spot not necessarily designed for it. That's expensive. More important than the expense, perhaps, is the fact that it takes a long time to effect such changes, whether you do them yourself or hire someone. There's something psychologically disabling about a wait of months or years between the time you buy a home and the time when it's reasonably close to what you'd hoped it would be. What seems like great fun in the first few months — spending weekends in search of just the right moulding and evenings scraping two generations of pink paint off the living room woodwork — can turn into sheer drudgery by the end of the second or third year. And while you may justly consider yourself to be better educated and more clever than any licensed plumber in the state, there's no substitute for experience. That unlettered plumber has probably sweated 10 miles of pipe into place in his day; the chances are he's seen every problem your home has to offer a hundred times over. Your experience — connecting the garden hose to the sprinkler and changing a sink washer once — doesn't put you in the same league. What will take the plumber an hour will take you a weekend. Don't overestimate your skills.

In some cases, of course, other factors may overshadow such considerations. There are, for instance, two latter-day programs that attempt to change the whole financial picture for the purchaser of a rundown home. They are the "sweat-equity" and the "urban homesteading" programs, and they have been tried with varying degrees of success in many cities. Generally, they have two purposes: To make homes available to families who would not otherwise be able to afford home ownership, and to help stabilize or improve declining neighborhoods. Both programs are usually underwritten with government or foundation money. In a sweat-equity program, a low-income purchaser is allowed to substitute his own labor for part of the down payment on a home, usually a condominium or cooperative apartment in a building that is in need of rehabilitation, but sometimes a detached home he will help build. Some such programs represent attempts to teach construction skills to their participants. Since the sponsoring organization can buy a rundown building for little or nothing, and since most of the labor involved in the rehabilitation is free, the monthly carrying charges for the resulting apartment are — in theory, at least — modest enough for even a poor family's budget. Sweat-equity savings, the experts say, can range from 20 to 60 percent, depending on how much of the work you're willing or able to do. Beyond that, the theory goes, a rundown neighborhood is improved because one building has been rehabilitated and its residents are its owners, so they will see that it is properly maintained. If in addition some of the residents have learned new skills that open to them new job opportunities, the benefits of the program are multiple. If you're interested in such a program, check around for an owner-builder school, which will teach you the necessary skills, from acting as your own contractor to doing it all. Try to find one run by licensed architects, construction engineers, or builders. Check 'em out with the local building department and the Better Business Bureau. The local planning department, building department, or real estate department may be able to tell you where there is a sweat-equity program for buyers of modest income.

The same officials may be able to steer you to urban homesteading programs, in which run-down but salvageable buildings are sold for nominal fees to buyers who pledge to rehabilitate them and live in them for a specified number of years. The idea is that the improvement will turn a decaying area around, attracting new middle-class residents and the businesses that serve them. It's a sort of do-it-yourself urban renewal, though there is normally no requirement that the buyer perform the rehabilitation work himself. He can hire someone to do it if he chooses, just so it gets done. These programs have run into considerable difficulty in many places when slum neighborhoods resisted change and buyers found themselves strangled in red tape and rising costs. In at least one instance the homesteaders, plagued by vandalism, surrounded themselves with a chain-link fence designed to keep the rest of the neighborhood out. Their influence seems unlikely to "turn the area around" any time soon, and they seem less than likely to stay when their obligation expires.

Obviously, a critical factor to study if you're interested in a sweat-equity or homesteading program is how susceptible the neighborhood is to being upgraded. Studying the patterns of change over recent years and seeking out the forces that will produce change in the near future are even more important than in other home purchases. Decisions on the soundness of the structure and the cost of refurbishing can wait until you've decided whether there's any point in investing any money at all in the area.

NEW AND OLD APARTMENTS

There's one added consideration in a discussion of age if your goal is a condominium or cooperative apartment. Older structures will probably have been built as rental properties rather than as apartments intended for individual ownership. And all the professional real estate men concur that you have to build a better apartment if you plan to sell it than if you plan to lease it. The older apartment will have extra grace and charm — high ceilings, solid walls, and lush woodwork — just as the older house will. And the older apartment may have inadequate wiring and obsolete plumbing, just like an older house. But it's also possible that the genius is not yet born who could put a washer and dryer in an old rental apartment that has been converted to condominium or cooperative ownership, that no architect alive could create a dining area or an adequate kitchen no matter how many walls you're willing to tear out. The rental apartment may, in other words, be beyond conversion. If an apartment is what you have in mind, study the old very carefully before you reject the new.

Obviously, there's no way to say how old your home should be. That depends upon what you want, what you can afford, and what you're willing to put into it. One thing is sure, though: No matter what the age of the home, you will ultimately discover in it a few quirks that defy correction — a door that won't close tight, a room that cannot be made as warm as the rest of the place, a spot in the floor that squeaks when the cat walks by. Every home, new or old, has a few such things, and sooner or later you just learn to live with them.

12

If It's New, Should It Be Custom-Built or a Developer's Home?

Just as new and old homes have their pros and cons, so do custom and development homes. A custom-built home will fit your taste and lifestyle much more closely than anything offered by a developer. In a true custom home, you will be able to choose not only the colors and details, but also the materials, the layout, and everything else. Because you'll be dealing on a one-to-one basis with a builder, not as one of a thousand faceless customers, or because you'll be represented by an architect, you'll probably have much more control over the quality of the materials and workmanship than you would in a development home.

THE CUSTOM HOME

The custom-built home will be more expensive than a developer's home of the same size. The developer spreads his design and site-preparation costs over a hundred units or so. In a custom project, you have to absorb all those costs in one dwelling. The developer also buys land wholesale — in large tracts that have been or will be subdivided into lots — and that's cheaper than buying one lot at a time retail. The developer will standardize things as much as possible to allow the wholesale purchase of lumber, appliances, hardware, and everything else. Your whole purpose in custom building may be to avoid standardization, which means you also avoid the economy of massive buying.

IF NEW, CUSTOM-BUILT OR DEVELOPER'S HOME?

The custom home may be more to your liking than its development counterpart, but it's just about certain to cost more.

And while dealing with a developer can certainly be a large pain in the neck, seeing a custom home through to completion may produce the sort of psychological uproar that would drive a nun to drink. To begin with, there may be problems with zoning or other local regulations. The logical spot for a house on your lot, for example, may be too close to the street as far as the law is concerned, and the municipal fathers may not be anxious to make an exception in your case, no matter what logic suggests. The building code may wreak aesthetic havoc on your design. Too bad. It may be expensive or impossible to obtain sewers on your property, and the land may not lend itself to a septic system. Public water service may not be available, and you may drill to Mongolia without finding so much as a damp spot. The electric company may demand a king's ransom to run a little wire out to your corner. You may have financing problems, for financing is often much more difficult with vacant land — which is what you'll be buying — than with a completed home. There will be no developer to worry about construction financing — the loan that buys the materials, pays the labor, and sees the thing through until permanent financing (a mortgage) can be arranged on the completed home. It is most unlikely that your contractor will find or help you find a mortgage, as many developers do. Once work gets under way, the builder may discover something like unstable subsoil, adding a few thousand to the cost and a few weeks to the construction schedule. The contractor and subcontractors may not be as reliable as you'd hope. Some of them, of course, are as dependable as the calendar, but as a class they are notoriously poor managers of their own time and resources. Each of them may be trying to juggle several jobs besides your own — all of which were scheduled for completion yesterday. You can expect to hear a lot of evasive answers, to see very little progress on the first day of the hunting or fishing season, and to be told ad nauseam that it is, naturally, the other guy's fault.

The construction period will be, in case you haven't guessed, longer than you expected, even after you've revised your expectations in view of the fact that delays are inevitable. And if you never learned before that time is money, you'll learn it when you build a home. The cost will be higher than you expected, even after you've increased your estimates. The prices of some building materials may go up daily, not monthly. When inflation hits, it can run absolutely rampant through construction. Moreover, after everything's been completed just the way you'd dreamed it would be, the day will probably come when you'll want to sell, and you may then discover that you've built a magnificent white elephant. The potting shed, interior waterfall, and bathtub-built-for-three may be what you've dreamed of all your life. But they may not appeal to anyone else in the world. In such a situation, you'll simply have to accept fate. Slashing your wrists in the bathroom will only make the home that much harder to sell.

THE DEVELOPMENT HOME

A developer's home, on the other hand, will probably be readily salable, precisely because it wasn't built to suit an individual. All of the designs and details will be what the developer thought would appeal to the widest audience in a given economic class, and developers don't stay in business long if they're not good judges of such things. When you want to sell a development home, there will probably be many potential buyers who will find it acceptable, if not exactly overwhelming. In the meantime, even before you sell it, you are likely to find that the fittings and replacement parts are of standard types and sizes, that local merchants have them in stock if there are hundreds of homes in the neighborhood that sooner or later will need the same parts.

But a developer's home will not have — for you, at least — the charm and convenience of a home you've designed yourself or have had designed for you. In a development, you will have relatively little latitude to make personal choices — it will vary according to the price of the place. Those choices you can make will probably have more to do with details than with the basic design. If you don't like the design, your option is to choose another model or another development.

In a development home, you will have little control over the quality of the materials and virtually no control over the quality of the workmanship. You will not have an architect making regular visits to the construction site to look after your interests, though you may be able to hire an engineer to make periodic checks, and you will probably have difficulty getting onto the site to watch the work yourself. The developer will undoubtedly subcontract some or all of the actual construction work, and his budget for quality control may be about the size of your budget for sun-tan lotion.

You may need a lot of sun-tan lotion, though, because it will probably take the landscaping 15 years or so to catch up with everything else the developer hath wrought. Developers tend to buy farm land for two reasons: in most areas, that's what's available for development, and it's largely clear land and therefore easier (which is to say cheaper) to build on. Once the developer has had his way with the fields, he offers the home buyer a landscaping "package" that is usually minimal at best — a handful of grass seed, a couple of shrubs, and some twigs that, with years of care and lots of luck, may someday be trees. You can buy your own trees, of course, but there are only two kinds — small ones and expensive ones. It takes forever for the small ones to grow to the point where they provide something that might be described as shade, and in the meantime you will sit there on the prairie, braving the sun and the wind and paying for the heat and air-conditioning.

Moreover, all new homes are subject to a shakedown period, and that period in a development home can be especially traumatic. Custom homes are still built in the traditional way, more or less. Small crews do the work, largely by hand, and that means that the home is closed in, or made weathertight, only gradually — say, over a period of weeks. That allows time for the new lumber to dry — to twist and warp, shrink and expand — before it's sealed up completely. It can breathe, if you will. But big developers hold down their costs by using mass-production methods. They can close in a house in a couple of days, and once it's weather-tight, they lose no time in getting the plumbers, electricians, sheetrock men, and flooring crews to finish the job. Then when the framing lumber moves, as it inevitably does when it dries, the walls and floors move, too. That process can go on long after the buyer has settled into what he thought was a completed home. You may be dealing with "popped" nails — nails that back out of the wall when the wall and its framing move — and cracked joints for months or even years to come.

Despite such drawbacks, however, there is something to be said for the mass-production methods adopted in recent years by big developers, even something beyond the money they save. If the pride and precision that used to characterize the construction trades have disappeared — and who is arguing otherwise? — then it is the wise builder who assigns each crew one small task that is to be repeated over and over, a task that the crew will fairly soon learn to do very well, even when it's half asleep or entirely hung over. The man who installs the bathtubs in a big development constructed by a major builder can probably install bathtubs in a comatose state as fast as anybody in the history of plumbing. The problem occurs when the man who does the "rough" plumbing (installs the pipe that leads to the bathtub) is not only comatose but clumsy as well. If the pipe is three inches out of line and doesn't connect with the bathtub drain, that's not the bathtub man's responsibility, right? Right. And the plumber is by this time nine houses down the street, right? Right. The first one to discover the error is the buyer, whose initial morning shower in the new home is interrupted by a small child asking why that water is dripping from the ceiling into his cereal and why it tastes like soap.

The real fun begins when that buyer tries to get the developer to send a crew to fix the defect. It's like getting a brain surgeon to make a house call. In the first place, when one section of a development is completed, all the buyers move in at once, and they all discover their problems at once. Most of them are relatively minor problems — popped nails, loose moulding, faulty paint jobs. If the developer is to succeed, he must have most of his employees busy on the next section, building new homes that will generate new revenue rather than fixing old homes that will generate nothing more. He may be glad to come back and make good, but he'd like to do it once — say, in 30 days, when everybody's discovered all his problems and they can all be taken care of in one trip. In the meantime, it might be wise to shop around for a brand of soap that tastes good on cereal.

All those disadvantages notwithstanding, development homes do cost less than custom jobs, and they are more readily salable in many cases. They have another advantage, too: They usually age well. Custom homes are built for people who know what they want, who want it now, and who can afford it. Development homes are built for people who may know what they want and may want it now, but who can't quite afford it. The custom home is built for today, and it starts getting dated or outmoded tomorrow. Chances are that the development house will improve as it gets older, though of course it, too, gets dated. The landscaping will mature, first of all. And the buyer's income will probably grow, too. More often than not, he will decide to add something here or change something there as his finances permit and his needs require. In 10 years or so, the intense homogeneity that marks new developments will have disappeared. Every home will have a bit of landscaping that looks like something other than last week's special at the garden center, and every home will have been added to or remodeled in its own way. The place will have become a neighborhood, not a development. And values may well have doubled. You can't knock that.

THE SPECULATIVE HOME

There is also the possibility that you can find something between a true custom home and a development home. One alternative is the speculative single house, one constructed by a builder — usually on an isolated lot in an otherwise built-up neighborhood — in the hope that he would find a buyer during construction or soon after completion. If you find such a place while it's still under construction — the earlier the better — you may have a much better chance of tailoring it to your needs than you would in a development. For one thing, you will have a closer relationship with the builder, who's dealing with only one or two customers, not a hundred. For another thing, the builder will not be buying components by the carload, so he probably will not be concerned if you want something a little different, as long as he's not committed to a specific item. You are unlikely, however, to be able to make really major changes — adding a basement, altering the floor plan, or increasing the size in a radical way — and in that sense it will not truly be a custom home. It will be cheaper than a custom place, though, if somewhat more expensive than one in a development. You may have to wait 15 years for the landscaping to look like much, as you would in a development, but your house won't look like every other one in the neighborhood, and most of the utilities and other public facilities will probably be in operation and long since paid for.

INDUSTRIALIZED BUILDING

Another form of housing that is halfway between the custom and the standard development is the industrialized, or factory-built, home. It is also a form that applies to single-family attached and multiple-family homes as well as single-family detached houses, though you may be aware of its use only if you're buying a detached house. In a way, the industrialized home is a marriage between the mobile-home and traditional home-building businesses. The product looks more or less like conventional construction, but many of the methods used to build it may be closer to those commonly associated with automobile factories than those of construction. Most industrialized homes are ordered, in part or in whole, from catalogs, and they are built, in part or in whole, in factories.

If you're in the market for an attached home or an apartment, you may never know whether the place was built with industrialized construction methods. Indeed, it may not make any difference. If, however, you're looking for a detached single-family home, something cheaper than custom-built but a little more original than the usual development job, you will probably be aware of the differences between industrialized and conventional methods. You may not see any difference when the house is finished, but you will during construction. How much difference you see will depend upon what industrialized method is used. In any of them, you may have to buy your own lot and build your own foundation, though many factory houses, as they are called, are sold through builder-dealers who have building lots and are willing and able to construct the foundations. Broadly speaking, there are three categories of industrialized housing: pre-cut, panelized, and modular.

Pre-cut houses consist of lumber that is cut and marked in a factory, then delivered to the site. What arrives is like the kits kids use to build model planes and boats. The pieces and the directions are all there, but they remain to be assembled into a house. You, a contractor you hire independently, or the builder-dealer through whom you buy the house will have to prepare the site, construct the foundation, and put the thing together. The electrical, plumbing, and heating systems may not be included in the kit, you may have to take care of such extra touches as a fireplace or a patio, and you may have to supply interior paint, wallpaper, and paneling. You may also be responsible for grading, landscaping, and the construction of sidewalks, driveways, and other exterior doodads. Or you may not be responsible for any of that; all of it may be in the package you're buying. The wise buyer will therefore be extremely careful to find out exactly what materials and services he is getting and what will have to be done at extra expense. Obviously, your choices will be more limited than they would be in a custom house — materials and dimensions have to be standardized to some extent if they're to be subject to factory production methods — but everything that's left out of the package will represent a choice you can make yourself. And you may be able to negotiate a lower price by deleting some things from the package — interior paint, say, and paneling for the family room — then buying exactly what you want locally. It'll probably cost a bit more when you're finished, but the end product will be more a custom house.

One step beyond pre-cut construction is the panelized — widely known as prefabricated or "prefab" — home. In this type of building, the pieces are cut in a factory and some of them are assembled into panels — walls, perhaps, or roofs or floors — before delivery to the building site. You or a contractor or your builder-dealer will have to prepare the site, construct the foundation and fasten the panels together into the boxes that make up a home. The same conditions that apply to the purchase of a precut home apply to that of a panelized one. Be absolutely sure you know what you're getting and what you're not getting. The opportunites to customize the design may be more limited in panelized than pre-cut housing because factory methods, which imply standardization, are taken one step further. But factory methods — for the most part, the use of unskilled production-line help rather than skilled carpenters and other craftsmen — imply greater economy, too, and that may be carried one step further as well.

The ultimate in industrialized housing (apart from mobile homes, of course) is modular construction. It goes a step beyond panelized housing: The pieces are cut in a factory, then assembled not just into panels but into boxes that constitute rooms or groups of rooms. The boxes, called modules, are then shipped to the building site and fastened together or piled up to make a house, a row of townhouses, or an apartment building. The degree to which such a home is finished at the factory can be remarkable. Off the back of a truck may come a virtually complete home: appliances, light fixtures, plumbing and electricity, paint, wallpaper, carpeting — everything in place. You or a contractor or builder-dealer will probably have to prepare the site and build the foundation, but after that it may be like piling up blocks rather than assembling a kit. Your choices are severely limited, of course, if even the paint and the carpeting go in at the factory, but this is the ultimate (again, barring mobile homes) in production-line housing, and the savings should be obvious.

On the theory that mobile homes are a whole other bag that appeals to a whole other audience and is fraught with a whole other set of problems and possibilities, we'll deal with them in a whole other section. Later.

Whether the home you're contemplating is pre-cut, panelized, or modular, it is well to realize that you are embarking on a relatively uncharted course. These are comparatively new ways of doing things and, like all new ways of doing just about anything, they present problems as well as solutions. No matter how attractive an industrialized building system may be, there is probably a building code somewhere that will prevent its use. Building codes tend to be archaic things. Most of them are based on theories developed before there was any possibility that factories could produce homes. They are usually based on "common" building practice, and common building practice in the small-scale residential field has probably developed less in the last 100 years than any form of technology this side of fly-swatting. Carpenters built houses that way because that's the way their fathers, who taught them carpentry, built houses. Lawyers and politicians, who produce building codes, decided that if that's the way carpenters built houses, that must be the way they should be built, since very few of them fall down. So the way houses were built became law; you had to build houses that way. And once there was a law, it was in the interest of the people who built houses according to the law and the people who supplied the materials to do so to see that the law was not changed in such a way that other people could build houses — maybe cheaper! It remained for the industrialized housing types to ask why studs (the vertical framing members in the walls) had to be 2 x 4's and 16 inches apart when 2 x 3's that were 20 inches apart seemed sufficient, and why piping had to be copper when plastic was so much cheaper and seemed to work as well. You can predict for yourself the reaction from the folks who brought you copper pipe and 2 x 4's. The politician who didn't know a 2 × 4 from a brick was left at the mercy of the local carpenters and plumbers, and the building code remained inviolate. Industrialized homes don't get built in some municipalities because they are held up as a threat to motherhood, democracy, and copper pipe.

All this presents a major problem to the industrialized housing folks. They can succeed only if they can manufacture homes the way Detroit manufactures cars — by the thousands. But they can't manufacture thousands if they can't sell thousands, and they can't sell thousands if hundreds of cities, towns, and villages make their homes illegal. But the industrialized housing crowd is, after all, just one more manifestation of good old American know-how, so it did the logical thing. It started bombarding state governments with reasons to set up statewide building codes that would supersede local codes and would be based upon scientific data rather than tradition. That campaign has succeeded in some states and not in others. Some states even have inspectors in out-of-state factories that are producing homes for shipment to their citizens.

The restrictions are gradually easing, but the lesson for the potential buyer is clear. Be very sure that what you have in mind is legal. Ask the building inspector. That caution is particularly appropriate when you're thinking about modular construction, which relies more heavily on modern technology than does any other form of building.

Nor are building codes the only problems you may encounter with industrialized housing. Transportation of your components may be very difficult and expensive — perhaps even impossible, if the home you've chosen is modular, and to get to your lot the modules will have to go through a tunnel en route from the factory. Housing modules are, after all, oversize loads. There are places they simply can't go, and their movement may be severely restricted in other places.

The transportation problem is most serious for modular construction, but all of the industrialized systems — whether pre-cut, panelized, or modular — share the disadvantage of unfamiliarity. They are relatively new to contractors, subcontractors, inspectors, lenders, and lawyers, so such people may be getting an education by working on your place. They may learn from their mistakes, all right, but you may have to live with those mistakes. Therefore, the choice of builder-dealer or contractor may be as important as the choice of manufacturer and model. Check the potential builder-dealer as you would a contractor if you were having a custom home built. Try to figure out, in addition, whether he got into industrialized construction solely because he couldn't make it as a conventional or "stick" builder. Failure in that business is not a high recommendation for this one. Look at the manufacturer, too, as you would a contractor, checking financial institutions, suppliers, subcontractors, old customers. Then study the home you're thinking of buying just as you would the model in a conventionally built development. Be sure that you know what is included in the package, what delivery will cost, what erection will cost, how long it will take, and what services are included. Finally, make sure you can get the financing you need at a rate you can pay.

13
If You Decide on a New Custom House, How Do You Find the Land?

Whether you're looking for a completed building or the land on which to put one, the process of choosing an area and a neighborhood is pretty much the same. If you're looking for buildable land, though, some factors are more important than they otherwise would be. In fact, what may look like an advantage if you're in the market for a completed home can be a disadvantage if you want to build a new one. Local regulations may, for instance, rule out the kind of construction you have in mind or perhaps any construction at all. Despite the long-standing theory in this country that bigger is better — that growth in itself is good — local restrictions on growth have become routine. Such "no-growth" or "slow-growth" laws are particularly common in areas that have seen very fast rates of growth previously and have experienced the pain that comes with municipal expansion — the pain of disappearing wilderness, crowded schools, and skyrocketing tax rates.

GROWTH RESTRICTIONS

The oldest and most popular form of growth restriction is probably the minimum lot size; in certain zones, no home can be built on less than half an acre or three-quarters of an acre or two acres. The over-all effect of such a zoning regulation is to reduce the number of homes that can be constructed in a given area, thus holding down growth in the school population, traffic congestion, and demand for extra police and fire protection. At the same time, such laws raise the price of each available home, and therefore restrict potential buyers to a more "acceptable" (that is, richer) group. If building lots in town are going for $20,000 an acre and you need two acres to build a house, you'll have $40,000 tied up before you hire a lawyer, consult an architect, or stick a shovel in the ground. A very small proportion of all potential buyers can afford that, so growth is automatically curbed. There are other ways to limit growth, though. One way is to stipulate a minimum construction price for each home. That, perhaps, is a more direct method of doing the same thing that large-lot zoning does. Another way is to limit the number of bedrooms in each home. This sort of regulation usually applies to large developments — most often, multiple-family developments — but there's no reason that a sufficiently clever and persevering municipal government couldn't make it apply to individual houses as well. It may not limit the buyers to the upper financial reaches, but it does disqualify large or growing families, and that's the idea behind it — to hold down the school population.

Though it can lead to incredible legal hassles, some local governments have turned to the building moratorium, a broader form of growth restriction. This is a policy saying, in effect, that there will be no building whatever until we have worked out a master plan or built a new school or extended the sewer system. While legal action has brought many local officials to the realization that they must tie moratoriums to such specific projects for the provision of public services, they can be maddeningly slow in dropping the other shoe, even when the courts step in to prod them. A far fairer, but more complicated and less widely used method of matching growth in demand for public services with growth in the government's ability to provide them is the timed development plan. Such plans are usually based on a system of points. A landowner must accumulate a minimum number of points before his property can be developed. Points are awarded for proximity to all sorts of public services — roads, sewers, water service, a fire station, and so forth. There is also usually a time limit — after a given number of years, one can build on the land, whatever its point score.

All of this means that if you're looking for land rather than for a completed home, zoning and building regulations are much more important to you. And in such matters, a real estate agent's word is not sufficient evidence on which to make a commitment. If you can't go down to city hall personally to find out from the planning or building department what the situation is, hire a lawyer — you'll have to hire one anyway, sooner or later — to tell you or find out for you.

ENVIRONMENTAL RESTRICTIONS

The same sort of caution should be exercised with regard to ecological regulations. Get a knowledgeable local lawyer or go to the governmental source yourself. It might also be wise in the area of ecological regulation to consult an architect before you are absolutely committed to the land. A local architect may be more aware of some of the technical ramifications of environmental regulation than a lawyer would be, at least when the regulations are fairly new. There are areas where environmental restrictions are more likely than elsewhere — coastal areas, for example, and flood plains, sites adjacent to wilderness, and sites of striking natural beauty. While ecological rules have always seemed like a good thing, they are no small matter if you want to build, even though they may sound harmless enough. Conservationists — and, to their chagrin, developers — have learned that the environmental-impact statement is a potent weapon in any campaign to halt building. All it asks for is an outline of how the proposed construction will change the natural environment. That seems fair, but it can be fantastically complicated, and the time and expense of producing it have been enough to convince more than one developer that he should simply drop a project. Bear in mind that on a smaller scale you are planning to do just what the hated developer does — cut down trees, deprive animals of homes, pollute streams, dig up land, burn fuel, produce sewage. Do not fail to find out from a lawyer or the responsible local authorities what the environmental restrictions are before you commit yourself to the purchase of land.

The lawyer is not half the story. Expert advice is essential in many facets of all home-buying decisions, but it's more than essential if you're starting the process by buying vacant land. The strengths and weaknesses of a house or apartment are much more likely to be apparent to the untutored eye than are the strengths and weaknesses of a chunk of rock and topsoil. The rock you so admire may be the contractor's Waterloo. Find out before you own it.

FINANCIAL ADVICE

A real estate broker can advise you on the availability of land. A good broker or his agent will know what's on the market and generally what prices are like. He can make your search much more efficient. He will also know something about zoning, environmental restrictions, and other technical matters, and, though his word should not be the last one in these areas, his advice can be very valuable while you're still in the process of choosing. You can't hire a lawyer, an architect, and an engineer to look at every lot that comes along. Bear in mind that a real estate agent works on a commission — he is paid only when property is sold. Most of them are honest, hard-working people who want to find things that will please their clients. But the agent's personal interest is in making a sale, so even the most honest one may tend to dwell less upon the defects than the advantages of a property. Real estate brokers and agents are not — and do not pretend to be — architects, engineers, lawyers, or contractors. Don't expect them to be. Consult an expert when you need advice. The one field in which many brokers and agents are expert is appraisal. Even there, you would probably be wise, if there's any doubt in your mind about the value of the thing, to consult two of them before you commit yourself to a price. At least one broker will have to be paid an appraiser's fee, since he will get no commission on the sale.

Another source of expert advice is lenders — commercial banks, savings banks, and above all, savings and loan associations. They're the folks who supply the money that makes homes possible, and if you're not going to be able to get the money, there's not much point in going on with the pipe dream. An official of a lending institution — he's usually called a mortgage officer, but he may be called almost anything — can tell you whether his institution is making mortgage loans in the area you have in mind and, if you've got fairly firm ideas about what you want, whether it is interested in making loans on that sort of project. Lenders take a lot of heat for their refusal to make loans, and in many cases it's more than justified heat. Many a bank or savings and loan is eager to accept the deposits of the poor folks who live near its slum branch, but is willing to lend money only to the relatively rich folks who live near its suburban branches. There seems to be something morally wrong with that. But that doesn't mean there's something morally wrong with every lender's decision not to issue a mortgage. There are lots of good reasons: The institution doesn't have the money to lend (don't laugh; it can happen). The applicant seems unlikely to be able to meet the payments (the lender has an obligation to protect the funds of his depositors and stockholders; he's not doing so if he regularly approves loans to applicants whose income is obviously inadequate to make the payments or to applicants whose income seems unpredictable or likely to evaporate). Another valid objection is that there is something wrong with the collateral for the loan, in this case, the home you propose to build or the land on which you'll build it.

It's entirely possible, in other words, that the local bankers know something you don't know about the area where you're thinking of buying or about the kind of home you're thinking of building. Without being an engineer or a geologist, for instance, an experienced banker may know that, no matter how deep they've drilled, nobody's ever been able to find water within five miles of your lot. He may know that there are serious flooding or erosion problems in that part of town. He may be a member of the board of directors at the local glue factory and therefore know that the glue combine is thinking of moving its hoof-grinding operation to a new plant right next to your dream house. The moral to be learned here is that lenders don't turn down loan applications solely because they are heartless and greedy. They may be that; but they may have other reasons, too. If you find that lenders are making mortgages but won't give you one, ask why, and listen to the answer. Whatever it is that they know or think they know, you should know it, too. You may decide that the bankers have come to the wrong conclusion on the basis of the facts they have, and you may be right. But before you go through with the deal you should be aware of the reasons for the lenders' reluctance. Believe it or not, they often know what they're talking about.

TECHNICAL ADVICE

Beyond such preliminary legal and financial advice, you should also have some technical advice. What are the chances that the subsoil will prove to be too unstable to support construction? If there is no public water service, what are the chances that you can drill a good well at reasonable cost? If there are no sewers, is the ground suitable for septic tanks? The only way to be sure is to take what's called a "percolation test," a test of how fast liquids seep into the earth. An architect or an engineer can advise you on such matters and steer you to the specialists who can take the appropriate tests if they seem indicated. Your lawyer can help you insure that the seller has title to the land and that no one has an easement across it, and he can draw up an agreement with the potential seller that contains the appropriate "contingency clauses" — provisions that let you back out of the deal if, within a reasonable time, you discover factors that make building impossible or outrageously expensive.

An architect can also advise you on the aesthetics of the thing — help you visualize how the house you have in mind will fit on the land, precisely where it should be built, what the potential zoning and code problems are. Even if you don't plan to have an architect design a home from scratch, you may be able to hire one to advise you on the technical and aesthetic problems involved in building on a particular lot. He may see a way to turn what looks like a disadvantage into an asset, to turn a pedestrian lot into a remarkably attractive homesite. And he may see a problem with soil stability, rock formation, topography, water table, or drainage that will guarantee a disaster later on. Either way, you're ahead for having had his counsel. And if you've already got a contractor in mind, you'd better have him take a look at the site, too, before you commit yourself. He may tell you that he'll never be able to get a truck or a bulldozer in there without knocking down all the trees and destroying the lot. You can guess for yourself what it would cost to have the foundation dug by hand and the materials hauled in by mule or dogsled.

LOOKING AT THE LAND

In fact, you can guess a great deal about the whole proposal just by taking a walk around the land you have in mind. You may be able to save yourself the trouble and expense of consulting lawyers, architects, and engineers if you look closely for yourself first. Even if you retain such experts after simply driving by, you should get your feet on the ground before the deal is closed. When you do, be sure to use your eyes and your head as well as your feet. Is the place so sandy or rocky that you'll never be able to grow anything but cactus or moss? Is it so steeply sloped that most of it will be useless, even if you can build a house on it? A house on a hilltop can provide beautiful views in summer, but it can be a disaster in winter, when the wind whistles through it and the driveway is a foot deep in snow. Walk all around what you envision as the boundaries of the land; the exact boundaries may be virtually impossible to find. Does the place have enough trees to provide shade? Enough sunshine to make it pleasant? Are the views good? Are there any swampy areas or large areas of rock outcropping? Either can present a construction problem. Where would a house go on the lot? What would that do to views? To the trees or other wild plants already there? Where would the house be in relation to the street? In relation to nearby homes or other buildings? Are there signs of serious erosion? Is ground water likely to run from the house to the street or vice versa? Is it likely to run from your land to that of a neighbor or vice versa? If it runs from the street toward the house, you'll probably have flooding problems. If it runs from a neighboring tract toward yours, the same may be true. If it runs from your land to someone else's, you may have legal problems. It should run toward the street or to a creek, pond, sewer, or other collection point.

You might ask the owners of nearby vacant land whether they have building plans or would like to sell in the near future. Ask the owners of nearby homes, if there are any, whether they found fill, ledge rock, unstable subsoil, a high water table, or other problems when they built. Obviously, your investigation of the future of the area — zoning and planning provisions, the information and instincts of local planners, your own observations of what's likely to occur — should be much more careful when you're buying land in an undeveloped area than when you're buying either land or a home in a relatively built-up area. A built-up area is on a course toward somewhere or other. It is possible that an obvious course has not yet been chosen for an undeveloped area. It can go in any direction at all, and you should be careful in your study of what that direction is most likely to be.

Finally, such things as a survey and a title search are more important in the purchase of vacant land in relatively undeveloped areas than they are in the purchase of a home in a more populated place. The more rural the spot, the more informal transactions are likely to have been in years gone by. It may be that no one is quite sure just how big the tract is or precisely where it begins and ends. And it may be that some previous owner forgot to get divorced before he remarried and sold the land, and that his first wife is about ready to pounce on it. Too bad if you happen to have paid for it.

14

How Should You Get a Custom Home Designed?

If you're really adventurous, you can hire a carpenter, a plumber, and the other appropriate tradesmen and let them design a home as they go along. You might wind up with a sumptuous home, though it probably would not be exactly to your taste and it might look a bit odd. Would it be wiser to design it yourself? Well, maybe. To do that properly, you'll need a great deal of specialized knowledge. You'll have to know what sorts of materials and fittings are available, what they cost, and what their relative advantages and disadvantages are. You'll also have to know something about loads and stresses, about soils and their stability, about building codes and zoning regulations and about the traditions and habits of local craftsmen. On top of all that, you'd better know something about cost estimating unless you're interested in a ticket to the welfare office. It's probably easy to design a home that's the biggest, most solid place in town — just take everything you see other people doing and double it — but it's hard to pay for a home like that. Every time you depart from the convention, the usual way of doing things, you will encounter what might be called the "head-scratching factor." The contractor or a subcontractor will have to stop to try to figure out just what it is you want and just how it should be done. That wastes time, and time, you will soon discover, is money. When you're the client, it's your money. So unless you have lots of money or lots of special talent and knowledge, don't attempt to design your own home. Find someone who has the qualifications and can design something to your specifications, or find a design produced by such a person that fits your specifications.

STOCK PLANS

Every small builder has a few stock plans in a drawer someplace or knows somebody who has a drawer. But choosing that sort of plan is hardly better than drawing your own. The chances are that the contractor won't have any problem understanding the plans because he will have built them a hundred times before. But the result will hardly be a custom home, even though it was built to your order. It will look much like any other house, perhaps with an extra bathroom or a larger living room or gingham siding, if that's what you specified. It won't be an individual expression of the owner (or of anybody, for that matter) and it won't blend particularly well with your land unless you're very lucky. The design probably will not have been drawn with local conditions — zoning and building codes — in mind, and it may be out of date, making little or no use of newer, more efficient systems and materials.

There are other sources of stock plans, however, and their plans may be more up to date and more imaginative than those a small builder happens to have in the trunk of his car. Most newspapers these days flesh out the real estate section with a "plan of the week" for which detailed drawings and materials lists are available. And where is the suburban newsstand that is not flecked with magazines bearing such titles as "Custom Home Guide" or "Tomorrow's Homes Today" or "You, Too, Can Turn a Common Cave Into the Taj Mahal"? What they contain are lush renderings and small floor-plan diagrams for dozens of houses, together with brief descriptions that are sweet enough to leave you with diabetes. If you can ignore the sales pitch and concentrate on the facts, which may be few indeed, you may find a sound and fairly imaginative plan that is close to what you require. Unlike a plan you draw yourself, a stock plan from a magazine or newspaper will probably have been drawn by a professional who has the proper technical background. Unlike the stock plans a builder may have, the ones from magazines and newspapers will probably be reasonably up to date. They will not, however, have been drawn with an eye to your lot or to local variables — the building code, the weather, supplies of materials, and construction traditions. They probably will not reflect precisely your tastes and desires; they will not produce a custom home in the narrowest sense of that term. They may not even produce a custom home if you hire an architect on an hourly basis to tailor them more closely to your needs, though that may improve them a great deal. Stock plans will, however, be considerably cheaper than complete architectural service, even if you retain a professional to modify them. A typical package — five sets of blueprints and materials (specifications) lists — should cost about $100, maybe less. It should contain enough information for a contractor to make a bid on the job and for a lending institution to decide whether it will issue a mortgage. Before you order any stock plans, be sure they meet the minimum standards of the Federal Housing Administration, the FHA. That's no assurance that the plans will produce an enviable home or that the place will conform to local regulations, but it does suggest that it probably won't fall over in the first good storm, and it means that the home will qualify for financing insured by the federal government if that's what you decide you need.

In one sense, industrialized homes — pre-cut, panelized, and modular homes — are stock plans taken one step further. Like stock plans, they will probably have been designed by qualified professionals, and they will probably be up to date, perhaps more so than other stock plans. Most manufacturers publish catalogs that contain dozens of designs and variations on designs, so over-all you'll have a wide selection. The manufacturers advertise heavily in magazines aimed at a homeowner or potential homeowner audience; you should have no trouble compiling a list of names and addresses. Because their catalogs are relatively expensive to produce, they may charge for them. It's a small investment compared to the thousands you're contemplating spending on a home. Like the builder's stock plan, the plan offered by a housing manufacturer will have been used before — the bugs will have been worked out of it. It will probably not be a design you can expect to see duplicated on every block, and in many cases it will be relatively adaptable — you can ask the manufacturer to alter some details to make the home better suit your needs. But in only a few cases is it likely to be a strikingly original design, and it will hardly be a custom home in the strictest sense, one designed with both your tastes and your lot in mind. Moreover, marketing, production, and transportation problems can produce some strange design compromises. Still, it will probably be a lot cheaper, room for room and square foot for square foot, than a home designed to your order by an architect.

ARCHITECTS AND DESIGNERS

Ultimately, the only way to get a custom home is to hire someone qualified to design it to your specifications. The chances are that the professional you hire will be an architect, a man or woman trained in both the technical and the aesthetic aspects of housing design, a combination engineer and artist, if you will. In some areas, you may find "building designers," people who have — or at least maintain that they have — the proper technical and aesthetic training, but who are not licensed architects. Some of them are trained architects who lack only the license — perhaps because they choose to act as both architects and contractors, and some professional groups and licensing authorities have, at least until recently, seen that combination as a conflict of interest. That system, like some of the newer arrangements that architects are setting up, eliminates one of the checks built into the traditional architect-contractor-client relationship, but if you find a competent and honest designer, you may get as good a home as an architect could produce, and save money as well.

Economy aside, an architect is probably your safest bet if you want a true custom home. Because of licensing requirements, you have some small assurance that his training has been sufficient, and if he has been in practice locally for a while, he can be expected to know the building and zoning codes, the strengths and weaknesses of local workmen and contractors, and the peculiarities of the supply situation. He can take the time to study your land or to help you find an appropriate lot, then design a home to suit it. He can take into consideration your own tastes and needs. He may be able to build into the design some economies that you or a builder would never have thought of. He can help you choose a contractor, then supervise the construction, making sure that the specifications are met and the laws adhered to.

Probably the best way to start looking for a design or for the professional who can create one for you is to talk to friends who have recently had homes built. Find out where they got their designs and how pleased they are. Did their design present any unusual problems? Did it work out as well as they had expected? Were costs in line? Did the architect or designer, if there was one, listen to their thoughts and apply them to the design? Did he have some good ideas of his own? Don't rely solely on friends, however. Look around for yourself. If you see a relatively new home that looks appealing, find out where the design came from. It's a rare owner who will not be flattered that someone else admires his home enough to want to imitate it. Keep your eye open as you read magazines or newspapers, too. You may stumble across a feature story about a home that's just what you have in mind.

The local chapter of a professional society — the American Institute of Architects, for example — may be able to refer you to a list of members who specialize in or are willing to accept commissions for custom homes. The bigger, older architectural firms may want to confine themselves to large commercial, industrial, or institutional projects, which offer a different challenge than a home — and usually a larger fee. But the younger or smaller firms, and even some of the big old ones, may like the idea of doing residential work or may be in the position of having to accept any reasonable commission that comes along. That need not mean that this firm is any less competent than others, especially in times when building is slow and everybody in the industry has to scratch a little harder to make a living.

Once you have a list of prospective architects or designers, shop around. Make appointments with a few of them to discuss what you have in mind, what you can afford, and what they have designed in the past. Does the architect seem to understand what you want? Does he have some useful suggestions? Do you feel comfortable talking with him? Has he had other projects roughly similar to your own? Does he seem to be proud of them? Is he so busy that he won't be able to get to your project for several months or will have to sandwich it between phases of a larger job? Will he work with you and design the home himself, or will the actual work be taken over by a partner or associate? If the latter is the case, try to meet the associate who will be doing the design work and to get a feel for his approach; he may have other ideas than the partner in charge. Ask each architect or designer you interview for a list of clients for whom he has designed homes more or less similar to the one you're planning. If you get serious about one of the firms, call some or all of the clients on its list. Ask to see their homes and discuss the experience they've had with the architect and with the home itself. Look at the home critically, the way you would an existing home you were thinking of buying. Ask the owners what they'd do differently if they had it to do over. Did the architect supply some useful ideas beyond what they knew they wanted? Did he warn them away from things that later proved to be mistakes? Were his cost estimates accurate? Was the project completed on time, more or less? Was the architect helpful in choosing a contractor? If you wind up with several architects or designers who are highly recommended and whose design philosophy seems to complement your own, you're lucky. Try to choose the one with whom you feel personally most comfortable, to whom you can talk most easily about your dreams and finances. If you don't feel at ease talking to the architect, find a different one. No point in paying to be ignored.

DEALING WITH AN ARCHITECT

Even before you settle on an architect, you should understand what he will expect of you and what he will be able to provide. He is offering expertise in the areas of design, siting, costing, bidding, and construction supervision. He may also have contacts in the local financial community and in the appropriate areas of government — the building department, for instance — and those contacts may be sources of more good advice. The architect will expect you to provide frank, clear and concise explanations of your needs and resources. Part of his job is to get you the maximum home for every dollar you spend. It will help neither him nor you to hide the true state of your finances. If you can really spend $10,000 more than you told him you can afford, you might never hear about some options that would have increased the beauty or value or utility of your home far beyond the extra cost involved. The architect might never mention such things because you've told him you can't afford them. If you overestimate your resources, the problems are predictable. You gain nothing if he designs you a home you can't afford to build. The lender will soon discover whether you can swing the deal, and it's a waste to have to go back at that point and scale things down. The architect or designer will also have to know something about the way you live and the size and interests of your family. He will have to know, for example, how many bedrooms you need, how important a separate dining room is, and whether there should be room for a workbench in the garage. He will also have to know something about your tastes — the styles and materials that appeal to you and those that don't. He will not, however, expect you to design the home. He is better equipped than you are to produce a design that meets your needs and budget if he understands what the needs and budget are. If you cannot abide asbestos siding, tell him so, but don't tell him that you want red brick here, fieldstone there, and cedar shakes in between. Let him come up with the design; you can always suggest modifications before you approve it. Once the design is agreed upon, however, the modifications should pretty well end. The architect will not expect you to change your mind every time you drive by another attractive home or read another magazine. Once the design is set, changes are expensive as well as annoying for the architect. Once construction begins, they can be expensive for the contractor as well. In either case, they'll be expensive for you, too. You can have a second thought as the thing begins to take shape and make some alterations in portions of the home not yet complete, but if you plan to stay within your budget, you'd better plan to keep changes to a minimum.

How much your budget will have to allow for an architect will depend upon what you want him to do. In the traditional arrangement, the architect sees the project through from concept to completion. The process usually begins with meetings between client and architect so the architect can get an idea of what the client wants and what the budget is. Then the architect usually prepares some rough drawings for the client's approval. Gradually, the drawings get more detailed and specific. The client may be asked to inspect and approve them at several stages. At several such points, too, the architect may supply rough cost estimates, each a little more detailed and accurate than the last. When the design is set and the client has approved it, the architect produces working drawings and specifications that describe the structure in great detail. It is on the basis of these drawings and specifications that a contractor can make a bid for the construction work, the zoning and building authorities can issue approval for construction, and a lender can decide whether he will accept a loan application. The architect usually advises his client on the selection of contractors who will be invited to bid, on the evaluation of the bids, and on the final choice of a contractor. Then he makes periodic visits to the site during construction to insure that the plans and specifications are being met and to interpret the plans, where necessary, for the contractor or subcontractors on the job.

There's no law, of course, that says you have to hire an architect to do all of those things. And there's no law that says he can't adjust his fee accordingly. If you ask an architect to modify a stock plan rather than start a design from scratch, his fee should be lower than it would be for the whole job. Even if the design is made from scratch, the architect can in theory drop out of the process anytime you want to take over. If you feel able to do so, you can conduct the bidding and supervise the construction yourself, though you'd better know what you're doing. You wouldn't be the first hopeful homeowner to see a fine design damaged or destroyed by an incompetent or unscrupulous contractor. Also be sure that the architect understands at the outset what you're planning

HOW SHOULD YOU GET A CUSTOM HOME DESIGNED?

to do, and that he agrees to it. Don't surprise him with an announcement that he's through just when he thinks he's got the project rolling.

Some architects are adapting to residential construction an arrangement long used in larger projects — the construction manager system. When it's used in small projects, the client and the architect usually divide between themselves the normal duties of the general contractor. Instead of signing just one agreement with a general contractor, who then negotiates with the subcontractors, the client takes bids from and negotiates directly with the electrical, plumbing, roofing, excavating, and other trades. That can be a complicated process, and it means that the client must be skilled in negotiation and willing and able to become more involved in the project than he otherwise might. The architect does all the design work, as he would in the traditional arrangement, and then acts as construction supervisor. He must make more frequent and thorough inspections of the construction in progress because there is no general contractor to oversee the work of subcontractors. Because he must spend more time on the job, the architect's fee is likely to be higher. But the client saves on the overhead and profit of the general contractor, and some architects who use the system say that the over-all saving can amount to 20 percent. Whatever the saving — and it probably won't be 20 percent — if you act as your own general contractor, you'll have to deal with the hassle involved in coordinating and overseeing a construction project. You'll also have to insure that your architect-construction manager (or one of his associates) has the kind of "hands-on" building experience required for construction management. Not all architects do.

What you pay the architect will depend upon how his fee is calculated as well as upon what tasks you expect him to do. Traditionally, the architect is paid a percentage of the project cost — about 15 percent is common, but the actual percentage is worked out in negotiation with the client. This system has been criticized on both sides. Some clients fear that a fee based on project cost encourages the architect to build as expensively as possible in an effort to run up his fee. Some architects argue, on the other hand, that if a client is particularly difficult or fickle, the architect can spend an inordinate amount of his time in planning — or changing plans — and that this additional time never shows up in the construction cost. Architects also complain that if the contractors' bids are low — perhaps because they need some work to keep busy during a slack period — the architectural fee is automatically and unfairly reduced.

Because of those complaints, other forms of compensation are coming into more general use. In some cases, the architect may be paid a negotiated lump sum for all his services on the project. This system works best — certainly from the architect's point of view, and perhaps from the client's as well — when the broad outlines of the project are understood at the outset and are unlikely to change. If the project may change radically before it's completed, it would be fairer to negotiate at the outset a fee that will be paid in addition to expenses. In small projects like homes, it is also sometimes possible to hire an architect for an hourly fee, with the understanding that his services will end when the client thinks he can carry on alone, perhaps when drawings and specifications are complete or when a construction contract has been signed.

With almost any method of compensation, you can expect to make an initial down payment when you sign a contract with an architect, then to make periodic payments in proportion to the services rendered. In the traditional arrangement — the one in which the architect handles the design, helps with the bidding and contract award, and oversees the general contractor — the last installment on the fee is usually paid when construction is completed. Beyond his fee, the architect will expect to be compensated — perhaps monthly — for travel in connection with the project (one reason to hire a local architect) and for such miscellaneous expenses as long-distance telephone calls, reproduction costs, and, if you want them, scale models.

The American Institute of Architects publishes sample contracts that cover the usual arrangements involving architect, contractor, and client. Copies are available through local chapters of the institute or through its national office at 1735 New York Avenue N.W., Washington, D.C. 20006. Such contracts are the result of years of experience with thousands of building projects, large and small. They are probably fair to all parties concerned with typical building processes. Nonetheless, they were drawn up by architects, not clients. It is extremely important to have a lawyer examine any agreement before you sign it. Your project may not be typical, and your lawyer can advise you about tailoring the contract to your specific situation. He may also spot some legal loopholes that you might miss.

15
How Should You Find the Right Contractor to Build Your Home?

Obviously, if you're going to use a contractor's stock plans, the search for the design and the search for the contractor will be one. If you're inclined toward an industrialized home — a modular or pre-fab structure — the two processes may also overlap. Many such homes are sold only through builder-dealers who do the site-preparation and erection work after you've bought the package. Whether or not the design and the contractor go together, the choice of the company that will erect your home is one of the most important you will make in the course of building. Do it carefully.

GETTING ADVICE

If you have retained an architect to design your home or to assist in its design, seek his advice on the contractors from whom you should solicit bids. He's probably dealt with a lot of local contractors for a long time. He's therefore likely to know which ones customarily deliver good homes without a big hassle and which ones usually deliver problems.

But don't rely solely on the architect. If you have friends who have built homes locally, ask about their experiences. Was the contractor on time? Did he complete the job within the budget? Were there extended and bitter arguments over costs, quality, and changes? Did the work seem to be of a high standard?

While you're at it, ask bankers and savings and loan officials, real estate agents, and municipal inspectors about their experiences with local contractors. A banker may be reluctant to commit himself, but he just might let you know that his institution is very slow to lend money on any home a certain contractor is building. It may be that the contractor simply does his banking elsewhere or is a member of the wrong political party, but it also may be that he builds lousy houses or doesn't pay his bills. In either case, it's useful to know that the bank doesn't like him, even if you don't know the reason. Real estate agents and inspectors may be equally reluctant to tell you frankly what they think of a contractor, but their knowledge is no less valuable.

Perhaps the best source of information about small contractors is subcontractors — plumbers, electricians, tile and drywall installers, carpenters, and so forth. If you know some of them — it's unlikely that they'll level with you otherwise — find out what contractors they like to work with, what ones they avoid and why. Though the sub-contractors rarely confide in outsiders, they know which contractors are doing a schlock job and which are doing a good one. They know the quality of the materials they're called upon to install and the quality of the work that's going on around them. They also know which contractors do not pay their bills on time, an oversight that seems to be epidemic in the industry, even during the best of times. The contractor who has a reputation as a late payer may have trouble getting materials and hiring subcontractors unless — and perhaps even if — the customer pays in advance. He's not the contractor you want to sign up, for all of his problems will ultimately become your problems. You have enough trouble worrying about your own bills. Why should you have to worry about his, too?

If you're really stymied on how to check out contractors, scout up some fairly new homes and ask their owners what they thought of the contractors they worked with. Be sure to ask whether the job was completed on time or within a reasonable time, whether it was reasonably close to the budget, and whether there were major disagreements over quality, costs, or changes.

It should be emphasized, by the way, that contractors are not at fault every time a job is delayed, runs over budget, or results in bitter recrimination. That's why it's wise to check with a broad cross-section of former customers before writing off one company. It's not unusual for a client, particularly one who has never built before and who does not have an architect or other professional advice, to make wholly unreasonable demands upon a contractor. In such cases, argument and delay can be expected, but the contractor is not necessarily to blame.

Once your conversations with architects, lenders, brokers, inspectors, and former clients — or, if worse comes to worst, a perusal of the Yellow Pages — has produced a list of likely contractors, check their backgrounds carefully.

For what it's worth (probably not very much) ask the Chamber of Commerce and the Better Business Bureau what they know about the contractors you're considering. What they know is likely to sound like a eulogy, but the way it's delivered can be revealing if you're alert.

Ask the local consumer affairs office, if there is one in the municipality or county, whether they've had a lot of complaints about the people on your list. If there is no consumer affairs office — and maybe even if there is one — it might be a good idea to ask the district attorney's office or the state attorney general's office the same question. It's unlikely that a small custom-home builder will have come to the attention of such people unless he's outrageously dishonest or incompetent, but it's worth a call, just for the peace of mind that's in it.

Call the local builders' association and ask whether the people on your list are members and whether the local group is affiliated with the National Association of Home Builders (NAHB). Membership in such an association is no guarantee that a man knows how to build homes, but it is an indication that he's been trying for a while, takes the matter seriously, and intends to keep trying. The national association is not made up entirely of angels, either, but it tends to attract the more professional and experienced builders. It is, however, generally limited to the larger operations, ones at least large enough to afford the annual dues. The most competent and honest one-truck, father-and-son companies will probably not be members; not because they aren't good enough, just because they aren't big enough. All things considered, membership is probably better than nonmembership, but neither really proves anything at all.

If the local group is affiliated with the national association, ask about a program in which its member-builders may or may not participate, the Homeowners' Warranty program, or HOW. It is something between a guarantee and insurance against defects in a home built by a participating company. Because the insurance company that stands behind the program doesn't want to go broke paying claims, the participating builders have to meet certain standards. That means there are some built-in assurances for the potential customer that the participating builder is fairly responsible. At bottom, though, HOW was established and is administered by builders. It's hardly Ralph Nader's dream, but it's better than nothing.

Recognizing the shortcomings of the national consumer program, find out whether the contractors you have in mind are participants. Be aware, though, that membership in the national association — as well as participation in HOW — is for the most part limited to the larger companies, companies that are more likely to be building developments than individual homes. Nonetheless, it's worth asking about.

Call the nearest office of the Federal Housing Administration (FHA) and ask if they have rated the contractors on your list. It is again likely that the ratings will apply more to large-scale developers than to small builders of single homes, but it's still worth a call. The FHA's ratings are an indication of what you're likely to get for your money. The average rating is 100, and the top score is 105. The contractor or builder who gets a score higher than 100 is judged to have offered more for the money than the competition in general.

The one who scores less than 100 is judged to have offered less than the average for the money. Interesting statistics, those, but still no assurance that you'll get exactly the home you want.

INTERVIEWING THE CANDIDATES

By this time, you've probably developed a list of contractors who might be worthy of your consideration. Call each one and ask some questions:

How long has he been in business? Always under the same name? Always in the same town or area? Does he use his own name in the name of his company? The favorite trick of the shyster builder is to dissolve his corporation every year or so, then form a new one under a new name, thus avoiding all that bothersome legal nonsense when old customers get upset about defects in their homes. It's a very good sign if a man has been in business under the same name for a long time. It's an even better sign if the company name is his name; it's more likely that he's ready to stand behind it.

How many houses has this contractor built? How many like the one you have in mind? This question is especially important if your plans are unusual. Some contractors can be stopped cold by an unusual idea.

What is his bank and who are his major suppliers of materials? Call them, explain why you're interested, and ask about his credit, reliability, and general reputation. You may get some obtuse answers, but any answers at all may be revealing. If you're given the impression that this builder has trouble getting credit, beware. Trouble for him in this area is trouble for his customers. You're supposed to pay him in proportion to the work completed, but if he has no credit he won't be able to buy the materials to do the work in the first place. The result will be an endless stream of reasons why you should pay him in advance — "just this once," of course — and ultimately an incomplete home and a contractor nobody can find.

For whom has this contractor built homes in the last three or five years? Get all the names and call at least a random sample — some from this year, some from last, some from five years ago. Try to look at the homes and certainly talk to the owners. How satisfied are they? Did they have a big hassle to get the job completed? Does it sound as though it was the customer's fault or the contractor's? Was the workmanship sound? Are they still satisfied over-all with the job?

When you've narrowed the search down to one or two contractors, ask them for financial statements. Such statements may tell you more than anything else about whether the contractors will be in business long enough to complete your home and, if necessary, to come back and take care of the inevitable problems that remain. Consult your lawyer or an accountant on what the statement really means unless you're equipped to interpret it yourself.

THE RIGHT CONTRACTOR TO BUILD YOUR HOME

In one way or another, all of these questions apply to the builder-dealer who wants to sell you an industrialized home as well as to the contractor who wants to build a conventional one for you. The questions may have to be modified somewhat if you're buying from a catalog and the contractor is merely going to erect what's delivered, but it's still in your interest to learn how much experience he has, how satisfied his old customers are, and how good his financial health is.

Be aware throughout that custom-home builders and industrialized housing builder-dealers tend to be very small operations. There may not be one person on your list of potential contractors who is a member of the National Association of Home Builders or who has a rating from the Federal Housing Administration. That may be a reflection on their size, not their ability. If a contractor has good credit, is well thought of among his colleagues, can refer you to a dozen delighted clients, and is unknown to the D.A. and the consumer affairs office, his lack of membership in professional organizations is beside the point. Being small is no offense.

Ultimately, the FHA, the builders' association, the D.A., and even your own architect will not tell you what contractor to choose. You'll have to sift through all your information and make that decision yourself. It's your money and your life. Some of your decision should probably be based on nothing more than rapport. If you can talk to this fellow — if he speaks your kind of English, seems to understand what you want, and seems enthusiastic about building it — and if all the other indicators are positive, he's probably the contractor for you.

16
How Should You Deal With the Contractor?

To avoid painful and unnecessary problems later on, understand at the outset what the contractor will expect to do for you and what he will expect from you. He will offer a bid, a price for which he will build the home you want. When you and he sign a contract, he will be bound by the bid and you will be bound by the plans and specifications on which it is based. That is, the contractor will not be able to raise his price, but you won't be able to change the plans in such a way as to increase his costs. Changes can, of course, be made, but you will have to understand that they will increase the over-all price of the job in most cases. Under the usual contract, the contractor agrees to supply all the necessary materials and labor and to put them together to create the home — he agrees to do all of the purchasing, scheduling, and coordinating, and to provide day-to-day supervision of the actual construction. Again, there can be exceptions. You can supply certain materials if you can obtain better quality or lower prices than the contractor, and the final price should be adjusted accordingly. The same goes for labor. If you do some of the work yourself, the contractor's price should reflect that fact.

WHAT THE CONTRACTOR EXPECTS

Generally, the contractor expects to supply materials and labor, and that's all. He will not expect to function as your architect, engineer, designer, interior decorator, real estate agent, or lawyer. Even if he's willing to assume such roles, it's not in your interest to have him do so. If he knew enough law, he'd be a lawyer.

The contractor will expect you to understand your relationship with him and to cooperate. He will want clear, complete plans and specifications upon which he can calculate a bid, order materials, and schedule the work. He cannot be expected to commit himself to a price unless he has a reasonably firm idea of what you're planning to build. He will want a minimum of head-scratching time — time spent trying to figure out from unclear plans how to build something he's never seen before or how to use a material he's never encountered before.

Remember that Einstein was not a contractor. Most contractors are not geniuses, just as most of the rest of us are not. The function to which the contractor is accustomed is not creativity and imagination; his job is to follow the plans. Remember, too, that relatively few contractors have ever built a Frank Lloyd Wright home. Most of them are used to doing very ordinary things in a very ordinary way. If you alter that pattern, you had better be sure that your intentions are made crystal clear — that you, the architect, the contractor, and the man with the hammer all know what you're trying to do.

The contractor will want as little interference and as few changes as possible. If you didn't think you could rely on him, you shouldn't have signed a contract with him. Once you've signed the agreement, you should be prepared to leave him alone. He's built a lot more homes than you have; he should know what he's doing. This does not mean you must leave town during the construction or avoid the site as though it were a leper colony. On the contrary, you should make it clear that you're interested in what's going on and you should be available for consultation when necessary. But you should not interfere. And while changes should be held to a minimum, they are not absolutely forbidden. The contractor may even suggest a few himself that will make construction easier, save on materials, or add an extra little touch when the job is complete. But the changes you make should be confined to parts of the project that are not yet complete, and you must understand that changes can mean delays and extra expense. It's your money and your life; if you think a change is worth the price, go ahead.

The contractor's fee will probably be about 15 percent of construction costs, and he will expect periodic payments as the work progresses — that's the money he uses to buy materials and pay the subcontractors. He will hope for good weather, constant supplies of labor and materials, and fairly stable prices. The weather, supplies, and prices are factors largely beyond your control or the contractor's, and a problem with any one of them can mean big trouble for a building project. Be patient and reasonable if such a factor produces complications with your home.

NEGOTIATING THE AGREEMENT

Against that background, how do you negotiate with a contractor? The first step is to get several bids — say, three — from contractors who seemed in your investigation to be reliable and experienced. Be sure that each of the bids specifies certain things:

- The block and lot numbers of the land on which the home is to be built.
- The date and number of the plans and specifications on which the bid is based.
- The exact price of the complete job.
- How long the price is good — that is, how long you can think and debate before you have to accept the bid or see it expire.
- How much time will be needed to complete the home and obtain a certificate of occupancy.
- Who carries insurance during the construction, what kind of insurance, and how much.

When the bids are in hand, show them to your architect, if you have one, and to your lawyer (you'd better have one). Discuss with the architect the technical merits of the various bidders. Get the lawyer's thoughts on any legal differences there may be among the bids. He may also know something about legal or financial problems that some of the bidders may have had in the past. Using that information and the technical expertise of the architect, try to choose one contractor among the bidders, then do some more checking.

Be sure, for example, that the contractor has sufficient insurance. Get from him certificates of workmen's compensation, public liability, auto liability, and property damage insurance. Show the certificates to your insurance broker and get his opinion on whether the contractor's coverage is adequate. Consult the broker about your own coverage, too. You will probably have to have insurance to cover yourself, the contractor, and the subcontractors against fire, wind, vandalism, and malicious mischief. You can probably get a policy that provides coverage, from the beginning of construction, equal to the value of the completed home.

Tell the contractor that you want a performance bond, and insist upon a performance bond proof sheet, your assurance that he has the bond. The contractor applies to his insurance agent for the bond, which obligates the insurance carrier to complete the home if the contractor is for some reason unable to do so. The cost of the bond is a small percentage — as little as 1 percent, perhaps — of the cost of the project. If the contractor balks at the idea of getting a bond, offer to pay for it yourself (one way or another, you'll wind up paying for it anyhow). If the contractor is still unable to get a performance bond, you should probably start looking for a different contractor. The insurors apparently think there's a relatively good chance that he won't be able to finish the job.

If the bids turn out to be higher than you'd expected — everything else is, why not construction bids? — discuss the matter with your architect and the contractor you'd like to use. The architect may be able to help you negotiate a lower price without changing the plans or specifications. He may be able to explain to the contractor why some of the materials or procedures called for are not as expensive as they seemed at first glance. The contractor may also be able to suggest ways to reduce costs by eliminating nonessential items — perhaps things that can be added later — by substituting less expensive materials or by changing architectural details without doing great aesthetic damage.

When you and your architect, insurance broker, and lawyer have sifted through all the details and chosen a contractor, and when you and the contractor have settled informally the details of your agreement, have your lawyer draw up a contract. It should specify just about everything, including everything that was in the contractor's bid.

THE CONTRACT

The agreement should, for instance, specify the block and lot numbers of the land on which the home is to be built. This is to protect you against the possibility that the home will be built inadvertently on someone else's land. You wouldn't be the first to whom that has happened. The contract should stipulate the date and number of the plans and specifications to which it applies, and a copy of those documents should be attached to it. It should be very precise on what is included in the job — how much landscaping, what kind of sidewalks and driveway, what kind of termite protection, what brands of paint and wallpaper, what models of appliances.

The contract should specify that the contractor will use his best efforts to produce a structure that conforms in all respects to the plans and specifications and all other written understandings with the owner. It should provide that, upon request, the contractor will supply materials samples to the owner and such samples as well as shop drawings to the architect.

The agreement should state the exact price of the job and provide that the contractor will pay all costs of the work, including materials, labor, permits, license fees, and all other payments required by public authorities. It should be specific about any exceptions to these standards — an agreement, for example, that you will supply certain materials or do certain parts of the work.

The contract should stipulate that the contractor is responsible for compliance with codes, ordinances, rules and regulations, and that he will obtain (as well as pay for) the necessary permits, inspections, and certificates.

The contract should specify the date on which work is to begin and the date by which it is to be completed. It should allow a generous construction period — figure a month for each $10,000 to $12,000 in construction costs — so that the contractor will be able to deal with delays beyond his control. Ideally, there should be a clause calling for a financial penalty for every day of delay beyond the agreed-upon completion date. Contractors are notorious for their tardiness, and most of them will strenuously object to any such penalty clause. Those who do accept it can be expected to pad their bids so heavily that they will make a profit even after they have paid a large penalty. But a penalty clause is worth trying for nonetheless, and if you're willing to pay enough for it, you can no doubt get it. Your chances of seeing the job swiftly completed will be better if you can avoid the building industry's rush season — spring and fall — or if you build during a year when business is particularly slow.

The contract should provide that changes can be made only in writing, signed by both parties, owner and contractor. It should specify that the contractor is responsible for safety on the site and stipulate what insurance coverage is the responsibility of the contractor and what coverage must be obtained by the owner.

The contract should say what, if any, warranties are offered by manufacturers or suppliers for products, materials, or appliances to be installed in the home. It should specify who — manufacturer, supplier, or contractor — will stand behind the warranties and provide service. It should stipulate further that the contractor will guarantee for one year from the date of completion all workmanship and materials supplied by him that are not otherwise guaranteed. Here is where his financial stability becomes especially important. His guarantee is worthless unless he's around to honor it.

The agreement should state that the contractor is to deliver the home to the owner free of all mechanics' and other liens, and it should require that the contractor remove from the site all construction rubbish and debris.

It should stipulate that construction will not be considered complete until a permanent certificate of occupancy — the local government's stamp of approval — has been issued for the home. Without that certificate, it's illegal to live in the home, so the place is worthless, in a sense, until the document is issued.

The contract should specify the schedule on which payments will be made as the work progresses. A typical schedule might call for 10 percent when the foundation is completed; 30 percent when the rough enclosure is finished; 30 percent upon the completion of drywall and rough plumbing, heating and electrical work; 25 percent when the work is complete and a certificate of occupancy is issued, and the remaining 5 percent 30 days after completion. Generally, before a payment is made, the architect — or the owner or an engineer if there is no architect — inspects the project to insure that the specified work has been completed properly, then certifies its completion so the money can be released to the contractor.

For protection against the filing of liens by subcontractors after the job is complete — if, for instance, the contractor collects his money but skips town without paying them — the contract should specify that all periodic payments will be broken down among the contractor and subcontractors and will be made through checks payable to the contractor or jointly to the contractor and a subcontractor, depending on who did the work. The subcontractor's endorsement on a check then becomes an acknowledgement that he has been paid. If the contractor skips town, you are not on the hook. As an extra precaution, you can also stipulate in the contract that after each payment the contractor and each subcontractor will issue a receipt acknowledging payment for all work completed to date. And with the final payment, you can get from all hands releases waiving the right to attach liens to the property. Ideally, such releases should also be obtained from all suppliers, but there's a limit to the amount of time you want to spend collecting legal papers, so that may be asking a bit much.

SUPERVISING CONSTRUCTION

Once construction is under way, you should be interested and available, but you should not interfere. It's advisable to show up on the site now and then, to know what's going on, and to flatter the workmen with a few ingenuous questions and some naive exclamations about how interesting it all is. But show up only with the attitude that the people at work know what they're about. Even if they don't, making them nervous is not going to help. If you see what looks like a problem, take it up with the architect or, if there is no architect, with the contractor. Deal with the workmen only through the proper channels, and don't make accusations unless you're sure they're warranted. Start out by seeking guidance and assurance, not revenge. That will come later.

If you're tempted to incorporate into your plan every good idea you see, cancel all your magazine subscriptions the day the contract is signed. No point in encouraging costly temptation.

The contractor will probably have occasional questions for you — about things like the color of the tile in the bathroom or the pattern for the living room wallpaper. Some contractors will simply allow you a fixed amount of money for such things as interior paint, wallpaper, and light fixtures, expecting you to buy the stuff so they can install it. Try to anticipate all questions and choices. When the contractor asks what color tile, be ready with an answer. When he says he needs the light fixtures Thursday, have them Wednesday. They may hang around until two weeks from Tuesday before he picks them up, but any complication or delay on your part is another excuse for delay on his part. You'll quickly learn that he has enough excuses; you needn't give him any extra ones.

Another thing not to give the contractor is any unnecessary opportunity to build less than you bargained for — to cut corners where you won't be likely to see them. If you have an architect, he should look after your interests, insuring that the home is built according to the plans and specifications. If you don't have an architect but do have the proper technical knowledge, you can inspect the job for yourself, making sure that the materials used are those specified and that they are being assembled according to the drawings. If you lack both an architect and the necessary expertise — if you don't know interior plywood from exterior plywood or concrete blocks from cinder blocks — find someone who has the proper training and hire him to stand in for you.

Probably the most likely source of such talent is a home inspection service or building inspection service. These services, which are available in virtually every city in the country, concentrate on inspecting resale homes for potential buyers. The inspector, usually an engineer or a man of long experience in the building business, spends an hour or so looking over the structure and mechanical systems of a home, then fills in a written report for the potential buyer. Most of these services will also arrange to have an inspector go over a home at several stages during its construction, thus giving the owner some assurance that he's getting something akin to what he's paying for.

If you're working directly with a contractor and will rely on a home inspector or some other independent expert to keep tabs on the job for you, you would probably be wise to consult your lawyer about including in the contract a clause stipulating that periodic payments will not be made to the contractor or the subcontractors until the inspector verifies that the work in question has been completed according to the plans and specifications.

Ultimately, the target date for the completion of construction is almost sure to be missed. Keep calm. Be reasonable but firm. If your contract contains a penalty clause for delay, don't invoke it on the spot. Be a good fellow and give the contractor an extension — two weeks or a month — because you understand he has problems. Be especially generous if the delay is obviously the result of bad weather, materials shortages, or a statewide strike — factors that one contractor can hardly be expected to control. You may be able to get a home sooner if you're adamant, but it's unlikely that you'll get a better home. The contractor can always slap a few things together so you'll get off his back, but you may not be too happy with the results. And since it will be much harder to get him to return to correct sloppy workmanship than it is to get him to stay an extra day or two and do it right in the first place, patience is in order. You must, however, make it clear all along that, while you will be reasonable, you ultimately intend to enforce the contract, so he'd better be reasonable with you, too.

SETTLING DISPUTES

When you've been issued a certificate of occupancy and have moved in, but before you've made the final payment on the contract price, try everything and keep a list of all the things that don't fit, don't work or weren't finished properly. Two weeks before the final payment is due, send the contractor a registered letter listing the defects you've found, and add that you expect them to be corrected before the final payment is made. This should not be an outraged letter that calls the contractor's integrity into question. You have just purchased an enormously complex, custom-made machine. Like any other machine, especially any other custom-made machine, it will require some testing and adjustment before every component can be expected to work properly. Every new home has some small defects at first, no matter how much it cost. That's par for the course, and you should understand it. Understand it; don't be overwhelmed by it. While some defects are perfectly normal, having them corrected is perfectly normal, too. Keep after the contractor until he makes things right. And be very reluctant to part with that last 5 percent of the price until you're satisfied.

If you and the contractor have some rather basic differences about how much you owe him or about whether the home meets the specifications outlined in the contract, that will hardly be surprising. Unless the dispute is of overriding importance, unless it involves grand sums of money or the habitability or structural integrity of the home, you should make every effort to settle your differences through negotiation. Your architect and your lawyer can be extremely helpful in this effort; rely on their advice. It may wind up costing you a few hundred dollars more than you think is fair, given the contractor's obligation to deliver a certain home at a certain price, but that may be cheaper by far — both financially and psychologically — than fighting the thing to the bitter end.

The bitter end is, of course, court, but few such cases get that far. Most disputes that can't be settled through negotiation go to arbitration, and the arbitrator's decision is usually not subject to appeal. The decision of the arbitrator rarely pleases either the contractor or the owner, and the expense of getting it can be considerable. The best course is not to get to the point where you need such a decision, and the best way to do that is to be careful in choosing your contractor, be reasonable in dealing with him, collect your endorsements and receipts for every payment, and collect your waivers with the final one.

The ultimate weapon of the contractor, subcontractors, and suppliers of materials for your home is the lien. The lien is — like a mortgage — a claim on the property. It makes the property unmarketable and in certain circumstances can result in its being sold at auction to satisfy the claim. This is complex, messy business, worth some trouble to avoid. The laws vary from state to state, so legal counsel is essential in dealing with a lien. In fact, it's essential long before that. Proper legal counsel can mean there won't be any possibility of a lien.

SPECIAL ARRANGEMENTS

There are two other matters relative to your relationship with a contractor that ought to be considered. The first is whether you can do without the general contractor altogether, performing his function yourself or in conjunction with an architect. Doing so can save you some money — the contractor's overhead and profit — but it can also produce some headaches. The job requires skill and experience as a negotiator and a basic knowledge of construction costs and techniques. Subcontractors, anticipating that they will waste some time working with an amateur, may pad their bids, and you will be obligating yourself to work out with each of them all the details of his part of the job. If you do not have an architect or cannot find an architect or other professional qualified to act as construction manager — that is, to oversee the day-by-day assembly of the place — you may have to do that yourself, too. You will have to coordinate and expedite the project, making sure that the proper materials and people are in the proper place at the proper time and that everyone understands what's expected of him. Acting as your own contractor will mean that when a problem crops up — and problems will crop up with amazing regularity — you'll have to be available to deal with it. It will mean, in other words, that you must have not only skill, experience, and patience, but a good deal of free time as well. Unless you have all four, be wary of acting as your own contractor.

The second popular arrangement with a contractor — also designed to save money — is a contract that calls for a partially completed home that you will finish yourself. Again, your skill and experience are major factors in evaluating that approach. If you have trouble driving a nail without smashing two thumbs and splitting the wood, you probably should let the pros handle all the work. If your workshop consists of an old carton containing two broken screwdrivers, a tack hammer, and six used faucet washers, you may discover that you'd have to spend more on tools than you'd save on construction costs. And many of them are likely to be tools that you'll use rarely, if ever, again. But even more important than your supply of skill or tools is your reservoir of patience and perseverance. Moving into an unfinished home can be like camping out, not the sort of life most people care to put up with for more than brief periods. And do-it-yourself work always seems to take twice as long in fact as it did in theory, especially if it's confined to evenings and weekends. A project like completing an unfinished home can drag on forever, and before it ends the strain may be terrific.

If you're seriously considering completing your home yourself, calculate very carefully what that arrangement is likely to save you and very realistically how long the job is likely to take. Then double your time estimate, halve your savings estimate, and think about the strain under which you'll be living during that period. If you decide to go ahead, be very careful that your agreement with the contractor spells out precisely what he will do and what you will do, what he will supply and what you will supply, so there is no room for misunderstanding. As always, get everything in writing and sign nothing — absolutely nothing — without legal advice.

17

If It's a New Development Home, How Do You Find It?

Whether you're looking for a house, a boat, a car, or somebody to groom your pet fish, it's wise to keep your eyes and ears open wherever you go, to mention your search to everyone you meet — friends, relatives, neighbors, colleagues at work, the driver stopped at the traffic light in the next lane. One of them may know of just what you're looking for.

ADVERTISING

You can't, of course, depend solely on such accidental information. You'll have to have a more methodical approach. If what you're looking for is a new development home — whether it's a high-rise condominium apartment or a detached house on its own lot — the place to start your search is in the real estate advertising of a local or metropolitan newspaper.

Newspaper ads come in two general categories — display and classified. The real estate classified ads, the small ones in the tiny type, will be used by large and small builders trying to sell new homes and by brokers and individual owners trying to sell homes that have been lived in. The display ads — the big ones with large type and pictures or other designs — will be dominated by the relatively large developers who are selling relatively large projects, though a small operator may use some display ads to kick off a new development. All kinds of real estate ads, display and classified, for all kinds of homes will be more plentiful on weekends, especially Sundays, and just before most holidays. That's when developers, brokers, and individual sellers expect potential buyers to take advantage of a day off to look for a new home.

In most newspapers, the classified ads — and perhaps the display ads, too — will be broken down alphabetically by location. The East Side listings, for example, will appear together, and they will come before the North Side, South Side, and West Side listings. Usually, the name of the town, section, neighborhood, or development will be the first words in the ad, and sometimes those words can be misleading. Let's say the West Side is generally considered to be a desirable area in the city where you're looking. Some ads may start with the words "WEST SIDE AREA." That may mean that the place is really on the North Side or the South Side, but the seller is trying to cash in on the chic of the West Side and figures his place is near enough to qualify. In location or in anything else, be careful to understand just exactly what the ad says. People who write ads often play with words.

The typical real estate ad will tell you, in addition to the general area of the home being offered, its size and its price range. A developer's ad will usually state only the lowest price in the project while it extols the virtues of the biggest home. It may say that two-, three-, and four-bedroom homes are available "from $48,000." That means the cheapest, stripped-down two-bedroom shack on the premises — the one with the living room that floods whenever a cloud crosses the horizon — is on the market for 48 big ones. If you need four bedrooms, two baths, and a family room, you're going to be spending something like $60,000 in that development.

But you can still do a large part of your shopping for a developer's home right there in the ads. Almost every ad will tell you the price range, the size, and the general location. If the price quoted in the ad is beyond your means, if the home described there is not large enough to meet your needs, or if the location is not up to your standards, move on to the next ad. You can probably eliminate half of the available developments with just such a quick look at the advertising. That leaves you free to study the rest of the offerings more closely.

Compare them carefully. One ad may mention a feature that is especially important to you — a two-car garage, say — while another touts something you simply don't care about — perhaps a basement. It's a pretty safe bet, though not a sure thing, that if the ad doesn't mention a basement, there is no basement, if it doesn't say one-and-a-half baths, there is just one bath, if it doesn't mention garages, there are no garages. If you maintain that point of view, half an hour of looking should allow you to winnow a hundred ads down to half a dozen that might be worth looking at. Not that you won't have some questions. Most of the ads will contain telephone numbers, though some developers like to eliminate that detail so you'll have to come out and get the sales pitch to have your questions answered. If there's a number, call and ask your questions. As a last resort, go and look at the developments that haven't been eliminated by the ads or the phone conversations.

IF IT'S A NEW DEVELOPMENT HOME, HOW DO YOU FIND IT?

BROKERS

Advertising is without doubt the surest route to a new development home, but don't ignore real estate brokers. Some developers — usually small ones — retain brokers to do their selling, and some brokers simply list the development homes along with their resale listings. That may not be the best way to sell a development, but it may be the only way if the project is small and the budget is limited. And if that's the situation, the only way to find the home is to consult the broker who's listed it.

Visiting a broker will probably mean spending an afternoon or more at the mercy of a salesman or saleswoman. Most of what you see may be what you know you don't want. But it's not necessarily a total waste of time. Every home you visit — even one you wouldn't consider buying — should teach you something. You may notice some pitfall that you had never thought about before, but one you'll look for in the future. You will probably learn something about the area or the neighborhood. You will almost surely pick up one more impression of what's on the market at what price. And who knows, you may just come across a place that will make you decide you don't want a new development home, after all — one that has everything you need and a little something extra at the right price, just the home you're looking for, even if it isn't new.

VISITING MODEL HOMES

Obviously, if a new development home is your bag and visiting brokers can be useful, visiting new developments can be nothing less than invaluable. For one thing, you'll quickly gain some sophistication in the way you read the ads. When you see what "palatial colonial" applies to in this week's ad, you'll be a little less excited about the "luxurious contemporary" that's likely to be touted next week. You'll also, of course, get a better sense of the market with every visit to a development. You'll begin to see that one project offers excellent location but has small rooms, no basements, and tiny lots, while another, in a less desirable area, includes not only basements and larger lots but a selection of appliances and wall-to-wall carpeting as well. You'll begin to get a sense of what the trade-offs are, of what a buck will buy. That's a sense with which you really should be equipped before you set out to do battle with a development salesman. You'll be a much better bargainer if you have it.

In all of this, it is well to keep in mind that the homes you're inspecting are model homes, homes built for sales purposes as well as for ultimate livability. Any home obviously must be inspected carefully before you buy, but there are some extra pitfalls when the place you're traipsing through is a model.

The model house or apartment is, after all, the developer's pièce de résistance. The model will probably be on one of the best lots in the development, one with trees and perhaps a creek, one isolated from obnoxious neighbors, and one that offers good views. The lot for the model won't be chosen solely on aesthetic grounds — it also has to be a place that potential customers can get to fairly easily — but it is possible that no other lot in the project will be as attractive as the one on which the model stands. It's almost a sure thing that most of them will be less attractive.

Beyond the lot itself, consider the landscaping. There's liable to be much more of it than you will get on the average lot in the development, and it's likely to include some subtle tricks. Many developers, for instance, don't install driveways for model homes until the development is sold out and they're ready to sell the models. The absence of a driveway makes the lawn look much more expansive, and there's hardly a buyer who notices that there's no way to get a car into the garage.

Some developers take the best section of the project and build a model on every other lot, devoting the lots in between models to sweeping lawn. It creates the impression that you're buying a small estate rather than a ticky-tacky house on a postage-stamp lot. When the development is sold out, the construction crews will usually be back to put up houses on the lots between the models.

Inside, the model is likely to contain every available option — a central vacuum system, an extra-large refrigerator, a super-duper range, a freezer, a finished basement, perhaps two or three fireplaces, top-of-the-line carpeting. What you see isn't necessarily what you get. The standard refrigerator may be half the size of the one you see. You may get no fireplace — unless you order one and pay extra for it — although the model has two of them. You may get $2-a-yard carpeting, though the model is furnished with stuff that goes for $32.95 a yard. Look at the model with that in mind.

Also keep in mind the fact that the place will probably have been furnished and decorated by a pro — not just any pro, but one who specializes in making model homes look good. The furniture is likely to be small so the rooms will look bigger, and to be made in an open design so it won't block your view of the farthest reaches of each room. Wrought iron and wicker are popular for that purpose. What isn't wrought iron or wicker is likely to be very low, so you'll naturally look over it rather than attempt to look through it. In any case, the decorator will do his utmost to make the room look bigger than it will when you fill it with your neo-Salvation Army furniture.

The management is also likely to spend a lot of time and effort trying to make the room look brighter, which is another way of making it look bigger. The window "treatments," as the decorators like to call them — the draperies, curtains, shades and blinds — will probably be calculated to let as much light as possible into the room and to enhance the view, framing it with just the right colors and textures to make it look as attractive as possible. There's nothing dishonest about this approach, but when you move in you

IF IT'S A NEW DEVELOPMENT HOME, HOW DO YOU FIND IT?

may be more interested in privacy than view enhancement in the bedrooms, and that decision may result in a room that looks like a dungeon rather than the lavish hall you saw in the model.

The decorator is also likely to choose very light colors for the furnishings in an effort to make the place look brighter and bigger. If your furniture and rugs are dark rather than light, keep that fact in mind. The decorator may slap mirrors around the place as though he's trying to recreate Versailles. That's because he knows that mirrors make rooms look much larger, in some circumstances almost twice as large as they really are. Look for mirrors, but not to be sure that your ties or your seams are straight. Be sure that your impression of the room is straight.

Then there's the matter of closets, another place where the decorators of model homes like to do their magic acts. It's relatively easy — especially if you're a developer — to turn a living room or family room closet into a lavish bar or a bedroom closet into a smashing vanity. It's also relatively easy — if you're a developer and don't have to live in the place — to get along without closets. If you're a buyer, it's not so easy to transform closets, and it's even less easy to live without them. The closet question is important in any home, but doubly so in models. Closets are rather dull affairs, necessary but not exciting. Count them carefully in a model. Be sure there's a place near the front door to hang guests' coats. Be sure there's a place in the family room for the kids' toys. Be sure there's a place near the kitchen to keep the mop and the vacuum cleaner. Be sure there's a linen closet near the bathroom. Any one of them may make a great bar, but the chances are you can get along better without a bar than without a closet.

CHOOSING THE LOT

Some of the problems you're likely to face in looking for land on which to build a custom home have presumably been solved by the builder if you're buying a development house, but it might be well to consider them anyway. It's just possible, though highly unlikely, that the pirate who built your development forgot to get a building permit or zoning approval or electrical service. In any case, be very careful about the lot you'll get in a development. Unless you're one of the later buyers in the project, the chances are that you'll see no more than a large field where your home will be and a simple map cutting the place up into more or less rectangular lots and winding streets. It's very hard with such sparse information to tell just what it is you're getting, and you're likely to be discouraged from obtaining more information. Do not allow yourself to be discouraged. You can look at a model home, and — except for the optional extras and the decorating — it must be substantially what you'll end up with. But nobody's offering to show you a model of the lot. If you can't look at the real thing, buy elsewhere.

First of all, make sure you know where the lot is in relation to everything else — in relation to schools, traffic, shopping, noise, pollution, whatever will influence your comfort. The salesman's map is probably not going to give you much of that information, so you'll have to find it elsewhere. The most likely place is the local municipality. At city hall or town hall or whatever it's called, you'll find the office of the planning board or the zoning board or, in a very small town, the town clerk. One or another or all of them will have a map of the area that shows what the zoning is and where various public facilities are as well as where the streets are. You can find out where the railroad and bus stations are, where the schools are, where the factories and shopping centers are. You can find out where the areas zoned for industrial or commercial use are. That's where there will probably be factories or stores, even if there aren't any now. On the city or township map of the larger area, locate the lot you're thinking about buying and plot traffic patterns. Will you be living on the most logical route between a big residential area and the railroad station, the downtown area, the parkway, a shopping center, or the high school? If so, you'll have a great deal of traffic. That's all right if you're prepared to live with it.

You probably won't be prepared to live with heavy traffic, however, if you're the bucolic sort or if you have young children. So be sure you know where the traffic is likely to go before you plunk down your money. Be sure, too, that you know where you'll want to go. How easy is it to get from the lot you're going to buy — soon to be your house — to the railroad station, if you commute by train; to the school, if you have children; to the supermarket, if you have a wife (or husband or roommate) who doesn't drive?

While you're down at town hall, if you have questions about where the new school will be built or when the sewers are likely to arrive in your neck of the woods, ask the appropriate public officials. Don't rely on a salesman's word.

Traffic problems can, of course, be avoided by buying on a cul-de-sac, the developer's term for a dead-end street. But even on a cul-de-sac you can suffer with noise or pollution from an adjacent property. Look at the traffic situation and zoning on the next street as well as your own.

On every lot, there's a place to put a house, and the house will face one way or another — north or south, east or west. That may sound simple-minded, but it makes a difference whether your house faces north or south, east or west. How much difference it makes depends upon the design of the house. Its design and position will probably be fixed in a large development — the builder and his engineers and designers will have decided long ago which models would be built on which lots and in which positions they would be built. Changing that is incredibly complex, and you're not likely to be able to do it. When you choose one model in a development, in other words, you're likely to be limiting yourself to a certain number of lots on which that model will be built. After scratching from your list the lots that will be subject to heavy traffic or obvious noise and pollution, you want to find the one on which the model you've chosen will work best.

IF IT'S A NEW DEVELOPMENT HOME, HOW DO YOU FIND IT? 107

The first factor to consider is orientation, or the direction in which the house will face. Ideally, you want the living areas — the living room, dining room, family room, and perhaps the kitchen — to face south because they are the rooms in which you're likely to have the largest windows and in which family members are likely to spend most of their time. The windows are the key. If the large window areas face south, you should be able to take maximum advantage of the sun in winter and get the least abuse from it in summer. That's important when the cost of operating heating and air-conditioning units is high. You will probably be able to figure out the orientation of a given home by looking at the developer's map. If the map does not contain an outline of each completed home on its lot, you can presume that the front of the house will face the street. Then figure out where the biggest windows are in that model and the direction in which they'll be facing.

DEALING WITH THE SALESMEN

In dealing with any developer or development salesman, don't hesitate to ask any question that pops into your little head, no matter how silly it may sound and no matter how many questions there may be. The purpose of the exercise is not to impress the salesman with your sophistication; it's to learn as much as possible about this pig-in-a-poke he's asking you to buy. And after all, he is being paid to answer questions.

If you get vague answers, press for specific ones. If the salesman says that he's unable to answer a question immediately — reasonable enough if it's a technical question — make a note of it and tell the salesman that you'll expect to have the answer before you make any decisions. If you don't understand some of the answers you get, insist upon explanations. You're not supposed to be a construction expert; the developer is. Make him prove it.

Do not, however, take the salesman's word for what can be learned more reliably elsewhere. He may be the only one who can tell you what kind of roof the place will have, but he is not the best authority on where the new school is to be built or how big it will be. The school administration is the best — maybe the only — source for that information, though the salesman will no doubt be glad to talk about it for 20 minutes or so.

Once you have narrowed your choice to one or two developments, examine them just as you would a neighborhood if you were buying a resale home. But remember that many of the important facilities that will make up your neighborhood — even the homes themselves — may not exist when you have to make your decision. That means you'll have to do some crystal-ball gazing, some shrewd guessing about the future of the area. Again, rely on the responsible public officials — school administrators, planners, and zoners, for example — not on salesmen for your information. And again, ask every question you can think of. Pay particular attention to the probable timing of public facilities promised in the future. A new school will be of no use to you if it is completed after your children have graduated. And remember that public officials may be optimistic in their predictions. It takes a couple of years to construct a school. It may take a year or more before that to do the preliminary work and get the design approved. It may take a generation before that to pass the bond issue that will pay for the whole thing. Be wary.

When you have hit upon a model and a development that seem reasonably good over-all, compare some homes under construction, called "production units" in the trade, with the model. Then compare the lot you're thinking about with the lot on which the model stands. You will probably encounter some bureaucratic problems here, so it may take some perseverance. The salesman and the signs that surround the construction site will no doubt tell you in the most forceful terms that you're not allowed in there. Insurance problems, you know, and trouble with the workmen when they are interrupted in their meticulous, craftsmanlike labors. Make it very clear to the salesman — and the sales manager, if necessary, and the developer and anybody else who cares — that you will under no circumstances consider buying land you have not seen. And stick to that principle. It says under no circumstances. Without exception. Not ever.

INSPECTING THE HOME SITE

Sooner or later, if you are persistent, you will find your way onto the construction site. You will probably need the management's cooperation if you hope to find a specific lot, however, because the whole development may at this point look to the layman like no more than a sea of muck littered with junk and crisscrossed with bulldozer tracks. You'll probably need someone who'll take you to the lot in question.

When you get onto the construction site, before or after you visit the lot that interests you, pick a few production homes that are near completion and look them over, keeping the model in mind. Do things fit together as well in the production unit as they do in the model? Where walls or other surfaces have not yet been closed up, are the framing members and mechanical systems what you were told they would be? Even if you're no expert, does it look as though the visible work was done neatly and carefully?

On to the lot. The trick here is to learn everything you couldn't find out studying the developer's map. Is it, for instance, too sandy or rocky to grow grass? Is it so steep that you could climb it only with with a pick and rope? Is it swampy? Don't just stand back and admire the thing; get right into it. Find the stakes that mark its four corners and walk the boundaries. Study the soil, the topography, and the drainage just as you would if you were buying raw land.

If the place is topographically unsuitable — sloped so that all the surface water is likely to run in the front door or so that you'd need four-wheel drive to make it to the garage, the salesman may assure you that the grading will be

IF IT'S A NEW DEVELOPMENT HOME, HOW DO YOU FIND IT? 109

changed. In that case, you want to look at another map, one that shows elevations, and you may need someone to help you interpret it. Somewhere or other, the developer has to have a map that shows everyone from the architect to the bulldozer operator how the land will lie after the final grading. If it seems likely that there will be major changes on your lot, be sure to find out what that final grading will be.

If the final grading will require filling — dumping a few tons of earth into your lot to bring the house up to street level — or if there has obviously been filling on the lot, get professional advice before you buy. Building on filled land before the fill has been properly compacted or has had a chance to settle (a process that can take several years) can produce disastrous problems.

Finally, note any natural advantages the lot may have — a stand of trees, for example — and try to determine whether the home can be built without disturbing them. Remember that the builder will need room for a bulldozer and trucks, room to store material, and room to work as well as room for the structure itself. Remember, too, that what looks like a natural advantage now can, with a little diligent effort on the developer's part, be turned into a man-made eyesore. You wouldn't be the first buyer to have paid a premium for a lot next to a babbling brook, only to discover when you moved in that the brook had become a concrete-lined drainage ditch that cuts off half the backyard.

CHECKING ON THE DEVELOPER

When you're satisfied that the home, the lot, and the development have passed muster, it's time to take a close look at the builder. Your best assurance of getting a good home in a good development is dealing with a good developer, one who is reliable, honest, experienced, and financially sound. If you have friends who live in homes constructed by the builder you have in mind, even if the homes are in other developments, get their opinions. Find out whether they would try the next time to buy a home from the same builder rather than one of his competitors. Given 20-20 hindsight, what do they think is wrong with their homes? If they bought directly from the builder, was the place completed on schedule, more or less? Were there big hassles over defects? Did the builder return to correct the defects?

Ask local banks, real estate brokers, and the building inspector what their experience has been with the developer. Are bankers reluctant to make mortgages on homes he has built? Do brokers find those homes hard to sell when the original owners move on? Does the building inspector have constant problems with defects in the houses?

If you know some subcontractors in the area — plumbers, carpenters, electricians — ask whether they bid on the developer's work, whether they like working for him, and what they know about his practices. Subcontractors know better than anyone else what kind of materials a builder is using and how carefully he is using them. Subcontractors also know something about a developer's financial situation — whether he pays his bills on time. If he doesn't, he may have trouble getting materials and labor. And you may have trouble getting a home.

For lack of anything better to do some afternoon, call the Chamber of Commerce and the Better Business Bureau and ask about the developer you are considering. They often seem to have favorable reports on everybody this side of Adolf Hitler, but you might learn something useful all the same, maybe just from what they don't say. If the municipality or the county has a consumer affairs office, ask whether they've had complaints about the builder. If so, find out what kinds of complaints, how many, and how the matters have been adjudicated. It might also be worth asking the district attorney's and state attorney general's offices.

Call the local builders' association and ask whether the developer is a member and whether the organization is affiliated with the National Association of Home Builders. Membership in NAHB is no guarantee of honesty or competence, but the national association and its local affiliates tend to attract builders who have been in business for a while, who take the business seriously, and who intend to stay in business. Ask whether the builders' association has established a Homeowners' Warranty program and whether the developer you're interested in participates. Again, membership is no guarantee of anything, but it may be an indication that the company you're dealing with has a reasonable track record. The Homeowners' Warranty Program gives you a form of insurance protection against certain defects in homes constructed by participating builders. The insurance company that stands behind the program requires that the participants meet some minimum standards of experience and financial stability.

The builders' program is not the last word in consumer protection, but it's better than nothing. It should be noted in fairness that the smaller builders — perhaps even some who have one fairly large development — may not be members of the national association or the national consumer protection program. And their nonmembership need not be a reflection upon their competence, seriousness, or integrity. It may be simply a reflection upon their size.

The financial stability of the builder with whom you're dealing is an extremely serious consideration. If he goes out of business after he's collected your down payment but before he's completed your home, you may be out both the money and the home. The money may have been spent on what there is of the home, but that may belong to the bank that foreclosed the developer's mortgage on the incomplete project. Given that possibility, you want to be sure that the builder is in reasonable financial health. Ask your employer or your bank to get you a Dun & Bradstreet report on him, if possible. Bear in mind that there will not be one unless he's a pretty big operator. Many developers selling land across state lines must file "Statements of Record" with the U.S. Department of Housing and Urban Development, and the statement contains some financial data on the developer. Write to HUD's Office of Interstate Land Sales, 451 Seventh Street S.W., Washington, D.C. 20410.

Ask the salesman for the names of the company's bank and its major suppliers. Call them, explain why you're interested, and ask about the builder's credit, reliability, and general reputation. If his suppliers won't give him credit and the bank considers him a liability, you may have some trouble getting a home from him.

Call the nearest office of the Federal Housing Administration and ask for the developer's FHA rating. The FHA insures many mortgages on development homes, and it has set some minimum construction standards for those homes. Its rating is a measure of how well its experts think the developer is doing in offering a good home for the money. The average rating is 100, and the top score is 105. A rating above 100 means that the builder offers more than average performance for the money. A score of less than 100 indicates that you can probably do better elsewhere.

18
If It's an Older Home, How Do You Find It?

The easiest and most likely ways to find a resale home are to watch the newspaper ads and to call some real estate brokers in the area that interests you.

THE BROKER

Like everything else, consulting a real estate broker has some advantages and some disadvantages. The broker will have a good idea of what's available in his area and what's simply impossible. At first, his opinions may not come as good news to you, but the chances are that sooner or later you'll realize that he knew more than you did at the outset. The broker can probably save you time and effort because he will have done a great deal of looking before you arrive. After he's talked to you a while — discovered what sort of home you want and what you can pay — he may be able to rule out many available homes before you take the trouble to look at them. They simply won't be what you want or they will be too rich for your blood. In either case, the broker will be performing a service by saving you a trip to look at the place. (All this, of course, presumes that you've told the broker clearly and honestly what it is you want and what you can afford.)

The broker is also likely to know a great deal about the local financial situation — what kinds of mortgages the banks are making now — and about such things as where the schools are, how far it is to the shopping center, and whether there's a hospital nearby. The broker may also have a good deal of information about the seller — why he's selling, when he wants to close the deal, how long he's owned the home. That information will save you some time, and perhaps, some embarrassment. Some people just don't like to ask such personal questions; you can rest assured that the broker won't mind. Finally, when the time comes, the broker may be able to help you with the negotiations for the purchase and help you find a mortgage. They're all useful services.

On the other hand, the broker gets a commission; it's usually paid by the seller, but one way or another, it will be built into the sale price of the home, so you'll ultimately be paying it. There are exceptions, of course. Sometimes a seller simply has to cut the price and sell the home so that he can move quickly — to take a new job, get the kids in a new school, or for any of a dozen other reasons. And while most sellers will pad the asking price a bit if a broker is involved, one of the broker's most valuable — and, perhaps, most frequent — services is persuading the seller that he has overpriced his home, that the price must come down before there will be serious offers. So there's really no assurance that the absence of a broker means a bargain. You'll have much more to choose from with a broker than without, so you might as well face the music early on, while you're glancing through the real estate ads some Sunday afternoon.

Try to pick out the broker whose advertising offers the greatest number of homes in your price range and in the area where you want to buy. But don't let it go at that. If you have friends who have bought or sold homes locally, ask for their recommendations. Watch for brokers' ads listing members of the million-dollar sales club; they're folks who have some experience and should know the market. Call the mortgage departments of some local banks or savings and loan associations and get their suggestions. If you have a local lawyer, ask him. If you're moving from out of town and have dealt with a broker there, ask him for a recommendation in the new area. Many brokers — perhaps most of them these days — belong to nationwide cooperatives that have member brokers almost everywhere. The broker in the city you're leaving can send an outline of your requirements to a cooperative member in the area to which you're moving and even arrange an appointment for you. When you arrive to shop, the second broker will have lined up the homes that he thinks will interest you most. Ultimately, if you buy through him, he and the broker who referred you will share the commission.

Many of these broker cooperatives like to think of themselves as relocation companies, and some of them have ambitious programs for helping large corporations in transferring employees. There are other concerns that do nothing else. So if you're being transferred by your employer, ask whether he's got such an arrangement with a relocation specialist who will help you find a new home, sell the old one, and make the move. Some of these services will advise you on the various sections of a metropolitan area that would be of interest — offering information on schools, commuting, shopping, taxes, and so forth — and they may even hire an engineer to inspect the new home for you. (In which case, bear in mind that the engineer is ultimately working not for you, but for the relocation company or brokers' cooperative, and their interest is in making a sale, not in finding every last potential defect.)

If all else is equal, you're probably better off looking for a broker who's a member of the National Association of Realtors or the National Association of Real Estate Brokers. The former call themselves "Realtors"; the latter, largely minority group members, call themselves "Realtists." Both groups have codes of ethics to which their members are required to subscribe. And both have grievance procedures in case there are differences of opinion between the broker and one or more of the principals in a transaction. The Realtors, by far the larger organization, are made up of local boards that may also have grievance procedures. In case you are absolutely without friends and can't get a newspaper, you can call the local realty groups and ask for a list of brokers who are active in your geographic area and price range.

Again, if all else is equal, you're probably better off dealing with a broker who is a member of one or more multiple listing services. This is another form of broker cooperative, often run by the local real estate board. The member brokers share their listings of homes for sale. If a home is listed with one member broker and another finds the buyer for it, they share the commission. The disadvantages of the multiple-listing system are that the broker may work harder to sell his "exclusive" listings — the ones that are not shared — on which he gets the full commission, and that the broker may know less about a home he got from the multiple list than about one he inspected and listed himself. On the other hand, the broker who is a member of the predominant multiple list can probably show you most of the homes for sale in his area. And that's what you consult him for — to show you homes, not to advise you on whether to buy them.

In the area of real estate brokerage, as in almost everything else these days, there are some discount houses, cut-rate practitioners who will not provide all the services of their more traditional brethren but who charge less and therefore allow a seller to put a lower price on his home. In theory, anyway. If you consult such a broker and express interest in one of his listings, he is likely to give you the address and some directions, leaving it to you to find your way and leaving it to the seller to show you around and answer your questions.

Then there are "buyers' brokers," who will charge you a flat fee — say, 3 to 5 percent of the selling price — or an hourly rate to search the market in your behalf, screen the potential purchases with your interests in mind, and negotiate a deal for you. In many cases, these folks are very aggressive. They maintain that if the seller doesn't have to pay a broker's commission and they negotiate hard on your behalf, you come out ahead. If you're very unsure of yourself, maybe that's the way to go.

DEALING WITH A BROKER

Before you get too involved with traditional brokers and their salesmen, you should understand what their relationships are and how to deal with them. First of all, understand that the broker's services normally will cost you, the buyer, nothing, and that beyond some basic standards of ethical conduct you owe the broker nothing. Any broker or salesman who has been in the business more than a few days has seen a willing and able customer buy elsewhere. That's the way it is. You may feel free to do that. You may feel free to ask the broker or salesman any question that occurs to you. And you may feel free to consult as many brokers as you like. But there are some rules for the game.

Answer the broker's questions honestly and straightforwardly. There will be some fairly personal questions about how much money you have and how you live, but only through such questions can an agent decide what homes to show you.

Understand that, while it's perfectly acceptable to consult more than one broker, it's not ethical to let one broker show you a home that you've already visited with a competitor. Once a broker or agent shows you a home — or maybe even tells you about it — he or she has a right to a commission if you buy. As soon as you realize that you're about to be shown a place you've seen before, explain why you don't want to see it. The salesman will understand; he doesn't want to get involved in a fight over a commission, either.

Moreover, if you're dealing with one broker or agent who's a member of the local multiple list and who seems to understand your needs and to be reasonably energetic in attempting to meet them, there's little point in consulting a second local broker. They've all got the same listings, after all, and pitting one against another will merely prompt a frenzied competition to show you everything on the market, whether or not it meets your needs, before the other guy does. That's the only way a broker in such a situation can protect his potential commission, and it will waste a good deal of your time as well as his.

If matters get to the point where you're dickering with an owner over terms, keep the broker informed of what you've been discussing. Reject out of hand any suggestion that you and the seller get together and do the broker out of his commission, splitting the difference between you. That's not only unethical, it's illegal. The broker can sue for his commission, and most brokers won't hesitate to do so.

Ultimately remember that, whatever he calls himself — whether it's broker or agent or counselor or advisor or vice president and general manager — the person you're dealing with is a salesman. His interest is in making a sale; otherwise there's no commission. That doesn't mean he's out to bamboozle you or mislead you. It merely means that his comments and opinions should be understood for what they are. He may bring tears to your eyes with his gripping description of the structural soundness of a home, but if you can see that the place is leaking like a sieve and listing precariously to starboard, you'd better ignore his pitch and move on. After all, the salesman is not — and does not represent himself to be — an architect, engineer, or lawyer. Don't expect him to be. Though many agents may have learned, through training or experience, a great deal about construction or law, they are probably not licensed in those fields and therefore should not be relied upon for technical information. When you need legal advice — and you will — get a lawyer. When you need architectural or engineering advice, get an architect or engineer. When you want to know more about schools or taxes or zoning, talk to school administrators, tax assessors, or zoning officials, not to salesmen. But when you want to know where there are homes for sale and on what terms, talk to brokers. That's their specialty.

OTHER SOURCES

Beyond consulting brokers, you should spread the word about your search for a home. Talk to friends, relatives, colleagues at work or school. One of them may know of a suitable place that has not yet been listed with a broker; you might save that commission, after all. Be especially careful to mention your plans to friends who live in the areas that attract you. They are more likely than anyone else to know of something that's coming on the market.

Drive around the areas you like, keeping an eye peeled for "For Sale" signs. That's hardly the most efficient way to find a home, but it'll help you get a "feel" for the neighborhood, if nothing else, and you just may come across the perfect home. Stranger things have happened. Be aware that the lack of "For Sale" signs doesn't necessarily mean that nothing's available. Some owners are reluctant to display signs for aesthetic reasons. Others don't want them for reasons of bigotry. If there's no sign, such people reason, "they" — the targets of the bigotry, whether it's blacks or Spanish-Americans, Jews or Catholics, Chinese, Australians, or Tibetans — won't know the place is for sale and therefore won't ask to see it. And if "they" don't see it, "they'll" hardly buy it. The other side of the coin — a "For Sale" sign on half the homes in the neighborhood — is no less alarming. It means that the area is not stable, and you should find out why before you buy. It may be that the first black family has arrived and white homeowners are panicking, perhaps with the encouragement of some less-than-ethical brokers or other operators who see a buck to be made out of racial tensions. It may be that all the local residents know that a rendering plant is about to be built on the next block. Or it may be that the neighborhood is filled with employees of one large company that is moving its whole staff to Sheridan's Switch, Kentucky. The large number of signs, in other words, may or may not reflect social or physical trouble in the area. You should know what it reflects before you join up.

In addition to consulting brokers and driving around, you should, of course, watch the real estate ads in the newspapers. Some brokers may use display ads — the large ones with illustrations or other graphic devices. Almost all brokers and most owners who are trying to sell their homes without brokers will use classified ads — the small ones in the tiny type. Both kinds of ads will be most numerous on weekends, especially Sundays, and just before most holidays. These are the times when owners and brokers expect buyers to have the time to shop. Watch the ads in the local papers as well as the big metropolitan dailies. Many sellers — and even some brokers — favor them, at least in part because they're cheaper. In some areas, especially suburban ones, you may find in stores, banks, bowling alleys, bus stations, and other public places free booklets filled with real estate advertising, virtually all of it from brokers rather than owners. You might find there something that didn't appear in the newspapers, though the ads in such booklets are likely to be "staler" than those in newspapers because the lead time (the delay between the writing of the ad and its publication) is usually greater.

All real estate advertising — whether in newspapers, magazines, or booklets, whether placed by a broker or an owner, whether classified or display — must be read negatively. Assume that the good things not mentioned in the ad don't exist. If there's no mention of a basement, for example, it's a pretty safe bet that the place is built on a slab or at best a crawl space. If the ad doesn't rhapsodize about rolling hills and thick woods, you can expect a small lot and forget about the trees. If the ad does make a grudging admission of some small defect — "needs work" or "handyman's delight" — you'd better visit the dump on an empty stomach. Those terms can be translated as "about to collapse" or "a disaster area, get it before the health department condemns it." You can assume, in other words, that the author of the ad, whether it's an owner or a broker, has taken every permissible liberty in making a lean-to sound like something the shah just moved out of.

The ads do, however, have to stick to something bordering on reality. They generally do not mention a basement that doesn't exist or magnify the size of the lot or the number of bathrooms. So you can rely on them up to a point. You can, for instance, determine from the ad which of the places is worth a phone call if not a trip. Most ads contain telephone numbers at which more information is available, and that first call can be very useful. The information it produces may save you a wild goose chase. Beyond that, if the ad was placed by an owner rather than a broker, your warning call may give him an opportunity to get dressed and put the place in reasonable order before you arrive — not to redecorate it, just to pick up the kids' toys and put the laundry away. If the ad was placed by a broker, your call will give him or his agent a chance to go through the listings and find other, similar homes that may interest you when you finally do make the trip. It's conventional wisdom among brokers that no client buys the home in the ad he's called about, but he may buy the next thing he sees. If the agent is good and you've been honest with him, the other listings he has will be close to what you want, homes that are worth your time and trouble. Yes, the broker is trying to make a sale; that's what he's in business for. But he's not necessarily trying to trick you or force you to buy something you don't want. Take a ride with him. You may learn something. And he will probably have a very comfortable car.

TAKING A TOUR

When you do set out to look at homes — either for a tour with a broker or salesman or for a visit to a home being offered by its owner — allow yourself plenty of time. If you're really serious about buying, you'll want to look the thing over very closely. And it's sometimes extremely valuable to return after a few hours for a second look at a home that interests you. You can often see much more on the second — or third or fourth — visit. If you're the hot prospect they've been looking for, neither the owners nor the broker will mind the inconvenience of having you back.

On all such home-inspection trips, arrange to leave the dog, the cat, young children, and your aged grandmother at home. You want to be able to give the homes you're visiting your undivided attention without having to worry about juvenile or animal manners or about whether Aunt Martha can make the stairs. There will be plenty of time later to show the place off to the whole clan if you decide to buy it. And besides, the homes you're looking at aren't yours yet. It's really unfair to visit small fingerprints all over the walls that the seller has just scrubbed so they'll look as good as possible.

So hire a babysitter, be sure there's plenty of gas in the car, and get a red pencil and an early copy of the Sunday paper. You're off.

19
How Do You Tell Whether the Place Is Worth Considering?

Going through a home foot by foot to find its strong and weak points is a difficult and time-consuming process, one that you shouldn't attempt until you've narrowed your search to one or two possibilities.

In the meantime, however, as you visit a variety of homes, you can make some broad decisions, forming quick impressions of whether the homes will work for you, whether they're worth visiting again and inspecting more closely.

The trick is to keep your eye on the big picture. Never mind the popped nails in the family room wall. They're a small matter that can be dealt with later. At this point, you want to determine whether it's even worth looking for popped nails and dripping faucets or whether the place is simply so wrong for you that there's no use worrying about its small defects.

THE NEIGHBORHOOD

The first question to ask yourself as you approach a home for the first time is whether the neighborhood is right. Is it what you had in mind when you went through the general process of narrowing your search from a metropolitan area to one section, then a town? There's no need to run down to the zoning board this minute, but you can keep your eyes open and keep thinking. Are the obvious public services — the streets, streetlights, playgrounds — plentiful and in good repair? How close are shopping areas and schools? Are there obvious eyesores and hazards in the neighborhood? Are other homes in the area well maintained? Asking yourself such questions doesn't interfere with the ostensible purpose of your outing — looking at a few homes — and the answers may be enough to eliminate one or more places without even considering the plumbing or the wiring.

Every time you visit a home, start inspecting it even before you arrive. Is it easy to find? Is the address visible? Would it be impossible to find at night? Is the home as well kept as those nearby? Is the landscaping attractive? Can you park safely — on the street or in the driveway if it's a single home, and on the street or in a parking area if it's a multiple-family unit? Obviously, much of this doesn't apply if you're looking at a builder's model, which can be expected to have adequate parking and good landscaping and to be accessible.

THE EXTERIOR

Does the lot seem large enough to offer both room to live in and privacy? Is the driveway too steep to negotiate in ice and snow? Too long to shovel? Does the topography suggest that surface water will run toward the home? That could mean flooding. Does it indicate that water will run toward a neighboring property? That could mean legal problems. The water should run toward the street or toward a creek, storm sewer, or other collection point. Are there signs of erosion? Is there someplace to put the snow you've shoveled from the walks, or will you have to carry it into the bathroom and melt it?

Does the building have clean, pleasing lines? Does it seem to fit into its site or to have been dropped there arbitrarily? Is the approach to the entrance attractive? Does the exterior seem to have been well maintained? Is the paint blistering and peeling? Are there cracks in masonry walls? Is the roof smooth and even, or are some shingles curled or missing? Are there gutters and leaders in place? Do they seem from the ground to be in good repair? Are the patios and terraces cracked and heaving? Is there standing water on them or on the driveway and walks? Are there screens or storm windows and doors in place? On every door and window? Is there a garage? One-car or two-car? Is it big enough for your car? Is there room for a workbench? For the storage of bicycles, garden tools, and patio furniture?

THE INTERIOR

Does it look as though your furniture would fit into the place, both physically and aesthetically? Is there enough wall space for your art? Are the rooms bright and cheerful? Would they lend themselves — in size and arrangement — to the way your family lives? If you have small children, to cite one example, a steep, open stairway leading to a basement family room may not be best.

Does the place need remodeling or redecorating? That's no big deal if you just want to slap a coat of paint on a few walls. But it can be a big deal indeed if you can't stand the pink tile and fixtures in the bathroom or the purple cabinets and counter in the kitchen. Is the kitchen big enough to eat in? Is it modern and well equipped? What appliances are to be included in the sale? How old are they? In what condition? Is the dining room large enough for your furniture and your family?

Are there enough bedrooms and bathrooms? Are the bedrooms isolated from the living room and kitchen? Are the bathrooms modern? Do the major traffic patterns — from bedrooms to bath, kitchen to front and back doors, kitchen to dining room — seem direct and convenient? Do you have to walk through the living room to get to any other room? Picture yourself coming home from work or from shopping and imagine where you would have to go to do whatever it is you usually do at that point. Would you find yourself tripping over the kids or interrupting the dinner preparations every time you wanted to move?

Do the walls and ceilings seem to be smooth and in good repair? Do the doors and windows open and close easily? Do the doors latch and stay latched? Do the floors or stairs squeak? Do dishes or glasses in a cabinet rattle as you walk by? Are the stairs too steep or too narrow? Are there obvious stains on ceilings or walls from leaks? Look especially under windows. Do the closets seem adequate? Is there other storage space?

In the basement, if there is one, are there obvious signs of dampness? A pump would be one sign, stains another. Does the heating plant look modern and efficient, or like an octopus wrapped in asbestos bandages? Do the joists (the overhead beams that hold up the first floor) look solid and straight? In the attic, is insulation visible? If it isn't be sure it's in place. Are there water stains on the roof sheathing or the rafters? Do the rafters look solid and straight? Are there vents?

ECONOMIC CONSIDERATIONS

Over-all, is this an economical home for you? Is it cluttered with expensive things you don't need or want — too many rooms, say, or rooms that are too big. They can mean big heating and tax bills. Does it have sweeping staircases, lavish entertainment facilities or, perhaps, a swimming pool that you don't need and would just as soon not pay for? If there's a possibility that you might want more room later, is the place designed so that it can be expanded with minimal trouble and expense?

Ask the seller or agent, if it's a resale home, what the annual taxes are and how much the heating and electrical bills were last year. Ask as well the age of the roof, wiring, plumbing, heating system, and hot water heater. If it's a new home, you'll have to get utility estimates from the companies that provide the service and a tax estimate from the local assessor.

NARROWING THE CHOICES

It will make this winnowing process easier if you carry a small pocket notebook. At first, it's not necessary to keep detailed notes, just the address of the place or the name of the development and model, the name of the owner or developer, the name and phone number of the broker, if there is one, and a few phrases that will jog your memory. As the choice gets narrower, you may want to keep more detailed notes — on the tax and utility bills, for example, or on special features that set one home apart from the others.

As you move along in this process, you should begin comparing your entries and weeding out the lesser among them. Comparisons will often be difficult — it's hard to balance low taxes or less commuting time against good schools or new plumbing — but they're the only route to a sound decision.

There is one other question to ask about every home you visit: Does it turn you on? Does it have some inexplicable charm that the others lack? Are you almost willing to overlook its many obvious shortcomings just because it's the kind of place you always thought you'd like to live in? Well, maybe that's the home you ought to buy, but not before you're aware of all the shortcomings you're planning to overlook. Gird yourself. It's no small task.

20
How Do You Inspect a Home, New or Old?

Before you commit yourself to the purchase of a home, you'll want to have a professional examine it closely and report to you in detail on the defects he finds. Virtually every city in the country has home inspection or building inspection companies that perform such services for a fee — $100 or more for the average home. At those prices, most buyers obviously cannot afford to have an inspector look at every home that comes along. When you get it down to a yes-or-no decision on one home, that's the time to call the inspection service. Until then, you'll have to do your own inspecting, with its thoroughness depending upon how serious you are about the home in question and how many risks you're willing to take.

If you're buying a new home from a model, you'll want to have the inspector look over the model for you. Then, if you go ahead with the purchase, have inspections of your home at various points during construction and have the inspector walk through it with you, pointing out problems, before you take possession.

The inspection process outlined here is substantially what a professional will do if you hire him. Done right, it's a difficult, complicated, and dirty process, so it isn't something you ought to attempt until you're really serious about a place, interested enough to consider plunking down good money so a pro can make sure you haven't missed something calamitous. If you're really short of time or strongly disinclined to get involved in this sort of thing, read up on it, then tell the inspector you want to go with him during his inspection. You'll then be prepared to ask intelligent questions and assure yourself that he has not overlooked some grievous problem.

The result of the inspector's trip will probably be a detailed checklist and a page or so of written comments about the structural and mechanical condition of the home. Remember that he is being paid to find problems, and he can find some in any home in the world. Not every problem is a disaster, however. If the plumbing is 90 years old, that's potential trouble. If the faucets drip, that's some washers but no big deal. Many inspectors will, especially if you're along for the investigation, give you rough estimates of what repairs will cost and assessments of how necessary they are. That's a good way to keep the thing in perspective. There's no sense in turning down an $80,000 home because it needs a $50 repair, though the defect may sound like the end of the world when it's coldly noted without comment on an inspector's report.

Inspections like this, whether or not they involve a professional, are best made when the seller is elsewhere, though that cannot always be arranged. If the owner is on hand, keep your comments to a minimum, make notes as unobtrusively as possible, and try to be as understanding, deferential, and polite as you can. The owner is going to be nervous about this process, too — maybe more nervous than you are — and if this is your fourth tramp through his happy home he may be getting understandably impatient.

If the seller should be out of sight, there's no question that your kids, dogs and in-laws have no business there. The dog and the kids know nothing about construction and design; they can hardly make the process more efficient. Most in-laws, cousins, and uncles also know nothing. Your father-in-law is not going to live in, maintain, and pay for this place; you are. Let him choose his home and, unless he really is an architect or engineer, you choose yours. As soon as you've moved in, invite him over for his favorite dinner and listen politely as he tells you how to rip the place apart and rebuild it the way he would have done it. That will be less frustrating and expensive than having him disrupt the process through which you are trying to arrive very carefully at an important decision.

The process is described here in terms of a single-family detached home that is not new. That example was chosen because it's the sort of home most buyers will find themselves looking at, because it's more complicated than inspecting a new home, and because the layman can do a more complete inspection of a single-family home than of a multiple-family unit. Whatever the type of home you're after, the principles are the same. If the place is new, you obviously don't have to worry about the age of the wiring. If it's a unit in a high-rise building, you won't be able to crawl in the attic. But with a little thought, you can apply the principles here to housing of any type and age. You do the best you can with what you've got.

PREPARING FOR THE CHORE

Get ready in advance. If it's a house that's been lived in, make an appointment with the owner and tell him it will take several hours to complete your examination. Ask him whether he has a floor plan and a plot plan (a sketch of the lot with the outline of the building on it). If you're considering a new home, the builder should have both a floor plan and a plot plan readily available.

Dress in old clothes or bring a pair of coveralls. In even the best-kept home there are some dirty places, and that's where you're likely to be crawling. Bring your tools:

- A pair of work gloves because it may really get dirty.
- Pencil and paper, preferably some graph paper, so you can accurately sketch the floor plan and the plot plan if the owner doesn't have them available.
- Your notebook for keeping track of observations.
- A 50-foot tape measure to find out how big things really are.
- A compass to find out which way they face.
- A level — not a tiny, pocket-sized one, a real two-foot or three-foot one — to tell whether the place is standing straight or leaning.
- A pocket knife (probably the best because it's the most versatile) or an icepick or awl for poking things in which there may be rot or other damage under the surface.
- A magnet to tell what things are made of.
- A flashlight so you can see what things look like.
- A marble or a ball bearing to use in determining whether floors are level.
- A small hammer so you can tap things as though you knew what you were doing.
- If you really want to go whole hog and scare the living daylights out of the owner, a ladder. But not if bringing it means renting a truck.

GETTING STARTED

If you haven't been able to get a plot plan from the owner, start by roughly measuring the lot and the building, together with the distances from the lot line to the structures and major plantings. Don't forget to include garages, sheds, patios, pools, and so forth. Make a rough plot plan. You can refine it later if you're really interested. Using the compass you were smart enough to bring along, note where north is and mark it on the plan. Obviously, you can skip this step in examining a builder's model unless the model is the home you're buying. Even then, the builder should be able to give you a plot plan.

Inside, measure the rooms and make a rough floor plan containing the dimensions of rooms. Don't forget to mark windows, doors, counters, chimneys, and so forth, as well as walls. Get the dimensions right and make a rough sketch at this point. You can refine it later if necessary. If the home you're dealing with is a builder's model and the floor plan doesn't have dimensions, just measure the model and write the dimensions on the plan.

THE EXTERIOR

Now go back outside and really start inspecting. Are there enough trees to supply shade, muffle noise, and provide privacy? Deciduous trees help on the south side of the building, providing shade in the summer and losing their leaves to let the sun in during the winter. Evergreens are helpful on the north side, where they cut the winter wind. Beyond their practical advantage, trees are often the only difference between a pasture and a yard. Don't underestimate their value. But trees are another matter when they're dead. Are there dead trees that represent a threat to the home or its outbuildings or to neighboring properties? If so, and if the owner won't foot the bill for removing them, the cost of their removal must be added to the purchase price.

Is the driveway too steep to negotiate in winter or pitched in such a way that it's likely to flood the garage or yard during a heavy storm? Is it so long that clearing it of snow would be a big and expensive chore? Is there someplace to put the snow when you've cleared it? Does it provide turnaround room? Is it designed so that two cars can be parked and neither will be blocked? Is it designed in a way that forces you to back out into a blind curve or hill? What's the condition of the driveway? Is it cracked or heaving? In need of sealing? If it's crushed stone or gravel, is it rutted and washing away? Are the yard and walks littered with gravel and stone? Any standing water on the drive?

What's the condition of the walks? Any standing water? Are they smooth and even or cracked and heaving? That can be dangerous underfoot, and so can walks made of crushed stone or loose flagstones. Does there seem to be adequate lighting along the walks and at the entranceways?

Be especially alert for drainage problems. Does the land slope away from the home so water will run toward the street or some other safe place? Be sure that surface water won't run toward your home or onto a neighbor's property. Are there any signs of erosion? Is the lot so steep that it requires — or will require — retaining walls? Is it so steep that the lawn will be difficult to mow and useless for play? If there are retaining walls, what shape are they in? If there aren't any but should be, what will they cost? That cost should be added to the price of the place.

Is the patio, if any, properly sited for privacy and easy access to the living areas of the home? Does it get the sun? Is it pitched for proper drainage? Is it cracked or heaving? Any standing water? Is there lighting? Is the patio of permanent construction — concrete, say — or is it something less durable, like bricks or patio blocks on a sand base? If there is no patio, is there space for one?

Is there a suitable place for trash cans? Is it out of sight but handy to the back door? Is there a place for the storage of garden tools and bicycles? Is there a suitable play area, one that's safe if your children are young? Is there a place for a clothes line if you need one, and a barbeque or compost heap if you want one? Is there a sunny spot for a garden?

Don't overlook the garage. Is it a one-car or two-car affair? Is it oversized, to provide some storage space or room for a workbench? Is it big enough for your car? Will it be big enough if you buy that new Super Hupmobile station wagon you've had your eye on? Is there a sheltered route from the garage to the back door? Will using that route require you to climb over three bicycles, two skateboards, and the golf clubs?

Check the condition of the garage carefully, especially if it's not attached to the house. Detached garages tend to be allowed to run down more than attached ones, probably because they're not looked upon as part of the mansion itself. Does the garage door operate smoothly? Does it have a good lock? Is the hardware rusty or pitted? Is there any sag in the header, the heavy framing member over the door opening? Check it with your level. (See, you needed that level.) Are any wooden parts of the garage touching the ground? If there's no wood touching the ground, look for the vertical mud tubes that termites build on foundation walls to get from the ground to the nearest wood. With your knife or icepick, probe carefully along the sill, the flat wooden beam resting on top of the foundation wall, and the studs, the vertical framing members for the walls. If the knife or icepick goes in "hard," the lumber is probably sound. If it goes in "soft," there may be termite damage or the lumber may be rotting; be cautious. With your flashlight, look around inside the roof and along the upper walls for water stains that indicate leaks. Are there enough electrical outlets — the covered, three-wire kind — and lights in the garage? From outside, look the garage roof over carefully. Is it flat and smooth, or are shingles missing or curling? Are there gutters and leaders? Do they appear to be sound?

So much for the garage. But that was just a warm-up for the main attraction, the home itself. Start by standing back and taking a long, critical look at the thing. Are its lines clean and relatively simple, or does it look as though the carpenter made it up as he went along? Does the roof have one continuous line? Do the tops of doors and windows line up? The structure certainly doesn't have to be a box, but too many jogs and offsets are disturbing aesthetically, they are difficult and expensive to build, and they can produce chopped-up, inefficient interior space. Is there a clutter of colors, textures, and materials, or does the design seem to be uniform and consistent, without being boring? Does the structure conform to the terrain? Does it look as though it belongs where it is or as though there was simply no place else to put it? Are there roof overhangs? They're useful for keeping rain and snow off the walls, out of the windows, away from the foundation, and — especially on the south side of the building — for shading windows.

Now tip your cap to a rakish angle, spit on both hands, and step up for a closer look. The exterior walls should be solid and plumb. Stand at each corner and sight along the walls. If one is a bit out of plumb, that's probably nothing to get excited about, especially in an older building. But if you find a large bulge, excitement may be in order. The finish on the walls, whatever the material, should be smooth, firm, and weathertight. A long, open horizontal crack in a brick wall may mean that it's out of plumb and tipping out, even if you didn't notice the defect when you took a bead on it from the corner. Test the mortar in a brick or masonry wall with your knife or icepick. It should be hard and solid. If it's loose and powdery, it will need attention.

Clapboard siding should not be cracked, mismatched, or uneven at the joints. At corners, the ends should be mitered or should fit tightly against vertical corner boards. The exposed ends of siding will soak up moisture, which is to be discouraged. Nails should be noncorroding, countersunk (driven in below the surface) and filled (covered over with putty or a similar compound). Scratch one with your knife to see if it's rusted and if it's been countersunk and filled over. Obviously, if the nails and other hardware are noncorroding there won't be streaks of rust on the siding. Shakes should not be cracked, split, or curled, and should line up uniformly, though in some designs they are intentionally uneven at the bottom. You should be able to tell when it's intentional. Such new-fangled sidings as vinyl and aluminum should be in proper alignment with tight joints and should not be scratched, dented, or cracked. All metal sidings must be vented and grounded. Stucco should sound solid, not hollow, when it's tapped with a wooden object. Hairline cracks are not serious, but wide ones can be trouble if the lath beneath the stucco is not sound. The paint should be dense and opaque. The surface beneath should not show through, and the paint film should not be dull and chalky. Chalking indicates that new paint will be needed soon. Paint that is discolored, cracked, pitted, or blistering suggests that more will be needed than just another coat. It will require at least a great deal of elbow grease with a scraper or torch and sandpaper.

All joints — around windows and doors and between two materials such as wood and masonry — should be tight and fully caulked. An open joint between the building and the chimney can mean a serious problem, specifically, that the two are parting company. While you're inspecting joints, use your knife or icepick to probe windowsills for rot. They should be firm. And keep an eye out for cracked or broken glass. Watch for weatherstripping around windows. Doors should also be weatherstripped in cold climates, and they should fit well and open and close easily in all climates. There should be a light at each door. There should be flashing (a horizontal strip of sheet metal) above each window and door. Are the screens or storm doors and windows pitted or otherwise in need of attention? Are the windows the self-storing, triple-track kind? That will make life easier in the spring and fall. The exterior trim around doors and windows and at corners should be solid and smooth, and it should fit tightly.

Check stairs and railings for sturdiness and probe with your knife for rot and termite damage. Look for knotholes and other lumber defects that can weaken them. Notice whether there are hose connections in front and back and whether there are electrical outlets — the three-wire type that is protected from the weather — around porches, patios, and similar activity centers. Are the utility meters outside? They'll be read more frequently and conveniently if they are. The gas and electrical meters may be mounted on the wall of the building. The water meter may be underground, perhaps near the street.

Now look carefully at the foundation. It's important because it's — well, it's the foundation for the whole thing. Is there any standing water around the foundation? That can mean trouble, later if not now. Are there splashblocks under the downspouts, or do they lead underground to drywells or storm sewers? There should be one arrangement or the other. The foundation walls should rise at least 6 inches or so out of the ground, and there should be no wood touching the ground to attract termites. Check the foundation walls for vertical mud tubes leading from the ground to the wood. To a termite, that's not just a mud tube, it's an elevator to the cafeteria. To you, that's trouble. Look for termite shields — strips of sheet metal running along the top of the foundation wall. They should form a continuous, virtually seamless seal below the wooden part of the building. Unless the seal they form is just about perfect, they don't work, so they are not the best sort of termite protection. Treated soil and treated lumber are better, but not so visible.

Take a look at the foundation walls themselves. Uneven concrete and broken corners indicate poor workmanship or shoddy materials. Hairline cracks are not important, but big vertical cracks can mean settling and eventual dampness problems. If the foundation is built of block or stone, have a stab at the mortar with your knife. It shouldn't be loose or crumbling. Check the window wells, those semicircular enclosures for the basement windows. They should not be littered with leaves and other garden debris. They should be deep, and the bottom should be covered with gravel to facilitate drainage.

Now look up! To the roof! The chimney! The gutters! The roof is best inspected from a ladder or from the roof itself. If you are unequipped or reluctant to get up there, the professional inspector you call in later should do so before you buy. Whether you're looking from the roof or the ground, here are some highlights to notice. Is it light-colored? A light roof will help keep the place cool in summer. The chimney should be straight and solid. It should rise two feet above the ridge of a peaked roof and at least three feet above a flat roof. Give it the old knife-in-the-mortar test. Is the ridge line of the roof straight? There should be no visible sag. Are shingles warped, torn, curled, or missing? Are they self-sealing or interlocking — that is, are the lower edges firmly held down against the wind? Shingles should not bend over the edge of the roof; they're likely to break off. You won't be able to tell without getting up on the roof, but it's useful to know how many layers of shingles are there. If there's just one and it's not badly curled or warped, you may, when the time comes, be able to put a new roof right over it. But two layers is about the limit, so if there are two layers up there now — or if the one is in bad shape — you'll have to rip it off before replacing it, which adds to the cost. Flashing (sheet metal strips that fit under the edge of the roofing material) should be visible at all joints (around the chimney, for instance) and in valleys (the points where two sections of roof meet at an angle). The flashing should not look rusty or corroded. If you get up on the roof, give a squirt down the chimney with your flashlight, if it's not belching heat and smoke, and have a look. Unless it's very old, it should be lined with tile, not brick.

There's no law — except, perhaps, the law of averages — that says the roof on the home you're looking at will be asphalt shingles. If it looks like something other than the garden-variety roof, don't walk on it until you're sure it's safe to do so. Some roofing materials are brittle. There are a host of materials other than asphalt shingles that have been around a long time and will wear like crazy. Among them are asbestos cement shingles, tile, slate, and copper. They'll last approximately forever, but they're so expensive that you'll be paying them off for just about that long, and you may have some difficulty finding anyone able to repair or replace them. There are also wood shingles, which are held by some people to be superior to the asphalt kind, but which are banned in many places as a fire hazard.

If the home you're considering has a flat roof, the covering will probably be what's called a built-up roof, layers of roofing felt and an asphalt sealant, perhaps with a granular mineral material on top. Look for bare spots, spots where the granular material is missing, and for breaks or tears in the felt.

Does the building have lightning rods? They may not be needed in a densely settled area, though they may be advisable in a sparsely developed rural or suburban place. A tall, well-grounded structure is said to protect every lower structure within the radius of the taller structure's height. If the place you're looking at does have a lightning rod system, it must be carefully designed if it is to be effective. There should be rods no more than 20 feet apart along the roof ridge. They should also appear on dormers, and there should be two on each chimney. There should be arresters on antennas and power lines, and such metal rooftop devices as weathervanes and gutters should be tied into the system. The whole complex should be connected with heavy metal cables or straps to rods driven at least 10 feet into the ground. There should be additional grounds for clotheslines and other free-standing structures.

Are the gutters in place all around the home, and are they in good repair? Are they free of debris and covered with a wire or plastic mesh to keep them that way? Are there enough downspouts? Ideally, the gutters and downspouts should be inspected in the midst of a torrential downpour, but nobody will hold you to that.

What about the wires coming into the home? Are they underground or overhead? If they're overhead, are they free of interference from such things as tree limbs? How many wires are there? In addition to a telephone wire, there may be two or three for electric service. Two wires means only 120-volt service. Three means 240-volt service, which is required for such big appliances as ranges and large air conditioners.

If the home has a heat pump or central air conditioning, the condenser (the component that disperses the heat removed from the living area) will probably be outside, somewhere close to the building. Look it over for signs of rust or deterioration and be sure it's securely mounted on an adequate base. Its air passages should not be blocked by nearby foliage, though it should be in an inconspicuous place. It should not be under a bedroom window or in some other spot where its noise is likely to bother your family, but it should be positioned so the noise won't bother the neighbors, either. There are both air-cooled and water-cooled systems. Unless the place comes with its own lake or has a reliable well, the air-cooled type will be far cheaper to operate. Indeed, a water-cooled system should have two wells, one to take water out of the ground and another to put it back.

THE BASEMENT OR CRAWL SPACE

That's about it for the exterior. It's time to straighten your tie — or your bib overalls, anyway — and head for the basement, if there is one. This is likely to be the dirtiest part of the job, but it may also be the most informative.

The first problem to look for is one common to basements — water. If there's a pump in evidence you can assume, no matter what the seller or salesman tries to tell you, that it's there to remove water. A "sump" pump, the kind often used in basements with chronic water problems, is likely to be built into a hole in the floor. Don't miss it if it's there. Also look for water stains on the floor and walls. If there's a fresh coat of paint on an otherwise unfinished cellar, it may mean that there were water stains before the place went on the market. If there are mottled stains or pockmarks that look like white measles on the framing lumber in the basement, there is probably a dampness problem. On the other hand, an owner is not likely to keep good furniture in a basement that has a serious water problem, nor is he likely to stack valuable belongings on the floor there. Either one is an indication that everything is shipshape below, waterwise. In an unfinished basement, the floor should pitch gently toward a drain. When you find it, pour some water into it to see how well it works. It shouldn't be clogged.

While you're in the basement, you can examine the foundation walls from the inside unless the place is completely paneled or the walls are otherwise hidden. In general, all foundation walls look more or less alike from the outside. The ones that are made of concrete block or cinder block are often covered with a thin coat of cement to make them look better. Inside, though, what you see is usually what you get. Poured concrete is the best of the modern materials, then concrete block, then cinder block. And of course there are natural stone foundations that have been around for a century or two. Vertical cracks in the wall can mean settling or an inadequate footing (which is the base under the wall). Settling is a more serious matter in a new home than an old one. The old one may have finished settling, and it's still standing dry or you wouldn't be there. The new house may just have begun to settle, and there's no telling where it will end. A step-like horizontal crack in a block wall may suggest a weak foundation, a cause for extreme caution. Check the holes where pipes pass through the walls. They should be sealed with cement. Look for small cement patches in a row along the wall. They are an indication that the place has been treated with toxic chemicals (which have been pumped into holes drilled into the foundation wall) to keep termites out. Look for evidence of rotting around window frames.

Tap the concrete floor lightly with your hammer in several spots. It should sound flat, dull, and solid. A thin, hollow sound may mean that it's not thick enough or that there's a pocket of space between the floor and the cinder base below it. That can produce a water problem. If there are columns supporting the first floor, they should be steel or wood and should be directly under a heavy girder that spans the basement. The best column is probably a heavy steel pipe that's filled with concrete. You can tap it to see if it has been filled or is hollow. The column should rest on a concrete footing buried in the floor, not on the floor itself, and it should be bolted down so it can't shift. Wood columns should be securely anchored, too, and should rest on solid bases. Probe them with your knife in your never-ending search for rot and termite damage.

The girder that rests on top of the columns can be a steel "I" beam or wood. If it's wood it can be solid or "built-up" (that is, made of several pieces of lumber nailed together side by side). In a built-up girder, the joints between the components should be staggered and should rest on columns. The ends of the girder should rest on the foundation walls and should not be sealed in concrete or masonry; that will promote rot. If the home is new, the end of the girder should extend two or three inches over its support to allow for shrinkage as the lumber dries. Take out your knife and do you-know-what to the girder.

Above the girder and at right angles to it will be lighter framing members called joists, on which the floor above actually rests. The joists will be standing on edge. Measure them. They should be almost two inches wide and anywhere from 6 to 12 inches deep, depending upon the kind of lumber used, the distance the joists span, and the distance between them. They should probably be 16 to 24 inches apart. Do the joists look firm and true? Give 'em a stab here and there with your knife and use your level to see whether they sag alarmingly. Unless the house is more than 100 years old and built of rough-hewn lumber, there should not be bark on the framing members and there should not be a great many knots. Look around for grade stamps on exposed lumber. The joists and other members should be made of "construction" or "standard" grades of common lumber, not "utility" or "economy" grades. Most modern homes will have wood or metal "bridging" ("X"-shaped braces between the joists to prevent their twisting or warping). Very old houses are unlikely to have bridging.

The ends of the joists will be resting on the sill, which lies on top of the foundation wall and runs around the perimeter of the building. Notice whether the sill lies flat and tight against the foundation. Probe it every two or three feet for rot or termite damage, and note whether there's a metal termite shield between it and the foundation wall.

Above the joists and visible between them will be the subflooring, the lowest layer of the floor above. If the subflooring is composed of individual boards, they should be nailed down at a 45-degree angle to the joists. If the subflooring is plywood, which is more likely in a newer home, the grain should run at right angles to the joists.

In some of the newest homes, there may be no subflooring at all — tongue-and-groove flooring may be nailed to the joists and carpeting laid over it. That's a cost-cutting measure, and there are many others coming into common use. Among them are the elimination of bridging and the spacing of framing members every 20 or 24 inches rather than at the more traditional 16-inch intervals. Many of these new procedures result from tests conducted by national builders' organizations, sometimes in cooperation with government agencies. The builders maintain that the new specifications are perfectly adequate, and that may be right. The orthodox standards they replace are the result of tradition alone, not of any engineering tests or scientific studies. Only time will really tell. If homes start falling over more often or developing very serious structural problems, tradition will have been proven right. In the meantime, don't be alarmed because you don't find subflooring or bridging in a new home or because the studs are farther apart than you expected. That's the way the advanced builders are doing it these days.

Find the electrical entrance panel — what used to be called the "fuse box" — and open it. It will contain one or two circuit breakers or fuses (the circuit breaker, a sort of switch, is preferable) for each circuit. Each fuse or circuit breaker will be marked with its capacity in amps, a measure of electric current. Add them up. They should total at least 100, preferably 150 or 200. The rule of thumb is that with three or fewer large appliances, you need at least 100 amps. With four large appliances or with central air conditioning you need 150 or 200. Anything less than 100 is clearly inadequate if you live the way most people do. Each 120-volt circuit will have one fuse or circuit breaker. Each 240-volt circuit will have two fuses or a double circuit breaker. The 240-volt circuits are required for heavy-duty appliances — ranges, large air conditioners, and the like — and there should be at least two of them, probably more. You should have 12 to 16 circuits all told (though 20 would be better) with a few blank spaces in the box so you can add on later if necessary. One handy rule, if you want to take the trouble to do the arithmetic, is that there should be one circuit for every 375 square feet of usable floor area. There should be at least two 20-amp circuits for outlets; the rest may be 15-amp. There should be separate, marked circuits for the refrigerator, range, wall oven, oil or gas burner, washer, dryer, air conditioner, and electric space heater.

See if you can find markings on the wires leading out of the entrance panel. They will probably say something like "14-2" or "12-3." The first number indicates the size, and therefore the capacity, of the wire; the lower the number, the heavier the goods. On the wires coming out of the entrance panel, the number should be 12 or lower. The second figure indicates the number of conducting strands inside the insulation. Ideally, all of the wires should have three strands, but that will hardly be the case unless it's an unusual custom-built home or you're buying it from an electrician. Look over the rest of the visible wiring. It should be neat, workmanlike, and fastened securely every three feet or so. It should not loop gracefully from one support to the next. Grace may be fine for steelworkers; electricians are supposed to be down-to-earth. If the wiring is "tube and knob" (that is, if the wires are supported on porcelain knobs and fed through joists in ceramic tubes), it is very old and probably in need of replacement. If the wiring is "BX" (which means clad in a flexible, spiral metal armor) it's dated and subject to dampness and corrosion, but in some places the electrical code requires it. Modern wiring is usually clad in a flexible nonmetallic insulation. It's called "NM" (for nonmetallic) or "Romex." Some codes also require that wiring, especially where it is exposed, be enclosed in pipe-like casings called conduits. Keep an eye peeled for spliced wires. Splices should be made only in rectangular or hexagonal wiring boxes; the cable should be continuous from one box to the next.

Watch even more carefully for signs that the place has aluminum wiring, which is more dangerous than copper because it expands and contracts more as the temperature changes, and in doing so can loosen some connections. When that happens, the aluminum forms an oxide that resists electricity, causing heat that can melt insulation or a receptacle or start a fire. Aluminum wiring first came into wide use in 1965. Though the guidelines for its use were tightened in 1972, it continued to be a matter of controversy. The aluminum manufacturers have been singing its praises, consumer activists and some insurance people have been condemning it, and government officials have been coming down squarely on both sides. Its existence alone would seem to be sufficient reason not to buy a home, but finding it can be a problem unless you happen to be an electrician. If the home you're interested in was built between 1965 and 1972 and all wiring is insulated so you can't tell copper from aluminum, have an electrician look at the wiring before you make a final decision to buy it. In the meantime, if any bare wire is visible — it shouldn't be; insulation should cover it all — the difference in color between copper and aluminum is obvious. During your inspection, you might also try feeling an outlet plate or switch plate here and there to see if it's warm; keep alert for the smell of smoke or burning plastic around switches and outlets. Watch as well for lights that flicker inexplicably. All of those things are signs that the electrical system is awry, though the cause need not be aluminum wiring. And it need not be said that one shouldn't go around poking knives, screwdrivers, pencils, and fingers into electrical doodads. That stuff can be literally hair-raising. If you have any reason to suspect that the place may have aluminum wiring, have someone who knows what he's doing tell you the score.

The score should be easier to determine as far as pipes are concerned, if only because they're likely to be more visible. Pipes come in three classes: supply pipes, which deliver the water and distribute it around the home; waste pipes, which obviously collect the waste and remove it; and gas pipes. The water supply pipes and the gas pipes may in some cases be about the same size; no more than an inch or less than a half-inch in diameter; the waste pipes will be much larger. If there's any confusion about which is a water supply pipe and which is a gas pipe, trace it. If it goes to the range, it's a gas pipe. If it goes to the sink, it must be for water. The water supply pipes should be copper or brass (or, in newer homes, plastic). Water pipes should not be iron or steel, which corrode too easily, or lead. Your magnet will be attracted to iron or steel, but not to copper or lead. Lead will be soft and silvery if you scratch it. Rigid plastic pipe is used for water in some areas, but many plumbing codes do not allow it, especially for hot water. Plastic pipe is relatively new, and it is a case where you can pick your expert, pro or con, and believe as you please. (But, whatever the experts say, it's the best thing for doing it yourself since hammers grew handles.) Flexible plastic tubing is widely frowned upon except for such things as lawn sprinklers. If you find iron water supply pipes, you can plan on some expensive plumbing work sooner or later. The pipe is probably old and corrosion has had a head start on you. If you find both copper and iron pipe, the trouble is likely to come sooner rather than later. For one thing, the presence of both indicates that trouble has already begun; some of the iron pipe has been replaced. For another thing, the two materials can be expected to produce a corrosive chemical reaction wherever they meet. A good sign to look for in the water supply piping is the use of "unions" (joints between sections of pipe) in long runs. They make repairs easier and cheaper. Another good sign is the presence of insulation on hot-water pipes. It saves fuel by keeping hot water hot longer.

Gas pipes will probably not be copper, but steel, which is perfectly acceptable since gas will not corrode pipes the way water will. The waste pipes, which are larger than the others, may be cast iron — in which case they're likely to be as rusty as your golf game — plastic, or a synthetic composition material. Many plumbing codes ban the synthetic pipe inside a building or within a certain distance of the foundation but allow it underground elsewhere. If you're alarmed by the rust on a cast-iron pipe, just drop into a plumbing supply house, find the worst-looking section they have, and try to lift it. It'll take a lot of rusting. Like all other pipes, the waste lines should be neat and secure. Look for plugs (called "clean-outs") wherever a waste pipe turns a corner and midway on long runs. They facilitate just what their name suggests they'd facilitate. Very useful indeed. If you're looking at a two-story or three-story home and the waste pipes are plastic, try to figure out how close they are to the living room, dining room, and other areas where you may have guests. The sound that emanates from plastic waste pipes when an upstairs toilet is flushed can stop a D.A.R. luncheon absolutely cold.

Having disposed, as it were, of the plumbing inspection, you may feel free to trip gaily over to the water heater. It will probably have a plate on it that will tell you what it's made of and what its capacity is. It should have a tank that is aluminum or copper or has a ceramic or glass lining. Depending on its "recovery rate" (the speed with which it heats water) and the rate at which you use hot water, it should have a capacity ranging from 30 gallons for a family of two or three to 50 gallons for a family of six or more. There will probably be a small door or cover at the bottom of the heater. If it's a gas-fired model, that's where the pilot light will be. Open the door or cover and, using a flashlight, look for signs of rust or leakage at the bottom of the heater. That's probably where the first signs of trouble will appear. If you can't seem to find the water heater, it's probably the so-called domestic type, a coil built into the furnace or burner. Such systems save a bit of space but can be troublesome in areas that have "hard" water (water with heavy mineral content). During the winter, but not the summer, they are cheaper to operate than separate water heaters. The capacities of these systems are given in gallons per minute, or gpm. A small family in a home that has two baths is said to require at least 3.25 gpm; a large family in the same home would need 3.75 gpm.

Somewhere in the vicinity of the hot-water heater should be the burner or furnace that heats the home. If the place has baseboard electric heating, a heat pump, or solar heat, you may not find a furnace at all, but if the fuel is gas or oil you'll see some sort of heating contraption. It can assume a variety of sizes and shapes, depending upon the sort of system it is: hot air, hot water, or steam. If it's a hot-air system, sheet metal ducts or pipes will lead from the burner to all parts of the home. There are two types of hot-air heating. A gravity system makes use of the fact that hot air rises. It lets nature deliver the heat. A forced-air system, on the other hand, uses a blower or fan to push the warm air where it's needed. The forced-air type is more modern and by all means preferable. The fan can be either belt-driven or direct drive. Belt-driven blowers are regarded as better. Look for a belt like the fan belt in a car. Also look for a short fabric section between the heater itself and the main duct. It serves to insulate the blower from everything else. Without it, the vibration transmitted through the ducts is likely to drive you nuts. See whether the filter in a hot-air system can be removed easily for cleaning. If not, it's probably filthy. Also notice whether the ducts are insulated where they pass through unheated spaces. That's especially important if the ducts also handle central air conditioning during the summer. Also important in that case are dampers so the ducts can be adjusted or "balanced." Are the ducts in general neat and out of the way? If they run every which way at elevations that require you to duck to walk under them, the system is probably either ancient or incompetently designed. You can expect to have to replace it.

Whether the heating system is hot-air or another type, one indication of old age is an oil tank in the basement. That probably means that the thing started out as a coal-fired system, and when it was converted the oil tank replaced the coal bin. There is one advantage to a tank that's so accessible — you can look for signs, including odor and stains on the floor, that the tank or its fittings are leaking.

If the heat in the home you're inspecting uses hot water rather than hot air, it will have pipes rather than ducts. They are similar to water supply pipes, but a bit larger. The same rules apply to them as to supply pipes, though it is wise to remember before fooling around with them that if the system is working they will be (or should be) hot. Like hot-air systems, hot-water systems can be gravity operated or forced, with the force supplied by a pump rather than a fan. Again, the forced system is preferable. If it's a steam-heating system you're looking at, there will be pipes rather than ducts, but the pipes will be considerably larger than the water-supply pipes, and they should be insulated. In a steam or hot-water system, look for signs of leaks around and under the boiler. A steam system is likely to be relatively old; hot air and hot water (or electricity) have been popular in recent decades. If the system is either steam or hot water, a cast iron boiler is preferable to a steel one because it resists corrosion better.

Take an over-all look at the basement and the space it contains with a mind to what you would like to do there. If some of the basement is finished, of course, you should look at it the way you would other living areas. If it's unfinished but you have visions of converting it to a family room or some other use, study its potential. Is there adequate headroom? Seven feet is an absolute minimum. Measure it in several spots. Is it dry enough? Dry enough for a cellar may not be dry enough for a family room. Are there enough windows and are they large enough to supply adequate light and ventilation? Is the floor area large enough and open enough for what you have in mind? If you're considering the purchase only on the theory that you can convert the basement, you'd better measure it and draw a floor plan that includes all the columns, windows, the water heater and burner, and other obstructions. Don't discover after you've bought the place that you can't put your darkroom or laundry in the basement after all.

Examine the stairs from underneath. Do they seem to be solidly and carefully constructed? Are they free of knotholes or other defects that would weaken them? Are they too narrow or steep for safe use? A direct entrance from outside can be a distinct advantage in a basement, but not if it's too narrow, steep, or rickety to be of any use. What about the door at the top of the stairway? Does it open into the stairs, requiring you to bend over backward to get out? Is there a light switch at the top of every stairway? Does every stairway have a handrail and a light?

Well, that's the basement. If you think that was a dirty and unpleasant job, pray that there isn't a crawl space rather than a basement under the next home you inspect. If part or all of the place is built over a crawl space, you should have a look in there, too. If there's no basement at all, the crawl space may provide your only opportunity to inspect the foundation walls, sill, joists, subflooring, wiring, and plumbing. All the same tests that would be made in a basement should be made in a crawl space, the big difference being that you may have to make them lying on your back. Beyond that, there are a few extra things to look for in a crawl space. First of all, it should never be built in a place where there is a danger that it will be flooded. It should be 18 to 36 inches high. There should be screened vents on all outside walls. They should provide a square foot of opening for every 300 square feet of floor area and should remain open all year unless the space is heated. If there is heat in the space, the vents can be closed during the winter. The ground under the crawl space should be covered with a vapor barrier, probably a sheet of plastic. Unless the space is heated, there should be insulation under the floor above it. Any exposed pipes or ducts that run through an unheated space should also be insulated. If the space is heated, the walls around it should be insulated. If the vents or the vapor barrier are missing, be especially careful in looking for signs of moisture or rot in the framing lumber above the crawl space.

If the place is built on a slab, with neither a crawl space nor a basement, you will still want to examine the heating system, the water heater, and wherever possible, the plumbing, wiring, and framing. Some of that equipment will probably be accessible in a first-floor utility room, and some may be reachable in the garage or attic. Wherever you can examine the framing — the joists and studs and so forth — give it a poke with your knife.

THE LIVING AREAS

Well, you may look and feel like a coal miner, but the worst is over. You're ready to inspect the living areas of the home, and, even in the most slovenly places, they're usually cleaner than the crawl space. Besides, by now you probably know more about this home than the fellow who's selling it.

Generally, as you go through the living areas, look for indications of good planning and workmanship (or the lack thereof) and, in a resale home, for signs of excessive wear and tear. Sight along some walls. Do they look plumb and true or do they wave? Waving can mean poor workmanship, shoddy materials, or settling. Run your hand over the walls here and there to see if they're smooth. Are they plaster or wallboard? Plaster absorbs sound and adds rigidity but is expensive. Rap plaster walls with your knuckle to see if the plaster is loose. Check corners to see if the wallpaper has cracked or buckled. If the interior is of drywall construction rather than plaster, are the joints obvious under the paint or wallpaper? How about the ceilings? Bad joints can mean poor workmanship or settling. "Popped" nails (nails that have backed part way out of the wallboard) can mean settling, excessive vibration, or excessive moisture in the studs. Hairline cracks are probably the result of settling, but wide cracks can mean poor construction. When you find wood paneling, tap it in several places to see whether it's solidly nailed or glued in place. Sight along it for bulges. Whatever the wall material, be alert for stains that indicate leaks, especially under windows. Watch for stains on ceilings, too.

Notice baseboards, mouldings, the trim around doors and windows. Are they smooth? Are joints tight, without a lot of filling to cover poor workmanship? Do the floors squeak? Are they level or do they sag? Sagging can mean that the home has settled, that the framing lumber has shrunk, or that the joists or other framing members are too weak for the load they're carrying. One way to check for sagging is to put your marble or ball bearing on an uncarpeted floor — preferably upstairs if it's a two-story home. If the marble or bearing rolls quickly in one direction, the floor is not level. If the floor is sagging and you put the marble in the middle of the room, of course, it won't roll; it can't go uphill. Try several spots in several rooms, if possible. Do the glasses or dishes in a cabinet rattle as you walk by? They shouldn't. If the home has hardwood floors, the nails should be hidden. Exposed nailheads can mean poor materials or just lazy workmen. Be wary of linoleum anywhere except the kitchen, bathroom, laundry room, or family room. If you find it in an unusual place, it may be hiding a bad floor. You may not be able to lift the linoleum to see the floor below. In that case, walk on it and crouch down and feel it to see if you can determine whether the floor is level and firm. Try to find out what's under wall-to-wall carpeting — what kind of padding, floor, or subfloor, and what shape it's in. Is furniture strategically placed to hide damage or wear to the carpeting or floor?

Do the doors open and close easily and fully? When they're closed, do they latch and stay closed? When a door is partially opened, does it stay that way or does it swing shut or open further? A door that is not equipped with a closing device but still closes or opens on its own is probably out of plumb. That could be the result of poor workmanship, settling, or just age. Do some doors bump one another when both are opened? Are closet doors high enough and wide enough so you can see and reach everything inside? Are there dangerous doors on or near stairways? Are all sliding glass doors shatterproof? Are the exterior doors solid? Are there deadbolt locks on all exterior doors, including those in the garage and basement? Are there peepholes or intercoms so you can tell who's there?

Do the windows open smoothly and easily — especially those in hard-to-reach places, the one over the kitchen sink, for example? Is the window hardware in good condition? Do all the windows lock? Does the glass distort your vision? Is the glazing compound around the outside of the glass dried and crumbling, or is it solid and painted? Are the window frames steel, aluminum, or wood? The metal ones require less maintenance, but all except the most expensive of them get cold in winter and cause condensation on the glass. Are there jalousie windows (windows made of adjustable glass louvers to control ventilation)? They tend to be a leaky, balky nuisance.

No matter what the weather, ask that the heat be turned on; adjusting the thermostat to 80 or 90 degrees should do it. Wait 15 to 30 minutes if the system has been off. If it's a hot-air system, notice whether it's noisy, whether the ducts rattle. Check each of the registers, (the grilles through which the air passes) to be sure they're connected and working. In cold climates, the registers should be low on exterior walls, preferably under windows, and the return registers (the ones that carry air back to the burner for reheating) should be high on interior walls. In warm climates, where air conditioning is more important than heating, they should be reversed — that is, the registers that are delivering cool air should be high and the return registers low. Notice whether there are streaks of black soot around the registers.

If the place has central air, you'll want to turn that on, too. Feel each register to be sure it's working, and notice whether they're adjustable. They should be for use in air conditioning. Generally, the fan in a more efficient system will continue to operate, even when the compressor shuts down. That way, whatever "cold" remains in the system will be distributed and the temperature and humidity will remain more uniform.

If the heating system is steam or hot water, check whether the radiators are iron, which is preferable, or finned copper or aluminum. If nothing else tells you, your magnet will. Are there water stains on the floor near steam radiators, suggesting leaks? Are the radiators baseboard or upright? Upright ones are probably older and almost certainly more of an eyesore. Is there an automatic thermostat, one with a clock that will set the temperature back at night and up again in the morning? Is there more than one thermostat? That indicates zoned heating, which allows you to heat one part of the home more than another. The thermostat should not be in a draft, in the hottest or coldest part of the home, or in a spot where it will interfere with furnishing or decorating. The thermostat should be on an inside, not an outside, wall.

Keep an eye out for extra heating devices — typically, electric baseboard or wall heaters. They suggest that the main system is not adequate to heat all parts of the home, and they can be expensive to operate. Such auxiliary heating devices may have their own thermostats, but they do not constitute real zoned heating. These additions to the heating system are most likely to be found in a room over a garage, crawl space, or some other unheated area. They also tend to crop up in finished basements, and they may be used in conjunction with solar or heat-pump systems.

As you go through the home, try to notice whether the top floor is roughly the same temperature as the first floor — hot air rises. If the weather is cold, hold your hand against the inside of an exterior wall, then against an interior wall. A big difference in temperatures indicates insufficient insulation.

Does there appear to be enough light in each room? Is there a light switch at each entrance and exit to a room and at the top and bottom of every stairway? Are the switches the newer, silent type, or do they go off like a shot? Are there dimmers on any of the lights — in the dining room, perhaps? Are the outside lights — those on walks, patios, porches, and the garage — controlled from inside, too? Are any of the light switches hidden when doors are opened? Are there enough outlets? They should be no more than 12 feet apart (most appliances have 6-foot cords), and there should be one on either side of a door, arch, fireplace, or other wall obstruction. Notice whether the owner uses many extension cords and multiple plug-in outlets. If so, there probably are not enough outlets. Where you do see outlets, notice whether they are the three-wire, grounded type. Such devices are essential for heavy appliances like ranges and big air conditioners; they are useful elsewhere as well.

Be aware of the layout of the home as you move through it. If you've made a careful floor plan you'll be able to study it later and learn a lot; but there's nothing like being there, so keep your eyes open. Can you get from any room to any other room without going through a third room? Do you have direct access to a bathroom from any other room? Is there a bathroom on every floor? Are they shielded from general view? Are there buffers between the sleeping area and the living and working areas? Is the kitchen easily accessible to almost everywhere? Are the halls, doors, and stairways high enough and wide enough? High and wide enough to get your furniture into the joint? Are there two escape routes, even from the second floor?

Is the place attractively decorated? Are the colors and patterns things you could live with? Is there carpeting that will be included in the sale? How about draperies, mirrors, and other decorative items? Are there special lighting fixtures or such luxury extras as a central vacuum system or fancy door chimes? Would they be an asset or an embarrassment to you? Are there fire or smoke and burglar alarms?

Keeping all these things in mind, go through the place room by room, examining each room specifically. Is there a hall or vestibule to shield the main entrance, or does it open directly into the living room? Is there an adequate coat closet? Is there room for a table to hold hats, purses, and parcels? Is there a window near the entrance so you can see who's knocking at your door? Is the window far enough from the knob and lock or small enough so that a burglar can't break it and reach in to unlock the door? If it's too big or too close, is the window unbreakable?

Does the living room picture window put the whole place on view to anyone who drives by? Is the room large enough for your usual entertaining? Will it accommodate your furniture and your vast collection of the erotic art of Byelorussia? Is there a fireplace? Look above the front opening for soot, an indication that the fireplace is smoky. If there are ashes in the grate and the firebrick inside the fireplace is blackened, that indicates it's been used recently, a good sign. The damper should work. Open it and see if you can see up into the chimney. The chimney should be lined with flue tile; you shouldn't see brick inside unless it's a very old double-thick chimney. If you do see brick, have an engineer take a look. You may not be able to see into the chimney because of a smoke shelf, a projection above the fireplace proper. In that case, you'll have to be content with a look down from the top.

Before you leave the living room, notice whether it has places — or space for places — to store books, magazines, records, a card table and chairs, TV tables, and firewood. If it has all that, you've got quite a living room.

Is the dining room big enough for your family and your furniture — including a buffet or hutch or some other serving and storage area? Is it convenient to but screened from the kitchen? Is the chandelier positioned properly so you can center a table under it and still have room for a hutch at one side — not to mention chairs on both sides?

Is the kitchen large enough? Is it large enough to eat in, if you plan to do that? Are there enough cabinets? Do they have adjustable shelves? Check metal cabinets for rust and wood cabinets for warping. Try all the drawers and doors. They should work smoothly. Is there enough counter and work space? Is it well lit? Is it covered with a material that resists heat, water, and grease? Is it cut, scratched, or discolored? Does the backsplash, the wall immediately behind and above the counter, extend all the way up to the bottom of the wall cabinets? Are there plenty of electrical outlets along the backsplash? Are they of the three-wire, grounded type? Is there a broom closet? An exhaust fan? Try it and see if it's noisy. See if the hood over the range is clogged with grease, a fire hazard. Check the sink for chipped enamel, rust stains, and scratches. Put some water into the sink and see how it drains. Look under the sink for signs of leaks, rust, and rot. What appliances will be left in the kitchen after the sale? How old are they, and in what condition? Try whatever you can — the oven and the range burners, for instance. Is the floor material easy to clean and maintain? If there is no dishwasher, say, or freezer, and you hope to buy one, is there room for it? If you have small children, can they play in the family room or backyard and still be supervised conveniently from the kitchen? Is there easy access to the garage or driveway for unloading groceries? Is the wallpaper water-resistant? Beware of metallic papers, which may be electrical conductors — especially dangerous in a room where quantities of water are used. Before you sign off on the kitchen, be sure that your floor-plan sketch indicates the sizes and positions of the refrigerator, sink, range, counters, and cabinets.

Are the stairs in the right proportion for safe, comfortable use — the treads deep enough and the risers high enough? Are the railings sound? Steep, narrow, and especially circular stairs are both tiring and dangerous. Is there headroom and sufficient clearance to get furniture up to the second floor? Do the stairs squeak? A squeak at the top or bottom may mean poor construction, but one in the middle is probably caused by a loose tread. Easy to fix.

Are there enough bedrooms for your family? Are they large enough for your furniture? Is there sufficient closet space? Are the bedrooms convenient to a bathroom and isolated from the rest of the home? Does each bedroom have cross ventilation? One school holds that bedroom windows should be high enough so you can place some furniture beneath them and they provide some privacy. Another school holds that in children's rooms the windows should be high enough so the little fellers won't fall out, low enough so they can see out, and low enough, large enough, and easy enough to open so they can climb out in an emergency. It's one of those cases where you can pick your expert, measure your kid, and take your choice. Another safety matter: If you're wandering around second-floor bedrooms in an old home, feel the walls in the rooms near the chimney. Try to determine whether there's a metal plate in there covering an old flue opening; it may be a fire hazard.

Does the place have enough bathrooms for your family, even at the peak of the morning rush hour, when bathrooms are most in demand? Are the bathrooms convenient to the bedrooms? Is there one in or next to the master bedroom? Is there also access to it from other rooms? Are the bathrooms shielded from the front door? From the living, dining, and family rooms? Are they big enough so you can use them without bumping into everything? Sit down and try the toilet on for size. Are the fixtures modern? Are they and the tile of an acceptable color? Are there tubs and showers, or just stall showers? Do the showers have doors or sliding-panel enclosures? If so, they should be safety glass or plastic. Are there adequate medicine cabinets, vanities, or other storage areas? Is there sufficient light for shaving and make-up? Is there an outlet near — preferably not above — the mirror? Are the light switches out of reach of the tub and shower? Do the tub and shower have non-skid bottoms? Are there hand holds above the tub? Is the caulking around the tub firm and solid? What's the condition of the "grouting" (the "mortar" between the tiles)? Is there an exhaust fan or a window in every bathroom? Is there a sun lamp or other heater? They're safest when they're recessed. Are there shut-off valves under the toilet and lavatory? Are all the cold-water faucets on the right? That sounds like a small matter, but more than one person has been scalded while discovering that what he thought was the cold water was hot. Is there a window over the tub? If so, you'll have trouble opening and closing it unless you want to tramp across the tub in your clodhoppers. Is the bathroom wallpaper waterproof? Be wary of the metallic types; they're waterproof, but they may conduct electricity, especially when they're wet, as they're apt to be after a steamy shower in a small bathroom. Turn on all the faucets in the bathroom at once, then flush the toilet. If the water flow falls off to a trickle, the place does not have adequate water pressure. Be sure to try this in the highest bathroom in the place, the one on the top floor. And if one bathroom looks particularly ancient, try it there, too. Those old galvanized pipes can get clogged with rust, which does nothing for the water pressure. Put some water in the tub and the sink, then drain it out. If it drains slowly, the pipes are probably clogged, a problem that is relatively easy to correct. But if it gurgles and bubbles as it's draining, there may be inadequate venting in the plumbing system, an indication of shoddy construction. Finally, before you leave the last bathroom, taste the water. If you buy the place you'll have to live with that water supply unless you're amenable to buying bottled water or installing a purification system. Might as well find out right now what you're up against.

Is the family room large enough to accommodate both your children and your regular Friday-night beer busts? Does it have provision for toy storage? Is it finished with childproof, easy-to-clean materials? Does it have an exterior as well as an interior entrance? Is it sufficiently isolated from the other rooms? Can it be closed off to hold down the noise of a teen-age party? Is it handy enough so that young children playing there can be supervised from the kitchen or wherever it is you're likely to be while they're playing? You probably can't have it both ways — it can't be both isolated and handy. The status of your family will determine what is important to you. Just remember that children grow with striking determination; today's toddler is tomorrow's rock collector. So plan ahead a little. If there's a lavish bar in the family room, check to see that it has what a bar needs — running water, a sink, provision for a small refrigerator. Is the surface of the bar resistant to water, heat, liquor, and grease? It should be as good as the countertop in the kitchen. If the family room is in the basement, are there enough windows to ventilate it, even during a crowded party, and to make it bright and cheerful?

Is there a utility or laundry room? There had better be if there's no basement. Is it convenient to the kitchen? Is it convenient to the bedrooms and bathrooms so laundry can be delivered and distributed with little trouble? Does it have an exterior door so that it can also be used as a mud room? Is it large enough for a washer and dryer and for the storage of laundry supplies and the laundry itself? Is it also large enough to handle a freezer, perhaps, or an extra refrigerator? To store cases of beer, soda, or canned goods? For the boots, rubbers, and umbrellas that have to go someplace during the winter? Is there a utility sink? Are there grounded outlets on separate circuits for the appliances? Is the dryer vented outside? Is there a clean, comfortable place to sort and fold laundry? Is the light good? Is there room for a sewing machine and an ironer or ironing board? Are there outlets for such appliances?

Is the storage space sufficient? You'll need a place for sleds during the summer and the lawn mower during the winter. You'll have to find a place for clothes that are out of season, for the leaves from the dining room table, the vacuum cleaner, a broom and toys, toys, toys. Not to mention your camera, skis, outboard motor, high school dink and old Navy uniforms. What about your saddle shoes and that swell statue of Pan that Aunt Edna gave you last Christmas? Have to have a place for them. And the place had better be handy enough so you can get the thing out if Aunt Edna decides to show up for dinner some night. Do the closets have lights and adjustable shelves? Do they open from inside as well as outside, so trapped children can escape?

THE ATTIC

Now just a short traipse to the attic and you needn't ever look at this rathole again — unless, of course, you decide to buy it. The first question to ask as you begin the trip is whether you'll risk breaking your neck every time you try to go to the attic or whether it's so difficult that you'll just skip it more often than not. The older the place is, up to a point, the easier the climb is likely to be. Years ago — though not as many as 200 years ago — builders put in permanent staircases to the attic, just like the staircase to the second floor. After World War II, the developers discovered that they could save some space and some money by doing away with the regular staircase and using a set of disappearing stairs, the kind that pull down from the ceiling, which could be installed in a hallway or bedroom. Then the trapdoor, for which you had to use a ladder, became the vogue. Recently, trusses have begun to replace rafters as roof supports, so there isn't any space up there anyway. If there's any access at all, it's probably through a trap door in the garage or a closet. You'll have to be the judge of how valuable the attic space is and how difficult it is to reach, but it's a safe bet that the newer the home, the less useful you'll find the attic.

In any case, once you get up there, if you can, look at the rafters (the framing members that support the roof). Measure them and the distances between them. They should be 2 × 6's or larger — almost 2 inches wide and almost 6 inches deep — and they should probably be 16 to 24 inches apart, depending upon the kind of lumber used, their length, the weight of the roof they have to support, and the likelihood that they will have to support snow. The joints between the rafters and the ridgepole (the beam that runs the length of the roof at its peak) should be tight and accurately cut. Look for the grade mark stamped on the rafters, just as you did on the joists in the basement. It should be "construction" or "standard" grade, not "utility" or "economy."

In newer homes, the rafters and the ridgepole may be replaced by trusses, which are constructed as units before erection. A truss looks like two rafters joined together with wooden bracing that assumes the geometric patterns of the steel you see in the framing of bridges and big buildings. Trusses pretty well destroy the attic space, but the engineers say they are lighter than rafters and ridgepole for the same load, and they allow more flexibility in the placement of walls on the floors below because the walls don't have to carry the load. They are also easier and cheaper to erect. You give some and you get some. There's no free lunch.

While you're looking at all that lumber up there, look as well for signs of leaks — stains on rafters or trusses or on the sheathing (the boards just above the rafters or trusses that form the bottom layer of the roof). Ventilation is extremely important in attics. There should by all means be cross ventilation. The best arrangement is a combination of vents at the ridge (the peak of the roof) and in the soffits (the horizontal surfaces under the eaves). Vents in the ends of gables can be perfectly adequate if they're big enough. Generally speaking, there should be a square foot of area for every 300 square feet of floor. Vents should be above the insulation. If the weather is cold while you're making your inspection, feel the insulation — carefully, because fiberglass can be mean stuff if you get it in your skin. Dampness in the insulation is an indication of inadequate ventilation.

You might as well look at the insulation, too, wherever you can. There should be plenty of it in an attic, more than anywhere else, either up between the rafters or trusses or underfoot. It it's underfoot and the place has a complete floor, you may not be able to see it, but you'd better make sure it's there, one way or another. Every time oil prices go up a nickel, the engineers revise their thinking on how much insulation is necessary, so there's no point in setting down a rigid rule here. Find out how much this place has and drop in at the nearest lumberyard or home-improvement store. They'll be glad to tell you how much more you need. In general, the batt or blanket type of insulation is better than the loose type. It should have a vapor barrier (a sheet of foil, plastic, or treated paper) on the side that faces the heated area.

One note of caution on insulation: Avoid a home containing urea-formaldehyde, a type of insulation that can be blown into the cavities in the walls of existing buildings. While no one seems to dispute its effectiveness, the fumes it gives off have been linked to skin and eye irritation, headaches, dizziness, nausea, respiratory problems, and even cancer. Those effects are the subject of some dispute, but at least one survey of appraisers concluded that urea-formaldehyde's presence reduces the value of a home by 14 percent, on average. So who needs it?

If the chimney runs through the attic, you'll want to have a look at that, too. Haul out the old knife and give the mortar a stab or two; it should be firm and hard. Look closely around the edges of the chimney, the places where the framing of the building comes closest to the masonry. Except in a few extremely old buildings, which were designed that way, the home should not be leaning on the chimney — or vice versa. They should be independent structures, standing next to one another. If that isn't the case you may have problems so serious that you simply shouldn't consider buying the place. One of the best indications of such problems is charred or burned lumber around the chimney, especially at the floor or the roof line. Very dangerous. If you're at all in doubt, have a pro look at it. The periphery of the chimney is also a good spot to look for the stains that suggest leakage. They're more likely to occur there than at most other places on the roof.

One of the positive things to look for in the attic is an exhaust fan. It can be mounted in the attic floor — that is, in the ceiling of the living space below — or in the end of a gable or on the roof. Some of them, the type designed to cool the living spaces below, are huge; they look almost like the propeller on an airplane. The critical factor to consider is the amount of air they can move, whatever their size. That capacity, usually given in cubic feet per minute, or cfm, should about equal the total volume of the living area in cubic feet. Another type of attic ventilator, much smaller and installed in the roof or a gable end, is designed only to exhaust air from the attic. The best of them are thermostatically controlled — when the attic temperature reaches a certain point, the fan turns on and expels the hot air. An attic fan or ventilator can make your air conditioning much more efficient, and it can keep the living areas markedly cooler without air conditioning. It should be mounted in such a way as to keep the weather out — under a weatherproof housing if it's on the roof, or behind shuttered louvers if it's in the end of a gable.

Now descend as gracefully as possible from the attic, dust yourself off, be gentle with the owner of this dump, and beat a hasty retreat with all the notes you've made on your inspection. The notes will remind you of all the negative things about the place, every defect you were able to find. Have yourself a shower, a drink, and a good meal before reviewing them. And keep two things in mind when you do study them: First, there were many good things about this place or you wouldn't have gotten interested enough to give it all that time. Second, not every defect is a disaster; every home has defects. You've found most of the detectable defects in this one, but many of them are defects that can be fixed with a screwdriver or a little putty. And don't write off the home on the basis of things that puzzle you, things that don't seem quite right but may be acceptable, until you consult someone who really knows for sure.

21

How Should You Evaluate What You've Seen?

After you've washed the crawl space out of your hair and collected your thoughts, it's time to decide where you stand and where you're going. It might be best to start by making two lists of questions you'd like to ask — one list for the owner if it's a resale home or the salesman if it's new; the second list for someone who knows construction, probably the building inspector you will soon retain if you remain serious about the purchase. The lists needn't be completed in one sitting. Other questions will crop up as time passes, and you can add them when they do.

On the list for the engineer, note everything you saw during your inspection that didn't seem right, even if you're not sure it wasn't right. Ask for rough estimates of the cost of repairs or changes you have in mind. Don't question every loose screw in the place, but try to hit all the important things.

QUESTIONS FOR THE SELLER

The list of questions for the seller or salesman will be longer for an old home than a new one because you will want to know just how old many things are. The list should include such questions as these (you can figure out which ones to skip if it's a new home):

Precisely how old is the place and who built it? Are the original plans and specifications available? Who were the previous owners? How long has the seller owned it? Why is he selling? Has the place been treated to protect it against termites? Is there a certificate proving that this service has been carried out? Ask to see it. What sort of treatment was it? The most effective is the use of toxic chemicals in the soil around the building. Next best is the use of chemicals to make the wood itself toxic to termites. Least effective is the use of a metal shield around the top of the foundation. Faulty joints, which make the shield virtually useless, are extremely difficult to avoid. How long has the exterminator guaranteed that the home will be free of termites? Is there a charge for an annual inspection to insure that there is no termite infestation? What is the charge?

How old are the roof, plumbing, wiring, heating system, and water heater? How long are the burner and water heater guaranteed? It should be 10 or 15 years. When was the burner last cleaned? When was the place last painted? Be aware that most paint used before 1950 contained significant amounts of lead and should be removed or covered, especially if you have young children. What appliances are to be included in the sale? How old are they? Are any of them still under warranty? Is the warranty transferable?

Does the home have city sewers and water, or does it rely on a well and septic tank or cesspool? If the sewers are in, are they paid for or is there an outstanding assessment? Are there assessments outstanding for sidewalks, curbs, or other improvements? If there is a well, how deep is it and how old? How much water does it produce? A flow rate of six gallons a minute is about the minimum. The average home uses 75 gallons a day for each occupant. Where is the water storage tank, and how big is it? The minimum is about 80 gallons. If there is a septic tank, how big is it? It should have a capacity of at least 100 gallons a person, and, if you have a garbage disposer or automatic washer, 125 gallons a person. Another rule of thumb is that a two-bedroom or three-bedroom home needs a 750-gallon tank and a four-bedroom home requires 1,000 gallons. When was the septic tank last cleaned out? It needs attention at least every two years. If there's a cesspool, plan on replacing it. It's unhealthy. Ask for precise locations for the well, the septic tank, and its drainage field, and for any drywell, cesspool, or other underground facility. The well should be at least 50 feet from the septic tank and at least 100 feet from the drainage field. The septic system should be on flat land if possible and as far as practicable from buildings; it should drain away from rather than toward the well.

Ask the seller for last year's tax bill and for the utility bills for the last few years. Heat and electricity are the big items, but you can also ask for water and sewer bills, if there are sewer bills. If it's a new home, the salesman should be able to give you utility company cost estimates. Be sure to find out who collects the trash, the municipality or a private service, and whether there is a charge for the service.

WHAT THE PLANS SAY

While you're dreaming up other questions to ask the seller, the salesman, or an engineer, make a couple of neat copies of the floor plan you sketched when you started the inspection. Feel free to mark them up as you study the details of this home and how it works. You might, for example, want to use colored pencils to mark one of them with the zones in the home: The living zone (living, dining, and family rooms), the working zone (kitchen, laundry, utility room, workshop, and perhaps the den if it's used as an office) and the sleeping zone. Study the floor plan to insure that those zones are more or less isolated from one another and that there is some sort of buffer — closets, a hall, or a bathroom — between the living and sleeping zones.

Plot on the floor plan the kinds of trips your family makes most often — from the kitchen, say, to the front door or the living room or family room. Can those trips be made conveniently and efficiently? How would guests move through your home from the front door to the living room, the dining room, the family room, or powder room? Would they get lost? Would you get embarrassed? How would the kids move from the yard, family room, or bedroom to the bathroom? Would those trips disrupt everything else that's going on?

If you have expansion in mind, study the floor plan for its possibilities. Would adding a new room mean chopping up some existing ones with hallways or doors? Would you have to go through one room to get to another? If you're thinking about adding a second floor, would there be room on the first floor for a stairway? What would the addition do to the zoning and organization of the home?

Go over the floor plan room by room, bearing in mind some general principles. The living room should be centrally located, with good access to the front door, dining room, family room, and kitchen as well as to the porch, patio, or other outdoor living area. One study concludes that a living room should be at least 12 by 20 feet, with 10 to 12 feet of unbroken wall space for furniture. But you know your habits and your furniture better than the experts do, so don't make that an iron-clad rule.

The dining room should be convenient to the kitchen and living room and, naturally, big enough to accommodate a table that will seat your family and guests, a chair for each, and storage and serving facilities, with enough room left over to allow serving and the vague sort of moving about that goes on in dining rooms.

The kitchen, as you may have heard somewhere, should be convenient to everything but the septic tank and big enough for anything this side of the Civil War. Perhaps more important than the kitchen's size or location, though, is the way its space is used. The things to watch other than the obvious are the relative positions of what the experts like to call "work centers" — the refrigerator, sink, and range — and the amount of counter and cabinet space. The "work centers" should form a triangle with 4 to 7 feet between the refrigerator and the sink, 4 to 6 feet between the sink and the range, and 4 to 9 feet between the range and refrigerator. If the oven and the range top are separate, the range top is what counts. Between the refrigerator and the sink there should be 4½ feet of countertop, and the refrigerator should open toward the sink (otherwise, you have to walk around the door every time you want to open a beer). Between the sink and the range there should be 3½ to 4 feet of countertop, and there should be at least 2 feet of it on the other side of the range. A couple of extra feet are all to the good, of course, especially near the range. These minimums should produce about 12 to 14 lineal feet of base cabinets and 14 to 16 lineal feet of wall cabinets, presuming all the space is used in the typical way. The experts say you need about 10 feet of base cabinets and 15 feet of wall cabinets.

Bedrooms, which seem to be shrinking faster than anything else in the modern home, should be at least 8 by 10 feet, according to one study, and no smaller than 9 by 11½, according to another. There should be 3 to 4 feet of closet space for each occupant. The bedrooms should, of course, be near a bathroom and not too near anything else.

Theoretically, at least, there should be at least one bathroom for every two bedrooms, and in a two-story or split-level home there should be at least a half bath on or near the main level. How many baths you actually need depends upon how many of you there are and how long you spend primping in front of a mirror each morning. You know that better than anyone else. If the master bedroom has its own bath, it's sometimes advantageous if the bath is accessible from outside the bedroom, too. When the boss is coming for dinner, the kids can be encouraged to use that bathroom, preserving some semblance of order in the main one.

Family rooms, the planners say, should be at least 12 by 16 feet, though many families get along with none and others need a stadium. Especially if there are young children, the family room should be reasonably close to the kitchen and, probably, a bathroom. It should be isolated from the sleeping zone and ideally should be accessible to outdoor living areas.

The laundry room should be at least 6 by 8 feet, according to those supposed to know. Obviously, its size can vary, depending upon what you want to do there. You'll need more space if it's going to double as a utility room or sewing center than you will if it's merely a place to park the washer and dryer. It, too, should be close to the kitchen.

In a home without a basement, the utility room and other storage space become especially important. The minimum recommended size for a utility room in a place without a basement is 8 to 10 percent of the living area of the home. It should, of course, be close to the kitchen. As to storage space, there should be at least 30 square feet in addition to closets and the garage, carport, or other outdoor storage.

Now think about the place from the outside rather than the inside. Using both the floor plan and the plot plan (your sketch of the lot with the buildings and plantings on it), evaluate the way the house is positioned in relation to its environment. In most of the country, the main living areas should face south and at the same time face the best views — not always a combination one can arrange. The windows on the south side will get the most sun during the winter, when the sun is low in the sky, and are easy to shade with a roof overhang, trees, or awnings during the summer. Bedrooms, which are used mostly at night, work well facing the north or east. With an eastern exposure, they get the sun in the morning — a pleasant way to wake up. On the west, they get the sun in the late afternoon and heat starts to build up when you least want it. Garages do well on the west, where they block the sun during the summer, and the north, where they block the wind during the winter. Porches and patios are often too hot on a summer evening if they face west. They're better on the north or east. All of this presumes, obviously, that the home you're looking at is in an area where winter cold is a problem. If you're shopping in a warm climate, you may want to look for a different orientation — living areas on the north, bedrooms on the east, garage on the south or west, and porch or patio on the north or east. And whatever the climate, be aware that no home will fill the bill perfectly. These are guidelines, not graven-in-stone laws.

Putting aside the floor plan, use the plot plan to consider the grounds of your potential estate. Is the building properly sited on the lot? Its position should produce a limited public zone (the front yard), an efficient service zone (the walks, driveway, storage areas, and so forth), and a large and secluded private zone (the patio, play area, and backyard in general). The private zone should be convenient to the living areas of the home. If you're planning or someday may plan an extension, is there room for it? Be careful here, not only that there is the physical room for expansion but also that local regulations will permit it. If adding on is an essential part of your plan, check with local zoning and building officials — not merely with the seller or salesman — before you commit yourself. And double check with your lawyer before you sign anything. Be just as careful if the sort of expansion you're planning is a swimming pool. Understand the local regulations before you get inextricably involved.

While you're looking at the plot plan, think about the size of the lot and its relationship to the rest of the neighborhood. Is it the highest and therefore probably the windiest spot in town? Is it the lowest and therefore the most flood-prone? Be aware that "bigger" is almost surely more expensive but not necessarily "better." A bigger lot offers more prestige and privacy and perhaps a chance to expand later without regulatory problems. But it also offers higher taxes, bigger fertilizer bills, and the opportunity to do a lot more lawn mowing and snow shoveling. Least of all, perhaps, does bigger mean better when the lot in question is on a corner. Corner lots usually cost more, and they waste space since much of the lot is devoted to two front yards. That means more street traffic, more walks to shovel, more lawn to care for. It may mean less backyard, less private space of your own. But if you're planning to move your chiropodist's office into the place, you'll be better off on a corner, where the halt and the lame can find you more easily.

MATTERS OF OPINION

Now think about a few of the loose ends having to do with the home you're considering, and you'll soon be ready to get out your checkbook and do business. First, there's the question of basements, crawl spaces, and slabs — matters of great emotion indeed. In some places, everyone knows absolutely that a home with a basement is best. In other places it is common knowledge that slabs are superior. Your prejudices aside, there are a few facts you should keep in mind. Basements add useful space and make the upper floors easier to heat. But basements add to construction costs, too, and soil conditions sometimes make it impossible to build them. They are most economical in cold climates, where foundation footings have to go below the frost line anyway and digging deeper doesn't add much to the cost. Crawl spaces provide very little in the way of storage space, but they are cheaper than basements and can help make heating in the living areas more efficient. A slab adds no room and does nothing to improve the heating efficiency, but it may be more aesthetically pleasing because it allows the building to sit closer to the ground. And it is cheaper than anything else. A slab may render termite protection infinitely more difficult because the critters can work their way up through almost any crack in the thing. A slab will also mean that equipment normally found in the basement—wiring, heating ducts and pipes, for example—will have to run through the attic. That reduces the space available for storage in the attic. It also renders pipes more liable to freezing than they would be in a basement. And there's no comparison between the damp floor a burst pipe will produce in the basement or a crawl space and the soggy mess it will create if it happens to be in the attic when it chooses to burst.

Then there's the exterior siding material, another matter on which there are many opinions, all firmly held. Brick and masonry, for example, have wide appeal because of the appearance of solidity they give. As a result, they usually add value to a home, all else being equal. But they are not, despite what your mother told you, better insulators than wood, and they are more expensive. As to their solidity, most masonry walls in homes built now are veneers, coverings put over the wood frame walls that are the real structural components of the building. Masonry in new homes is merely decoration. Stucco offers both fire resistance and insulation value, but it is extremely expensive and it requires more maintenance than a masonry wall. You know about wood siding. It is only a fair insulator, it burns more or less readily, and in most cases it is forever needing another coat of paint. But it is pretty reliable stuff, all things considered, which is why it has been used so widely for so long. And wood shakes may eliminate the paint problem, though they can split. Metal sidings are usually made to look about like wood and require very little maintenance, though eventually, like a car, they will need refinishing, and, like a car, they can be scratched and dented. Synthetic siding materials such as vinyl are maintenance free but subject to cracking or shattering. Both metal and vinyl sidings get most of their insulating properties from backer boards, not the siding itself. Finally, there are asbestos cement shingles, which are economical and hold up well but are not widely thought to be handsome.

And what about heat? Which kind is best? Forced hot air systems are most popular because they can be so easily converted to central air conditioning — the ductwork is largely in place. A hot-air system responds quickly and lends itself to the addition of such things as filters, humidifiers and dehumidifiers. But it is more difficult to install than a hot-water system and more difficult to zone. Beyond that, the registers may interfere with furnishing or decorating. Older, cruder systems can be noisy and may produce uneven heat, too. Hot-water systems take longer to respond to a call for heat and do not lend themselves to the addition of central air conditioning or humidifiers, filters, and the like. Baseboard hot water heaters can also be a pain in the neck when you're trying to furnish a room without blocking all the heat. Steam systems — except in some big cities where steam is piped under the street to consumers, just like gas and water — tend to be old, noisy, and cumbersome. The average steam or hot-water system lasts 25 or 30 years, the average hot-air system 15 to 20 years. One type of heat that may be either hot water or electric is the radiant system, one in which the heating element — a pipe carrying hot water or an electrical resistance heater — is buried in the foundation slab or some other surface. A radiant hot-water system in a slab can produce disaster if it leaks; digging up that pipe is like digging up the street, but it's happening in your living room. Beyond that, such systems can make a floor uncomfortably hot, and their response time is extreme. A good system should be coupled to an outside thermostat so that the system starts working even before the home gets cold; it takes a long time to heat or cool a concrete slab. Heat pumps — electrical devices for transferring heat from a warm place to a cool one — are relatively new and complex and are typically used with hot-air systems. They are more efficient for air conditioning than for heating and may require a supplementary system for use when temperatures drop into the 20's. At the moment, they're probably a better bet in the South than in the North.

As to fuels, it's likely to be more a question of what you can get than what you want. Gas burners tend to require less service and to last longer than oil burners, and you don't have to have a bulky tank stored in the basement or buried in the yard. But you do have to have gas, and there are times and places where it is simply not available. Relative fuel costs vary from one area to another, but electricity is generally the highest. Electric heat pumps are more efficient than resistance electric heat, but both require particularly good insulation. Resistance heat, on the other hand, is cheap to install, requires little space and virtually no maintenance, and makes each room a zone of its own.

All of that is largely academic, however, if you don't have a choice of fuels available where you want to buy. About the only energy source you can be sure will be available is the sun, and even that is so far not a very good bet for heating your home. There may be a few thousand solar heating installations flourishing in various parts of the country, and there's no question that solar heating works and is gaining popularity. There is, though, a serious question of whether it is yet economical. The latest designs are really no more than supplements to conventional heating systems, at least in the colder parts of the country. They still can't cope with long periods of cold, cloudy weather. And they're expensive supplements, too. Beyond that, there remain some legal questions for which there are not as yet reliable answers. What recourse would you have, for instance, if a neighbor were to plant a tree that grew to the point where it shaded your solar collector, cutting off your heating system?

While you're pondering that, sharpen a pencil and start to figure out what this dump will cost you every month if you buy it.

22
How Do You Estimate What It Will Cost You to Keep the Place?

Much of the information you'll need to estimate your monthly expenditures is already in hand; you've gathered it as you've gone along. If it's a resale home, for example, the seller has shown you last year's utility bills — for electricity, gas, oil, water, sewers, and trash collection. If it's a new home, you've gotten from the developer or the utility an estimate of those costs. Throw in your telephone bill and there you have your estimated utility costs. Take account of the fact that your phone bill may be sharply higher if you're moving some distance and are likely to make frequent calls to friends or relatives back home.

The seller, if it's a resale home, has shown you last year's tax bill and the municipality has told you whether the place will automatically be revalued when it's sold. Whether it's a new home or an old one, you've found out at city hall what the tax rate is and at what percentage property is evaluated. So even if you can't depend upon last year's tax bill, you can calculate roughly what next year's would be if you bought at a given price. If it's a resale home that will not be revalued after the sale, last year's tax bill should be a pretty good guess, though of course there's always the possibility that the tax rate will go up. If it will be revalued or it's a new home, use the asking price as the theoretical true value of the place. If the municipality assesses at 90 percent of true value, find 90 percent of the asking price, then apply the tax rate and there's your tax. An example: The seller is asking $50,000 and the town assesses at 90 percent and has a tax rate of $2.50 per $100. If you paid the full asking price — you won't, of course, if it's a resale home — the new assessment would be 90 percent of $50,000, or $45,000. At $2.50 per $100, the tax on a home valued at $45,000 would be

$$\left(\frac{\$45,000}{100} \times \$2.50\right)$$

or $1,125.

You've made inquiries about the rest of the tax situation — income or wage taxes, sales, personal property, or other types. Here you'll have to make an educated guess, but the instruction booklet from last year's federal income tax return — and the return itself — may be of some help. The instruction booklet usually contains tables that show what the impact of a given sales tax is at your income level and how much the gasoline tax will total if you drive a specific number of miles (more in a minute on why you shouldn't assume that you'll drive the same number of miles as you did last year). This will necessarily produce a rough estimate, but that's all you need. If the place has a flat rate wage or income tax, apply it to what would be your federal taxable income from sources in the jurisdiction levying the tax.

You know how much you have in the kitty and the asking price for the home you want. The difference — plus, say, 10 percent of the asking price to cover such things as closing costs, moving, and other initial expenses — is roughly the size of the mortgage you'll need. Again, bear in mind that you won't pay the asking price for a resale home. If you want to be picky, knock 5 percent off that price and calculate from there.

Now you'll have to dredge up some more information. If it's a new home, the developer's salesman will be able to tell you in a trice what financing terms are being offered — what interest rates and how long you have to pay off the mortgage. If it's a resale home, the real estate broker, if one is involved, or the mortgage department at any savings and loan association or bank will be able to tell you what terms are prevalent locally. Then you can turn to the table back yonder in Chapter 3 and figure out roughly what mortgage principal and interest will set you back each month.

INSURANCE

Your next call should probably be to an insurance broker or agent to find out approximately what homeowners' insurance will cost. The price will depend upon the sort of home you're buying (the materials of which it's built and its value), where it is (location determines such things as proximity to the nearest fire hydrant and the quality of the fire protection that's available), and what kind of coverage you want. Though all you need at the moment is a rough estimate of insurance costs, at some point you'll have to sit down with an agent or a broker and discuss in detail the kind of policy you want, so you might as well start to think right now about what's available.

Unless your circumstances are unusual, you should probably buy a homeowners' "package" of insurance, one that combines policies covering you against several hazards or risks, usually at bargain rates compared to separate policies. In general, there are six kinds of homeowners' "packages":

- Homeowners 1, or HO-1, also known as the Homeowners A or standard form, provides basic personal liability protection — insurance against a suit by someone who is injured on your property or injured by a member of your family (except in an automobile accident) — and coverage against fire, theft, and several other risks. This is minimal insurance, suitable only for those who can afford no more.

- Homeowners 2, or HO-2, also known as the Homeowners B or broad form, protects you against an expanded list of risks. Most homeowners should probably consider this the minimum coverage they'll accept. It costs about 10 percent more than an HO-1 policy.

- Homeowners 3, or HO-3, also known as the Homeowners B-plus or special form, offers coverage against the same expanded list of hazards as an HO-2 policy with regard to your personal property — generally, what you would take with you if you moved — but is markedly better in its coverage of the home itself. On the structure itself, an HO-3 policy provides "all-risk" coverage; it protects you against any damage except that caused by fewer than a dozen specifically excluded hazards. That's much better coverage than you'll get from an HO-1 or HO-2 policy, so much so that an HO-3 policy is probably what your insurance broker or agent has on his own home. It costs about 15 percent more than an HO-2 policy.

- Homeowners 4, or HO-4, is not homeowners' insurance at all, but a tenants' policy, one that provides coverage only on personal property, not on the structure itself. It's of little use if you're buying your own home, unless you're buying a cooperative.

- Homeowners 5, or HO-5, also known as the Homeowners C or comprehensive form, is the top of the line and priced accordingly. It provides all-risk coverage on both personal property and the structure, with the same exclusions as an HO-3 policy. The cost, however, is likely to be so high that it's not worthwhile unless you have very valuable furnishings or other possessions or you travel frequently with very expensive luggage, clothing, and so forth (most homeowners' policies offer some sort of coverage for personal property away from home).

- Homeowners 6, or HO-6, is a policy designed specifically for the owners of condominium units, about which more anon.

No matter which of the packages you choose, there are some fundamental principles to keep in mind. Be sure, for example, that you have enough insurance. That means your home should be covered for at least 80 percent of its replacement cost, minus the value of the land and foundation, which are not likely to burn down or blow away. Notice, that's not 80 percent of what you bought it for or would sell it for; it's 80 percent of what it would cost to rebuild it now. If the insurance totals at least 80 percent of the replacement cost and the place is damaged by a covered peril, the insurance company will pay the full cost of repairs up to the limit of the policy. If the coverage totals less than 80 percent, many companies will consider you a co-insuror of your home — that is, you'll have to share the repair costs with the insurance company. The company may deduct from its contribution to the replacement cost whatever it considers to be reasonable depreciation on the portion of the home destroyed or it may peg its payment to the ratio between your total coverage on the building and the 80 percent figure. Either way, you lose.

Be sure, in particular, that you have enough personal liability protection — coverage against suits by people injured on your property or by members of your family. The average homeowners' policy, even the top-grade HO-5, offers only $25,000 in personal liability insurance, hardly enough in view of the huge judgments often awarded to accident victims. For a relatively nominal fee, your coverage can be raised to as much as $500,000.

Be sure that your valuables are protected. The usual forms are not likely to provide adequate coverage for such big-ticket items as paintings or other art works, furs, jewelry, camera equipment, stereos, stamp and coin collections, antiques, silverware, stocks and bonds, boats, trailers or professional tools and equipment (including even office equipment). You may need a "floater" to provide added coverage specifically for such possessions.

Then, too, be sure you're covered against the right perils. Virtually every homeowners' policy excludes damage caused by: flood, surface water, waves and tidal waves; water seepage and the backup of sewers or drainpipes; war and nuclear radiation; mechanical breakdowns; normal wear and tear or deterioration; existing structural defects; smog and smoke from factories or smudge pots; landslides, and earthquakes. The lower-priced, more basic policies are even narrower. Coverage against some of those perils — nuclear war, for instance — may be simply unobtainable at reasonable rates, and some of it may be a waste; few desert residents are interested in tidal wave insurance. But flood or earthquake coverage, to mention two, may be advisable where you're buying. Earthquake insurance can often be purchased as an extra, and in many places — the municipality has to qualify by adopting certain flood-control measures — federally subsidized flood insurance is available through private companies. If you need it, ask your broker or agent.

The home you're thinking about buying may be in what the insurance companies see as a high-crime area, not a place where they like to gamble. In that case, you may have trouble getting coverage against burglary and robbery. If so, you can apply through a private company for federal crime insurance or, in some places, for state coverage. You may even have trouble getting basic fire insurance in such areas, which means you'll have to ask about "pool" coverage. It's similar to the assigned-risk automobile insurance provided in many areas for drivers with poor records or drivers who happen to live in the wrong neighborhood. Pool insurance is expensive, but if it's all you can get you're stuck. The nature of insurance is that it's cheap only if you don't need it.

Bear in mind, too, that if you're buying a multiple-family home — a brownstone or rowhouse containing three or more apartments, for example — you'll need somewhat different coverage. Among other things, you'll want to insure your rental income in case an accident renders the building uninhabitable for a while.

When it comes time to actually buy an insurance policy — which is to say, before the closing, when you take possession of the place — shop around a bit. Prices can vary sharply, and so can the coverage you're offered and the attention you get from a given broker or agent. The attention you get will be especially important when you have a claim. All else being equal, you may fare better in this regard with a broker, an independent businessman who can place your insurance with a number of companies, than with an agent, who may represent only one company. The attention you get may increase in direct proportion to the business you place with the broker or agent. In that regard, it's often a good idea to put all your insurance business — auto, home, and even life — in the hands of one competent man. On the other hand, a buck is a buck, and some companies, particularly the "direct writers," the ones that don't deal through brokers, may be cheaper. And there's the matter of claims practices. Some companies are notoriously slow and stingy when it comes time for them to pay, though they don't hesitate to let you know when the premium is due. If you don't have an insurance relationship, you should probably establish a local one where you're going to buy. All you can do, beyond knowing the reputation of a company, is ask friends and relatives what their experience has been. Pay particular attention to the opinions of those who have filed claims against their insurance companies. If such people are still happy, their brokers or agents and their insurance companies ought to be pretty good risks.

In all your shopping, take advantage of deductibles, the provisions that in case of a loss you pay the first $50 or $100 or whatever. The purpose of insurance, after all, is to protect you against major losses, not small ones, and the deductibles can reduce your premiums sharply, perhaps enough so that you can get better coverage for the same money.

As the home-buying process develops, you may find that you're being told to accept an insurance policy along with a mortgage. That policy will be designed to protect the interests of the lender, not your interests. If no other mortgage is available and you can't talk the lender into substituting a policy that protects you better, but still protects him, find some supplementary coverage for yourself. You may also find yourself under some pressure to take over the existing insurance on a resale home. Don't agree to do so unless you're sure that it's what you need. A seller is not likely to watch a hot prospect walk away for the sake of his insurance policy.

There's one more type of insurance that you should consider (there are some specialized kinds that will come up by and by, but things are complicated enough as it is) — mortgage life insurance, which is really no more than decreasing term insurance. Unlike whole life, term insurance does not build in value — you can't borrow against it. You pay premiums for a given number of years — the term — and when you stop paying, the insurance stops. There's no such thing as a paid-up policy that still provides coverage, as there is in whole life insurance. But term insurance is much cheaper than whole life. In a decreasing term policy, the amount of insurance in force drops gradually until it disappears at the end of the term. If it's structured to keep pace, more or less, with the remaining principal on a mortgage, its effect is to pay off the mortgage if the family breadwinner dies. This is insurance that you may or may not need, depending on your circumstances. If the sudden lack of your income or your spouse's income would not endanger your family's ownership of its home, mortgage life insurance is probably a waste. If you're heavily insured otherwise, it may be unnecessary. But if you're the working head and sole support of a young family that is living from one paycheck to the next, you probably ought to look into mortgage life insurance. Buy it only if you need it, but if you need it, don't fail to buy it.

COMMUTING COSTS

All right, you've figured out roughly what insurance will cost you. Now turn your attention to matters that are, at least momentarily, simpler. The railroad or bus company can tell you the price of the commutation ticket you'll need. Don't ask just about the round-trip fare; they may have special weekly, monthly, or — who knows? — lifetime fares. And don't forget, even if it's required only in winter, the cost of local bus, subway, or cab at either end of your commute. Also in the realm of transportation, don't forget the second car that may be part of the great suburban migration. Better find out what car-loan rates are and what the extra insurance will cost.

Then do some calculating. Calculate, for instance, what it will cost to drive that second car. You know approximately what kind of mileage the model you have in mind will provide, and you can easily find the price of gasoline if you haven't suffered at the pump already. You know the beast will have to be serviced every 1,500 or 3,000 miles, and you know that every two years or so you'll have to spring for a new battery and tires. That may not be what the salesman says, but you know it's true. Well, estimate the distance to the railroad station, the grocery store, the dry cleaner's, church, and wherever else you're likely to go regularly. How often are you likely to go? Multiply. (If you need help, ask one of the kids. If you don't have kids, find a kid; they can all multiply, and they're proud of it.) Don't limit the calculation to a new second car. Figure what the first car will cost, too. The supermarket that was down at the corner when you lived in an apartment in the city may be four miles away in the suburbs. While he's driving the new subcompact to the railroad station, she'll be piloting that big old barge to the butcher shop, the drug store, the PTA meeting, and the supermarket, none of them within a good Ozark holler of home. It costs. Figure it. A move over a long distance may also mean that you'll be making frequent trips back to the old town to see the old folks. Add the cost of that, too.

OTHER EXTRA COSTS

A move — especially if it's a move from the city to the suburbs — may also mean that the kid who was doing all that multiplication to figure your travel costs will transfer from private to public school, or vice versa. That'll make some difference. Don't ignore it.

Entertainment and recreation — movies, golf, dinners out, tennis, riding lessons, and the booze — may cost more or less after the move. Have a drive around and see what it costs to do what you like to do. Then estimate how many times a month you'll probably do it, even with all that lawn to mow. (Don't ask the kid, just give a rough estimate. What the kid doesn't know won't tempt him.)

There are other things. Household help, if you're into that sort of thing, may cost more or less after you change households. If the move means that a second spouse is going to have to work and babysitters or some other form of child care will be necessary, that's one of the costs of the new home. If the change will mean you can finally do without the day-care center or maid, chalk one up for you. Medical care may cost more or less. Ask the seller, if it's a resale home, about his doctor's charges for an office visit and compare that with what your old sawbones demands. If you don't have a seller, ask the salesman. Ask the local druggist. Ask anyone. You won't get better than a rough estimate anyway. Food and clothing may also be priced differently than they were in the old place. Drift through the supermarket, the boutique, and the haberdasher's, and have a squint at the price tags. Then make a boldish estimate. (Call the kid if you need him for multiplication.)

Moving may also mean getting or giving up a rental income, which will probably be a major factor in your financial equation.

Now throw in a nice round number — say, 2 percent of the cost of the place — to cover your annual maintenance expenditures, such things as painting the living room every few years and fixing the pipe that will sooner or later spring a leak. That figure should cover the day-to-day upkeep once the place is in shape, but don't count on it to finance major remodeling. That's not enough to add a bathroom, but it should be enough to keep the one you have from flooding the dining room. Keep in mind as well that if you're buying a new home you may not have to repair so many things at first but there may be some extra initial costs, things like landscaping or towel racks — the big and little things that a developer sometimes overlooks.

Before you go any further, be sure to reduce everything to the same basis. You may have figured annual educational costs, monthly mortgage payments, and weekly food bills. See that they're all stated in comparable terms — weekly, monthly, or yearly — before you try to add them together. Once they're all the same, add 'em up. Then add up the corresponding expenses in your old home or apartment. Ultimately, you're probably interested not in either total but in the difference between them. If you're financially afloat now and the home purchase won't markedly increase your expenses, it seems a safe bet that you can swing the deal and survive. Your allocations may change — you may give more to transportation and less to education — but that's immaterial if the big picture looks bright. Also bear in mind that this exercise is based on the presumption that your income will remain relatively stable in the immediate future. If, on the one hand, you're about to be fired and to start living on unemployment compensation, it hardly seems the time to be buying a home. If, on the other hand, the purchase is related to a transfer that means a big promotion or your godfather's will is about to be probated, you may be able to take in stride a rather healthy increase in your recurring expenses. It all, as somebody once said, depends.

INCOME TAXES

One major factor has been ignored so far — the effect of home ownership on your income tax burden. Just thinking about trying to unscramble such a complicated mess is enough to produce a nervous tic in the calmest man, particularly if his move will be accompanied by a change in income, but there it is. If you normally consult an accountant, by all means dump in his lap your collection of estimates and calculations and promise to buy him a new eyeshade if he figures out how much the purchase and move would save you or cost you in taxes. If you don't have and can't find an accountant and don't have accounting expertise yourself, haul out copies of last year's tax returns and substitute for last year's real numbers this year's estimations and calculations. Don't forget to consider such things as potential changes in local taxes (property, sales, income, and others, not to mention the extra gasoline tax if you'll be driving more), the extra interest you'll be paying on your mortgage, perhaps the loan for a second car, and possible changes in medical costs.

If you've been renting out part of your home but won't be after the move, or if you've not been renting but will be, the tax impact of your purchase will be even greater than usual. If your home is also a rental property, some portion of almost all direct housing expenses — utilities, maintenance and so forth — is probably a business expense and therefore deductible. What part of your expenditures will qualify and how great the tax relief will be depend upon your circumstances and the sort of home it is, not to mention the ever-changing tax law. If the place is a rental property, you may also be able to depreciate it to some extent for tax purposes. How and how much are questions best discussed with accountants or tax lawyers.

The same sort of situation prevails if you have been or will be maintaining a home office that meets the Internal Revenue Service's qualifications. Be careful here because, like everything else about tax laws, the qualifications seem to change every now and then. If you pass the test, you can probably deduct from your income taxes a portion of your utility bills, maintenance costs, and homeowners' insurance premiums as well as the direct costs of operating the office — for instance, the premium on a special insurance policy on your office equipment. You may also get a tax break if the home you're buying is a historical structure and you rehabilitate it. It is all very complicated, however, so don't count on any tax advantages unless an expert in that field tells you that you qualify for them.

Well, now you've got a head full of numbers and have probably used up every slip of scrap paper available. Find one more scrap and figure out the ultimate financial impact of your contemplated move. It will almost certainly mean that your expenditures will be different, and it will probably mean that they'll be higher. If you've carefully and honestly calculated a lower expense projection, be sure your kid's multiplication is right and thank your stars. If you've calculated a higher projection, consider realistically where the extra money will come from. What will you give up to pay your higher housing costs? Cutting down to one pack or quart a day will hardly carry the freight. Is the money going to come out of the food budget or what's set aside for the kids' shoes? Will the strain be so great that the thing just isn't worth it? Confer with your spouse or your roommate on this question — unless the idea behind the purchase is to get away from your spouse or roommate. Two further cautions: Don't count on income that you expect but are not assured of; and leave yourself a cushion. All bills have a way of being higher than you expected, and in any case you don't want to spend every last dime just keeping a roof over your head. There's more to life than staying out of the rain.

Believe it or not, you're in the home stretch (if you'll pardon the pun). You've found a neighborhood and a home that suits you and you're reasonably certain that you can afford them. Now it's a question of determining whether the place has any hidden defects, whether you can get it on the right terms and conditions, and whether adequate financing is available. You'll be a burgher yet.

PART THREE
Closing the Deal

23
What Professional Help Do You Need?

How much advice you're likely to need along the way to home ownership — and what kinds — will depend upon your own background and skills, the type and condition of the home you're buying, and the complexity of the transaction. It is virtually certain, though, unless you're a lawyer, that you'll need legal advice (even if you're universally told that it isn't customary), and the time to get it is before you sign anything or agree verbally to anything. When matters heat up, the bank will have a lawyer, the seller will probably have one, and the broker will have one available if not on the scene. Those lawyers will be representing their own clients, whose interest won't necessarily correspond to yours — and indeed may be diametrically opposed to yours. When you get down to the nitty gritty, you need just as much protection as the bank or the seller with whom you're negotiating. That means you need a competent lawyer whose only concern is your welfare.

THE LAWYER

The lawyer's largest contribution to your welfare will probably consist of advice not to do something that will later prove to be troublesome. That means you need his advice before you do anything that might later be troublesome, which is just about anything at all except looking. Don't give the broker or the seller or salesman anything but polite conversation until you have a lawyer and have discussed the deal with him. Above all, don't sign anything, no matter how meaningless it's supposed to be, until you've discussed it with your lawyer.

When you begin searching for a lawyer, look for one who is active in residential real estate work in the area where you're buying. Like other professions these days, the law has — to some extent, at least — become a business of specialties. Hiring a specialist in estates or divorces to handle your real estate transfer is no more sensible than hiring a chiropodist to perform your lobotomy. Specialization doesn't mean that the lawyer must do nothing but real estate work. In small towns and small firms especially, lawyers have to be generalists of a sort. But it does mean that the lawyer has handled cases like yours for some time, that he has some experience with the problems you're likely to face, and that he knows the law in that area. It also means that if you're buying something more complicated than a simple single-family home — a condominium unit, say, or a three-family, income-producing home — the lawyer is familiar with that particular kind of sale.

On the other hand, a simple home transfer is a relatively basic legal exercise, and the critical question is probably not whether the lawyer is competent to deal with it but whether he will devote to it the time required to insure that the details are in order, that your interests are fully protected. In that sense, you may be better off with a young, hungry lawyer than a successful and secure one, with a small, general firm than a large, specialized one. In a large firm, you may have no idea who your lawyer really is. Your transaction may be handled by a secretary or other paralegal employee until 10 minutes before the closing, when a young staff lawyer will leaf through your folder to be sure all the necessary papers are on hand. If he discovers something amiss at that late date, he is liable simply to cross his fingers and hope nobody notices. Usually, nobody does, but that's hardly what you'd call adequate legal protection.

Whether you choose a big firm or a small one, it should be a local one. Each state has its own laws on real property and each area its own customs and traditions, which often dictate the form and content of certain documents and the parts of a contract that are considered negotiable. After a while, those customs can assume almost the force of law, so your lawyer had better be familiar with them if he is to advise you adequately.

The lawyer you hire should be someone you trust and feel comfortable with. If you can't explain your situation to him easily and fully, he won't be of much help. To that extent, hiring a lawyer is like hiring an architect — if you don't feel comfortable with him, find a different lawyer. Ideally, your lawyer should also be an astute bargainer and psychologist, one who can sense when to press for advantage in a negotiation and when to hold back, when to intervene so you have a moment to think and when to sit by and let you run the show.

Finding such a genius is not necessarily an easy matter, especially if you're moving into a strange area. It may take a bit of shopping. If you're in a familiar area, you can start by asking friends, colleagues, and relatives for their experiences with lawyers in home purchases. Be particularly attentive to the opinions of those who had some complications or entanglements. Try to figure out whether they got into trouble because they received bad advice or because they acted against good advice or without any advice at all. If a friend experienced difficulty because of bad legal advice or because his lawyer failed to see a pitfall in a document, say, you obviously don't want his lawyer. But if he got into trouble for some other reason and the lawyer seemed to extricate him skillfully, perhaps you do want his lawyer.

When you're checking with lending institutions on the mortgage situation, find out what lawyers represent them in real estate matters. You don't want the same lawyer as the bank or savings association that is making your mortgage, but a lawyer who represents a different lender is no doubt experienced and may be just the one you want. While you're at it, ask the lenders for an estimate of typical legal fees for a home transfer in your price range. You can also ask brokers who their lawyers are. Again, you don't want a lawyer who represents a broker involved in your transaction, but one who represents other brokers regularly is likely to be experienced. Brokers will also be able to give you an estimate of typical local lawyers' fees.

If you're employed by a company that has a legal department in the area where you're buying, you might ask them for a suggestion, though they may be most reluctant to make one on the theory that you will blame them for any mistake the lawyer might make. The same goes for a local law school. They may be hesitant to make an official recommendation. But you can get the catalog and see who teaches real property law. A full-time professor will probably not have time for much else, but an adjunct professor will probably have a regular practice, and if he's teaching real estate law he ought to know what it's all about and have some experience using it.

In the event that all else fails, find out whether the state or local bar association operates a legal referral service. The telephone book will probably tell you whether such a service is available. If it is, it will give you the names of a few lawyers who claim expertise in the appropriate area. Be warned, however, that the only thing you can be assured of from such a service is the name of a lawyer who claims expertise; there is no guarantee that he has the expertise. The same thing is true of legal advertising. The ad will tell you only that the lawyer in question claims expertise; no one but he is necessarily saying that he has it.

Once you've collected a few likely names, consult the Martindale-Hubbell Law Directory, which is available in most good reference libraries. It's a set of fat tomes, organized by geographic area, that lists many, though hardly all, of the lawyers in the United States. Martindale-Hubbell will tell you the year a listed lawyer was born and the year he began to practice law; where he went to college and to law school and what degrees he has earned; whether he's a member of the American Bar Association, and what the name of his firm is if it isn't simply his own name. The directory also rates many lawyers in two categories. A general recommendation indicates diligence, professional reliability, and faithful adherence to ethical standards. The rating of legal ability can be "very high," "high," or "fair." The ratings are based on confidential recommendations from lawyers and judges who are asked to consider the general ability of lawyers in the area as well as the individual lawyer's age and experience and the nature of his practice. To qualify for the top rating, a lawyer must have at least 10 years of practice behind him. To win the second and third ratings, he must have at least 5 and 3 years of experience. For the larger or more prominent firms, the directory may also contain some additional details on the lawyers' backgrounds as well as their specialties and perhaps a list of representative clients.

Not every lawyer is listed in Martindale-Hubbell, and not every lawyer who's listed is rated. While a lawyer may have declined a listing because he knew he would get a poor rating, the fact that he isn't listed or rated isn't sufficient reason in itself to conclude that the fellow you've hit upon is an utter cad and bounder. If he's listed, he may be too young to qualify for a rating and still be more experienced in residential real estate than some of his older peers. And he may have chosen not to be listed because he's already busy and doesn't want to encourage the new business that a listing is designed to generate. Really good lawyers in small firms can usually depend upon reputation alone to produce all the business they can handle.

Once you've found the Clarence Darrow of your choice, arrange a conference with him to discuss your case and his fees. Don't be afraid during that meeting to ask him whether he has experience applicable to your problems and what that experience is. Give him all the details of your case, with special attention to things that may mean more work for him — your intention to seek a second mortgage, perhaps, or the fact that you don't want your wife (or husband) to know you're buying this place solely to stash your lover. Be frank and open with the lawyer. If you don't give him all the facts, he can't properly advise you. And it's unfair to hide from him some potential complication, then complain later that his bill is higher than his estimate of the fee.

Legal fees vary widely, depending upon the area, the nature and complexity of the work, and the social panache of the lawyer. In some places — but not many — fees may be as low as $20 an hour, but they can range well beyond $50 or $100 an hour. Often, lawyers charge a flat fee for a residential real estate transfer or one based upon the value of the property — say, 1 percent of the sale price. Be aware, though, that such fixed fees may not apply to more complex deals, for instance, those involving multiple-family buildings in which the owner plans to be both a resident and a landlord. Be forthright in asking about fees, and do it at your first meeting so there will be no surprises or recriminations later. This is a guy you want in your corner all the way; don't try to bamboozle him. If he doesn't charge a flat fee or one based upon a percentage of the sale price, ask how the fee will be calculated and whether he will itemize it in writing. Then get a rough estimate of what it will be, realizing that there may be unpredictable complications that will cause it to change. If you're really pinched, ask whether you might be able to hold down the fee by doing some of the legwork for the lawyer — collecting data or documents from the assessor's office, the courthouse, or the bank.

In this and all subsequent meetings, give the lawyer all the pertinent information you have and rely on his advice. But don't be timid about asking questions or speaking up for what you want. If the lawyer says you can't do what you'd been planning on doing, find out why. He may have a very good reason, but you should understand the reason and he should be willing to explain how you can modify your plan to make it legal or safe or fair. Unless, that is, you simply plan to steal a house someplace. If you and the seller have agreed upon a mutually acceptable closing date, don't shrug your shoulders and resign yourself to fate if the lawyer wants to change the date because it interferes with his vacation. Speak up; he's working for you, after all. If he can't find any other open reservations in Borneo, he can at least find another lawyer to sit in for him at the closing.

Finally — yes, you've heard it before, but it bears repeating — promise nothing, in writing or verbally, until you've discussed it with your lawyer. Don't even autograph your picture for the broker until your lawyer sees the picture. It might not be a flattering one.

THE ACCOUNTANT

Your lawyer will be able to advise you on the tax implications of your purchase, but — especially if you're buying a multiple-family building that will represent both a home and a business — you may want to have an accountant or other tax advisor as well as a lawyer. He'll be able to keep track of your tax situation in much greater detail than a lawyer can, helping you maintain the proper records and prepare the proper forms. He can also study those records and advise you on what you can do from year to year to minimize your tax burden. Whether you need such a specialist depends upon the complexity of your tax situation and your own patience and sophistication in this area. If you're the meticulous sort who keeps excellent records and likes to fiddle with numbers and complex problems, an accountant's fee might exceed any savings he would produce by invoking an obscure part of the tax law. You might be just as well off reading a book or two and doing it yourself. But if the mention of deductions and depreciation sets your palms to sweating and you're never quite sure that you can figure the sales tax properly when you buy a pack of chewing gum, the chances are that you can benefit from professional advice.

The process of finding a tax advisor, once you've decided you need one, may be easier than that of finding a lawyer because there are so many practitioners who can be eliminated at the outset without so much as an interview. There are fast talkers and obvious charlatans who operate out of their hip pockets or out of storefront offices that will certainly be vacant come next

April 16. They are not the people you want. Nor is anyone who promises, even before he knows your situation in detail, that he'll save you money. A responsible, professional accountant may indeed save you money, but he won't promise to do so until he's sure that it can be done legitimately. You remain responsible for the contents of your tax returns, no matter who fills them out and co-signs them for you. So you don't want a tax advisor who's going to be less careful of the facts or the law than you would be yourself. Like your lawyer, your tax advisor should be someone you trust, someone on whose integrity you can rely.

Finding him is likely to be a hit-or-miss proposition at best. You'll probably have to rely on the experiences of friends in similar circumstances. Don't just ask whether they saved thousands of dollars with one accountant. Ask whether he or she had useful ideas for saving or budgeting money. Then visit the accountant and talk to him the way you would a lawyer. Ask what he thinks he can do for you and what it's likely to cost you. Try to get some idea of whether this is somebody you can talk to and rely on. If it seems to be, go ahead, but don't expect miracles. No matter how good this accountant is, the chances are that the money will run out before the month does.

THE ENGINEER

Now that you have the law and the money seen to, you need someone who can tell you whether your prospective castle will last until you get the bills paid. You need an expert who can assure you of the physical soundness of the place. It's not yet necessary to send him scurrying off for an inspection; that time will come when you're sure that you and the seller can arrive at a reasonable sale agreement. But when you want such an inspection, the chances are that you'll want it in a hurry. So now is the time to shop around, to find out what sort of experts are available, what their qualifications are, what services they offer, and what they charge.

The type of expert you're most likely to decide upon is an engineer who specializes in examining and reporting on buildings for prospective buyers. They are available in most areas of the country, and they are usually listed in the Yellow Pages of the telephone directory under building inspection or home inspection services. For a fee that will vary according to the size, value, and location of the property, they will inspect the home you're looking at for structural and mechanical defects and give you a written report on its condition. Though there are some local practitioners, most such engineers are affiliated with one of the several chains that operate all over the country, using standard procedures and checklists developed during thousands of inspections. The promotional literature for these big national companies tends to be very slick, and their reports are often impressively bound. That need not reflect ill upon the individual engineer who is operating his own local inspection service. The quality of the product depends not upon its promotion or packaging, but upon the knowledge and perception of the man providing it. If he doesn't know what he's doing or isn't careful about it, it won't matter how fancy the binding on his report is.

What you're principally interested in, therefore, when you're choosing a building inspector is the qualifications of the man who'll do the job. Some of the big companies say they use as inspectors only licensed professional engineers, a good sign. Others also use architects or men with long but unspecified experience in the building business, which may turn out to be good or bad. Most of the big companies have toll-free telephone numbers that are widely advertised. Maybe the best way to begin is to call them and ask what minimum qualifications their inspectors have. In many areas, they have only one affiliated engineer, so you may be able to find out from the national company precisely who would inspect your home if you were to hire them and what that man's specific experience and qualifications are. You might also ask whether the company's inspectors are insured or bonded.

Bear in mind that a man with good educational and professional credentials will probably become a better, more observant inspector as he gains experience in the field. So you ideally want a man who's been an inspector for a while as well as one who has the more esoteric qualifications. You also want one who's been working awhile in the area where you're buying. He's more likely than a newcomer or an outsider to know something about peculiar local conditions — soils, building practices, and water tables, for example. A local man is likely to be cheaper than an outsider, too, for the inspector will have to consider travel expenses in calculating your bill. Getting a local man doesn't mean avoiding the national chains necessarily, for their affiliates usually work in just one area. It merely means that you try to insure that your boy knows the territory.

Building inspection is a relatively new business, and there are as yet no national standards, licenses, or codes of ethics for inspectors. One reason for that situation is that there has been no public clamor for reform in the industry; if the average customer has had complaints about the service he's received, he's kept his complaints to himself. But one result of the lack of regulation is that the consumer is pretty much on his own in a technical thicket, just as he is in hiring a lawyer or accountant or physician. It may help to seek the advice of relatives or friends who have dealt with home inspectors in the past, and your lawyer or the bank's mortgage officer may have some recommendations, though the bank is more likely to suggest an appraiser than an engineer. Be suspicious if a broker involved in the transaction recommends one engineer; that engineer may see his function as praising any home the broker hopes to sell. If the broker gives you a list of qualified engineers, he may be providing a genuine service, but the broker is probably not the best source of advice in this area.

In addition to an inspection and written report, some of the national companies offer — for an extra fee, perhaps — a limited warranty against defects in certain systems that their inspector has found to be in good condition. The warranty will apply only to specified components of the home — the heating system, roof, and plumbing, for example. It will be good only for a specified period, perhaps a year or 18 months. It will probably have a deductible clause providing that you pay the first $100, say, in repair costs, and it will probably set a limit on the company's liability. The warranty may or may not be backed by an insurance company. If it isn't and the inspection company goes out of business during your warranty period, the warranty will disappear with the rest of the company. Because of all those limitations, the value of such warranties is debatable. If the idea interests you, find out what it will cost, consider carefully the likelihood that your repair costs will exceed that premium during the warranty period, understand all the limitations, and be sure that the warranty is backed by an insurance company. Find out, too, whether in the event of a claim you are free to choose your own contractor to make repairs or have to accept a contractor specified by the inspection service or insurance company. It's an advantage to be able to choose your own man.

Warranties offered by building inspection companies should not be confused with the blanket warranties offered by some brokers on some or all of the homes they sell. The broker's warranty, which is likely to have all the limitations common to the inspector's guarantee, is usually paid for by the seller, who will pass the cost on to you in the price of the home. This sort of warranty is not generally based on an inspection, but on the law of averages; the company that stands behind the warranty has calculated its risks and priced the policy accordingly without having the faintest idea what this specific home is like. Its warranty is therefore no indication that the home in question is in good repair and is, all things considered, not worth much. Don't rely on such a warranty to take the place of a professional inspection, and don't rely on any warranty to relieve you of all maintenance and repair costs for the first year or so.

With or without a warranty, your agreement with a building inspector needn't be limited to one inspection and a written report. If you're buying a new home, you can have the model inspected, then get periodic checks on your "production" home as it's being constructed. If you're buying an older place with a view toward major renovation or rehabilitation, you may be able to arrange for an inspector who will also act as a renovation consultant, suggesting necessary replacements or repairs and checking periodically to insure that the work is being done properly. If the renovation you plan is to be so extensive that an architect is involved, you should probably rely on him rather than an outside engineer to make the prepurchase inspection. He'll have to do the same thing anyway before he plans the project in detail.

It's always possible, though hardly probable these days, that you're buying in an area where a building inspection service is not available. If that's the case, you'll have to assemble your own team of experts and put their findings together to produce an over-all view of the property. The most likely candidates for the main structural inspection are licensed professional engineers, architects, and experienced contractors. You can ask for recommendations from friends and relatives, bank or savings and loan mortgage officers, or the municipal building inspector. The process of choosing the man is much the same as that for picking an inspection service. Ask about his qualifications and experience. Such people may tell you in the course of their inspections that they are not qualified to evaluate certain systems — the heating, say, or the wiring or central air-conditioning. That means you'll have to call in a reputable plumber, electrician, or other specialist to give you a supplementary report. Again, you want experienced tradesmen with good reputations in the community. However, you probably don't want the seller's plumber. He may know about the heating system because he's been out there tinkering with it every cold day since 1912. But he's got a conflict of interest; to say that the heating system is a mess is, in a sense, to say that his work is a mess. Try to find experienced, reliable people who have not been supplying the chewing gum and baling wire that's keeping the place together, people who can render an objective opinion. The report you get from this process won't be as smooth and comprehensive as one prepared by a specialist in building inspections. In fact, there may be very little, if anything, in writing. It will be up to you to ask the questions that will produce enough information to form a reasonable opinion of the home's condition.

No matter what sort of inspector you hire, you can expect to meet some resistance when the time for his investigation rolls around. The seller may not like the idea of having some stranger poke through his home, especially when the stranger's purpose is to find defects that might provide leverage for you to negotiate a lower price or even call the whole deal off. For the same reasons, the broker may not be ecstatic, either. The potential lender — the bank or savings and loan association that will make a mortgage — probably won't offer much support here. The lender is interested only in value, in whether the place can be sold for enough to return his money if you default. He can learn what he wants to know from an appraiser, who needn't have much construction expertise to judge value. Besides, the lender regularly does business with brokers, and they may not be happy if the lender insists upon inspections that may destroy their deals. Despite this widespread lack of enthusiasm, however, you should stand your ground. You are, after all, buying a big, complicated and by all means expensive structure. You have a right to get expert advice on its condition before you're committed.

A good professional inspector will understand that you may be in a delicate position. He will therefore be prepared to move quickly when you give him the nod and to conduct himself with discretion and professional detachment. If at all possible, you should accompany the inspector on his tour, and you should be just as tactful as he. Be sure, for example, that either you or the inspector makes an appointment with the seller if it's a resale home you're buying, and be sure that the seller understands what you're going to do. During the tour, don't be shy about asking the inspector questions; pick his brains while they're available. Ask for estimates of repair or replacement costs — such figures may not be in his written report — and of the life expectancy of such major items as the roof and the heating system. Before you part company with him, arrange to call him after you receive his written report if there are any further questions; they try to write clear reports, but even the best of them sometimes lapse into technical jargon.

When it arrives, the written report will probably tell you things you didn't know about the home you've been studying, all manner of things about the strengths and weaknesses of the structural and mechanical systems, but it will not tell you whether to buy. That's a decision you'll have to make yourself. It's your money and your life. The information in the inspector's report will, however, make the decision easier.

OTHER EXPERTS

In addition to an engineer, an accountant, and a lawyer, you may be well advised — or even required, in some cases — to find other technical experts. In some areas, for example, the Veterans Administration and the Federal Housing Administration insist upon an inspection by a termite expert before they will guarantee or insure a mortgage. If you're buying in such an area, you'd do well to follow the example of the VA and FHA. You may also want extra technical advice on septic tanks or wells if your new home will depend upon them. In fact, you may need specialized advice if the place has any unusual characteristic — if it's on the beach, where wind, water, and corrosion can be special problems, or if it's of unorthodox construction, a geodesic dome, maybe, or an igloo.

Friends and relatives may be able to supply recommendations for such experts. You can also try local public health officials if the problem is water supply or waste disposal. And, of course, there are the building inspector, your lawyer, and mortgage officers. If the inspection is required in your area by the VA or the FHA, call the nearest office and ask whom they use. As in all other areas, be wary of a single recommendation from a broker. The broker's friends may not be disinterested parties.

The engineers and other technicians can tell you whether the home you're looking at is sound, but they won't tell you whether it's worth what you're about to pay. If you've done some careful shopping, you may not need further advice in this area. You've seen what's available at what price; presumably, if this place were wildly overpriced compared to others you've seen, you wouldn't be interested. You also get an indication of value when you go looking for a mortgage. The chances are that a lender will appraise the place or have it appraised before he makes a mortgage commitment; that's his only assurance that he'll get his money back if you default on the loan and he has to sell the place. If the lender's policy is to finance no more than 75 percent of the value of a home and he'll give you a mortgage for 75 percent of the sale price, the chances are you're not paying an outrageous price. Even if the lender's appraisal is designed solely to cover his equity, not all of yours, the chances are that inflation will soon cover your investment. Within a few years, you'll probably be able to sell at a profit unless there's something very wrong with the home, the neighborhood, or the economy. If, on the other hand, the lender's policy is to make loans up to 75 percent of value, but you can't get a mortgage for more than 50 percent of what you're planning to pay, you'd better calculate carefully.

If you have serious reservations about the value of the home — either because of the lender's caution or your own — you can get an expert opinion in the form of an appraisal. An appraiser will give you a report on the design and condition of the building — though nothing so detailed as an engineer's report — the prices of comparable properties, the character of the neighborhood and community, and economic trends in the area. Those are the things that determine the value of the place, and that's all an appraiser will measure. He will not give you much specific detail about the condition of the structure or mechanical systems, and he will not tell you whether to buy. He will give you an informed opinion on what it's worth on the market, that's all.

That can be plenty important, though, if there's some question about the price, so don't hesitate to get an appraiser if you need one. You can ask friends and relatives to suggest appraisers they've dealt with, and you may be able to get recommendations from your lawyer, the building inspector, the tax assessor or brokers, bankers or builders. Obviously, you should be suspicious if the broker in the deal recommends just one appraiser, and you should not use the appraiser who represents the lender who will make your mortgage. Many brokers are themselves qualified appraisers, which is fine, provided you don't use as an appraiser either the broker who is trying to sell you the home or one who shares an interest in the sale because he originally listed the property. Their opinions might not be precisely objective.

Appraisers are usually listed in the Yellow Pages of the telephone book. Try to find one who's a member of a recognized professional group — the American Institute of Real Estate Appraisers or the Society of Real Estate Appraisers, among others. Some of the professional organizations require that their members pass examinations and meet other professional standards. That's no guarantee of expertise, of course, but it's some minimal indication of experience and seriousness of purpose.

Bear in mind throughout this process that there's nothing immoral or illegal about paying more than the so-called market value for a home if you can afford it and it's worth the extra money to you. Paying too much is likely to mean that you'll have some trouble getting financing, but if you have the money and find yourself among several bidders for a home that's just what you've always wanted, it may be worth whatever it costs you. Just because it's not a good investment doesn't mean it won't be a good home. Besides, as you've heard somewhere before, the chances are that, if you've chosen well, inflation will soon vindicate you.

There is one other professional with whom you may come in contact during these proceedings — the broker — and his value should not be understated, even though he will probably be working for the seller, not for you. You're about to enter the phase of the deal that gives the broker his best opportunity to prove his worth. During the delicate negotiations that lie ahead, a good broker or salesman may earn his commission several times over by keeping you and the seller on the track, finding ways around what seem to be insurmountable obstacles, isolating you from some of the more distasteful aspects of the wheeling and dealing, and running countless errands to gather information or documents for one side or the other. He can be worth his weight in plot plans.

There is, of course, the chance that the broker with whom you find yourself dealing will be an oafish lout who does nothing more useful than chew on his unlit cigar and ogle his secretary. In that case, console yourself with the knowledge that this dolt did, after all, lead you to the home you were looking for. There will be plenty of time after the closing to tell him that his secretary is ugly and his cigars smell.

24
How Should You Handle the Preliminary Negotiations?

Details may vary with circumstances, but generally just about everything is negotiable in a real estate deal — the price, how it will be paid, the time of delivery, the condition of the property, extra items to be included in the deal, the circumstances under which it will be called off.

From whom you're buying (a big developer, a small builder, the owner of a resale home or a single lot) and what you're buying (raw land, a lot prepared for building, a new house, a resale house, or a condominium or cooperative apartment) will determine some of the small points of negotiation, though the over-all process will be much the same no matter what the property or who the seller.

Deep thinkers in the field seem to agree that the negotiation process begins the moment you see something that you like and express an interest in it. It may be very subtle at first, but from that moment on both you and the seller will be fending off a growing list of psychological pressures while trying to make some swift calculations and press an artful line of bargaining. That's a tall order, and the process can begin — at least in your own mind — almost before you know it.

It is therefore wise to decide before that moment comes, before you see something you like, what items are simply not negotiable as far as you're concerned. If you're committed to making the move at a certain time — because you start a new job or the kids start school or you have to move out of your old home — the closing date (the day on which you will take title to the new place) may not be negotiable. Make that fact clear to the builder, seller, or broker at the earliest possible moment, as soon as the serious talk begins with the seller or as soon as you visit a broker to look over his wares. If your position on nonnegotiable matters is understood at the outset, you and everyone else concerned may avoid much effort and worry over a deal that was doomed to failure before it began. Who needs that?

In many ways, the negotiation for the purchase of a resale home is more complex than others. A big developer is not likely to be flexible on price, as an individual seller is; a lot or a new home will not raise questions about the age of equipment and the way the structure has been maintained, as an older home will; a builder can't throw in personal property to sweeten the deal, as the seller of an older home can; there's less likely to be a serious question about the closing date for a lot or a new home than there is for a resale place in which someone is living, someone who has scheduling problems of his own. So perhaps the best way to look at the negotiating process is to study the typical bargaining for a resale, even if you're thinking about a new home or a lot, then simply ignore what doesn't apply to your situation.

THE BASIC RULES

Whatever your situation, remember that this is a negotiation, not a bludgeoning. The successful negotiation is one in which everybody wins — the seller receives a reasonable return, perhaps even a handsome profit, and the buyer gets the property he wants at a fair price. Neither one attempts to beat the other insensible, to take all the marbles and run. Both sides give a little, both sides gain a little, and both sides go away happy.

In these circumstances, the thing to do is keep your eye on the big picture, even when you're haggling over small details. A small detail can make a difference of $100, say, and that's not lunch money, but it also isn't much when you consider the size of the total deal. Don't lose a $100,000 home you really want for the sake of a $100 detail, a difference of one-tenth of one percent. Keep things in perspective.

This is not to say that you should be a pushover, agreeing to anything the seller asks. You should be firm in seeking the deal you want but reasonable and realistic, aware that you're trying to buy a home, not steal one, and that compromise is the order of the day, though compromise is a two-way street.

It is also not to say that you should be argumentative or abrupt. Don't argue, discuss. Don't demand, request. Cajole. Delay. Bargain. Always give the other side a way to save face. And at all costs, be polite.

The surest way to achieve this stance is to remain cool. Don't be hurried, no matter what the seller or broker tells you. You have the upper hand; the seller has only one place to offer, but there are thousands of lots or homes for you to buy if this deal falls through. Don't be overly enthusiastic, even if you feel enthusiastic. If the seller knows that you can't wait to get your hands on his palace, he'll be in a stronger negotiating position, less likely to grant the small concessions that will make the deal work for you. If you are a couple and one partner has difficulty hiding emotions while the other can remain outwardly placid in an avalanche, let the cool one do the talking, even if the other one does the thinking.

If it helps, you can use the "good cop-bad cop" or "partner-in-the-back-room" approach: You'd gladly pay more, but your husband or wife or whoever has been unsure of the thing all along and would suffer cardiac arrest at the suggestion that the offer be raised. Or Uncle Paul, the doorstop magnate, who's helping you with the down payment, will withdraw altogether if you give another inch.

Try to remain flexible as long as possible, always leaving the door open for further discussion. Don't make "final" offers or demands unless you're genuinely ready to drop the whole thing. Let the seller sing the praises of the place as long as he likes; let him talk first at every opportunity. He may be willing to grant you more than you thought you could ask for or expect. By the same token, of course, a clever seller will try to keep you talking as long as possible while he looks for signs of weakness or interest — say, an admission that you've been looking for six months and this is the first home that's tempted you even slightly. To the seller who's an able negotiator, that's a sure sign that he's got a live one. His position will begin hardening. Thereafter, when you raise an objection he'll find a way to remind you that if you don't close this deal you'll have to resume your tedious and frustrating search. The way to deny him that negotiating weapon is simply not to tell him that you're getting tired of looking at homes you don't want. What he doesn't know won't hurt you.

In general, try to get some concession whenever you give something up — if you agree to close sooner than you'd like, for example, try to get the seller to throw in the carpeting or to agree to make some needed repair. Don't be afraid to mention, but politely, defects you've noticed or maintenance that's been neglected. And of course you can turn the tables on the seller, putting on him the kind of pressure he's no doubt been applying in an effort to move you to a decision quickly. You can mention casually that there's this other home you're interested in, and while you like his place better the other one is cheaper, so it's a difficult decision. But don't overdo it. That ploy will have no effect if the seller doesn't believe it, and this is, after all, a negotiation in good faith, not a spitting contest.

HAGGLING OVER PRICE

It will come as no surprise that the biggest bone of contention in these talks is likely to be price. If you're dealing directly with a seller — if you were not introduced by a broker — but the home is listed with a broker at the same asking price, the seller is obviously willing to accept the asking price minus the broker's commission. And it's sometimes possible to persuade a broker to give up part of his commission to insure a sale. That's easier to speculate upon than to achieve, however. It probably will not happen unless the broker is fairly desperate.

As soon as you mention a price that's even remotely acceptable, the seller or broker is likely to ask if you're willing to put it in writing. That is a critical question. If you say you're willing to put your offer in writing — never mind for a moment the legal complications of that move — the seller will probably consider that figure a floor for future negotiation; he'll spend the rest of his time trying to get you to raise your offer. If your response to the question is negative, the seller may lose interest on the theory that you're not serious.

For legal as well as economic reasons, this is a time for extreme caution. The document the seller wants you to sign — putting your offer in writing — is a binder, which can be fraught with problems. The moral is clear: Agree to nothing, and above all sign nothing, until you have discussed it with your lawyer.

While the seller is pressing for a written offer, your goal should be to delay that step as long as possible, to keep negotiations open and moving but not to commit them to a binding form until you've had time to consider all the angles. Keep looking for new approaches that may break a logjam. If an impasse is reached over one question, suggest that it be tabled for a while so the discussion can move on to some other detail. If tempers start to run short, suggest a recess of a day or so. The delay may allow both sides to cool down, to assess the situation and regroup, then return with a more reasonable and optimistic outlook. In that atmosphere, a compromise — even one that would have been rejected out of hand a day earlier — may produce a quick and happy agreement.

In all of this pushing and shoving, be careful about raising your offer too quickly. Go up in steps of $100, say, rather than $1,000, unless the asking price is very high and the gap between it and the original offer is huge. Small increments at frequent intervals help preserve your leverage but still serve to indicate progress and keep hope alive on the other side. And be wary of increasing your offer much in exchange for the inclusion of personal property. Remember that virtually all the personal property likely to be included — such things as draperies, carpeting, furniture, and appliances — is used, and the depreciation on this sort of property is usually considerable. Check the ads and compare the prices of new and used refrigerators if you have any doubts. You'll discover that a $500 used refrigerator had better be some refrigerator.

STAND-IN NEGOTIATORS

And be aware that you may be dealing with a vastly experienced horse trader, someone with years of negotiating experience. If the seller is a lawyer, an insurance adjuster, an automobile or real estate salesman, a labor mediator, a purchasing agent, perhaps an accountant or a businessman in certain industries — among them, horse trading — he may participate in or monitor negotiations every day. He may be able to dance circles around you. It is therefore extremely important, especially before you know the lay of the land, to be careful of what you say and how you say it and to listen closely to what the other side is saying.

If you happen to know that the seller recently concluded a deal to unload the Brooklyn Bridge on a combine of Siberian crabapple merchants, or if you simply abhor dickering over money under any circumstances, you can have someone else do your bargaining for you, though that course has some serious shortcomings.

An able and trusted friend or relative may be able to negotiate for you, but he will probably not be familiar with all your plans and desires and so may miss some opportunities you would have leapt at. And he may not be as skillful at bargaining as he seems. He may, for example, know nothing about real estate traditions and practices, though he's always been able to get you a great deal on a used overcoat.

The traditional broker, if there is one involved in the sale, will know real estate and will probably be a skilled and experienced negotiator, but he's likely to know even less than a friend about your needs and desires, and he's hardly an objective participant. The broker has his legitimate interests in this deal, and you have yours. They are not identical.

Your lawyer, while he may not be intimately familiar with your tastes, may be an experienced negotiator, and he had better understand the sale process. He also had better have your interests uppermost in his mind while he's representing you. On the other hand, a lawyer has only one thing to sell, his time. He is perfectly justified in charging you for whatever time he spends negotiating on your behalf, and lawyers don't come cheaper than auto mechanics, glassblowers, or notaries public. To justify his extra fee the lawyer will have to do markedly better than you could have done yourself in the bargaining. You're the best judge of how much better he's likely to do, but you'd probably be wise to give yourself the benefit of the doubt here. Just about the same thing can probably be said of buyers' brokers.

THE PRESSURE TO SIGN

No matter who's doing the bargaining, if the broker or agent is competent or the owner is sophisticated in the ways of selling, the first expression of interest on your part will start a campaign to close a deal right now, before it's too late. A good salesman will want to take advantage of your enthusiasm to move you along the path toward a final decision before you have time for second thoughts. This can be a powerfully annoying process when you're the pigeon, but it is not illegal, immoral, or unethical. In fact, it's not even fattening. It's just salesmanship, and that's what makes the economy go 'round.

The pressure will grow every time you return for another look or ask another question that produces a positive answer. And the salesman will struggle mightily to insure that every question produces a positive answer. The broker, agent, or sophisticated seller knows that the closer you get to making a decision to buy, the harder it will be to back off. He will therefore proceed as though you had made a final decision, even if you don't think you've done so, and he will continue on that course until you stop him. The longer you wait, the more difficult stopping him will be.

If you're with an agent and see something you like, the campaign will probably begin with his suggestion that you return to his office immediately to "work out the details." There will no doubt be repeated suggestions that you had better act fast if you want to snare this gem. Why, that's probably the home the broker would buy himself if he were in the market. You certainly know a good property when you see one, but many other people do, too, and this one surely won't last long. Once you're at the agent's office he will probably start as quickly as possible to fill out a binder, a written offer. His comments and questions will be leading ones — not "Do you want to make a deposit?" but "How big shall we make the deposit?" or "Is $1,000 acceptable for the deposit?" When you waver, the agent will remind you that prices and mortgage interest rates are going up, that mortgage money is getting tight, that other buyers are interested in this place and may snap it up if you don't act.

All of that may be literally true, but it's no reason to abandon common sense. You're buying an extremely complex machine "as is," a process that requires thought and study. Stay cool. Be polite, but be firm. Don't be hurried.

If you haven't already done so, now would be the ideal time to inspect and evaluate the home closely, though the seller may not be too keen on that idea until he sees the color of your money. Be honest with the agent or seller. Say that you're genuinely interested, if that's the case, but that you'd like to inspect the property again in more detail or investigate the mortgage market or confer with your lawyer or have Cousin Glenn, who's going to live in the coal bin, look the place over. Emphasize that for obvious reasons you'd like to take that step before you commit yourself, but emphasize as well that you really are interested.

While it's clearly safer to sign nothing at this point, the seller may be reasonably reluctant to give you the run of the place until he has some assurance of your seriousness. He may, as a matter of fact, refuse to discuss price at all until you give him a written offer. The seller may be perfectly justified in taking such a position, but that's no reason for you to be stampeded into signing something, no matter how innocent it looks, before you've discussed it with your lawyer. There are times and places where the market is so tight that buyers fight over homes and sellers literally auction them off. But such times and places so rarely exist that you probably should not even consider the possibility until you've had at least one prospective home — two would be more reasonable — snatched from your grasp at the critical moment. If you haven't seen newspaper and television stories about people camping out in line the night before a development opens, you can be fairly sure people are not camping out in such circumstances. Public relations men being what they are, that kind of news can't get overlooked. And if people are not camping out, you can be fairly sure — no matter what the agent tells you — that you can take a few days to think and still be the lucky buyer of the home you want.

MAKING AN OFFER

Obviously, if the seller with whom you're dealing insists upon a written offer before he'll discuss details of the transaction or allow you to inspect the premises to your satisfaction, you'll have to spend your thinking days deciding how much to offer. Start with the premise that it's a rare seller who won't negotiate on price. Mass market developers usually won't, and neither will private sellers who describe their asking prices as firm. But virtually every other seller expects to come down a bit from his asking price before he concludes a deal.

There are two kinds of sellers with whom you might negotiate for a resale home: institutions that happen to own real estate, such as banks that have taken homes in foreclosure or companies that have purchased the homes of transferred employees; and individuals. Unlike institutions, individuals may have emotional as well as financial commitments to homes in which generations of a family may have lived, in which children have been raised or spouses have grown old and died. Selling such a home can be a profoundly frightening experience, and that's a factor you should not ignore if it's present in the deal you're trying to negotiate. Be cognizant of such circumstances and tread softly.

Institutional owners may be more skillful than individuals at negotiating, but they can't be insulted by a low offer. To them, this is just a pile of lumber, pipe, and wire that represents a certain investment. All they want is to recover the investment or make a little on top. To the individual seller, on the other hand, an offer that's too low — even if it's a perfectly reasonable offer, given the market at the moment — can represent a condemnation of his taste and social standing, not to mention the memory of his great uncle Sherwin, who built the place out of old pump handles after the blizzard of '86. The seller's choices of landscaping, decoration, and furnishing can be an expression of all his personal beliefs and standards. To offer less than he thinks they're worth is to attack the basis of his respectability. You can easily insult such a seller, and if you do, he's likely to turn you off completely, no matter how much you want his home. You — and he — lose that negotiation before it's really begun.

Moreover, an individual seller is more likely than an institution to insist upon recovering every cent he's ever put into the place, even if that means it's priced at twice the market. Or he's likely to insist upon realizing from the sale every dime he needs to buy the retirement home he wants in Palm Beach, even though prices in Palm Beach are triple those in Jones's Junction, Colorado, where he's trying to sell. With such a seller there's little you can do except humor him — that is, pay an inflated price for his home — or wait him out, knowing that after the home has been on the market long enough he'll realize he must cut his price if he ever hopes to sell. If he's a stubborn man, you may finally buy the place from his estate.

Whatever the type of seller, remember that your first offer will almost surely be rejected out of hand. Just as buyers virtually never pay the asking price without negotiating, sellers virtually never accept the first offer without dickering further.

Obviously, in view of all this, it is useful to know before you make an offer where the seller's head is at. Without being overly inquisitive, try to learn some things that will indicate how much psychological freight this deal is carrying. Try, for instance, to find out how long the seller's family has owned the place. How long has he lived there? Did he or one of his forebears build the thing? If one of them built it, did he literally do so with his own hands or did he hire someone to do the work? The longer the home has been in the seller's family, the more emotion-laden it's likely to be. It will be more valuable to him if he or some member of his family built it, and he'll probably consider it without peer in the realm of human shelter if some relative, however unskilled, actually piled up the bricks and drove the nails himself.

Even if the seller or his family did not build the place, has he made major additions or alterations? If so, he's likely to want his money back when he sells. Has the seller raised a family here? That may add to his assessment of the place. If he has school-age children, though, he may be under pressure to move in time for the next semester, and that may give you an advantage in the negotiations.

Why does the owner want to sell? If it's because his wife just died or he's been forced to retire, this may be a delicate psychological situation. Don't push too hard. If, on the other hand, he's selling because the home is no longer large enough for his family or has become too large, he's taken one step in your direction, deciding for himself that the place has at least one defect. If the owner has found a job elsewhere or is being transferred, he probably has a deadline to meet. As the deadline approaches, his growing concern may make him much more willing to negotiate. But many companies agree to purchase the homes of transferred employees if the employees are unable to sell them at agreed-upon prices. A seller who knows that his employer will bail him out is not likely to be in a hurry to cut his price, and

HOW SHOULD YOU HANDLE THE NEGOTIATIONS?

he'll never drop it below the price his employer has agreed to pay.

Where is the seller planning to move? If it's a much more expensive area, he may need every dollar he can get out of this sale and therefore may be most reluctant to dicker. If it's a much cheaper area, he may be very flexible. Is he planning to buy or rent? Another purchase may require all his equity in his former home for a down payment, while renting may mean that he has no immediate need for cash. Has he found a new home yet? If so, when does he close on it? That may be another source of pressure to strike a deal for his old home quickly.

How long has the home been on the market? The seller's patience may be wearing thin if he's been through four brokers, hundreds of shoppers, and months of anguish. Has he thought several times that the place was sold, only to see the deal collapse? That experience can do wonders for one's willingness to be reasonable. Even a seller who says his price is firm and who has no stomach for dickering will entertain lower offers when he's sufficiently frustrated.

Weighing all those conflicting and unclear factors, you'll have to try to come up with a first offer that's high enough to keep negotiations open and low enough to leave you some room for flexibility. Every transaction is different, of course, so there are no hard-and-fast rules. But there are some guidelines. For example, if the asking price is an odd sum above a multiple of $1,000 — $34,500, say, or $68,900 — the chances are that the true asking price is the next lower multiple of $1,000 — in these cases, $34,000 and $68,000.

It's widely suggested that you can always reasonably offer 10 percent less than the asking price for a resale home, but that's often a dangerous assumption. It probably applies to most sales in the lower and middle price ranges, but not when the asking price is unrealistic or the home has some serious defect or an extreme buyer's market prevails. And it rarely applies to the upper price range; when the asking price is stratospheric, virtually anything goes. Offers 50 percent lower than asking prices aren't uncommon in that range, and sales at such levels aren't rare, either. The higher the price, after all, the fewer the potential buyers for a home and the harder it is to sell. Low-priced homes, for which there are more potential buyers, tend to sell at or above their true values. Very expensive homes tend to sell for less than true value, sometimes much less.

Probably the best way to decide upon a first offer is to figure out what you think the home is worth to you. How much can you afford to pay? How does this place compare with other homes you've seen? If you've been looking for a while, you should have a sense of the market, of what's being asked for a home of this type and size in this sort of neighborhood. The figure you decide upon as the value of the home to you should be your final offer when all is said and done. If that won't be enough to buy the place or if it will be too much for your budget, you should be prepared to walk away.

Presuming that your projected final offer is within your means and seems to have a reasonable chance of acceptance, work backward toward a first offer that will allow you some negotiating room. Don't attempt to split hairs. The seller's reaction is not likely to change if your first offer is $100 higher. But remember that you want the offer to "sound" as good as possible. Be aware that there are psychological barriers at every multiple of $1,000 and extra barriers at multiples of $5,000 and $10,000. The difference between $34,900 and $35,000 "sounds" much greater than $100. That's why so many asking prices are at such odd levels. By the same token, the difference between $50,000 and $49,000 "sounds" much greater than $1,000. Since your first offer will almost surely be rejected, throwing in the extra $100 or even $1,000 that will insure a warmer reception will probably not materially change the final selling price of the home. If, because of your own financial limitations or because of defects you've noticed in the home that will require extra expenditures, your offer is low from the seller's point of view, do what you can to make it "sound" convincing and reasonable. Explain the sources of your hesitation, emphasize your interest, suggest that you might be willing to revise the offer if the seller were willing to make certain repairs or improvements. Remember that the purpose of your initial offer is not to buy the home but merely to get the seller sufficiently interested to begin negotiations.

Remember, too, that in making an offer you are, in effect, putting a floor under the selling price. While it's possible, it's extremely difficult to negotiate a reduction in that figure later on. The seller has committed himself to an upper limit — his asking price — and you're now committing yourself to a lower limit — your offer. If a deal is to be struck, it will almost certainly fall somewhere between those extremes.

THE BINDER

Your offer, if it's a written one, will be a document that is in many ways insidious. It may look innocent, even informal, but it can be as binding as the longest and most complex contract. It can in some circumstances be a lethal legal weapon, so it should be approached warily.

The written offer parades under different names and takes somewhat different forms in different places. It can be called a binder, a deposit receipt or earnest money receipt, a binder receipt and option, an offer to purchase, an agreement to purchase or to buy and sell, a preliminary or conditional sales contract, a land contract, or an offer and acceptance. It is usually accompanied by earnest money, a token payment — anything from $50 to several hundred dollars, depending on local custom — designed to show the buyer's serious intent. The binder is supposed to be a temporary agreement between the buyer and seller that obligates them until they can work out the details of the transaction and their lawyers can draw up a more formal and complete contract. The binder is, in effect, an agreement to negotiate a formal contract.

HOW SHOULD YOU HANDLE THE NEGOTIATIONS?   191

It helps the buyer by taking the property off the market during the negotiations, and it helps the seller by committing the buyer to a price.

In some places, the broker may swear on his Great Uncle Ebenezer's bones that there is no such thing as a binder, that if you want to buy a home you have no choice but to sign a full, formal contract. Well, the broker may be correct that binders are not customarily used in his area, but they are hardly illegal or immoral (though they may be inconvenient for brokers). Binders are simply short contracts that provide for the thoughtful, methodical negotiation of the sale.

Typically, the broker prepares the binder agreement, and typically he'll tell you that it's a standard form that can't or shouldn't be changed. It is no such thing. The binder can take virtually any form, and its form will depend upon who prepares it. One written by a broker and his lawyer will see to the broker's interests first; one prepared by the seller's lawyer will emphasize the seller's interests; and one prepared by the buyer's lawyer will see to his interests. You need not reject out of hand any binder form prepared by the broker or seller, but any binder not prepared by your lawyer deserves his attention — and probably some alteration — before you sign it. Yes, before you sign it.

Usually, the binder describes the property and the agreed-upon price and specifies the amount of the earnest money (for which the binder is a receipt) as well as the deposit to be paid when a formal contract is signed. It usually gives the date and place for the contract signing, specifies the closing date — the date on which you will take title to the home — and the balance of the down payment that comes due then. It usually outlines how the remainder of the purchase price is to be paid and stipulates that the earnest money will be returned if the seller does not accept the terms and will be forfeited by the buyer if he does not comply with the agreement. The typical binder — or at least the typical one prepared by a broker — also specifies the commission due the broker at the closing.

The problem with all of this is that the binder may indeed be binding, and you may be called upon to sign it before you know or can iron out many of the critical details of the purchase — before you've been able to inspect the place thoroughly, for example, or have been able to shop for the mortgage you need. To avoid putting yourself into an impossible position — having to buy a home without sufficient financing or having to buy one that termites are about to fully digest — you need some contingencies, some escape clauses, written into the binder. If he's wise, the seller should want some, too. But by definition, the binder is not the final contract. It does not contain all the details that will be worked out in negotiation and written into the formal agreement. Indeed, you may be called upon to sign it before you have had a chance to figure out what the relevant questions are, let alone the answers. So what you want in the binder is some broad, over-all escape mechanism, one that presumes both you and the seller will be reasonable but that will let either of you bow out if something crops up that makes the sale impossible for one or the other.

What you want, in other words, is a binder that says you will pay the seller a specified amount for his home — your offer — provided you and the seller are able to negotiate a full, formal contract satisfactory to both parties before a stipulated date. It should specify that the earnest money, for which it is a receipt, will be held in escrow — by the broker or his lawyer if there is a broker, or by the seller's lawyer if there isn't — until the closing or until the home is available for occupancy, whichever comes later, or until the deal is called off. It should say that the earnest money will be returned to you if the seller fails to perform but forfeited by you if you fail to perform. The binder should specify that if the seller does not accept the offer within a certain number of days, it is to be automatically withdrawn and the earnest money is to be returned to the buyer.

Those provisions, set down in proper form by a lawyer, give you and the seller a decent interval in which to negotiate a full contract containing all the necessary details and contingencies, but also allow either of you, provided you're reasonable and negotiate in good faith, to get out of the deal if you can't come to an agreement. They also prevent the seller from using your offer as bait for other bids while refusing indefinitely to either accept or reject it.

The seller will naturally try to win from you as much earnest money as possible, and the broker may join him in that campaign; it is in their interest to get you as deeply committed as they can, and every buck gets you in a little deeper. Even though you fully intend to go through with the deal and will presumably have to pay the money sooner or later anyway, it's in your interest to tie up as little of your fortune as possible in such unproductive places as other people's escrow accounts. How much or how little you can get away with paying will depend upon several things. Most important, perhaps, is local custom. In some places, earnest money is traditionally a flat, more or less nominal sum — say, $50 or $100. But in some places that sum is traditionally increased, perhaps to $500, when the seller accepts your offer — that is, when he signs the binder. Your skill and energy as a negotiator will also help determine the size of your earnest money deposit, as will your determination of how far you can push the seller at this early stage without destroying the deal or at least making things much more difficult later on.

If there's a broker involved in the transaction, he'll probably insist that the binder specify the commission due him at the closing. Since the commission will usually be paid by the seller and will not change the selling price once that price is agreed upon, you should have no objection to the inclusion of such a clause. Though it's hardly the most important question that's likely to arise, you should be on the broker's side rather than merely neutral when it comes to a decision on who will hold the earnest money in escrow. That's because the broker is more vulnerable to pressure from you or your lawyer than is the seller or the seller's lawyer. That pressure can be exerted directly or through the Better Business Bureau, the Chamber of Commerce, the local real estate board, consumer affairs offices of local or state government, and state licensing authorities. The amount of money in question is relatively small, and it's a rare lawyer who is less than scrupulous in the operation of an escrow account, but you might as well try to keep the earnest money as accessible as possible.

Since signing a binder can be so tricky, be absolutely certain to get competent professional advice before you sign. Advice rendered before you make a mistake costs no more than that delivered after the damage is complete. And it's much more useful.

Don't simply hand to your lawyer the broker's standard binder form and wait for him to tell you that it seems hunky dory, just like a thousand others that have crossed his desk without incident. Read it before you give it to the lawyer and try to understand it. Ask the lawyer about anything in it that puzzles you. Ask him to explain the obligations the binder places on you and on the seller. Be pointed and specific in your questioning, and don't settle for vague or evasive answers. You're paying for advice; get your money's worth.

Because custom seems to have more than anything else to do with what's in things like binders, it's not very likely that your lawyer will be surprised by what he sees in a prepared form that's used locally. And since most transactions are completed without trouble — or at least without major trouble — it's not very likely that the lawyer will advise you not to sign. He may suggest that you alter a few phrases, but he'll hardly be alarmed.

If you want more protection than the law of averages — if you want a binder that obligates you to no more than a minimum price and negotiation in good faith toward a full contract — your lawyer will have to produce the document, but you will probably have to suggest that he do so and tell him in broad, layman's terms what you want. The lawyer may have serious legal objections to some of your suggestions, and if he has, you should accept them. It's crazy to pay for his advice if you're not going to take it. But the fact that "it's always done this way around here" is not a serious legal objection, and you need not accept it. If you get that kind of response regularly, you probably need a different lawyer rather than a different approach to your legal rights and obligations.

Once this sometimes-painful process has produced a binder that seems acceptable to you, you're ready to make your offer. Sign the form and enclose with it your check, bearing a notation that it is earnest money to be held in escrow and returned if the transaction is not completed. Give the binder and the check to the broker, if there is one, or the seller. Either one may object that this isn't the standard binder. Refer all such complaints to your lawyer. If there is a broker involved in the deal he will probably sign the binder. He is obliged to transmit your offer to the seller, even if he doesn't think it's a reasonable one. If the seller signs the binder without making any changes in it, your offer has been accepted. You have a deal, at least in principle.

If, as is more likely, the seller changes some term on the binder — moving up the date by which a formal contract must be agreed upon, for example — he is considered to have made a counteroffer, which he or the broker will transmit to you, and which you are free to accept or reject. You can make a counter-counteroffer by changing the terms again — suggesting a compromise, perhaps — and sending it back. This process can go on indefinitely, as long as you seem to be making some progress, until you strike a deal or one of you decides it's hopeless and rejects the latest proposal without suggesting anything new.

This sounds like a rigid, formal process that will drag out for weeks, but it usually isn't. Once you've made an initial offer in writing, the seller may decide that you're serious and conduct the rest of the offering and counter-offering by telephone. The whole thing can be concluded in an hour or so, with the binder then updated to reflect the modified agreement.

Once you and the seller have signed the binder, the detailed negotiating that will produce the formal contract can begin. Since the binder contains a contingency — a stipulation that your obligation to buy is dependent upon the negotiation of a satisfactory contract — the "For Sale" sign may not disappear from the property, and other prospective buyers may be shown around. If the binder is properly drawn, however, and both sides negotiate in good faith, no other sale can be completed unless you and the seller are unable to agree on a contract within the specified time.

Ultimately, if you have a valid binder and the seller fails to perform according to its provisions, even though he returns your earnest money, you can sue him for damages or for performance — that is, for the completion of the transaction. You may actually win the suit, but it's rarely worth the trouble. The broker, of course, may take a different view in such a case, electing to sue the reluctant seller for his commission. And the lawyers, who are often anxious to grapple with legal niceties and usually willing to collect the extra fees that a suit will produce, may also counsel a tough stand on the merits of the case. Nonetheless, litigation is a difficult way to buy a home, and unless there is something very unusual about your situation, you would probably be better advised to shrug your shoulders, mutter a few obscenities about the seller, and start looking for a different home.

If you're dickering for land rather than a home, the worst of your negotiating chores may be behind you now; there's relatively less to argue over in a land purchase than there is in a deal for a home that, on the day you want to move in, may be incomplete or occupied, full of rubble or falling down. Price is the major factor in any sale, but in a land deal it's perhaps more dominant than in others. And you've made an agreement on price.

If, on the other hand, you're butting heads with a developer over the purchase of a new home, all the fun may still lie ahead. You've really attempted to negotiate nothing so far except price, and developers usually won't give an inch on that. They will, however, often bargain with varying degrees of flexibility and enthusiasm on a host of other things that should concern you.

It is likely that the developer, who's in a different marketing position than an individual seller, will not care a hoot about a binder, insisting that you get right to the signing of a final, formal contract. In one way, that's to your advantage. It helps not to have to plunge into all the legal folderol involved in signing something before you have some idea of where you stand, of what the seller's concerns are, and of how they might affect your interests. You learn that sort of thing only in patient negotiation, and binders usually get signed before such give-and-take begins.

In another sense, of course, you're better off with a binder, especially in a resale transaction. A resale home always seems somehow unique. It bears the stamp of someone's personality and taste; it has evolved over the years. A development home, by contrast, is one of a dozen or a hundred similar places. If this one eludes your grasp, there's one down the street that's almost identical. Not so with a resale home, and if you don't sign a binder, you're taking a risk. For without some written commitment, the seller is free to accept any offer that comes along, no matter how much time and money you've spent inspecting his home, shopping for a mortgage, and negotiating a sale.

What you have in a binder is a foot in the door — some assurance that the home won't be sold out from under you — and some certainty about the biggest variable of all, price. It gives you the freedom to turn your attention to the dozens of other variables that should be specified precisely in the final, formal contract.

25
How Should You Negotiate the Contract?

Your goal now — and presumably that of the seller as well — is to negotiate a contract, a formal agreement that will set out every detail of the transaction you're about to undertake. If you signed a binder, you probably set yourselves a time limit; you and the seller agreed that you would negotiate an acceptable contract within a specified time or either of you could back out of the deal. There is an element of risk in that sort of agreement, for it's based upon the presumption that both sides will be reasonable. Obviously, if either you or the seller digs in his heels halfway through the process and vows not to give an inch, no agreement can be reached. When that happens, everybody loses — you lose the home you wanted as well as the time and effort you put into finding it; the seller loses the sale he's been hoping for and working toward; the broker or agent, if there is one, loses his commission.

Everybody involved has more tied up in this deal now than ever before, so it's doubly important to keep firmly in mind the rules upon which you operated earlier. Be reasonable. Discuss, don't argue. Ask, don't demand. Cajole. Persuade. Compromise. Be your usual charming self.

If negotiations seem to be going fairly well, but it becomes clear that you will not be able to meet the contract-signing deadline you've set yourselves — suppose you're unexpectedly called to Washington to perform your famous harp concert on roller skates at a White House dinner — stay cool. You can probably negotiate a reasonable extension if you have a decent excuse such as business commitments, illness, or unforeseen complications in the negotiations despite agreement in principle. The seller, after all, is likely to be just as anxious about this thing as you are and just as interested in seeing it proceed smoothly and end amicably. If you do arrive at an agreement to extend the deadline, treat it as you would any other facet of the transaction. Be sure it's in writing. Be sure it commits you to nothing except more discussion. Be sure your lawyer reads it before you sign. Be sure everybody concerned has signed it — including the broker or agent, if there is one hunkered down in a corner slavering over the commission to come.

As in your earlier negotiation over price, you should try to gain something every time you give something up. You probably won't be able to reduce the agreed-upon price, but there are plenty of opportunities to save a buck here. And there are places where you can pick up a little insurance — the seller's warranty that something is in working order, say — or a little convenience — the seller may agree to move out early so you can move in and get the kids started in school even before you actually own the joint.

Such things may seem like petty details to be negotiating in a contract for the sale of a home, but in real estate what's really important is what's in writing. And the only writing you're likely to get between now and the day you take title is the contract, so everything that's important to you — no matter how seemingly trivial — had better be in the contract. Basically, the contract should cover five areas: what you're buying; how much you'll pay for it; how you'll pay for it; when you'll get it; and under what circumstances you can cancel the agreement. It should also, of course, contain all those abstruse niceties that keep lawyers in regular work and make the agreement a contract that's enforceable against the seller — or, for that matter, against you.

WHAT YOU'RE BUYING

It is both a legal requirement and common sense that the contract contain an accurate and specific description of the property in question. You've heard stories about demolition contractors who tore down the wrong building. It can happen. Don't buy the wrong home. In addition to the street address, the contract should contain a full legal description of the property you're buying. That will probably include the name of the map from which the data were taken, the date the map was made, the block and lot numbers of the land and the metes and bounds (that is, compass directions and exact dimensions from some starting point, often a nearby street intersection). Sometime before you sign the contract — especially if you're buying in a large city and he may never see the property — give your lawyer a layman's description of the place and ask him to be sure it doesn't conflict with the information in the contract. It needn't be a fancy, detailed description, just something like this: the third house east of Kovach Court on the north side of Conway Lane, a three-story brick house with a two-car garage behind it (the one with the statue of Mae West in the front yard).

The contract should specify who will pay for a survey of the property if one is required before the closing. Even if the place was surveyed six months ago by a reputable practitioner, a mortgage lender may insist upon a new survey. You should negotiate with the seller now over who will pay for it. If it's not in the contract and the bank later insists on a survey, you'll have to foot the bill. Even if the lender doesn't demand it, a new survey may disclose encroachments — invasions of this lot by neighbors' fences, driveways or structures — that didn't exist six months ago or that were overlooked in an earlier survey. And it's one more assurance that you're getting what you're paying for — that the lot is what the contract says it is. Your lawyer will know whether local lenders customarily require new surveys, even if recent ones exist, and if there is a recent one, the lawyer may know something about the reputation of the surveyor who made it and about the likelihood that there have been changes since it was made.

The contract should specify all the covenants, restrictions, easements, and encumbrances on the land. Covenants are agreements or promises, and they can be good or bad from your point of view. The seller can, for example, covenant or promise the buyer absolute ownership with quiet enjoyment of the land. That's good. But there can also be restrictive covenants, agreements that curtail the use of the property — limiting the size of buildings that can be constructed there, perhaps, or prohibiting the operation of certain businesses. That can be good or bad, depending on your plans. Restrictions can be clauses in the deed that limit the use of the land — their effect is that of restrictive covenants — or limitations beyond the deed. Zoning regulations, for example, are restrictions, and so are easements. Easements are limitations on an owner's use of his property in the sense that they allow someone else to use it in a specified way, permanently or temporarily. Utility companies often have easements to run their wires or pipes over or under other people's land, and sometimes a land owner with a narrow lot has an easement to use a neighbor's driveway. Encumbrances are outstanding mortgages, liens, attachments, or assessments. They are claims of such legal status as to make the land unmarketable until they are satisfied. Such claims can be filed by various government agencies and by creditors, most notably mortgage holders, craftsmen, and materials suppliers.

Some restrictions that were once common — those that prohibit the ownership of land by certain religious or ethnic groups — have been ruled unconstitutional and therefore cannot be enforced in the courts, no matter how impressive they sound on paper.

If you learn of any covenants, restrictions, or easements — whether they sound good or bad — discuss them with your lawyer. Be sure to understand exactly what they mean and get his opinion on whether they can be enforced.

The contract should specify the kind of deed — the document that actually transfers ownership — you will get. There are several types. A general warranty deed or full covenant and warranty deed is the best. In it, the seller agrees to defend against all claims arising before you purchase the title he's granting you. If trouble appears, you can sue him. Of course, that guarantee is only as good as your ability to find the seller if disaster strikes 15 years after you bought the place, and, if you find him, only as good as his financial ability to defend you and your willingness, given the hassle involved, to sue him rather than simply pay off the claimant and forget it. Not much of a guarantee, perhaps, but the best available.

A similar but more limited guarantee is contained in a special warranty deed, sometimes called simply a warranty deed. A seller who gives such a deed promises to defend the title only against claims that arose during his ownership, not those that result from the carryings on of previous owners.

A bargain and sale deed can be written with or without a covenant against grantor's acts. The deed itself merely conveys to the buyer the seller's interest in the property. The covenant is the guarantee of the seller (the grantor) that he has not done or allowed anything that would encumber the property or reduce its value in any way. Obviously, the deed is better with the covenant than without it.

Finally, there is the quitclaim deed, the least desirable form of conveyance. It does not even specifically say that the seller has any rights or interest in the property that he can transfer to you. It merely stipulates that if he has any such rights, or any claims to such rights, he is granting those rights or claims to you. This type of deed is often used to remove a "cloud" on a title — the suspicion that someone has a claim on the land — by having that person sign a quitclaim deed in favor of the buyer. But in some places quitclaim deeds are commonly used in the sale of property.

Such common use — the local custom — will have a great deal to do with the kind of deed you'll get. So will the kind of deed the seller has. It's a truism of the real estate business that the seller can't convey a better deed than he has. In case of questions, see your lawyer.

The contract should require that the seller convey to you a good and marketable or merchantable title, one so free of encumbrances that it would raise no doubts in the mind of a reasonable person — a title, in other words, that a court would force a buyer to accept under the terms of a valid contract. A good and marketable title need not necessarily be a clear title, one free of any defect whatever, but its defects must be so minor that they do not present a serious question as to the ownership of the land.

Defects in a title are any encumbrances, any claims or apparent claims against it. They may be mortgages, tax bills, or assessments that have not been paid, mechanics' liens — that is, claims by workmen against the owner — or certain creditors' judgments against the owner. Another sort of defect is a contention of a former wife of a former owner that the place was improperly sold without her signature. Any suggestion of illegality in the handling of the title is a defect. An otherwise good title that has been sold illegally is probably not a marketable one.

Not all defects are fatal, however. An easement is a defect, but the fact that the electric company has an easement to run some wires across your backyard

25 feet off the ground does not make it unmarketable. Some defects may even be benefits. If you hope to assume the seller's mortgage, that mortgage is a defect in the title, but not one you necessarily want to remove. And if you are not going to assume the seller's mortgage, it will probably remain as a defect until the closing, when you actually take title and pay him so that he can pay off the mortgage. Although some such defects will hang around until the last minute, the contract should require that the seller pay off — out of the proceeds of the sale, if not before the closing — all liens, assessments, encumbrances, and loans not to be assumed. If the seller is fighting a claim — contending, for example, that a workman who has filed a mechanic's lien has been paid and is due nothing more — the contract should require that he post a bond to guarantee the payment of the claim if he loses his legal fight.

Whatever the status of the title and the seller's plans for making it good, rely upon your lawyer's advice. If ever there were an area in which he should be more expert than you, this is it.

The contract should stipulate what evidence the seller will supply to demonstrate the marketability of his title and the conditions under which you can reject it. In a typical transaction, a title search, an examination of all the public records relating to the ownership of the land, will follow the signing of a contract. The search can be conducted by anyone who knows what he's doing. It's sometimes done by a lawyer, but more often the lawyer or the lending institution making the mortgage hires a title company or abstract company, a concern that specializes in this sort of thing, to do the legwork. The search can lead to several types of documents, any one of which may be produced as evidence of a good title. The most basic one is an abstract of title, a summary of the history of the land's ownership and the encumbrances on it. This is the raw material turned up in the title search. The next step is a title report, a summary of the condition of the title, based upon an examination of the abstract. It is sometimes called a preliminary title report because it is typically prepared by a title insurance company before the company issues a policy on the land. Then there is the certificate of title, a written opinion by a lawyer or title company saying that the title to the land is apparently good and marketable. If a title company issues such a document, it is usually also willing to insure the title. And that's the last link in this chain of documents, a title insurance policy.

Title insurance provides protection against hidden defects in the title. If you're covered and someone comes along with a claim on your land, the title insurer will fight that claim legally and, if you suffer a loss, will reimburse you for it up to the face amount of the policy. Such policies usually do not protect you against defects turned up in the title search; the theory is that the search gives you fair warning and you can make up your own mind whether to assume the risks it discloses or reject the title. Title policies also generally do not protect you against zoning or other exercises of governmental power that restrict the use of the land, and there are usually some other exceptions listed in the policy. Discuss with your lawyer the exceptions in any title insurance policy offered to you.

Be aware that there are two categories of title insurance. Many mortgage lenders require that you buy a policy that protects their interest in the land but offers you no protection. If you want your interest insured, you'll have to specify that and pay extra for it. Such coverage is usually cheaper if you get it at the same time the lender is getting his. You pay only one premium for this insurance, and it remains in force as long as you or your heirs retain your interest in the land. The rates depend upon the amount of coverage you want, how well maintained and accessible the land records are in your area, and how difficult it is to trace the ownership chain of the land you want. Like homeowner's insurance, title insurance should be updated periodically to keep up with inflation. Some companies offer policies that contain automatic escalator provisions. Ask your lawyer; who else?

The ideal title evidence to get from a seller, of course, is a title insurance policy that protects you as well as the lender and that the seller pays for. If he will arrange the policy but won't pay for it, the evidence is just as good but the pain is a little greater. Pay for it yourself. You may be able to save a bit by asking the company that already insures the title for a "reissue" policy, which is usually cheaper than a new one. If the seller offers less than a title insurance policy as evidence of good title, you and your lawyer have more work to do. An abstract is obviously the least valuable of the supporting documents, nothing but the raw facts. A title report, even a certificate of title, is only as good as the judgment of the man who made it out, though a certificate that carries with it a willingness to insure is the next best thing to the policy itself. If the evidence is anything less than that, make sure your lawyer examines it and gives you his best thinking on the validity of the title. Make sure, too, that the contract gives you a specified period to examine the document in question and accept it or reject it. If you reject it, the seller should be allowed a limited time in which to correct the defects. If he fails to do so, you should then have the right to cancel the deal. Ideally, you may be able to write into the contract a title insurance contingency, a provision that if you are unable to obtain title insurance coverage within a specified period, you can back out of the purchase. Local custom will have a great deal to do with what you can expect in this area. Discuss it with your lawyer before you make too many demands of the seller.

Whatever the local custom, the contract should be specific about the condition of the property when you take possession. Presuming that the place was in reasonable shape when you looked at it, the contract should require that the seller maintain it in its present condition until the closing, when you take title. It might also require that before the closing the seller correct all outstanding code violations, violations of the building, plumbing, or electrical codes for which citations have been issued. This provision may not be applicable if you're buying a wreck with the idea of gutting and rebuilding it, but even then, writing into the contract a list of all the code violations can be a useful negotiating ploy.

You can try to work into the contract a clause saying that the seller will make certain improvements or repairs before the closing or that such improvements and repairs will be made by the buyer at the seller's expense. The seller may not be too keen on that idea, but he should go along with a provision that until the closing he assumes all risk for fire or other hazards. It is, after all, still his place. You can also try to get the seller to pay for your fire insurance — the policy that will provide coverage after the closing — in the amount of the selling price. He's likely to balk, but it's worth a try.

Write into the contract a provision that until 30 days after the closing the seller guarantees all appliances, mechanical systems, and structural components to be in good working order and in compliance with all applicable codes, and that he will repair or replace anything that does not meet those standards. The seller would have to be fairly naive to accept that code compliance provision, but it doesn't hurt to ask.

If you're buying a multiple-family property to gut and remodel, have the contract specify that the property is to be delivered vacant — that is, without tenants. Evicting tenants can be as big a headache for a landlord as it is for tenants, especially in a city that has strict rental regulations designed to protect tenants. That is true, for example, in New York City — so much so that vacant multiple-family buildings there are often worth more than buildings filled with tenants. If your plans include the removal of tenants for whatever reason, discuss that aspect of the deal with your lawyer, and be sure you understand before you sign the contract what the tenants' rights are.

If you're buying an old hulk filled with discarded furniture and debris, try to enter into the contract a provision that the seller will remove the junk before you take title. If you're buying a place in good repair that you hope to move into yourself, work in a clause requiring that it be delivered broom clean and that personal property not to be included in the sale will be removed before the closing.

If personal property is to be included in the sale, it should be itemized in the contract and, where possible, described accurately enough so that no substitution is possible. Local custom on what is included in a sale varies, so be sure you know what the seller intends to take with him and what he will leave. Appliances, storm windows, screens, carpeting, draperies, and the TV antenna may all be considered personal property and removed unless the contract specifies otherwise. Negotiate to pay extra for the things you really want, but remember that it's all used — just one step this side of junk — and therefore not worth much. Try to work into the contract a stipulation that the seller will supply bills of sale and warranties still in effect for the personal property included in the transaction.

Though it may sound like inviting trouble, you should probably question the seller closely about what he does not want to include in the sale. A striking light fixture, for example, may look like real estate to you, but he may not consider parting with it because it was given to him by his great uncle Holcombe just before the old man perished in a vat of candle wax. You may want that light fixture, too, on the theory that it's the only thing that makes the dining room attractive. Better to have your brawl over it now and get its situation decided in the contract than to move in and discover it missing, replaced by an old kerosene lantern that was hanging in the garage.

The contract should provide that you'll have the right to inspect the property on the day of the closing to insure that it has been maintained in accordance with the agreement.

WHAT YOU'LL PAY AND HOW

How much you will pay for the place and how you will pay involve much more than the price, and the details should be given precisely. The contract should, of course, state the price you and the seller have agreed upon and the steps in which it will be paid: the earnest money, if any, which will probably have been paid by now; the down payment, usually made when the contract is signed; and the balance, which is due at the closing and will probably be paid through one or more mortgage loans.

The size of the down payment is negotiable. As with earnest money, it's to your advantage to keep it as small as possible and pay it as late as possible, and to the seller's advantage to get as much as possible as soon as possible. A down payment of 10 percent, including the earnest money, is common in many places and commonly paid when the contract is signed. No matter how much it is or when it's paid, the contract should require that the down payment be held in escrow by the broker if there is one, by the seller's lawyer or by a third party, an escrow agent, until the closing or the date on which the home becomes available for occupancy, whichever comes later, or until the deal is called off. That requires you to commit yourself — to put up some money to demonstrate that you're serious — but it prevents the seller from getting his mitts on the cash until he delivers the goods. If there's an escrow clause in the contract, ask the lawyers involved about having the money put in an interest-bearing escrow account, with you and the seller to share the income. The lawyers are not likely to leap at your suggestion. They are often anxious to maintain cordial relations with bankers, who don't go out of their way to pay interest when they don't have to.

If the balance of the purchase price that will come due at the closing is to be paid in anything other than cash, the contract should give the details. You will probably have to find a mortgage to meet that obligation. If so, specify in the contract the minimum acceptable terms — the amount you will need, the maximum interest rate you will pay, the minimum term (number of years) for which you need the money. If you've determined that you'll need an FHA mortgage (one insured by the Federal Housing Administration) or a VA or GI loan (one guaranteed by the Veterans Administration) put that in, too. Remember that you're trying to be realistic and reasonable here. If the prevailing interest rate in your area is 14½ percent, don't insist that you need a 9 percent mortgage. That's simply insisting that you really don't want to buy this place or are unable to do so.

If the seller becomes outraged at the suggestion of an FHA or VA mortgage, be wary. He may be legitimately concerned, as are many sellers and lenders, about the delays and red tape involved in the processing of such loans. But he may be more worried about the required inspection and appraisal than he is about the paperwork. It may be impossible to learn what prompts his chagrin, but look the thing over carefully.

The contract should allow you a specific time to find the mortgage you need. If you fail to do so, it should allow the seller a short time to find one for you, to offer you a mortgage himself on the stipulated terms, or to back out of the agreement. Once the seller's time limit is up, you should be able to drop the deal.

If you are not willing to pay "points" — a discount on the mortgage principal — or an "origination fee," the contract should say so. The same for a mortgage broker's fee. If you're willing to pay any of them but have limits in mind, put them into the contract among the mortgage terms you're willing to accept.

If you're going to get a purchase money mortgage (a loan from the seller to cover part of the purchase price), all of its terms should be spelled out precisely in the contract: the amount, the interest rate, the term, prepayment provisions (penalties if you pay the loan off early), and whether the loan will be assumable — and on what conditions — if you sell the home in the future. If this is to be a second mortgage, one that represents a lesser claim on the land than the mortgage you plan to negotiate at the bank, the contract should say so.

All of the same terms should be spelled out if you're planning to pick up the seller's existing mortgage. You can either assume it (that is, step into the seller's place and pick up the payments on his mortgage) or buy the home subject to his mortgage (make the payments on the loan, although the seller remains responsible to the lender for it).

All of these arrangements are subject to negotiation, as well as to the cooperation of the lenders, and they may be some of the most important points in the whole deal, especially when money is tight and mortgages are hard to come by. They are also very complex, in case you hadn't guessed, and deserve the rapt attention of your lawyer.

Those details explain how you'll pay for the home itself, but the contract should also specify who will pay the expenses of the sale other than the purchase price. Who, for example, will pay for inspections by an independent

HOW SHOULD YOU NEGOTIATE THE CONTRACT?

engineer and an exterminator who can tell whether the place is infested with termites? Who will pay for an appraisal? The title search and abstract? Who will pay for the credit report when the bank wants to find out what sort of risk you are? Who will pay the legal fees, escrow fees, broker's commission, mortgage broker's commission, mortgage origination fee, and title insurance premium? Who will pay for the tax stamps on the notes and deed and for the recording of the mortgage and deed? There are traditions on who pays what — the seller pays the broker's commission, for example, and the buyer pays for his own credit report — but all things are negotiable here.

Beyond the expenses of the sale itself, the contract should specify who will pay the cost of keeping the place between the signing of the contract and the closing — such bills as homeowner's insurance, real estate taxes, special assessments, and utilities. Generally, such things are the seller's responsibility, with prepaid items — taxes, for instance — prorated at the closing so that you reimburse the seller for the portion of the prepaid taxes that covers the period thereafter. You might also agree to pay the seller for any fuel oil remaining in the tank on closing day.

The contract should say who will be responsible for the repair or replacement of major items found to be defective in the various inspections that will take place after the contract is signed. Perhaps the most reasonable way to handle that problem is to devise a clause that says the seller will correct any defects found in subsequent inspections up to a specified dollar limit — perhaps $500 or $1,000 — or will reimburse the buyer for the correction of such defects up to the same limit. Beyond that limit, the contract should provide that the seller can refuse to make repairs and the buyer can withdraw from the agreement. This approach is fairer than making the deal contingent upon your approval of an engineer's report. With such a contingency you can back out at will, simply because you don't approve of the paper on which the report is written, if nothing else.

As a last point in your discussion of financial responsibility, why not ask the seller if he will guarantee those taxes and utility bills he has been so proudly minimizing — that is, guarantee you that they will not rise beyond a certain point for a year after the closing, and promise that if they do he'll pay the difference himself. The seller is liable to faint at the suggestion. The only one likely to agree is a seller who's been having trouble making a deal because buyers object to his high taxes or utility bills. But even if he doesn't agree, his reaction will provide a story you can tell your grandchildren someday.

WHEN YOU'LL GET IT

So much for what you pay. As to when you get it, the contract should set out the date, time, and place (usually a lawyer's office or the office of a mortgage lender) for the closing, the actual transfer of money and title. That date, like the contract-signing deadline, can probably be changed through negotiation and written agreement if some serious obligation or complication crops up.

In addition to the closing date, and even if it's the same as the closing date, the contract should specify the date on which you want to take occupancy. It should set the rent the seller will pay you if he has not vacated the property by the closing date, and if you're in a hurry it should probably be a high rent, more than the market rent for such a place. You might even try to negotiate a clause that will set damages beyond rent that the seller will pay you if the home is not vacant at the closing. This is an especially valuable provision if the seller is planning to move to a new home that may not be finished by the time you want to close. You might also write in an upset date, a date beyond which you can cancel the agreement and get your money back if the home is not available for occupancy. Tying the escrow to this date rather than a closing date puts a lot more muscle behind it.

The opposite arrangement can also be negotiated. Suppose you want to move in and the seller is prepared to move out a few months before you'll have the funds to close. You can negotiate a contract clause that sets the rent you'll pay the seller between the day you occupy the place and the day you close. It need not be so high as the rent you would want from the seller if he failed to vacate because there is no punitive intent here; the fair market rent will do.

It is also useful, especially if you're planning extensive remodeling or other work, to try to get a clause that allows you reasonable access to the property before the closing. You might save some carrying costs this way if you can begin your planning even before you own the thing. You run a risk of losing your planning investment if the deal falls through, but that may be a reasonable risk if it looks like a fairly straightforward transaction. Do not, however, begin your actual remodeling work before the closing unless you and your lawyer have worked out a legal way to do so. Not only might you lose your investment, but you also might be sued for damages and lose much more.

Finally, if timing is important to you, include in the contract a clause saying, "Time is of the essence." That's a legal way of saying, "I'm in a hurry, and I mean it."

HOW YOU CAN BACK OUT

The last major area the contract should cover is the circumstances in which you can withdraw from the agreement. Those circumstances are embodied in contingency clauses, clauses that provide a loophole for you or the seller. In general, you want contingency clauses that will protect you against any serious legal or physical defects that might be found in the property after you sign the contract and against serious economic developments beyond your control that would make it impossible for you to buy.

HOW SHOULD YOU NEGOTIATE THE CONTRACT?

No contract can protect you against every evil possibility, of course, and the seller, understandably enough, will want a little protection, too. In a sense, every ounce of protection you win is an ounce he loses, and vice versa. He's not going to agree to everything you want any more than you're going to agree to all that he wants. Nobody's going to be fully protected; everybody's going to share the risk. With that in mind, set yourself some priorities. Some possible contingencies are such that you probably shouldn't even mention them. Others you should drop quickly if they meet strong resistance. But some of them you should fight like hell for. Which ones those are depend upon your circumstances. You will have to make your own list, perhaps in consultation with your lawyer.

Generally, it is unfair to make contingencies dependent upon your approval. A sale that hinges on an engineer's report "acceptable to the buyer" is no sale at all. Every engineer will find something wrong with every home, including his own. That's what you sign him up to do — find what's wrong. But some of the faults he discovers will be things that take 20 minutes and $3.60 to correct. Insisting upon the right to cancel a $70,000 sale over such an item simply isn't reasonable. The clause should be worded in a way that limits the loophole to major defects, that gives the seller a fair chance at correcting them, and that puts a ceiling on everybody's expenditure of time and money.

Applying those rules to a contingency for an engineering report would produce a clause containing the following stipulations: The home will be inspected by an independent engineer of the buyer's choice. The correction of defects uncovered during that inspection in the major appliances, mechanical systems, or structural components of the home will be the responsibility of the seller up to a specified dollar limit. The seller will have the option of correcting the defect or reimbursing the buyer for the work. Beyond the agreed-upon limit, the seller will have the right to refuse to correct the defects, and the buyer will have the right to abort the sale.

The list of contingencies you might try to negotiate is about as long as a lawyer's imagination. Choose sparingly and carefully. There is no perfect contract.

If you have doubts about the value of the home you're negotiating over, you can have it appraised; for some kinds of mortgages, you'll have to have it appraised. In either case, you can make the sale contingent upon an appraisal that is reasonably close to the sale price. If the mortgage lender requires the appraisal, it'll have to be close enough to suit him. If you're the one who wants it, you can set some arbitrary limit — say, that the appraisal be no more than 10 percent lower than the sale price. In any event, you should allow the seller a reasonable time in which to consider reducing his price to a level in line with the appraisal. Only after that period and only if he refuses to comply should you be able to disappear.

You can write a contingency clause that lets you bail out if the survey shows the land to be substantially different than the description in the contract. Not 6 inches narrower; substantially different. You can make it contingent upon an inspection by an engineer, of course, or upon a study by an independent contractor or exterminator qualified to determine that the place is free of termite infestation and has not suffered structural damage at the hands of the li'l fellers. Again, you should not be able to withdraw if the seller is willing to end the infestation and repair the damage.

The sale can be made contingent upon your obtaining a mortgage commitment — a letter from a lender saying that he will make the loan you need. The contract should state the amount you will need, the minimum term or number of years for which you will need it, the highest interest rate you can pay, and the length of time you have to track the thing down. It should provide that when your time runs out with no mortgage in sight the seller will have some options: he can cancel the deal, he can offer you a mortgage himself on those minimum terms, or he can find you a loan elsewhere. After the period set aside for the seller to act, the contract should allow you to waive your conditions and accept a loan on less advantageous terms or withdraw from the agreement.

If the sale involves your assuming the seller's mortgage, you can make it contingent upon that loan's matching the terms given in the contract; what it says you'll get should be what you get. Again, it's necessary to keep your head about you. If the contract says that the principal remaining on the loan is $20,000 and in fact the balance turns out to be $20,136.84, you do not have reasonable grounds for canceling the agreement. That's not a substantive difference. If the principal is really $28,000 or $15,000, on the other hand, you have a point worth pursuing.

You can make the sale contingent upon your ability to obtain title insurance at reasonable cost — that is, close to average cost for the type of property involved. If nobody will insure your title, after all, it's fairly certain there's something wrong with it. If the cost of insurance is unusually high, the reason may be that things are simply a mess down at the courthouse and a title search takes forever; it may have nothing to do with the quality of the title. Whatever the cause, you can set a limit on the cost in the contract, then give the seller the right to pay the excess or refuse, and if he refuses, retain the right to drop out. You should be allowed a decent interval in which to examine — with your lawyer, of course — any title evidence submitted by the seller before accepting or rejecting it. Then the seller should have a reasonable time in which to correct any defects before you can walk off in a huff.

You can write a clause that allows you to get out of the deal if you discover after the signing of the contract substantive covenants or restrictions not previously disclosed. That doesn't mean you can change your mind because the electric company has an easement for those overhead wires. That hardly seems substantive unless you're planning to build a roller coaster in the yard. It means that if you discover a restriction that prevents your reasonable use of the land — let's say the neighbor who has the right to use your drive is a drive-in theater — you can scratch the deal.

You can produce a clause that makes the sale contingent upon your gaining access to the property by a certain date. You should probably build a little leeway into that, specifying the rent the seller will pay if he is still in possession after the closing, then a final date upon which you can pull out if you don't have occupancy.

If there is expansion or major improvement in your plans, you can make the transaction contingent upon your winning the approval of the zoning board or the building department for what you have in mind, provided you're willing to make reasonable modifications to get the nod.

Though the seller is likely to balk, you can try to make the purchase of a new home contingent upon your ability to sell your old home within a specified period — say 60 to 90 days. If the seller resists, you might suggest a clause that allows him to keep his place on the market and, if he gets another offer, allows you a short time — perhaps a week — to waive the contingency and close the deal or drop out and allow the other buyer to get the home.

In case you haven't guessed, you can write a clause that makes the sale contingent upon almost anything — death or serious illness in your immediate family, the sudden loss of employment, anything. It is best, however, not to fill the contract with contingencies. A few should be sufficient to give you reasonable protection. And whatever contingencies there are should probably be written in a way that assumes you have approved the latest development unless you inform the seller within a specified period of your rejection. You'll have to inform him in some official way — by sending him a registered letter, for example, or throwing a rock through his living room window precisely at noon — so don't lose track of time and get caught with your contingencies down.

CONTRACTS FOR LAND

If what you're dickering over is land rather than a resale home, the negotiating and contract-writing process may be simplified in the sense that there's less to negotiate over. The major items of discussion are likely to be price and the method of payment. There probably won't be any personal property to haggle about, and the closing date is less likely to be an issue than it is in the purchase of a home that must be completed or vacated before you can move in.

The seller of land may be more flexible on price and more willing to take a purchase-money mortgage or make some other financing arrangement than would the seller of a home, who may need his equity right away to buy another place. The land seller may even be willing to give you better mortgage terms than you could hope to get from a lending institution.

Though a willing seller will probably let you have the land any time you want it, he may for tax reasons want to conclude a transaction in one year or stretch it out into another. In such a case, you may be able to arrange interim financing or some other device that allows both your needs and those of the seller to be met. Talk over all the details with your lawyer before you agree to anything, and be sure that everything is stated precisely in the contract. This sort of special arrangement may ultimately cost you more money. Keep tabs on what it's costing, and if it's for the seller's convenience, use the extra cost as a lever in your bargaining.

You will probably have to accept the land "as is." But if there's some problem that lends itself to fairly direct solution — let's say the place is littered with trash or will require extensive grading or drainage work before anything can be built — you might be able to persuade the seller to absorb some or all of the cost. There should be a reasonable ceiling on what he has to pay, however.

Then there are the possible contingency clauses, some of which are about the same as those for a home — a construction mortgage contingency, for example, or one that hinges on an engineering report on drainage or soil and rock conditions. You can also try to negotiate a contingency on zoning board and building department approval for your plans. This will take some careful phrasing to describe the kinds of plan changes you are willing to make to win approval. You should be willing to move the structure 6 inches, say, to satisfy lot line requirements, but you should not have to double its size or change it from a two-family to a one-family home. Let your lawyer tinker with that.

One contingency that would not normally be in a contract for a resale home but might be included in one for the sale of vacant land would make the sale dependent on public health department approval for sewage and water supply systems, which may require percolation or other test results that meet minimum standards. Time limits and a cost ceiling should be part of the clause, with the seller having the right to absorb the excess cost if he chooses. Another contingency peculiar to a land purchase might concern commitments for the installation of utility service to the lot line at a cost not to exceed a stipulated amount.

CONTRACTS WITH DEVELOPERS

And if you're negotiating with a developer for a new tract home, the pitfalls to avoid and the concessions to expect are a whole new thing. The developer is not in the same position as the seller of an older home. The latter has only one place to sell, and he's probably in a hurry to get it done and just as nervous about this strange process as you are. The developer may have hundreds of homes to sell, and if he doesn't sell one to you, someone else will probably come along, someone not nearly so choosy. He may be feeling the burden of rising costs and therefore be in a hurry, but he's not likely to be nervous about a strange and complex process; he's been through it scores of times.

For all those reasons and others, the developer is not likely to budge on his price. He knows what it cost him to build the place and what he has to make on it to stay in business, and that's that. He also does not have a lot of personal property he can leave around to make you happy. Anything extra he puts in adds to the cost, and he'd better cover his costs if he wants to keep building. But the developer does have one advantage over the seller of an older home: He's just building the place, and to one extent or another he can change what he's building to suit you. That and some assurance that he'll deliver what he promises are the areas where your negotiating efforts should focus.

The first order of business in negotiating with a developer, however, is to be absolutely certain you understand the basic contract he's offering. What is standard and what is extra? Is the refrigerator you saw in the model the same one described in the contract? Be sure the contract specifies exactly what model is "standard" for every appliance. What is the standard landscaping package? Get it spelled out. What about decorating? Specify the wallpaper, the paint, the number of coats.

After you've got the basic offer down, investigate the available options and what they cost. Then start probing to find out what changes you can make. Because he knows salesmanship, the developer tends to put the quality where it will do the most good — that is, where it can be seen. If he has to cut corners to hold down costs, he tries to cut corners that no potential buyer is likely to notice, corners that are hidden behind wallpaper, paint, or paneling. The result may be stunning kitchens and lavish baths connected to plumbing and electrical systems that barely meet minimum FHA standards. Such minimal systems can be expected to give trouble sooner or later, and changing them after the home is complete will be much more expensive than upgrading them in the first place, when all the components are easily accessible.

Try hard to get the developer to agree, even at extra cost, to install a bigger, higher-grade water heater, heavier wiring with more circuits and outlets, more insulation, a better quality furnace or burner. Ask about double-glazed windows, heavier roofing, thicker wallboard, and a better air-conditioner. See if he'll upgrade the landscaping package. When the costs mount, consider doing without the intercom or the central vacuum system in favor of more reliable plumbing or heating.

Insist upon termite protection. The most effective kind is chemical poisoning of the soil around the home, but there are also methods that depend upon the use of treated lumber and the installation of metal shields around the top of the foundation. Ask if the termite-proofing is guaranteed. If so, be sure you get the guarantee.

If the lot you've chosen has some natural advantage — a stand of trees, perhaps — try to work into the contract a stipulation that it will not be disturbed during construction. Insist upon a clause requiring that the topsoil be left on the lot. In some areas, topsoil is so valuable that developers scrape it off and sell it, a practice that does not produce the lushest of gardens for unwary home buyers.

Tell the salesman or developer that you want a copy of the plans and specifications for the home, even if you have to pay for them. Have an engineer or architect go over them and suggest improvements, and be sure they meet the Federal Housing Administration's minimum property standards, which can be inspected at the nearest FHA office. The chances are good that the home will conform to those standards because developers are usually anxious to qualify for FHA financing. Conformance doesn't mean a good home necessarily, but it probably means the thing won't fall over the next time the wind blows. When you, all your knowing neighbors, and Uncle Evan, who was once the general contractor on the pyramids, are finished poring over the plans and specifications, file them away. They may be invaluable someday when you decide to add on, remodel, or repair.

Insist that the developer and the contract be specific about guarantees and warranties. What materials, components, and appliances are covered by manufacturers' or suppliers' warranties? For how long? Who services the warranty — manufacturer, supplier, or developer? Insist upon a contract clause saying that the developer guarantees for one year from completion everything not otherwise covered by a warranty.

Get into the contract all the details on price, financing terms, and closing costs. Scream bloody murder if the developer's standard contract will allow him to raise the price before the home is completed. Many big developers offer their own financing, often on better terms than you're likely to find elsewhere. Do some comparison shopping to be sure the developer's deal is the best you can get, and if it is, be sure all the terms are listed in the contract precisely. Also be sure that the contract contains the same kind of mortgage contingency clause you would want if you were buying a resale home. Many big developers include closing costs — all the fees and payments incidental to the sale — in the price of the home, but some do not. Make sure that the contract is specific on who pays what at the closing.

See if you can get the developer to guarantee the taxes and utility bills for a year after the sale — that is, agree to pay anything above a specified level. Developers sometimes do so when business is slow and taxes and fuel costs are rising.

Insist that your deposit and down payment must go into escrow until the closing or until the home is ready for occupancy, whichever comes later, or until one of the contingencies is exercised and the deal is called off. If the money is not in escrow and the builder gets into financial trouble — hardly an impossible situation — you may never see the money or the home. In some areas, escrow is traditional for deposits on new homes. In others, it's unheard of. If the developer shudders at the suggestion of escrow, ask him to post a performance bond or get an insurance policy that will guarantee the completion of the home. Either one may be cheaper for him than escrow. You might even offer to pay for the bond if you really want this home and no other. If the developer still won't go along, it's probably because he can't get a bond; he's too big a risk. That would suggest you'd be better off doing business elsewhere, on the resale market if necessary.

Be sure you understand the construction and delivery schedule. Try to get into the contract a clause setting a financial penalty for every day of delay beyond the agreed-upon closing date. After the developer gets up off the floor, offer to delay the start of the penalty until 60 days or so after the scheduled closing — long enough to give him a fair chance to cope with unexpected delays. He won't like that much, either, but wait'll he hears that you want a contingency clause allowing you to cancel the deal if the home is not available for occupancy by some specified final date. You may not get the contingency clause, but you'll have the fun of watching a developer turn red and sputter.

He's not likely to be so upset when you ask to put into the contract a requirement that you be able to inspect the home before the closing; that's more or less standard. His reaction will vary if you suggest such contingency clauses as those based on an appraisal (the place was probably designed with an FHA appraisal in mind), a survey, an engineer's inspection and report, a title report or insurance, easements or restrictions, or the sale of your old home (many big developers have trade-in programs under which they will buy an old home that is standing in the way of a sale).

In general, you'll find the developer less flexible than the individual seller of an older home. He's more likely to be willing to see you walk away, less likely to let you have the contract you want. But there's nothing wrong with your accepting the developer's terms, within reason, as long as you know the risk you're taking. Weigh the risk against the benefit — this home rather than some other one — and make your choice. It's your money and your life.

LEGAL NICETIES

Your choices are likely to be in the nature of second guesses. Normally, the basic contract is drawn by the seller or builder and his lawyer, then submitted to you and your lawyer for amendment. You will, naturally, have to rely on the lawyer's advice as to what should be there and in what form, though you can feel free to make suggestions or to give him goals you'd like to reach, then allow him to find ways to reach them. Your lawyer will know the local law and custom relative to real estate contracts, but in general they should include, in addition to all the details of the property and transaction, such legal niceties as the date, the identification of both parties, the buyer and seller, and the signatures of both parties.

In some places, a contract signed by only one party can be enforced by the other party, but not vice versa. Obviously, if you're interested in completing the transaction, you want both sides signed and committed. If a married couple is buying or selling, the signatures of both spouses should probably be on the contract. This gets complicated, but in certain circumstances the failure to get both husband's and wife's signatures can mean that the title conveyed won't be marketable. Even if the home is held only in one name, it's a wise precaution to insure that both signatures are on the contract.

The contract should also include an assertion that it contains all the agreements between the buyer and seller relative to the transaction, and that no other representations were made. Before you sign it, of course, you want to be sure that's true. If the seller promised on the side that she'd throw in her husband, you'd better be sure that's specified in the contract if you expect to find the old boy on the premises when you arrive. Any detail that's important to you should be in the contract.

When it's completed, the contract should contain no blank spaces in which, after you sign, someone might insert details you don't know about or would not agree to.

HOW TO TAKE TITLE

The final detail that should be covered in the contract is how you'll take title to the place. If you're buying this thing all by yourself, with no spouse, lover, roommate, partner, or fellow investor, you can take title in your name as the sole tenant or tenant in fee or fee simple. That means you'll own the land absolutely and can dispose of it as you see fit during your lifetime and pass it on to whomever you wish when you die.

If you're happily married and buying a home with your spouse, you may be able to take title in both your names as tenants in the entirety. This is a form of ownership, common in many states but not recognized in others, that is reserved to married couples. It provides that each spouse has an undivided interest in the property — since two spouses are one legal person, each of them owns all of the property. Neither of you can dispose of his interest without the other's consent, and if either one dies his interest automatically passes to the other. One advantage of tenancy by the entirety is that it provides a measure of protection if one of you is sued by a creditor. The creditor can't take the other spouse's property along with that of the debtor, so the home is safe as long as the other spouse lives. A second advantage of tenancy by the entirety is that the home need not go through probate if one spouse dies. It passes automatically to the surviving spouse, and the probate bureaucracy will not have a chance to cluck and rub its hands over that part of the estate. The disadvantages of this form of ownership are that you can't do anything with the home unless your spouse agrees, and you can't leave it to someone other than your spouse when you die.

If your state does not allow tenancy by the entirety or if you're not married but planning to buy a home with your roommate or roommates, and you'd like the advantages available to tenants by the entirety, you can take title in both or all your names as joint tenants or joint tenants with the right of survivorship. Under this form of ownership, two or more people own equal and undivided interests in the property. When one owner dies, his interest automatically passes to the surviving owners. While he's alive, however, one joint tenant can sell his interest where a tenant by the entirety cannot.

If you're planning to buy with someone to whom you're not married or if you're buying with your spouse but wary of letting him or her get a permanent lock on the turf — assessments of the wisdom of that course will be left to the philosophy faculty — you may want to take title as tenants in common. In this form of ownership, two or more people own property, not necessarily in equal shares, with each holding a separate, undivided interest that he may sell or otherwise dispose of without reference to the other owners. When one owner dies, he may leave his interest to whomever he chooses; it does not automatically go to the surviving owners. That gives each owner a measure of freedom, of course, but it also means that his interest in the property will probably pass through probate when he dies.

Unmarried couples and childless married couples who hate their in-laws should give some thought to the survivorship provisions of joint tenancy and tenancy by the entirety. Let's suppose you fall into the chicken-plucking machine today and are killed, then your spouse or roommate, naturally despondent, stands in the shower with an electric curling iron and suffers a fatal shock. The minute you died, your interest in your home passed to your spouse or roommate. By the next day, your interest might belong to some people you never heard of — your roommate's relatives and heirs — or your spouse's despised relatives, who no doubt started packing the minute they heard of his or her untimely demise. In the same situation, your aged Uncle Warner, who was always good to you before his accident with the windmill and whom you and your wife had agreed to help in his declining years, might be left out in the cold if your wife hadn't written a will when she died. Whatever is left of her possessions after the state and the lawyers got finished with them would go to her next of kin, the distant cousin who's been terrorizing the nursing home ever since he finished his 45-year stretch in the slammer. If such a development seems at all possible, you and your consort can buy a home as tenants in common, with each of you owning 50 percent. Then each can make out a will leaving his or her interest to the other or to anyone else.

If you're an unmarried couple contemplating a purchase in only one name, the unnamed partner may be in for a disappointment if the relationship breaks up later. Since there's no contract between unmarried cohabitants, as there is between married people, the owner of record has no obligation in the event of "divorce" to share his or her possessions, including the home, with the other partner. This problem can be solved with a written agreement, independent of the sale contract, worked out before the purchase. It should stipulate that the purchase is an equal partnership and that the spoils will be divided equally in the event of civil war. The agreement should spell out both parties' rights and responsibilities during ownership, and one right should probably be that of first refusal if only one partner wants to sell. Each partner will need a will covering the disposition of the property. And by all means you need a lawyer — at least one.

Whatever your marital state, tax considerations may have a bearing on the way you take title. That, too, is fodder for discussion with your lawyer. Don't let him get away with easy answers to hard questions. Make sure you understand what every part of the contract means, what it requires of you, and what it requires of the seller.

Once you've gotten all that down pat, have thought it over, have haggled and negotiated yourself into a swivet, and have completed a contract that more or less fills the bill, you'd better sign the damn thing before the seller changes his mind.

Then you'd better trot off and have a nip of something to steady the nerves and ward off the cold. If you're typical, you're about to be struck by Thibault's Lament — an absolutely thunderous attack of doubts, second thoughts, twitches, self-hatred, rickets, beriberi, and palpitations of the heart.

Never mind. It'll pass. After all, it's only money, and at that most of it will probably be someone else's money — a mortgage loan.

26
How Should You Finance It?

Few of us, unfortunately, are so well fixed as to be able to buy a home without borrowing money — for most people, as the pundits are so fond of remarking, a home purchase is the biggest transaction of a lifetime, involving the equivalent of several years' income. But even if the price of a 10-acre place with a pool, paddock, and tennis courts looks to you like pocket money, you might be well advised to consider financing. After all, you can't have so much money that you wouldn't mind saving a little.

THE ADVANTAGES OF FINANCING

The reason a loan may be advantageous even if you don't really need it is leverage — essentially, the ability to make a profit while investing other people's money rather than your own. Let's say you want to buy a $100,000 home and — thanks to the generosity of Uncle Dean, the leek king — you have $100,000. If you have that kind of cash lying about, you're probably in a pretty high tax bracket — perhaps 50 percent — and the deduction you make for your real estate taxes is welcome. You're a clever dude, so the place appreciates; in five years it may be worth $125,000. That means that in five years your $100,000 investment has produced a return of 25 percent — the growth in the value of the home — plus the half of the real estate taxes that you saved on your income tax returns. Not bad at all.

But suppose you'd found a 90 percent mortgage, one that provided you with $90,000 of the $100,000 purchase price. That would make your investment only $10,000. You could invest your remaining $90,000 elsewhere, earning who knows how much. You could subtract from your income taxes half of the mortgage interest payments as well as half the real estate taxes.

And the $25,000 increase in the value of the place would represent a return of 250 percent, not 25 percent, on your investment. Not bad? That's downright good, if you'll pardon the strong language.

Congress flirts passionately if unpredictably with the idea of curbing the deduction for mortgage interest and real estate taxes, which could throw a wrench in the works here. Still, there's something to be said for a return of 250 percent, tax savings aside. Beyond that, your payments to the mortgage lender will be made over the life of the loan in dollars that, if history is any teacher, will constantly diminish in value. If you get a 30-year loan in 1985 dollars, you'll make the final payment in 2015 dollars, and you know what they're likely to be worth.

Mortgage lenders have been busy in recent years developing ways to neutralize some of those advantages for the borrower, but the principle, one hardly lost upon professional real estate men, is clear: Debt can be a tool as well as a burden. Which is not to say that debt cannot be lethal; dynamite is a tool, too.

There are situations in which the smallest possible down payment and the largest possible loan are especially advantageous: if you're an active investor likely to find other places for your money that will return more than a mortgage costs; if you're likely to sell the place and move within a relatively short time, especially if the mortgage is assumable — that is, can be picked up by the buyer; or if your tax situation is such that the extra deduction for interest payments will represent major savings.

All of this financial derring-do has a major disadvantage, of course. If you keep the home until the mortgage runs its full course, the total price, including interest payments, will be nothing less than astounding. If this place looks with reasonable certainty like your last stop, think carefully before you take a bigger than necessary mortgage. Do the same if your income is subject to wide variation or if you're facing retirement before the mortgage expires. And be aware now — as you inevitably will be later — that anything you don't pay up front in the form of a down payment will come out of your hide, with interest, in the monthly payments. There is, as someone once said, no free lunch.

SOURCES OF MORTGAGES

By far the most common form of home financing is the mortgage loan supplied by a lending institution. The majority of such mortgages are made by savings and loan associations, also known as building and loan associations, and, in some areas, by savings banks. They are also often available from commercial banks, insurance companies, mortgage companies, union and other pension funds, college and university endowments, and even credit unions.

Savings and loan associations and savings banks tend to be specialists in mortgage lending; it's their principal business. But they also tend to be fair-weather friends because they are dependent upon their depositors for the money they put into mortgages. When interest rates for other investments rise, depositors withdraw their savings and go elsewhere. That means the savings and loans may not have money for mortgages when times are bad and interest rates are high. In good times, though, when interest rates are within reason, the savings and loan or the savings bank is the most likely source of a mortgage. Commercial banks may have more money, but they tend to be more conservative than the so-called thrift institutions when it comes to mortgages, at least in part because they are more interested in the businessmen who are their best customers than they are in the little guys who borrow only rarely and barely manage to keep their checking accounts solvent.

Insurance companies, pension funds, and endowments do make mortgages, but they usually look for big investments because it's cheaper and easier to put a million clams in one office building than to divide them up among a hundred bungalows, each of which represents another small problem. If an insurance company will make a mortgage, it may offer a low interest rate but require that you buy mortgage life insurance — insurance that will pay off the loan if you die — with premiums that would knock your hat off. Check insurance rates elsewhere before you plunge.

If you already have a good deal of insurance, it may be cheaper to borrow against its cash value than to get a mortgage; but that can leave you dangerously short of insurance coverage, so proceed with caution.

Because insurance companies, pension funds, and other large investors are interested in committing vast sums at one fell swoop rather than in operating retail businesses, they often place their residential mortgages through mortgage companies or mortgage brokers. Though many real estate brokers are also mortgage brokers, the two terms are not synonymous. A real estate broker arranges sales by getting sellers and buyers together. A mortgage broker arranges financing by getting lenders and borrowers together. A mortgage company often functions as a mortgage broker and in addition "services" the loans it places — that is, collects the payments, keeps track of the defaults, and chases the deadbeats — in return for a fee paid by the lender. Some mortgage companies also function as mortgage bankers, investing their own funds as well as those of others in mortgages they arrange.

The mortgage broker should probably not be your first choice when you go in search of financing, for, like everyone else, he wants to make a living. He charges a fee for his services, and if you can avoid paying it by finding a mortgage without him, you might as well. In some cases, however, they've got you before you start. Some lenders charge a "mortgage origination fee" whether or not a broker is involved in the deal, but share the fee with the broker if there is one.

When mortgage money is hard to find, the broker may more than earn his fee. Many lenders depend upon brokers they know, relying on the brokers' judgment to bring them only good risks. That could mean that your application will get a more sympathetic hearing if it's submitted through a broker. Beyond that, when money is tight, the mortgage broker or company may represent the only way to get a mortgage backed by the Veterans Administration or the Federal Housing Administration because the broker will be familiar with all the red tape involved in dealing with such government agencies.

If you decide that a broker is the way to go — you can find them listed in the Yellow Pages of the telephone directory under "Mortgages" or get the recommendations of your real estate broker or lawyer — remember that a broker is paid only if he succeeds in arranging a deal. You can therefore shop around and pay only the one who gets you the best terms. You might also be well advised to have your lawyer draw up a simple contract outlining your relationship with the mortgage broker, what you expect him to do for you, and when and how much you will pay him.

A relatively new device that may ease your mortgage shopping chore is a computer network designed to tell you in a trice what sort of financing is available and where. Some real estate brokers have terminals plugged into such networks, and the services they offer — along with the fees they charge — vary as widely as a prima donna's mood. Some will merely tell you what is being offered by the lenders who have themselves paid a fee to advertise on the network. Others will "prequalify" you, massaging much of the data about your financial situation and searching for the deal that will best meet your needs. The effectiveness of the network is, of course, limited by the number of lenders who join it, and you should be aware going in that for reasons of competition and tradition many lenders are reluctant to sign up. So you may be better off searching for yourself.

In any case, though the vast majority of home purchases are financed with loans from such institutions as savings and loan associations or banks, any source of sufficient money will suffice. If you have well-to-do friends or relatives, they may be more likely sources of financing than any institution. If your aged relatives don't happen to be wading around in spare $20 bills but you already own a home, you may be able to use it for the financing through a trade-in program, an arrangement under which a builder or a broker will give you some specified period after you sign up for a new home — say, 60 or 90 days — to sell the old one, and then will take it off your hands for 85 or 90 percent of the appraised value if you've been unable to sell. The big disadvantage here is obvious: The broker or builder is promising to pay you a reduced price for your old home. Less obvious is that the broker or builder probably won't consider taking your old home in trade if its value even approaches that of the new home or if the old place needs major improvement or repairs. On the other hand, trading does relieve you of the hassle of selling the old dump, and if you're building a new home, it guarantees that you'll have a place to live until it's finished. It may also save you some expenses while the old place is vacant awaiting sale, and it may save you some commissions and other closing costs. The opportunities for less-than-ethical dealings are rife here, however, so if you're considering a trade, ask the builder or broker how many such deals he's made and for whom. Then call some of the old customers to see whether they're still pleased. Get your own appraisal of the old home and have your lawyer read everything carefully before you sign.

Even though you don't own a home to use for financing, the seller does, and you may be able to borrow from him the funds you need. In general, there are two ways to do so — by using the seller's own money or by using the money he has previously borrowed on his home.

PURCHASE-MONEY MORTGAGES AND ASSUMPTIONS

The device through which you can use the seller's own resources is known as a purchase-money mortgage. Under it, the seller complements or even takes the place of the bank or savings and loan association, becoming the lender. In exchange for a mortgage note, he allows you to defer some of the purchase price and make regular payments on it over a specified period. Sometimes, purchase-money mortgages are offered on older properties that the sellers own free and clear — that is, without mortgages — and that may need extensive remodeling. The need for repair may reduce the value of the place and make it difficult to get regular bank financing. Such mortgages are also common on overpriced properties because a traditional lender will probably object to the inflated price. The moral is simple enough: Be doubly careful about appraisal and inspection if a purchase-money mortgage is in the offing.

But purchase-money financing is not by any means limited to such troublesome situations. When inflation or high interest rates have made selling difficult or when institutional mortgages are in short supply, purchase-money loans may be the only way. Indeed, during the worst of times you may be well-advised to look first for homes on which some seller financing is available, then decide which of them is most attractive. You may be the one promoting with the seller the idea of a purchase-money mortgage. And it may not be a bad idea. After all, the seller is not likely to charge origination or processing fees like a big lender. He probably will not require a title search or title insurance (though you should get both for your own protection). Moreover, the seller can probably earn a reasonable return on his investment in the home and still charge a lower interest rate than a big institutional lender. If he snorts at that suggestion, remind him that he doesn't have the overhead of a bank or a savings and loan. He isn't, for example, offering teddy bears and clock radios to anybody with $500 in a sock.

Not all purchase-money mortgages are on properties owned free and clear by their sellers. Some are used in addition to institutional loans that are not large enough to make the purchase possible, thus becoming "junior" or "second" mortgages, a class of financing with some serious pitfalls of its own.

A purchase-money mortgage is most often secondary financing when the buyer is assuming the seller's existing mortgage — in effect, picking up the payments. Such assumptions are the means through which you can use the money the seller has previously borrowed on the home. Assuming a mortgage — with or without a purchase-money loan — has some distinct advantages for the buyer. To begin with, some of the fees lenders charge for new loans — so-called closing or settlement charges — may be eliminated in an assumption because it is not, after all, a new loan. That may also mean that there will be less paperwork and delay in processing the thing. The interest rate on a loan made some years ago may be lower than that prevailing today (though the lender may retain the right to adjust the interest rate in the event of an assumption), and the total interest payments over the life of the loan will be lower if only because it is likely to have fewer years to run than a new mortgage. Compute the true interest rate, however, using the outstanding balance as the principal and the remaining life of the loan as the term.

In general, you can probably figure that an assumption will be a good deal if the mortgage has 20 years or more to run and represents 75 percent or more of the selling price. Even if it doesn't meet those criteria, it may be advisable if it's part of a very attractive package, or if times are such that there's simply no other way to obtain financing. Obviously, if you're planning to assume the seller's mortgage, you should find out how much rope the lender will allow you. That information should be available in an "estoppel letter," a document that sets out the conditions upon which a loan is assumable, the time remaining in its term, the outstanding balance, the interest rate, the monthly payment, and the amount in escrow for taxes and insurance. You will also want to know about any special fees the lender charges in an assumption and whether the original agreement allowed for the alteration of some conditions — say, the interest rate — in the event of assumption. The extra charges may parade under any number of names — origination fees, prepayment penalties, points — but what they're called is immaterial. It's what they total that counts, and you'd better find out (from the lender, not the seller) what the total is before you agree to take on the loan.

All this, of course, leaps merrily to the conclusion that you will be able to find an assumable loan in the first place, and that's an increasingly difficult quest. Lenders, burned by volatile interest rates in the past, are extremely reluctant to allow assumptions, and virtually every "conventional" loan — every loan that has no government backing — written since the early 1970's contains a "due-on-sale" clause. This is a provision that the entire balance outstanding on the loan is due if the home is sold. Forget about assumptions, in other words.

And if you can forget about assumptions (except for some loans backed by the federal government, about which more in due course), you can pretend you never heard about two variations on that theme — a purchase "subject to" the mortgage and a wraparound mortgage. In either case, the seller's mortgage remains in place, and he retains responsibility for it. If you buy "subject to" that loan, you make the monthly payments directly to the lender or to the seller, who forwards them to the lender. That may sound good to you, but it's not likely to mesmerize the seller, and certainly not the lender. Neither will a wraparound mortgage, a purchase-money mortgage that's larger than the original loan and probably bears a higher interest rate. The seller's original loan remains, and the new one "wraps around" it. You make monthly payments to the seller on the wraparound loan, which in some places may be called an all-inclusive trust deed, and he continues to pay on the original one, pocketing the difference. The wraparound mortgage is possible, obviously, only if the underlying first mortgage is truly assumable; have your lawyer confirm that it's so before you commit yourself. And if all else works out, press for an agreement under which you can make your monthly payment to the institution holding the first mortgage, which can then send the seller his share. That eliminates the possibility that the seller might make off with the whole nut, leaving you to face foreclosure.

Another form of seller financing is the land lease, an arrangement that can reduce both the down payment and the monthly outlays for the purchase. The land lease, which has been around since colonial times and is popular in Hawaii and Maryland, among other places, allows you to purchase a home while merely leasing the land under it. The agreement is usually written for a long term — perhaps 70 years — but the buyer often has the right to buy the land earlier. Some of the rent may be credited toward the purchase price, and some developers who sell homes this way write periodic price increases into their agreements to encourage the ultimate sale of the land. In other cases, owners may have very little interest in selling the land, hoping to retain it — and the income it provides — more or less forever. If you can, get a lease that gives you the ultimate right to purchase, even if that right is deferred for 20 years. Failing that, be sure the agreement provides for the renewal of the lease.

In theory, the seller might also agree to lease you the whole works — not just the land, but the building as well — for a specified term with the understanding that you will buy it by the end of the term. This arrangement, known as a lease-option or lease with an option to buy, will in any circumstances allow you to save up a down payment if you don't have one, and in times of tight money, it gives you the flexibility to wait until interest rates drop before you shop for a mortgage. It can also be useful if you need the equity from one home to purchase another. You can lease with an option, then exercise the option as soon as you have the money from the old place.

Of course, like everything else connected with real estate, it's not quite as simple as that. There are, first of all, two versions of this arrangement, the lease-option and lease-purchase. Under a lease-purchase, you are committed to buy at a specified price, but the sale is delayed for some agreed-upon time. If you fail to perform, the seller can sue. Under a lease-option, on the other hand, you are not committed to buy; you can walk away from the deal without fear of retribution, though it will probably cost you a few bucks.

In the typical lease-option, the buyer offers a nonrefundable "consideration" — say, $1,000 — for the option to buy at a given price. He also agrees to pay a specified monthly rent until the option is exercised. Either the "consideration" or the rent or both may be credited toward the purchase price if the option is exercised. If the "buyer" decides that he does not want to become a buyer after all, he can walk away, but he loses the fee he paid for the option and all the rent payments.

Options of this sort normally run for one to three years, and they are most often used when the home in question is vacant and has been on the market for a long time. If a lease-option interests you, try to ensure that you'll get credit for both the "consideration" and the rent when you actually buy. If the "consideration" is more than about $2,000, insist upon the right to assign the lease — sell it to someone else — if you decide during the term not to exercise the option. And remember that until you exercise the option you will probably enjoy none of the usual tax breaks associated with owning your home. It is the seller who will be paying the interest and taxes and taking the deductions.

Obviously, a lease-option demands a detailed agreement that covers everything a sales contract would mention and then some. It should specify who will be responsible for taxes, insurance, and repairs. It should state what will be credited toward the purchase price and what the price will be. It should provide for the extension of the lease if disaster strikes. Title searches, surveys, and termite inspections are just as important here as they are in a more traditional sale. And careful legal advice is perhaps more important.

That goes double if the sale you have in mind involves a long-term lease — one with a term of more than a few years. Some such arrangements are simply installment sales disguised as leases to get around a "due-on-sale" clause in a mortgage. It's hardly surprising that lenders have noticed, and they're not smiling. Be careful.

THE COMPANY AND THE GOVERNMENT

In the event that the seller is as strapped as you and your relatives and therefore unable to help finance your purchase, there may be some give at the office. If your move is a result of a company transfer, of course, your employer is to blame for all this hassle and can expect to be leaned on a bit. Some companies are very generous, paying all moving expenses, making allowances for decorating the new place, and even kicking in to ease the shock of higher interest rates and inflated home prices. Some will, in extreme cases, go the whole route and give a transferred employee — or perhaps a newly hired one — a mortgage at a favorable rate. Not many companies will go so far, but it's not unheard of. And even though you're not being transferred, if you're a valued employee, your company may be willing to do a little something in a monetary way to keep you happy. It's worth an inquiry, in any case.

Government agencies are also worth an inquiry, especially if your income is low or if you're buying in a rural area or the inner city. State and local housing agencies sometimes make mortgage loans at below-market interest rates to low-income and moderate-income buyers. Some lenders and builders will accept "sweat equity" — your labor rather than your money — for as much as half the down payment. You may have to demonstrate your ability, and your work will probably have to pass an inspection, but if you have the skill, the tools, and the time, you may save yourself a great deal or find yourself in a better home than you could otherwise afford. Some local redevelopment agencies have sweat equity programs that offer vocational training as well as monetary relief. They are most likely to be found in inner city neighborhoods.

Also to be found in the cities are urban renewal areas, neighborhoods in which various levels of government are attempting to join forces to turn decaying blocks into lively and attractive places. In many such areas, a gutted or neglected building can be purchased from a government agency very cheaply, and public aid in the form of a loan or a mortgage-interest subsidy may be available to help with the rehabilitation. In exchange for such help, the buyer usually must agree to fix the place up and to live in it for a minimum number of years. The problem with such projects is red tape. It may take two years to get your application approved and obtain title to the site. There may be monthly hassles over the inspection of the rehabilitation work, and once you're finished you may live in no-man's land for 10 years before the area starts to turn into what you'd call a neighborhood. If it still sounds good, look in the telephone book for the local redevelopment authority or urban renewal office to get information. Also check with the local office of the U.S. Department of Housing and Urban Development and with lenders in transitional areas.

If you're buying in a rural area rather than in the city, the governmental agency to consult may be the Farmers Home Administration. FmHA, as it's known in real estate circles, makes loans in rural areas, and it has special sweat-equity and low-income programs. Don't get your hopes up too high, however, because FmHA means what it says when it limits itself to rural areas and small towns, and it specializes in helping people with small incomes buy, build, or rehabilitate small homes. Moreover, dealing with it can be a memorably frustrating exercise in red tape, inefficiency, and delay. If you think you're up to it, you can get all the particulars at the FmHA office in the county where you're planning to live or by writing: Farmers Home Administration, Department of Agriculture, Washington, D.C. 20250.

THE VA AND FHA

There are two other government agencies that are far more active than the FmHA in the residential mortgage field, though they make almost no loans themselves. They are the Federal Housing Administration, popularly known as FHA, and the Veterans Administration, or VA. They lend virtually no money, but they do provide the lender with some assurance that his loan will be paid back. That assurance reduces the lender's risk, which allows him to make larger loans or charge less interest for them. At least, that's the theory.

The Veterans Administration provides mortgage help for veterans of the armed forces whose eligibility is based upon the length and dates of their service. Details can be obtained from any VA office or by writing: Veterans Administration, Washington, D.C. 20420.

In general, the VA guarantees repayment of a certain proportion of the loan, up to a specified maximum. The rules change from time to time, but there is usually a relatively low ceiling on the amount guaranteed, so VA mortgages, also known as GI loans, are most common on homes in the lower price ranges. From the lender's point of view, the VA guarantee is as good as a down payment, or at least a partial down payment, so you may have to produce little or no cash up front, and the VA doesn't charge you for this insurance. The first step in applying for a VA loan is to hunt through your old duffle bag and find your discharge or separation papers. They're necessary to get a certificate of eligibility, for which you can apply to the VA itself or through a bank or savings and loan that's willing to make GI mortgages.

Once you have the certificate of eligibility, you'll have to apply for the mortgage itself. The lender will want the usual information — financial statement, credit record, bank references, employment history, and so forth —and you'll have to promise that you intend to live in the place and will not discriminate when you sell it. You'll have to pay for an appraisal, which will produce a certificate of reasonable value, an estimate of a fair price for the home. That estimate will determine the size of the VA's guarantee.

If the purchase price you've agreed to pay is equal to or less than the appraisal set in the certificate of reasonable value, the VA will require no down payment, though the lender may. If the purchase price is higher than the official appraisal, you'll be allowed to pay the difference in cash, but you'll have to sign a statement saying that it was paid from your own assets. The VA will not allow a mortgage higher than the appraised value, and it is extremely wary of second mortgages to make up the difference.

The Veterans Administration may not allow the borrower to pay discount "points" (fees added by the lender to increase his return despite interest rate limits), termite inspection fees, or "truth-in-lending" statement fees, among other things. Check with the nearest VA office for the latest version of what you can and cannot pay.

Beyond the low down payment, GI loans have some other advantages.

Among them are the agency's provisions for mortgage assumptions. There is no penalty for paying the loan off early, and once a veteran has obtained a GI mortgage, it can be assumed by anyone he accepts when he decides to sell. The new owner need not be a veteran, and there are no minimum standards regarding his employment and credit history or his financial condition. There is, though, a small hook here. If the new owner defaults on the mortgage and the VA has to pay the lender, the original borrower will be liable for the agency's losses. He can escape that liability only by getting from the VA at the time of the assumption a written release that makes the new owner liable. Before the VA issues such a release, it will want a credit and financial statement from the new owner, who will have to pay for a credit report.

If you're using a GI loan to finance the construction of a new home, the VA may require the builder to warrant that the place was built in substantial conformity with plans and specifications approved by the agency, and if its inspectors oversaw the construction, the VA may reimburse you under certain circumstances for major flaws the inspectors failed to uncover and prevent.

In most cases, a mortgage guaranteed by the Veterans Administration can be used to buy a condominium unit, though the VA will probably want it to be in a previously approved project, and it can usually be used for the purchase of a mobile home as well, though the interest rates and other terms may be different from those for conventional homes.

Finally, the Veterans Administration does provide direct mortgage loans as well as guarantees, but only in times and places where private funds are genuinely unavailable. Those are rare cases, indeed. And whatever the VA is providing, you can be sure that it will arrive with more strings than a harp.

In that regard as well as others, VA loans are like mortgages insured by the Federal Housing Administration. It may take two months to find out whether either agency will deign to do business with you. They will be two months filled with forms, documents, and certificates, with excuses, delays, and confusion. If you make a mistake in filling out any of those forms or submitting any supporting documents, of course, you can expect to go back and start over. You will not find most lenders terrifically supportive, since they are less than anxious to get involved in any of this red tape. If you have to resort to a mortgage broker, you will also have to pay his fee. And the seller may — with some reason — insist upon a contingency letting him off the hook if you cannot get the necessary approvals within a specified time.

For all those problems, there are advantages, however. The FHA offers the lender insurance protection that usually allows him to increase the size of the loan on a given home, thus reducing the down payment. It also bars prepayment penalties, insists that loans be assumable, requires certain minimal construction standards, provides for standardized appraisal techniques, and insures that real estate taxes and insurance premiums will be included in your monthly mortgage payment, which may make life somewhat more convenient if no cheaper.

To apply for an FHA mortgage, go to a lender who makes such loans; find the ones that will make them by calling up and asking. You'll have to submit an application together with a credit report, a financial statement, and verifications — acknowledgments from your bank and employer, for example, that your statements of employment and financial history are accurate. You'll also have to pay some fees, perhaps an appraisal fee and a credit report fee; the amounts vary. The lender submits to the FHA all the data you and he have collected, then the FHA appraises the home, examines your background, and sends the lender one of two documents: a rejection if either you or the property is not up to snuff or a commitment if both you and the home qualify. The commitment will be good for a limited period and can be extended upon payment of a fee.

The FHA commitment will outline the terms and conditions for insuring the loan, and it may require that some repairs or improvements be made. If it does, you'll have to request a compliance report so the FHA can go back and inspect the new work before it issues its final approval and the money is made available to you. If repairs are required, the FHA will allow you to supply sweat equity — either labor or materials — in exchange for reasonable credit toward the down payment or the closing costs. The FHA will decide the value of your contribution and set a limit on the credit. The work must be completed and inspected before the closing, and you'd better not start it before you have the FHA commitment or you'll run the risk of losing everything you've put into it.

Generally, if the lender rejects you at the outset, before the matter goes to the FHA, you'll get your fees back. But if the FHA rejects you, you'll probably lose whatever service fees you have paid. Once a commitment is issued, it is the property of the lender who submitted the application. If you get a commitment and then decide to go to a different lender, you may have to pay a transfer charge to the lender who did all the initial paperwork.

The FHA has more rules than an elementary-school principal, covering such things as the maximum loan it will insure, the maximum loan-to-value ratio (the relationship between the amount of the loan and the price of the home), the minimum down payment, and the insurance fee the borrower must pay in addition to the interest rate. One or another of the regulations is always changing, so it will pay you to consult your nearest FHA office or write: Federal Housing Administration, Department of Housing and Urban Development, 451 Seventh Street SW, Washington, D.C. 20410.

The FHA doesn't much care what you pay for a home; it looks only at the amount of loan it's called upon to insure. The insurance will cover only the appraisal the FHA sets on the home or the maximum allowable loan-to-value ratio for the selling price, whichever is lower. And the appraisal you get from the FHA is not the same thing you get from the VA. The VA asks an appraiser to determine the fair market value of a home; the FHA asks an appraiser to estimate replacement value, or what it would cost to duplicate the home now.

The result of that FHA policy tends to be high appraisals for lower-priced homes and — perhaps because the process minimizes social or other factors that contribute to some higher market values — relatively modest appraisals for homes in the upper price ranges. The advantage the appraisal method offers to the potential buyer of an expensive home is neutralized, however, by the generally modest ceilings the FHA puts on the amount it will insure.

The FHA, which gets involved in the financing of everything from urban renewal to mobile homes, will often include in its loan calculations the closing costs customarily paid by the buyer in the area. The buyer need not plan to occupy the home himself to get an FHA loan, but an owner-occupant will be allowed a higher loan-to-value ratio. The maximum permissible loan will also be reduced if the home was not built to FHA specifications, unless it has been in existence for a year or more when the FHA enters the picture.

Time was when both the FHA and the VA closely regulated the maximum interest rate on loans they backed, and when market rates rose above those limits lenders often "discounted" the mortgages — that is, deducted from the amount provided the borrower enough to bring the lender's return up to about what it would have been at the market interest rate. Needless to say, times are achanging. The feds are less interested in setting limits on interest rates, so lenders are less quick to extract discounts. But they still exist, so you ought to understand them.

Such discounts are most commonly referred to as "points," with each point equal to 1 percent of the face amount of the loan. If, in other words, you borrow $100,000 with a discount of 5 points, you will get only $95,000, though you'll have to repay $100,000 and your interest payments will be calculated on $100,000.

The rules often restrict the payment of discount points by the buyer, though the lender can charge a loan origination fee or a service fee that does not exceed certain limits. Since the seller is likely to be stuck with the points in such a deal, he may resist the idea of a government-backed loan, and if he thinks one is inevitable, he will probably increase his asking price to cover the extra cost. The lender can charge the borrower discount points when the financing covers the construction of a new home for the borrower's occupancy or when the borrower is buying property from a government agency prohibited by law from paying a mortgage discount.

There are special complications if the object of a VA or FHA loan is the construction of a new home. The first step is to apply for and receive a commitment for the guarantee or insurance on the permanent financing, the mortgage that will be in force when the home is complete. Next you'll have to find — probably through a mortgage broker or banker — a lender willing to make a commitment for the permanent financing on the basis of the commitment for government backing. Finally, you'll have to find a lender willing, on the basis of both those commitments, to make a construction loan, a relatively short-term loan that will finance the actual building process and that will be paid off when the permanent mortgage is issued. During the construction, the government agency involved will probably require inspections at specified intervals to insure that the work conforms to its standards. And be forewarned: Bureaucrats who spend most of their time enforcing thick sheafs of rules and regulations are not noted for their eagerness to finance radical or wildly imaginative designs. If you're planning to build something unusual, you'll probably need conventional financing — that is, financing handled entirely in the private sector.

CONVENTIONAL MORTGAGES

Whatever you're planning to buy or build, the chances are that your financing will be "conventional" in the sense that it won't have government backing. And whatever its source, the chances are that it will take a fairly standard form: A loan as security for the repayment of which you will execute a mortgage (a pledge of the property) and a bond or note (a pledge of your own personal liability). The note is an acknowledgment that you are justly indebted to the lender and a promise to repay as scheduled. The mortgage is a document that can be recorded and that creates a lien on the property so that if you go into default, or fail to meet the terms of your agreement, the property can be sold and the lender reimbursed. The process of taking the property and selling it is called foreclosure.

Notice that in the standard deal the lender's recourse is not limited to foreclosure if you fail to repay. You have also signed a note creating a personal liability for the debt. If the property is sold but the sale does not fully reimburse the lender, you're obligated to repay the rest. Moreover, if you're going to buy a place jointly with someone else — a husband or wife, perhaps — the note will probably make you liable "jointly and severally" for the debt, meaning that each of you is liable for the whole thing and the lender can collect from any or all of you. If the lender sticks you with the whole nut, it will be your problem to chase your partner or partners and collect their share.

And that's not the half of it. The typical note or bond provides that the lender may call the entire balance of the loan if the borrower is delinquent in the payment of any installment or of taxes, assessments, or insurance premiums; if the borrower fails to assign (that is, make the lender a beneficiary of) and deliver to the lender a fire insurance policy; if the borrower so much as threatens to alter, demolish, or remove a building on the property; or if the borrower fails to execute an estoppel certificate (a waiver of the right to dispute the terms of the outstanding loan, a document usually sought by a lender who wants to sell a mortgage to some other institution). The mortgage itself, as distinguished from the note, will probably require that you pay all the legal fees in the event of foreclosure; that improvements you may add to the place after you buy it will become part of the collateral for the loan; and that you will keep the place in good repair and in compliance with all local codes.

Obviously, lenders are not taking any unnecessary risks here, which is not unreasonable. In the vast majority of cases, they never have to exercise all the rights they reserve to themselves. And that's just as well, for if the lender is forced to use his ultimate remedy, foreclosure, nobody benefits. It is a complex and expensive process for lender and borrower alike, one to be avoided if at all possible.

VARIETIES OF MORTGAGES

Mind-boggling as those complications may seem, they apply only to the basic mortgage loan. Beyond that, all manner of variations are possible. There are infinite ways to adjust the interest or the payment; there are mortgages that pay themselves off completely and mortgages that don't; there are mortgages designed solely to finance the construction of new homes and mortgages designed to finance the furnishings as well as the purchase of the home itself.

Given the reluctance of many lenders to make FHA or VA loans, there is private mortgage insurance that serves much the same purpose as a government guarantee or insurance. The processing is usually faster and more efficient for private mortgage insurance than for the government variety, but in many other ways it is similar. Both you and the home you hope to purchase will have to qualify for the insurance; there will be a small premium added to the monthly mortgage payment; the insurance will cover only the part of the loan that represents the greatest risk for the lender — say, the top 20 percent — and the effect of the insurance will probably be to encourage the lender to allow a higher loan-to-value ratio than he would without it. In some plans, the insurance premiums end when the covered portion of the loan is paid off, but in others they continue for the life of the mortgage. It is therefore wise to shop a bit before leaping in, and the way to start is with phone calls to a few lenders to ask what they offer.

The mortgage you find will probably be an amortizing or self-liquidating loan — that is, one on which the principal is repaid along with the interest in installments over a long period, typically 20 to 40 years. The most common variety was until recently the level-payment or constant-payment loan. In it, the monthly payment remains constant over the life of the loan with a gradually growing proportion devoted to principal repayment as the interest on the balance declines. There is a variation on that arrangement known as a straight principal reduction mortgage: You make fixed installment payments toward the principal, with added payments for the interest on the outstanding balance. Since the balance is always declining, the interest drops, too, and with it the size of your payments.

But, especially if you're young, your income will probably rise over the life of the mortgage, making larger payments easier to handle in the later years. Ever alert to your needs and the opportunity to make another buck, the mortgage industry has developed the graduated-payment mortgage, on which the payments are low at first but rise over time, usually leveling off after a certain number of years. In the early stage, you are borrowing money at less than the market interest rate. But the interest you don't pay in the early years is added to the outstanding principal, and later on you pay more than the market rate. The net result of all this fiscal legerdemain — sometimes also known as a deferred-interest loan — is that you will pay more over-all than you would with a level-payment loan. Moreover, adding unpaid interest to the outstanding principal may create negative amortization — the balance may be growing faster than you're paying it off. So if you sell the place under certain circumstances, you may owe more than you borrowed originally, perhaps even more than your selling price. Because of that risk and the possibility that your income may not rise as fast as you expected, the graduated-payment mortgage is a more dangerous proposition than the level-payment loan.

It makes the lenders a little nervous, too, because they have to wait so long to see the balance begin to drop. Even more alert to their own needs than to yours, they have therefore come up with a variation on the graduated-payment loan called the growth-equity mortgage. Under this arrangement, the initial payments are about what they would be for a level-payment loan but rise gradually so the lender is paid off quickly. This system offers some advantage to the lender, obviously, but little if anything to the borrower.

The graduated-payment loan has special attractions for builders of new homes who can lure unwary buyers by advertising very low monthly payments without explaining too clearly that those payments are going to go up, perhaps sharply, after a few years. Be careful in dealing with a builder, therefore, to understand whether you're discussing a level-payment or a graduated-payment mortgage. And if the payments will go up, be careful to determine when and how much.

As insidious as all this fancy financial footwork may sound, there is an even more risky variation on it—the graduated-payment adjustable mortgage. Not only do the payments rise on a predictable schedule, as in any graduated-payment mortgage, but in addition the interest rate changes from time to time with the market. It takes something less than mathematical genius to conclude that negative amortization, exacerbated by a sharply rising interest rate, can produce disaster.

This sort of interest-adjustment provision has become virtually standard in the mortgage industry since the late 1970's. Through it, lenders have been able to shift from themselves to borrowers one of the big risks of their business — the risk that interest rates will rise during the term of the loan. You will hear these mortgages described as variable-rate, flexible-rate, or adjustable-rate loans. They were not designed with your concerns in mind, but they may be all you can get and presumably they're better than nothing.

There are dozens of variations on the theme — one estimate is that well over 100 forms of mortgage are in common use — but generally the agreement specifies that the interest rate will be reviewed at certain intervals — every six months, perhaps, or every year — and adjusted according to changes in the prevailing market rate.

You should shop for a mortgage in which changes in the interest rate are tied to some index — not a regional index that a large lender may be able to influence, but a national one that reflects changes in long-term rather than short-term rates and that is widely published so you can verify it. If the index has dropped when your interest rate is up for review, the lender should be required to lower your rate. If the index has risen, he should be permitted (but not necessarily required) to raise your rate accordingly. You should ask to see a chart or graph detailing the performance of the index over the last ten years.

Among the indexes commonly used for adjustable mortgages are the national average of mortgage rates, which is published by the Federal Home Loan Bank Board, and the rates for one-year and three-year Treasury securities. The rates for the Treasury instruments are more volatile than the mortgage rate average—that is, they respond more quickly to changes in the market. So at a time of rising interest rates, a mortgage tied to the Treasury securities will probably hurt you faster than one tied to average mortgage rates. But when the cost of money is generally falling, a loan tied to Treasury instruments will provide faster relief, too.

And be aware that the initial interest rate on an adjustable mortgage is far less important than the rate after the loan has "matured" a bit, as the bankers say. As a sales tool, lenders have been known to advertise rates far below the market, mentioning only in the smallest of type (if at all) that those rates will prevail for only a limited time. Find out what the rate will be after the first adjustment or two. And find out what the lender's "margin" will be—what sort of cushion it will add to the index. If the margin is more than about two-and-a-half percentage points, you should probably keep shopping.

Then negotiate hard for as many "caps" or limits on change as you can get. There are several kinds, the most valuable of which limit changes in the interest rate. If you think you'll sell the home within a few years, try first for a cap on the increase the lender can get in any given year. If you think you'll have this mortgage for the full term, the most important cap is probably the cumulative one — a limit on the over-all rate increase during the life of the loan. If you can get both caps (why not?) so much the better. You can also get a cap on the monthly payment, a guarantee that it won't rise beyond a certain point, no matter what happens to interest rates, but a cap on the rate is more valuable. If there is a limit on the size of the monthly payment but not on the interest rate, the lender will probably extend the term of the loan (that is, require more payments over a longer time) whenever the rate goes up. And a term longer than 25 or 30 years generally benefits nobody but the lender. So do what you can to avoid having to extend the term.

And do whatever you must to avoid negative amortization. If it is a possibility, the lender may want a cap of his own, a limit on the size of the outstanding balance — perhaps 125 percent of the amount originally borrowed. If interest rates rise to the point where you exceed that limit, you could find yourself forced to sell the place just to handle the mortgage. Not much future in that.

Any truly adjustable mortgage should be assumable; another buyer who otherwise qualifies should be able to take it over if you sell. And there should be no prepayment penalty, no extra fee if you pay the thing off early.

The mortgage agreement should provide that the lender must serve notice of any change in the interest rate and offer you three options: paying the higher rate, extending the term, or refinancing and paying the loan off.

Before you settle on a specific loan, ask for a "worst-case" projection, an estimate of your payments if everything rose to the allowable limit. Then think carefully about your income prospects before you sign up.

One form of variable-rate loan is the convertible adjustable mortgage, which specifies that at several points during its life you will have the opportunity to convert it to a fixed-rate level-payment mortgage. One way or another, you will probably pay for that privilege.

Another variation is the rollover or renegotiable-rate mortgage. This is essentially a short-term loan (terms of three to five years are common) that can be "rolled over" or renewed when it expires. If it is truly renegotiable, you will have to haggle with the lender every few years over what the new rate will be. You're probably better advised to negotiate at the outset an agreement that ties changes in the rate to an index. Since the payments on these mortgages are usually calculated on the over-all term after several renewals, perhaps 30 or 40 years, you still owe a wad of money — a "balloon" — when the first loan ends after three or five years. It is therefore essential to have from the beginning a guarantee that the loan will be renewed and that only the interest rate will be subject to change or negotiation.

Most mortgages that require balloons offer no guarantee that the lender will renew at the end of the term, so they represent a considerable risk beyond that normally embodied in an amortizing loan. Such mortgages are common on commercial property and on cooperative buildings, but since the Depression, they have rarely been used for most types of ownership housing. The type widely used before the Depression, which saw millions of owners lose their homes in foreclosure, was the term mortgage, on which the installments cover only the interest, with all of the principal due in one payment — a balloon — when the loan matures.

A balloon mortgage is a risky proposition, since you're rarely assured that you will have a way to carry on at the end of the term. Some experts say that if you have one you should be sure to pay off at least 60 percent of the principal before the loan runs out so you can be sure to get a new loan that will cover your needs when the old one matures. That's fine advice, but few balloon mortgages require such amortization, and some may even prohibit it (though you're still free to make regular deposits or investments elsewhere during the life of the mortgage so that at the end of its term you have enough set aside to assure refinancing). Obviously, the longer the term the better.

Balloon mortgages, risky as they are, may be all that's available if you're buying a place that needs extensive renovation or is in an area that lenders consider too shaky to support the usual long-term, self-amortizing mortgage. The balloon loan is normally a short-term affair — anything from six months to five or ten years. If renovation is the name of the game, a balloon loan is often arranged as construction financing on the theory that an amortizing loan will be available when the work is complete and the place looks like a million dollars. But that's sometimes not the case, which often means that an owner is forced to sell in a hurry in order to meet a balloon payment.

A relatively new wrinkle in the financing fabric — one that may or may not ultimately produce a balloon — is the shared-appreciation mortgage, which may also parade under the names equity participation or appreciation participation. In this deal, you get better financing, but the lender or another investor gets part of the appreciation when your home is sold or the loan reaches the end of its term, usually in five or ten years.

If your partner in this sort of mortagage is an institutional lender, the chances are that the attraction for you will be an interest rate below the market. The rate will have to be well below the market and stay that way for the life of the loan to make the loss of appreciation worthwhile. You probably should not consider any offer that will cost you more than 20 percent of the appreciation. A shared-appreciation mortgage from an institutional lender may require a large down payment, and you'd better get some expert advice on whether the appreciation you must give the lender will be deductible as an interest expense. If it isn't, you may be better off with a higher interest rate and all the appreciation.

Not all shared-appreciation mortgages involve institutional lenders, however. Some of them are set up by brokers who find private investors willing to help strapped buyers in exchange for a share of the appreciation in the home. The investor may help you with the down payment as well as the monthly payments, though you will have to pay him a monthly rent for the use of his share of the property. In theory at least, this arrangement provides you with better financing, because the investor is sharing the burden, and a better home than you might otherwise have been able to buy. It provides the investor with at least some of the tax advantages of real estate ownership, with better financing than he might otherwise be able to obtain and with a more secure investment than a traditional rental property (because, again in theory, you are less likely to tear the place up or abandon it if you are a part owner). Since depreciation is one of the major attractions for investors in these mortgages, and since land does not depreciate, they work best with properties that include relatively little land — townhouses and condominiums.

When a shared-appreciation mortgage reaches the end of its term, you face a balloon of sorts. You have to repay the investor or lender and see that he gets his share of the appreciation. If you're ready to move, the solution is fairly easy: You sell the thing and split the proceeds as agreed. If you want to keep the home, you will have to get an appraisal to determine its value and find other financing so you can pay your partner off unless he wants to extend your agreement.

Clearly, this sort of deal harbors many pitfalls. Expert advice and a very detailed advance agreement are necessary. Among other things, the agreement should specify how improvements you make in the home will be valued when the time comes to divvy it up and how, in such cases, a value will be put upon the labor you invested in those improvements. You should press hard in negotiating this deal for the right to sublease in case, before the loan runs its course, you're offered a job as head of drip grinding at a coffee mill 1,000 miles away.

Still another new-fangled mortgage type is the pledged-account or reserve-account loan, which uses some security — a certificate of deposit, maybe, or an interest-bearing account — as extra collateral for the mortgage. This extra collateral, which may be provided by the seller, the builder, or your doting Uncle Wendell, the wok king, serves to reduce the down payment or the monthly payments in the early stages of the loan. If you default on the loan, the lender takes the pledged security along with the home. Be careful here; Uncle Wendell would not like that.

SECOND MORTGAGES

Balloons, along with a lot of other unattractive features, are common with so-called junior or secondary mortgages, mortgages made while one or more earlier loans are still outstanding on the property. The first loan is said to carry the primary lien. That means the lender can, if you don't meet your obligations, foreclose and take the property. Once that lien has been filed, it's first-come, first-served. If you've taken out a second mortgage — you're most likely to do so if you have a purchase-money mortgage from the seller or have assumed his existing mortgage — the secondary lender will be able to foreclose and remove you, but he will then own the property only subject to the primary loan. The position of the junior or secondary mortgage holder thus involves considerably more risk than that of the primary mortgage holder.

One result of that greater risk is that secondary financing is usually available only from individuals or mortgage companies that make it a specialty. Savings and loan associations and commercial banks usually want no part of it. In fact, on the theory that a second loan will make it harder for you to pay off the first one, the primary lender may prohibit secondary financing altogether or may demand the right to approve the secondary lender and the terms of any secondary loan.

You can guess how the secondary lender protects himself against the greater risk involved in this kind of mortgage: He charges more than a primary lender, often a great deal more, and his deal is likely to include a discount, a very short term — three to five years is not uncommon — and a balloon payment at the end.

And there are risks here for the borrower as well as the lender. While there are many reputable, honest, and able residential secondary mortgage lenders, just as there are many reputable, honest salesmen of used cars and home improvements, residential second-mortgage lenders are regarded in financial circles the same way home-improvement salesmen are regarded in architectural offices: As entrepreneurs meeting a need, perhaps, but not as professional colleagues. So be extremely wary of any second mortgage and especially careful to understand all of its terms and all the charges involved. Your lawyer and the bank that holds your first mortgage may be good sources of advice. Before you agree to a second mortgage, add up all the monthly payments for both mortgages and be sure the total is within your budget. And in negotiating for one, try to get a subordination clause, a stipulation that if the first mortgage is paid off and you want to obtain a new one, the second mortgage will remain a second mortgage rather than moving into first priority. If he agrees to such a provision, the second-mortgage lender may insist upon limiting the size of a new first mortgage and upon approving the new first lender. That's fair enough, since a little fast footwork on your part and on the part of your new lender could leave the holder of your second mortgage with virtually no security for his loan. He deserves a fighting chance, too.

CONSTRUCTION FINANCING

Another type of financing that involves special problems is the building loan or construction mortgage, which, as the name cleverly suggests, is used to finance the construction of a new home and is then replaced by the so-called permanent mortgage when the place is complete. The construction loan can be obtained in conjunction with permanent financing or as a separate deal. A construction loan usually has a relatively short term — about the time you think it will take to build the place — and in most cases, you don't get all of the money when you sign the loan agreement. Rather, the funds will probably be advanced to you in specified increments during construction according to the lender's "take-down" schedule. The lender is likely to require that the work be inspected and that the inspector certify the satisfactory completion of a particular phase before an installment is released. Interest may be payable on the entire amount borrowed or only on the amounts advanced. It may begin the day you sign the agreement, though you won't see any money for 60 days or more. Construction financing often involves discount "points," and the interest rates are usually fairly high. In general, construction loan amounts are something like 75 to 90 percent of what permanent financing will supply.

The chances are that, unless you're dealing with a fairly large and established builder who is selling you the land as well as constructing the home or who is able to help you with the financing, you'll have to own the land free and clear — that is, without a mortgage or other financing — and will have to have a fairly good nest egg in addition. That's because the construction loan will not provide you with any ready money until a substantial portion of the work has been done.

As a rule, your first concern should be arranging the permanent financing, even though you'll need the construction loan first. Lenders are generally less interested in making construction loans than permanent mortgages because construction financing requires so much hassle over inspections, certifications, and so forth. They may be more interested in a combination loan, one that includes both construction and permanent financing. Such a loan may require some amortization payments during the building period, which construction financing, a form of balloon mortgage, usually does not demand. If, on the basis of your plans and specifications, you can get a permanent mortgage commitment from a local bank, that bank is likely to be more willing than others to advance you a construction loan as well. If your permanent financing is to come from an out-of-town lender, you'll probably have to use its commitment as security for a construction loan made locally. There are a couple of disadvantages to that approach. For one thing, you're dealing with two lenders, so you're likely to face two sets of closing costs. Beyond that, once you have a commitment for permanent financing, you'll have to move fast in arranging a construction loan. The commitment will no doubt contain a time limit, and you'll have to obtain the construction financing and get the place built before the commitment expires. If you have steady nerves and are experiencing some difficulty in obtaining permanent financing, you can try a procedure used by speculation builders: Arrange for a construction loan with a term that extends beyond the expected construction period. The speculation builder uses the time cushion after completion to sell the place; you can use it to find a permanent mortgage. If you fail, of course, you will have a huge debt and no way to pay it, so you may lose the home before you ever get to live in it.

In general, beyond seeing that your own financial affairs are in order and that your plans are reasonable and sound, your best assurance of getting an attentive hearing when you go in search of construction financing is having a general contractor with good credit and a good reputation. Lenders will tend to rely on his track record as well as yours in making their decision. And in general the financing should be arranged before construction begins. Liens, or claims against real property, usually are given priority in the order in which they are recorded, and a first mortgage lender wants the first priority at all costs. But in some states, a mechanic's lien, or a claim filed by a tradesman, is considered to date from the beginning of construction, no matter when it is recorded. To insure himself of priority, therefore, the lender will want his mortgage and the lien it includes filed before there is any possibility of a mechanic's lien — that is, before construction begins.

PACKAGE MORTGAGES

Package mortgages, which finance some furnishings or equipment — appliances or carpeting, say — as well as the land and building, are most common in new homes being sold by builders who include the appliances, carpeting, or other doodads in the price, a price that is financed with a mortgage. What may or may not be included in such a loan varies widely from place to place and lender to lender. This sort of loan is valuable if you can just barely afford the home you want and the higher interest rates for the usual furniture and appliance financing would cause anarchy in your checkbook. The package mortgage also has the advantage of presenting you with just one bill every month rather than a series of them. But it has disadvantages, too. Technically, at least, nothing that is covered by the mortgage can be altered or removed from the property during the life of the loan, and those draperies will probably get fairly tatty within 15 years or so. The lender is not likely to insist that you cannot remove and replace things that have worn out during the life of the loan, but you will then be paying for that junk — and paying interest on its cost — long after it's been consigned to a rummage sale or palmed off on your brother-in-law, Humbach, who thinks he can repair anything.

On the other hand, the chances are you won't keep your mortgage until it matures — you'll probably sell and move long before then — so you won't be paying interest on things junked years ago. Besides, everybody has to replace the water heater, furnace, roof, paint and wallpaper before the mortgage is paid off, and nobody says that's a bad deal. Nonetheless, a package mortgage is not the most economic way to finance, and before signing up you should carefully compare the cost of buying appliances this way with the cost of doing so under more traditional financing. But if you need it, you need it. You only live once.

LAND CONTRACTS AND TRUST DEEDS

In some places, property is sold through land contracts rather than with mortgages. This sort of deal is especially popular among the developers of second-home or vacation communities, a crowd not noted for its vigorous advocacy of consumerism, and it is sometimes used when the buyer's credit is in question or when the interest rates are very high. In the deed-and-mortgage sale you take title to the property and begin to make regular payments on it, running the risk that you'll lose the title if you don't keep up the payments. Under a land contract — also known as an installment sales contract, a contract for deed, or an agreement to convey — the title is held by someone else, typically the seller or a mortgage lender, until the terms of the contract are met. What the contract requires, of course, are regular payments that are treated as installments on the down payment or on the full price of the property. If the contract provides only for the accumulation of a down payment, when it matures you get the deed and seek a long-term mortgage.

For the buyer, the advantage of a land contract is that little or no down payment is needed; it's much like renting with an option to buy. For the seller or lender, the advantage is that if you default he need not go through the complex, expensive, and time-consuming process of foreclosure. He can merely evict you and treat your previous payments as rent — that is, keep them. The buyer in this type of transaction — he's known as the "equitable owner" — usually pays the real estate taxes and takes the corresponding income-tax deduction. The seller generally continues to make the payments on the underlying mortgage, if there is one. That practice makes the land contract tempting as a way to get around the "due on sale" clause in an existing mortgage or the prohibition against secondary financing in an assumable first mortgage. That may or may not be legal. It certainly won't prompt the bank to send you a bigger, more lavish calendar next Christmas. So move very cautiously here, and get expert legal advice.

Whatever advantages there are in land contracts, there are a lot more disadvantages from the buyer's point of view. You probably will not be able to sell or borrow against your interest in the place before the contract has matured — a typical term is five to ten years, though you may be able to negotiate an extension — and if it's vacant land you may not be able to build on it before then, either. That means, in other words, that you're stuck — you can't sell it and you can't use it. In the meantime, you're likely to have trouble obtaining title insurance, and if the seller is holding the title there may be nothing to prevent him from encumbering it or even conveying it to someone else. Contract sales are sometimes used to unload properties with such serious defects that no institution would lend money on them. The contracts often involve high interest rates and outrageous prices. Abuses are rampant.

Find another way if possible. And if not, negotiate a very thorough agreement that stipulates your rights and obligations as to alterations and repairs, that guarantees you the right to sublet the place during the term of the contract, that prohibits the seller from doing anything to encumber the title, and that specifies what will happen if the seller dies before the end of the term.

In some states, the mortgage is replaced by a trust deed, which is similar to a land contract in the sense that the buyer does not get title to the property immediately. A trust deed — also known as a deed of trust or a trust deed mortgage — has the effect of putting the property in escrow until you've met your obligation as a buyer. It transfers title from the seller to an individual or corporation who acts as a trustee for the seller if the seller is granting a purchase-money mortgage or for the lender if you're getting an institutional loan. The trustee has the right to sell the property if you don't pay up as promised. For the lender or seller the trust deed has the major advantage of the land contract: The sale process is quicker and more efficient than foreclosure. For the buyer it has the same major disadvantage — you can't sell or borrow against what you don't own — but it's safer in that it puts title in the hands of a presumably disinterested third party, which at least prevents the seller from conveying it to someone else while you're dutifully sending off your monthly checks.

MORTGAGE SHOPPING

Whatever form your financing takes, be aware that there are almost infinite variations within a type, so it pays to shop around. The way to begin is to call a few lenders and ask about their policy on mortgages — what sort of mortgages they make, what sort of properties they look for, how much they will lend, what their terms are, and so forth. Make a list of the institutions that seem more receptive than others, then visit their mortgage officers for a more detailed interview.

In that interview or some subsequent discussion before you actually apply for a mortgage, you'll want to nail down all the variables about the loan proposal. Perhaps the first one to concern yourself with is the limits on the amount available. There will probably be two such limits — a flat ceiling, that is, a specific dollar figure beyond which the institution will not go, no matter what property you're mortgaging and no matter what your financial situation — and a loan-to-value ratio. That ratio is the relationship between the amount of the loan and the appraisal value of the property or its sale price, whichever is lower. The ratio is often stated as a percentage. The mortgage officer may tell you, for example, that his institution is making 80 percent loans. That means you'll have to have a down payment or other financing equal to 20 percent of the home's value, and the mortgage will cover the other 80 percent. Bear in mind that in the majority of cases the appraisal value of the place will be lower than its sale price, so the banker's 80 percent may be less than it seems at first blush. If building a new home is what you have in mind, a lot owned free-and-clear may be all the down payment you need.

Once you've established how much the bank will lend, find out how long you'll have to pay it back — the term of the mortgage. Terms for standard mortgages range anywhere from 20 to 40 years, with the average term probably getting gradually longer as inflation makes housing more expensive. Each lender is likely to offer several different terms and to set its own maximum. Obviously, the longer the term is, the lower your monthly payments will be but the higher your over-all interest costs will be.

An option that may prove valuable sometime later is the right to extend the term of the loan. You're sometimes allowed that privilege in "open end" or variable-rate mortgages. An open end loan is one in which, at some point after its inception, you can increase the amount, that is, borrow more money, perhaps to finance remodeling or a child's college education. Usually the additional amount you can borrow is limited to the amount you have paid off since the loan was made. If the lender will allow such shenanigans — not all of them will — he will probably require a new appraisal to insure that the value of the place has not dropped, and if interest rates have risen he will almost certainly require a higher rate on the entire outstanding balance. The chances are the lender will want to increase the monthly payments to cover the extra principal, but he may be willing to extend the term and keep the payments constant.

The same situation prevails with a variable-rate mortgage, one on which the interest rate rises and falls periodically with the market. When that rate goes up, the lender may want to increase your monthly payments, but you may prefer to extend the term instead of tinkering with your monthly outlay. The time to find out how flexible the term of your mortgage will be is now, before you sign up for it.

Beyond the amount you can borrow and the number of years you'll have to pay it back, the other major factor determining the size of your monthly housing payments is the interest rate — the cost of borrowing money. In general, interest rates are higher in the West than in the East, in part because more investment money traditionally originates in the East, but interest rates on mortgages vary widely from place to place and time to time.

There's no way to predict what the prevailing interest rate is likely to be when and where you want to buy. But it pays to shop around because there's likely to be some variation in what lenders are charging and even in what one lender charges for various kinds of loans. To cite a simple example, some lenders may give you a fractional break on the interest rate if your down payment exceeds a specified percentage of the purchase price. They will, in other words, lower the interest rate along with the loan-to-value ratio, but not much, so don't get your hopes — or your down payment — up too high.

If you're interested in a graduated-payment or variable-rate loan, be sure to get specific details on how much and how often the monthly payments or the interest rate can change. For a graduated-payment loan, you should be able to get a fairly precise schedule of what your monthly payments will be at various stages during the life of the loan. For a variable-rate mortgage, find out whether the interest rate is tied to some index or whether it can go up at the lender's whim. How much can it rise at one point? What is the limit on cumulative increases over the life of the loan? Is the lender required to lower the rate when the index drops, or is he merely free to do so at his own discretion? When the lender announces an increase, will you have the right to find a new mortgage and pay this one off? If you decide to find a different loan, will you have to pay a penalty? Will you have to give the lender notice of your intention?

If the variable-rate loan lacks strict ceilings on the increase the lender can make at any single point and on the cumulative rise in the rate over the life of the loan, you will almost certainly be better off with a level-payment loan, even at a higher interest rate. If you're faced with a choice between a level-payment loan and a variable-rate one that has the proper safeguards and a lower initial interest rate, assume that the lender will take the biggest allowable increase in the interest rate at every opportunity, then compare the over-all costs of the two loans.

The total cost over the life of the loan is not necessarily reflected in the size of the monthly payment, though you should be concerned about the size of that, too. If it exceeds your ability to pay, after all, it doesn't matter what the overall cost of the loan is.

Beyond your monthly payments and overall costs, you'll want to find out what it will cost you to get a mortgage in the first place — what you will have to pay up front in the form of discounts and fees. Though discounts are most common on government-backed loans, they are not unknown on conventional loans. The matter is further confused by the fact that discounts are usually discussed in terms of "points," with each point being equal to 1 percent of the principal, but some lenders also put their fees in point terms. It is therefore necessary to find out from a mortgage officer not only whether any points will be charged but also what they represent — a discount or a fee. When it's part of a discount, each point is roughly the same as increasing the interest rate by one-eighth of 1 percent.

When interest rates are high and lenders are requiring discount points, builders who are offering government-backed financing on new homes bear particularly close scrutiny. Since the builders are aware that buyers may be restricted in paying the discounts, they may cut corners in construction to save the amount of the discounts they'll have to absorb. Alternatively, they may have simply raised their prices enough to cover the discounts. In that case, you might be well advised to ask whether, if you find your own conventional financing, the builder will cut his price by the amount of the discount he would otherwise have to pay.

Points that are not discounts are most likely to represent an origination fee, a charge the lender makes to cover the cost of preparing the mortgage papers and processing your application. The mortgage officer can give you an estimate of that fee and other charges his institution normally makes — charges for the title search and survey, for recording the mortgage at the courthouse, legal fees, and so forth. Federal law requires that you be given an estimate of such so-called settlement charges after you file a loan application, but the mortgage officer can give you a pretty accurate estimate even before you apply. You might also ask about the lender's policy on late charges (the fees it collects when your monthly payments are not on time) and the grace period it allows (the number of days after the first of the month before it imposes the late charge).

Ask, too, about the lender's insurance requirements. Does the institution insist that you buy mortgage life insurance or mortgage cancellation insurance — a policy that pays off the loan if you die? Do you have the option of buying your own insurance or do you have to buy it through the lender? If you have the option of going elsewhere, find out what the premiums are for policies obtained through the lender; they may be group rates much lower than any you're likely to obtain on your own. Does the lender require that you have fire insurance? If so, how much?

Find out what the lender's policy is on surveys. Will it require that you get a new survey even when the seller has a recent one? Will it accept a recent survey — say, one no more than five years old — together with the seller's affidavit that there have been no changes in the structures or the boundaries of the property since the survey was made?

Ask whether the lender will allow you to choose the title company that will make the search and issue title insurance or whether the lender insists upon making that choice. If you can make the decision, you may be able to get a lower rate from the company that already insures the title. If the lender makes the decision, how long before the closing will you or your lawyer be able to get the title documents to inspect them?

Does the lender require photographs of the home before it will issue a commitment? That's most likely to be a demand when it's an out-of-town lender. If pictures are required, can you supply them? That may be cheaper than paying a flat fee for the bank's photographer.

Will the lender charge you an origination fee? A document preparation fee? Fees for appraisals, credit reports, termite or other inspections of the property? Will you be able to choose any of the appraisers or inspectors or do you have to play ball with the lender's team? Will you have to pay the fee of the lender's lawyer as well as your own? Will you have to pay an escrow agent or closing agent, the fellow who presides at the meeting where you pay up and where the seller produces the deed?

If the lender is a savings and loan association, will it charge you a fee to become a member before it will make you a loan? Will the lender's charges be payable in cash at the closing or will the lender deduct them from the amount of the loan, in effect making them a discount on which you'll be paying interest for 20 years or so?

Federal law requires that the lender give you a good-faith estimate of closing costs immediately after you formally apply for a loan and make available to you shortly before the closing all the information it has on precisely what your closing costs will be. That's the minimum. Will this lender tell you earlier exactly what some of your closing costs will be? How early? Will it tell you, too, what the seller's costs will be so you can be sure both of you won't be paying for the same thing?

Will your insurance premiums and real estate taxes be included in your monthly mortgage payment, will you have to pay them yourself, or do you have the choice of how to pay them? If the lender collects from you monthly, then pays the taxes and insurance premiums on your behalf, you're denied the use of your money while it's accumulating, but you're also saved some inconvenience when those payments are due. It's your choice which is better. If the lender collects your money monthly and pays the bills, your monthly contributions are put into an escrow account, also known in some places as an impound account, reserve account, trust account or trust fund. If you have an escrow account, will you be paid interest on its balance? In some places, the law requires it; in others it's up to the lender. It's a valuable advantage if you can get it, one worth asking for, even if it's not the law.

Find out whether the lender exacts a prepayment penalty, a charge levied if you pay off the mortgage before it matures or if you even pay ahead on it. These charges — usually calculated as percentages of the loan — are made because it costs the lender something to process the mortgage in the first place, and he doesn't recover that expenditure until he's collected interest for a few years. The penalty allows him to recover if you pay off before that point. Usually, prepayment penalties apply only if your extra payments exceed a certain proportion of the loan, and they usually have a fixed cutoff date; 10 years after the loan begins has been common, but it may be sooner. The right to prepay is a valuable one, one worth haggling to get. If you have it, you can pay off the loan and refinance on better terms or sell the place and pay off the loan anytime you want without being penalized. Even if you don't want to do that, in good times you can make larger than normal payments. That won't usually reduce your subsequent monthly payments, but it will reduce the number of payments you'll have to make, which may be very handy if you plan to retire before the mortgage runs its course or if your income fluctuates sharply and there may be some lean times ahead.

Another matter to ask about is the conditions under which the loan will be callable, under which the lender can demand full payment of the outstanding balance. These days lenders generally make mortgages callable whenever title transfers, even from a husband to his wife. That prevents a future buyer's assuming your mortgage or buying subject to the mortgage. A loan that some future buyer can assume might prove handy if you're forced to sell at a time when money is tight and mortgages are difficult or impossible to find. In such times, an assumption may provide the only way to finance a sale. But neither an assumption nor a wraparound mortgage will be possible if the original loan is callable when title transfers. Obviously, the narrower the grounds for callability, the better off you are, though lenders are not likely to be very flexible on such matters.

In general, bankers are not noted for their flexibility, but flexibility in whatever degree you can find it is a big asset when you're shopping for a mortgage. It may allow you to work out an agreement under which you can skip a certain number of payments — maybe one a year — if money gets short and extend the term of the loan. It might allow you to win a refinancing clause, a provision that if interest rates drop below a certain point you can negotiate a new, lower rate. It's not very likely. But it might.

It's also not very likely that the lender will be too flexible about the standards he looks for in a borrower or in the property being mortgaged, but you should try to find out what they are. The lender will probably want to be sure that your mortgage payments, taxes, and insurance premiums do not total more than about 33 percent of your income. And in calculating your income, the lender is likely to give more weight to base salary or wages than to bonuses, overtime, or even dividends, forms of income that may evaporate without much notice. What the lender is wary of is unstable income, and he'll see as signs of instability such things as a lack of experience in a new business venture or a new job; lack of seniority on the job; frequent employment changes, or employment in a seasonal business or occupation. While a mortgage officer is not likely to be so open in discussing these matters of borrower qualification as he would be in talking about prepayment penalties and interest rates, he may be able to give you some inkling of how your income compares with that of the institution's typical mortgage borrower.

The mortgage officer will be even less enthusiastic about discussing discrimination except to assure you that his institution has never practiced it. That's probably untrue. Lenders often discriminate against the aged on the theory that advanced age makes it more difficult to repay a large loan. They have traditionally discriminated against women, using stricter credit standards for them than for men on the theory that they'll work only until they're married or become pregnant. Lenders have required creditworthy women to have co-signers and refused to consider alimony or child-support payments in calculating income — though in recent years federal laws against sex discrimination in lending have become tougher. Lenders have not always been terribly fond of divorced or even single people, either. And, of course, financial institutions are no different from any other institutions in their tendency to discriminate against racial and ethnic minorities.

Though the laws may be stricter these days, the enforcement of prohibitions against discrimination in lending has been spotty at best. Your only defense is to know your rights and where to go with your complaints. In effect, the law provides that everyone must be treated like white Anglo Saxon males. That means you can't be denied credit or made to meet stricter qualifications because you are black, Oriental, American Indian, Jewish, Catholic, Hindu, Albanian, Icelandic, or female. Not even if you're all of the above. It means that a lender must take full account of a woman's primary income in determining her ability or that of herself and her husband or other partner to pay off the loan. It means that the lender cannot refuse to consider alimony or child-support payments or the income from regular part-time work, though he can consider the likelihood that such income will continue. It means that a lender cannot ask a woman if she's divorced or inquire after a couple's plans to have children. It means that a woman with adequate credit cannot be required to get her husband's signature on a loan for property she's buying herself.

Lenders may be reluctant to deal with a minority borrower who wants to purchase a home in an area that has no other minority owners, and they may resist lending to anyone who wants to buy in an integrated area. This practice of refusing to lend on properties in specified areas is known as redlining, supposedly because bankers drew red lines on maps around the neighborhoods from which they were going to cut off funds. No mortgage officer is going to tell you that his institution practices redlining, though he may concede that it does not look with favor upon loans in areas that are decaying or declining, areas that are therefore less financially secure than more stable neighborhoods. Your approach should probably be to determine whether the mortgage officer seems to think that the place you want to buy is in such a declining area. If there appears to be agreement among mortgage officers that the neighborhood is too questionable for them, ask whether there's a high-risk mortgage pool available. This is a fund to which several lenders contribute and from which mortgages are made in declining areas. The theory is that if all the lenders share the risks, nobody will be hurt too badly.

If the mortgage officer thinks your new neighborhood is right up to snuff, a veritable Park Avenue in the forest primeval, try to get a feel for the institution's attitude toward the kind of home you have in mind. In their evaluations, some lenders do not consider many of a home's special features on the theory that the average buyer would not require such luxuries and would not be willing to pay for them if the bank found itself trying to unload the place after foreclosing. Some lenders also steer clear of extreme features or the latest design for fear that such things will prove to be merely passing fads that will be difficult to sell in the future. Some lenders have prejudices for or against certain styles or designs — some, for example, wouldn't touch a two-family home. Others insist upon some pet feature — a two-car garage, say, or a family room — on the theory that everyone wants them and the place that doesn't have them will be difficult to sell.

In case you're planning on renovating the home once you own it, you'd better quiz the mortgage officer on that, too. Find out what plans, specifications, or other documents the institution will require before it will supply financing. When you're making estimates of the cost of renovation, it's probably wise to pad them slightly because inflation will drive them up before you get firm bids or get the work started. There's no point in going too far in this direction, however, since the lender will ultimately make his own estimates.

TWISTING THE BANK'S ARM

It's possible that if you're shopping in a time of tight money, you'll strike out at every bank in town, at least on the first try. That's when you should start to make imaginative use of the resources at hand. Your own bank should be more willing to help than others; after all, you're an old customer. Plead with them a bit. If you're moving from out of town and have no local bank yet, offer to open checking and savings accounts in the institution that will provide a mortgage. The more you have to deposit, the better that deal will sound to a lender (which is another way of saying that the less you need financing the more likely you are to get it). Whether or not you have a local banking connection, the seller probably does. Ask him to exert a little pressure in your behalf since it's in his interest, too, to get this deal closed. And while you're rattling the seller's cage, don't neglect to ask him to give you a purchase-money mortgage.

The real estate broker, if there's one involved in the sale, and the lawyers representing both you and the seller are likely to know half the lenders within a radius of 100 miles. Ask if they'll twist a few arms so they can collect their fees and commission. Your employer and the seller's employer undoubtedly maintain fairly large bank accounts, and when depositors like that clear their throats bank officers snap to attention. You might hint to your boss — and suggest that the seller hint to his — that you'd be much more stable, happy, and productive at work if a way were found to obtain financing and solve this personal problem that's been nagging at you.

Have your friends and relatives, especially the well-heeled ones, talk to their bankers. The institution that clips coupons for your Cousin Victor may find it worthwhile to lose money on a mortgage for you, as long as it keeps him happy.

Try the institution that already holds a mortgage on the home you want to buy, even if the seller does no other business there and the loan is not assumable. A lender who has had a profitable relationship with a property that seems to be increasing in value may be more willing than others to make a new loan on it, and he may waive some of the closing costs because he knows the place and won't need such things as a survey and title search. If he's in the throes of terminal generosity, he might even offer you financing at a "blended" rate — an interest rate somewhere between that on the existing loan and the higher rate prevailing at the moment.

When you really get desperate, ask your lawyer or real estate broker to recommend some mortgage brokers, or simply find some mortgage brokers in the Yellow Pages. You'll have to pay their fees if they find you a mortgage, but that may be a lot better than doing without the mortgage.

And if all else fails, try to negotiate with the seller a deal under which you can rent the home with an option to buy it when the mortgage market improves. You might, for example, agree to buy the place at a specified price a year from now, in the meantime paying rent, some or all of which will be counted as all or part of a down payment when the sale takes place.

In the event that even that approach fails, don't give up hope entirely. The mortgage market changes virtually from day to day, so you can wait a few weeks and, if you haven't committed suicide in the meantime, try again, even with the same lenders.

COMPARING THE OFFERS

The chances are that sooner or later — and probably sooner rather than later — you'll come across a few lenders willing to underwrite your escapade, but the deals they're offering are likely to prove difficult to compare. The one that offers the best loan-to-value ratio may have some obnoxious prepayment provisions, for instance, and the one with the lowest interest rate may involve many extra fees. Probably the best way to compare these apples and kumquats is to list all the provisions of each proposal — amount, term, interest rate, discount, fees, prepayment penalty, insurance requirements, and so forth — and then to cross off the features that are of no interest to you and translate the rest into dollars and cents. If you reasonably expect to own and live in this home for the rest of your life, prepayment penalties and assumability mean nothing to you. Forget them. If you know you're going to be transferred in two years and you're going to sell, prepayment penalties and assumability are very important, but total costs over the life of the loan are not. The things that are important you should evaluate in terms of cost from two points of view: the overall price of the loan during its entire term and the size of the monthly payments. Such things as fees and discounts should be figured in along with interest and principal payments, but tax deductions should be subtracted. For a loan of a given size, you'll find that the over-all cost rises as the monthly payments drop. In general, the best arrangement for holding down your long-term costs is to take the highest monthly payments you can afford now and get the right to prepay in the future.

In theory, at least, all of the details of a conventional mortgage agreement are negotiable. The lender will probably present you with what he describes as a "standard" form, and it will probably be the agreement he uses 98 percent of the time. But he's free — within the limits of the law and common sense — to change anything on it whenever it suits him. It's not likely to suit him very often since the thing was drawn up in the first place with an eye to giving the lender maximum protection. You are nonetheless free to suggest alternatives. Your lawyer and accountant are good sources of advice here, and a lawyer may be able to help you negotiate a more favorable agreement.

APPLYING FOR A LOAN

Ultimately, once you've made your choices and done your dickering, you'll have to fill out a formal application for a mortgage loan, a form outlining your financial situation and work history and giving the details of the property that will be the security for the loan. If it's a resale home you're buying, the lender may want a copy of the sales contract along with the mortgage application. If it's to be new construction, the lender may want one or more sets of plans and specifications and, perhaps, bids from one or more contractors. If you're self-employed, the lender may want a copy of your federal tax return and business statements.

Signing the loan application could under certain circumstances bind you to accept the loan if it's offered or to pay the lender's processing costs if the application is rejected. It is therefore important to ensure that the application states amounts and terms that are acceptable to you, and it is important to be sure that your lawyer reads the thing before you sign it.

After you've submitted your application, the lender will verify it, checking your work record with your employer and the size of your savings account with your bank and looking into your credit rating. The lender will also inspect and appraise the place and, perhaps, have a surveyor give it the cold eye. If it's an FHA or VA loan you're after, the government agency involved will assume some of those functions and you'll get your fill of delays and red tape.

Ultimately, the lender will either reject your application or send you a letter of commitment. If you're rejected, you may write to the lender and request an explanation of the decision and a list of the sources of negative information about you. The lender is required to respond. Call the sources he lists and ask to see your files. If any of the information in those files seems to you to be incorrect, ask for a review. Information that, upon review, is found to be inaccurate must be removed from your file. If that happens and the incorrect information was crucial, you may be able to try again and get a mortgage.

But if you conclude that you're being discriminated against on the basis of age, sex, race, religion, national origin, or marital status, you should write to the state banking and civil rights authorities and to the federal agencies concerned. Which ones are concerned will depend to some extent upon the sort of institution you've been dealing with. No matter what sort of lender it is, you might try the Civil Rights Division, United States Department of Justice, Washington, D.C. 20530. The Bureau of Consumer Protection, Federal Trade Commission, Washington, D.C. 20580, oversees the affairs of finance companies and other providers of consumer credit as well as credit rating agencies. National banks fall under the jurisdiction of the Comptroller of the Currency, United States Treasury Department, Washington, D.C. 20220; state-chartered banks that are members of the Federal Reserve System are regulated by the Federal Reserve Board, Washington, D.C. 20551; banks that are not members of the reserve system but are federally insured answer to the Federal Deposit Insurance Corporation, 550 Seventeenth Street N.W., Washington, D.C. 20429; and federally insured savings and loan associations are in the bailiwick of the Federal Home Loan Bank Board, 101 Indiana Avenue N.W., Washington, D.C. 20552.

Presuming, however, that the lender accepts rather than rejects your application, his letter of commitment should specify all the terms of the loan. It may, on the theory that you are a good risk but the property is not shipshape, specify different terms than you originally proposed, in which case the letter is a counteroffer that you are free to accept or reject. The commitment letter may also set out conditions for the loan — say, the making of certain repairs or improvements — and it may provide that some of the funds will be withheld until those conditions are met. The letter is also likely to contain a time limit, making the commitment good for a certain period, during which you must accept it in writing if you expect to get the loan. Once you've sent off that letter and informed the seller that you have financing, all you have to do is read a few boring papers and attend the closing, and you're a homeowner.

27
How Should You Prepare for the Closing and What Happens There?

The closing — it's also called a settlement — is a meeting at which the piper, among a million others, is paid and at which you actually take possession of the place for better or worse. In some cases, it's almost a ceremony, with a shiny conference table surrounded by appropriately serious lawyers and executives in three-piece suits. Such things usually happen in the office of the lender who's providing your mortgage, in the office of the lender's lawyer, or in the office of the seller's lawyer.

Where it happens is of little import — such little import, in fact, that in many cases it just never happens. In some areas (the West, mainly) you and the seller and your respective lawyers mail off the necessary documents, checks, and instructions to an escrow agent, a specialist in such matters, and some unseen gnome does all the required harrumphing and paper-stamping. As if by divine intervention — after a little greasing of palms — the seller gets his money in the mail and you get your deed.

The critical matter, of course, is not whether the meeting ever takes place, though it adds a nice little fillip if someone notices when you're blowing three years' salary. The important things are that you touch all the necessary legal and financial bases and that you make sure the seller has done so as well. If an escrow agent will handle the closing in absentia, as it were, you have to touch the bases in your written instructions to him. Make sure they're clear and complete. Make sure your lawyer makes sure, too.

CLOSING COSTS

The first base to touch, no matter how the closing will be handled, is a financial one. Shortly after you apply for a mortgage, the lender is obliged under federal law to supply you with what the bureaucrats have chosen to call a good-faith estimate of your closing or settlement charges — that is, the bank's best guess as to what you'll have to ante up on that fateful day, whether or not a formal meeting is involved — and a copy of a federal booklet explaining closing costs.

The size of the bill you face will depend in large measure on what the lawyers and lenders thereabouts think the traffic will bear and on — what else? — local custom. Generally, the closing costs seem to divide about evenly between seller and buyer. The American Land Title Association, the friendly folks who bring you title insurance, found on the basis of a nationwide survey that total closing costs, those paid by both buyer and seller, ranged from 5.24 to 15.85 percent of the sale price. A more recent study by the Department of Housing and Urban Development and the Veterans Administration concluded that the averages ranged from 6.08 to 14.4 percent. On that basis, you can figure, whatever the lender estimates, that your closing costs will be at least 2.75 or 3 percent of the price of the home and may go as high as 8 percent. Both those numbers are probably extremes; the chances are that you'll come out somewhere in the middle, and the lender's estimate will probably give you a fair idea of how close to the middle it's likely to be.

HUD found that closing costs were highest in the Middle Atlantic states, where both lawyers and title insurance were involved in the average residential sale, and surveys were often required. The study found costs much lower in New England and the upper Midwest, where independent abstractors or lawyers usually do the title searches and title insurance and surveys are the exception rather than the rule. But it's hard to make any generalizations because customs — and costs — vary all over. The HUD study found, for example, that in the District of Columbia, title companies handle most of the closing work and neither the buyer nor the seller usually hires his own lawyer. But in New Jersey, the buyer customarily pays for title insurance and coughs up the fees for two lawyers, his own and the lender's. In Chicago, according to the HUD study, the seller, not the buyer, normally pays for a title report as well as for deed preparation and the state transfer tax. In Los Angeles, the closing is usually handled by an escrow agent, with the buyer and seller splitting his fee.

The best indication of the customs in your area will be the "good faith estimate" of closing costs the lender gives you when you apply for a mortgage. Some of the items listed there may be open to negotiation — the lender's charges for processing the loan, for example, or the fee to be charged by your lawyer — but others are beyond the realm of discussion. If you can go down to the courthouse and negotiate a lower transfer tax or recording fee or if you can get the insurance company to give you a lower rate because you're such a swell fellow, you've found the secret to instant wealth and the rest of us would appreciate your letting us in on it. Call collect.

Your first step in preparing for a closing, then, will be to get together the scratch to pay for this rite of passage, at which everybody and his brother will seem to have his hand out. In general, the charges they're trying to levy will fall into five categories.

The first category involves the charges surrounding the loan, which the lender should be able to estimate almost exactly, since the lender is making them. If the lender's estimate contains obvious fudging in this area, question it closely and mutter under your breath, "Respa," the acronym for the Real Estate Settlement Procedures Act, the law that mandates these disclosures. Any intelligent mortgage officer ought to get the message. The loan charges may include: a finder's fee, also known as a broker's fee or commission, which is paid to a broker or someone else who brought the business in; an origination fee, also known as an application fee, commitment fee or service charge, which is supposed to compensate the lender for all the initial paperwork connected with your loan and which you should try to get itemized (it's almost always lower when the lender has to tell you how much went for notaries' fees, how much for clerical expenses, and so forth, rather than giving you one over-all cost); a document preparation fee, which is supposed to compensate the lender for making out all the subsequent papers (even including an amortization schedule, a list showing when you have to pay what and how much you'll owe after you pay it — that's like having Macy's charge you extra every month to make out your bill); discount "points" if they're being charged and you're eligible to pay them; an assumption fee if you're assuming an existing mortgage; a membership fee if you're borrowing from a thrift association that requires you to be a member before it will make a loan; and an escrow deposit if the lender will be paying your taxes, your homeowner's insurance premiums, or both (bankers like to get one month in advance, cautious fellows that they are, but that's as far ahead as the law allows). You may also be charged such strange things as a review fee (a payment for reading your file) or a warehouse fee (for keeping the file). Even if you have to pay eventually, squawk.

Any or all of these charges from the lender may be expected of you in cash at the closing, or they may be deducted from the funds the lender is giving you in the mortgage, in which case you'll have to produce the cash to make up the difference on the loan.

The second category of costs involved in the closing will be those for professional services, costs at which the lender may have to guess to some extent because they are the fees of other people, not the lender himself, though in some cases they will be people with whom the lender regularly does business and with whose fees he should be familiar. Among such fees are those for an appraisal, a credit report, a survey and termite or other inspections of the property, notary fees, the fee of an escrow agent if one is employed (the VA generally prohibits the payment of this one by the buyer), a closing fee if there's a closing agent who presides at the meeting and supervises the paper shuffling, and the fees of your lawyer and the lender's lawyer. If you're getting a purchase-money mortgage from the seller, it is customary in some areas for you to pay for the preparation of the bond and mortgage by the seller's lawyer.

Then there are the expenses connected with the title and various forms of insurance: the title search and premiums for title insurance; mortgage life insurance, which pays the thing off if you die; and homeowner's insurance. At the closing, you may have to pay the first year's premium on the homeowner's policy in addition to putting an extra month's premium into the lender's escrow account, which will be used to buy next year's coverage.

There will also be some money due the government, both federal and local — mortgage and deed transfer taxes and fees for the recording of the deed and mortgage.

You will, of course, owe the seller something, too. Most of it will represent the balance due on the sale price of the home, but you will also have to compensate him for such things as taxes, assessments, or sewer fees he has paid in advance, prepaid insurance premiums if you're taking over his policy, and prepaid interest or escrow deposits if you're taking over his mortgage. Such things are usually prorated so that the seller pays for the period before the closing and you are responsible for everything thereafter. You may also be called upon to pay for any fuel the seller has bought and is leaving with the home, and you may have to make a separate payment for personal property you're buying from the seller.

Finally, there may be some closing costs connected with the property itself — with a new home, for example, a utility connection fee or a deposit to be paid a utility company to cover service that will begin when you move in.

Armed with the lender's estimate of the total amount of the closing costs you'll face, you will know as the date for the closing approaches how many extra jobs you'll have to get before you can meet the bill.

TITLE INSURANCE

If you're going to pay for a title insurance policy, try to get a copy of it as far as possible in advance of the closing. With your lawyer, go over the exceptions, usually listed on something called Schedule B. The exceptions are the things the insurance company is saying it won't protect you against. They will probably include anything detrimental that's been turned up in the title search, things that you and your lawyer should be aware of. In some cases, those defects — for example, an electric company easement to run wires above the property — will be of no great importance. But others — say a mechanic's lien — you'll want to have removed before the closing or when the seller collects his money at the closing. You'll also want to ask the title insurer about the possibility and the cost of removing virtually all of the exceptions but those for inconsequential things like utility easements. Some of them are simply annoying and should be stricken without much fuss. There is a common one, for instance, that rules out protection against problems that "would be disclosed by an accurate survey." If you've paid for a survey you should get that one stricken. And if you're building or buying a new home, you might consider buying at extra cost coverage against mechanics' liens, which can sometimes be filed long after the fact, after you think all the problems have been solved.

GETTING READY

One business day before the closing is to take place, you have the right to inspect a Uniform Settlement Statement, a federal form that lists all the closing costs, filled out with whatever specific information the lender has at that point. By then it should be fairly complete, so you should know with some certainty what sort of nut you face on the morrow. If the lender is feeling cooperative, he may give you a peek at that document even earlier, which may help you in your financial preparations. Whenever you see it, you should take a look at the closing costs listed for the seller as well as those on your own account to be sure that you're not both paying for the same thing.

You will also have to visit your bank not long before the closing, for it's unlikely that you'll be able to pay the lion's share of your debt with anything less than cash, a certified check, or a cashier's check. Since it's dangerous to carry large amounts of cash around, some such fancy check is the thing. Get one drawn to your own order in the amount of your best estimate of what you'll owe. When the transaction is completed, you can endorse it over to the seller, but if a hitch develops you can simply deposit it in your own account. If the check proves to be too large — happy day! — the seller can write you his own check for the excess. If the certified or cashier's check proves to be too small, you can write a personal check for the balance.

On the day of the closing, as agreed in the contract, you should plan to inspect the home to be sure it's in the same condition it was when you decided to buy it. If the home is new, there are likely to be many small details still unfinished. Be sure you note them carefully, and if there's a builder's representative with you, have him note them as well and sign the list you've compiled at the end of the tour.

THE MEETING

Finally, the closing, a meeting that is likely to involve you and your spouse, your lawyer, the seller and his or her spouse or the builder, the lawyer representing the seller or builder, an official or lawyer for the lender, perhaps a real estate broker, a title company representative, and an escrow agent. Somebody in the joint will probably be a notary.

There is no fixed agenda for this sort of thing, but this is more or less what will happen. The contract may be reviewed by one side or both, just to keep the details in mind. The seller's lawyer will produce the deed for inspection by you and your lawyer, the lender's lawyer, and the title company representative. The seller may also provide an affidavit of title, a sworn statement that he owns the home in question, that he has been in possession of it for however many years, that he has enjoyed that possession undisturbed by others, that his title has not been questioned, and that there are no outstanding judgments against him. In addition, the seller may have to produce a termite inspection report, a bill of sale for the personal property and bills or receipts for taxes, assessments, and water and sewer service. If you're assuming the seller's mortgage or buying subject to it, he may produce an estoppel certificate, which sets forth the exact status of the loan, and a letter to his bank assigning to you the balance in his escrow account. If it's a new home you're buying, the builder should produce a certificate of occupancy and whatever warranties there are on appliances or equipment. If your inspection disclosed that the home is not yet complete, you and your lawyer should work out with the builder an escrow agreement under which enough of your money will be withheld from the builder and placed in escrow with your lawyer or the title company representative to insure that the work will be completed or defects will be corrected.

The same sort of escrow agreement may be necessary if the examination of the title documents at the closing turns up some encumbrance — a mechanic's lien, perhaps, or unpaid taxes — that cannot be cleared at once. In most cases, the seller can pay such things out of the money he collects at the closing. But he may be reluctant to do so if he is protesting the tax bill or contending in court that the mechanic in question has been paid what he is owed. In such a situation, you can have the seller place in escrow with your lawyer or the title company enough to discharge the encumbrance if he fails to do so otherwise. You should probably insist that the escrow include a little extra money in case interest or other charges have swelled the total. Your agreement can specify that any excess will be refunded to the seller.

The title company representative will produce an abstract of title, certificate of title, title policy binder (a temporary policy used when the permanent one is not yet ready), or the policy itself. You and your lawyer must be satisfied with the condition of the title, satisfied that it does not have any fatal defects. This

HOW SHOULD YOU PREPARE FOR THE CLOSING? 257

will be your last chance to get rid of some of the exceptions in the title insurance policy. Your lawyer will examine and compare the title documents, the survey, and the deed.

When everyone's happy, the seller — and, perhaps, his or her spouse — will sign the deed and their signatures will be notarized.

The lawyer or other representative of the lender will present the bond and mortgage for inspection by you, your lawyer, and the title company representative. Be sure you understand both documents; don't be afraid to ask questions. The lender may want to see your homeowner's insurance policy, and he may want from you a letter authorizing the tax collector to send bills to the lender for payment. Finally, you — and perhaps your spouse — will sign the bond and the mortgage and your signatures will be notarized. If it's an FHA or VA loan, there may be some government forms to sign as well.

The lender will produce a check, drawn to your order, for the amount of the mortgage. If the seller owns his home free and clear — that is, without a mortgage — you will endorse the check over to him. If he is paying off an old mortgage when he sells, you will probably be asked to endorse the check over to the holder of that mortgage. There may be a representative of that lender in attendance, too, ready to whip out a document known as a satisfaction of mortgage, which wipes the old mortgage off the books, clearing your title of one more encumbrance.

Your lawyer and the seller's counselor will then huddle over their calculators and pencils, mumbling the while about bills, receipts, and where's the damn eraser. They will ultimately come up with some numbers indicating what you owe the seller for personal property and for things he has prepaid and what the seller owes you for things he hasn't paid. The chances are that the balance will be in the seller's favor.

You give the seller or his bank the check representing your mortgage. You give the seller your certified or cashier's check and, probably, a personal check for whatever else you owe. The seller gives you the deed and the keys to the place.

The deed will soon disappear into the briefcase of a lawyer or the title company representative to be recorded at the courthouse and returned by mail. If the title company man seems to have his hand out, it's because he expects a tip, which is customary in some areas. Ask your lawyer for guidance.

Finally, you will get a copy of the Uniform Settlement Statement, the official accounting of all closing costs, but this time it should be completed, showing everything that's been paid, for what, and to whom.

The law says that if you or your representative attend the closing, you must be given the settlement statement then. If there is no meeting or you don't attend, the statement must be mailed to you as soon as possible after the closing. The Department of Housing and Urban Development can make exceptions to this regulation and to the one that requires a good faith estimate of closing costs when you apply for a loan if the seller pays all the closing costs or if the lender tells you when you apply for a mortgage exactly what they will be.

By whatever means, you now know what the closing costs are, and they're paid. You and all the other folks around that shiny conference table shake hands and congratulate one another on being so shrewd, honest, and agreeable.

You leave, shaken, poverty-ridden, but a man or woman of property, a homeowner, by George, and still alive to tell about it!

PART FOUR

Special Kinds of Homes

28
What Should You Look for in a Condominium or Co-op?

The purchase of a condominium or cooperative unit is at bottom much like the fee-simple purchase of a traditional home, but it's more complicated — physically, legally, financially, and socially. You'll have to scout the area and the neighborhood, just as you would with any other housing purchase, looking into the schools, churches, shopping, transportation, zoning, and so forth. You'll have to check on the background of the builder and be wary of the decorations and furnishing in a model, just as you would with any new home. But you'll have to be doubly careful, for condominium and co-op purchases are more complex than others and therefore more open to abuse.

Physically, for example, you're likely to be looking at one unit in a huge building or complex. You can't get a handle on the condition of your unit without understanding the condition of the whole project, and that's virtually impossible for the average Joe. Even those who know a 2×4 stud when they see one and can measure the distance between them have trouble distinguishing a good elevator from a cheap one. How do you judge sound steel-and-masonry construction? How do you assess the air-conditioning or heating systems for a 20-story building? How do you tell whether an access road for a 500-unit development is adequate?

If you're wise, you don't even attempt to make definitive judgments on such matters. You hire someone qualified to do so, a building inspector who has experience with projects of similar size. And if he seems puzzled about something serious or potentially serious, you even consider hiring another expert, a specialist, to advise you. It may sound expensive, but it'll be a lot cheaper than paying your share to replace the elevator and the heating system when they fail after you've moved in.

Legally, condominiums and co-ops may be more complicated than anything since your Uncle Fred explained how he happened to be playing a piano in a house of questionable repute. More than in any other kind of housing, what you're buying is as much a concept as a tangible object. You can't drive a nail into air space or stick a shovel into your undivided interest in the common elements. The whole transaction will hang on a vast collection of papers apportioning certain rights to you and to dozens, scores, hundreds, maybe even thousands of other buyers — outlining your rights and obligations vis-à-vis one another and vis-à-vis the developer or seller, the government, and the rest of the world. They will be papers that in most cases were drawn up long before you entered the picture, even if it's a new development, and that cannot be readily changed. You take 'em or leave 'em. Moreover, they are likely to be papers so freighted with "whereas" and "hereinafter," so riddled with "aforementioned" and "notwithstanding," that they may dumfound even the most experienced lawyer if he is not familiar with condominium or cooperative practices.

In other words, you need help. If you're unwise to buy a traditional house without competent legal advice — and you are, no matter what your cousin Blackstone tells you — then you're certifiably insane to purchase a co-op or condominium without it. Just ask all those big-shot Wall Street lawyers who retired to Florida a few years ago and now find themselves paying huge monthly rents for swimming pools they thought they were buying with their condominium units. Or ask the former chairmen of the board who are paying outrageous management fees under 25-year contracts slipped into their sales agreements by the promoters who sold them their places in the sun. Those folks would probably do it a little differently now. They'd find a lawyer, insist that he read everything and explain it before they signed, then look upon his fee as the best bargain in the whole transaction.

Beyond their legal complications, condominiums and co-ops involve financial complexity sufficient to boggle the most analytical of minds. Once you get into this thing up to your wallet, you're going to have money moving in several directions at once — sometimes faster than the eye can follow — and much of your money is going to get mixed in with other people's money, which makes it much harder to find. You may have a mortgage or other loan to finance the purchase of your unit; you'll have to pay monthly maintenance charges to an association or corporation, and you'll have to concern yourself with how that group handles and dispenses its money; you may have to deal from time to time with special assessments for big repairs or catastrophic losses; and you'll have to worry to some extent about whether your neighbors are paying their share.

Socially, too, condominiums and co-ops may be a can of worms because everybody has a vote in how the place will be run, and that means everybody has a say about how you live. It can get pretty hairy if the board of directors is not sufficiently competent, ethical, energetic, or sophisticated to insure that things happen when they're supposed to. That can be especially true if the board is saddled with a professional managing agent of less than rigid moral fiber. It can get even hairier if the pet owners and the animal haters have a showdown over whether to ban beasts from the premises, or if one group of owners wants to raise the maintenance charges so both the doorman and the elevator operator can be retained while another group wants to automate the elevator in an effort to avoid bankruptcy. Given such unpleasant possibilities, it's obviously more important in a condominium or a co-op than in other types of housing to get some idea in advance of the kind of people you'll be living with. That's easier when you're buying a resale unit in an existing development — you can just walk around and talk to people — than it is in a new project, but even in a new place you can figure out what sort of people the advertising was designed to attract and you can see who's wandering into the sales office and who seems to be staying around to sign some papers.

If at all possible, talk to the president of the homeowners' association or the chairman of the board about his plans and problems. Ask about the social functions the organization is planning, about the improvements it has made or hopes to make. Ask how active most residents are in the association. Track down the superintendent or an official of the company that manages the place and ask about his plans and problems, too. Then hunt up a few shareholders or unit owners to chat about their reactions to the maintenance and management of the development, the kinds of neighbors they have — how many retirees? how many families with children? how many young swingers with loud stereos? — the cost of living here, and the frequency with which they face special assessments or other unexpected charges. If you can, wangle an invitation to the next meeting of the shareholders or unit owners. There may not be one scheduled for six months, and even if there is the residents may not be delirious about the idea of having an outsider sit in, so the point may be moot. But if you can attend such a meeting, you may learn a great deal about how the place operates and what living in it would be like.

INSPECTING THE PLACE

While you're wandering around, even before you feel the need to call in a phalanx of engineers, lawyers, and accountants, you can make the same sort of visual inspection you would make for any other type of housing, with a few extra observations in deference to the nature of the place. Among the extra questions you ask yourself might be these: Is the roof pitched or flat? Pitched ones usually cause less trouble. Is there adequate soundproofing between the units — those above and below as well as those on either side? The best times to listen for bothersome noise in an existing unit are early in the morning and late at night. If the unit is under construction, you'll have to take the word of the salesman and the experts you hire. Check the points where pipes pass through floors. They should be sealed to keep your noise — and your neighbors' — at home.

Is there adequate privacy — are windows and patios shielded from public view? On a level site, there should probably be at least 100 feet between your windows or your balcony and those of the next facing unit, and there should be some trees or shrubs to offer screening. The units can be built closer together if the site slopes so that the view from one is higher than the roof of the next. If the project has not yet been built, you'll have to study the site and try to envision what will happen when the buildings, roads, and parking areas are complete.

And while you're thinking about privacy, think about a competing consideration — convenience. Do you want to be handy to or far from the pool, golf course, parking garage, and sauna? What are the traffic patterns? Will your front door be on the main route to or from everything? That's likely to be a busy, noisy spot. If you're looking at a high-rise building, the lower floors will obviously be more convenient, especially if you're elderly or handicapped, but the upper floors will be quieter and probably offer better views. Are there firewalls between the units? Are there sprinklers in hallways? Fire doors on stairways? In a high-rise building, is there a freight as well as a passenger elevator? Is there provision for a washer and a dryer in your unit? If so, are the necessary utilities in place? If not, how far is it to the laundry? Is the laundry one of those coin-operated affairs that seems perpetually to be out of order, even when you have a pocketful of quarters? (And while you're thinking about it, who gets the profit from the laundry — the unit owners or shareholders, the developer, or some anonymous suds conglomerate?) Have jacks been installed in the unit for telephones and cable television? Or is there a master television antenna? Is there an intercom connecting each unit with the front door? Does it work? How far do you have to carry your trash? Where's the mailbox? Will there be adequate parking for you and your visitors, even if many residents own two cars? Are public areas well lighted? Take a stroll at night. Are landscaped areas equipped with sprinklers? Do all the promised amenities exist, or are some of them merely drawings and projections? Do the recreation facilities seem large enough for the population of the completed project? For example, the deep thinkers say that a pool should be at least large enough to accommodate one person from every fourth unit in the development and even larger if the place has attracted or is likely to attract a lot of families with children. Are the streets wide enough for garbage trucks and fire engines? Are they through streets that will encourage heavy traffic or speeding?

Beyond looking around for yourself, there are some questions you can ask. How many tons of air conditioning have been installed, for instance, and what's the cubic footage of the space being cooled? The local utility can probably tell you whether the place has enough air conditioning. Who was the architect for this project, and what similar places has he designed? (You'll undoubtedly want to look them over.) If it's a new development, can you shop around for a loan or does one institution have an agreement to finance all the units? Do the square-footage figures in the builder's snazzy brochure refer only to interior living space or do they include the carport and the balcony as well? Are all the walls shown on the builder's floor plans real walls or are some just room dividers? Will the floor plans be reversed in some units, thus changing the orientation and ruining the view of the railroad yard next door? How high are the ceilings? If you will rent a parking place, are you assured that you'll get the same space every year or will you have to hassle over it every time the lease runs out? If all of the recreation facilities or other amenities in a new development do not yet exist, is there some iron-clad completion date? What assurances are there that they will eventually be built? Who will own the recreation facilities, the condominium or co-op or someone else? Will outsiders be allowed to use those facilities? If so, will they pay for the privilege? Whom will they pay? Who will own the land under the development? The parking areas? The streets and walks? The sewers and water supply? Are the sewers adequate to handle the runoff after a heavy storm? The city or town engineer should know. He should also be able to tell you if the streets and walks meet municipal standards. Have the sewer and water systems been approved by the health department? In general, anything that doesn't belong to the condominium or cooperative should belong to the local government. Things left in the hands of the developer or sold to third parties for lease to the unit owners tend to grow into large rip-offs.

If it's new, is there a strict limit on the over-all size of the project, so the recreational facilities won't become overcrowded? Has the zoning board approved the whole plan, which at least helps to ensure that early buyers won't find themselves unable to expand and stuck with a huge complex they can't support alone? What assurances are there that the place will be completed on schedule? When will control of the project pass from the developer to the unit owners? That should probably happen when 70 percent of the units are sold or within two years of first occupancy. It should never be dependent upon the sale of the last unit because that setup allows the developer to hold onto one unit and award lucrative contracts to himself and his friends for everything from collecting the trash to operating the laundry room. New owners often clamor for instant control of their own affairs, but many experts consider it the developer's responsibility to prepare the owners for the huge task of managing their complex by relinquishing control gradually.

Will your deposit go into escrow? Will you get the interest on the escrow account? You may have difficulty persuading a developer to put your money into escrow until you take title to your unit, but you may be able to arrange to have it put into escrow until a certain percentage of the units is sold and then stipulate that the money may be used only in the construction of your unit and the common elements in this project, not for any other purpose. Under what conditions will you be able to get your deposit back?

Who is the developer and what experience does he have with this sort of project? Has he built them before? Are the residents in those complexes happy — not with just the construction, but also with his handling of the initial transition to resident control? Does the developer have the financial strength to complete a project that is not yet finished? For a fee, some banks will run a credit check for you. Very helpful information.

Exactly what maintenance will you be required to perform, and what will be the responsibility of the association or corporation? Is the patio or terrace part of your unit or a common element? In a condominium, where does your responsibility for electric and plumbing lines end? Do you paint both sides of the door or just the inside? Are there prohibitions against pets or children? Some places will allow you to move in with the pet you already own but prohibit you from replacing it if it dies or strays. The ones that bar children don't seem to be nearly so understanding. The sort of communal living that goes on in co-ops and condominiums can seriously hamper all sorts of special interests. You may not, for example, be allowed to park your camper or boat at the door. You may be forbidden to wire your kiln or rig your ham radio antenna. You may have trouble practicing your trombone. And you will almost certainly be unable to breed dogs or use the parlor to sell perms to the neighborhood's beautiful people. Even if you're interested in nothing more exotic than eating and sleeping, you ought to ask about regulations that may cramp your style. Are there rules barring occupancy by anyone other than the members of an immediate family? If so, you may not be able to take your grandmother in after her next attack of double vision, thus insuring that she will cut you out of her will.

Are there restrictions against renting your unit? There should be because rentals, all the experts agree, tend to reduce the value of the project and make its management more difficult. After a nationwide study of condominiums and co-ops, the Department of Housing and Urban Development concluded that serious problems arise when 20 percent of the units are rented, but most informed opinion puts the breaking point much lower than that, at, say, 10 percent. Even more pernicious than renting is the practice of time-sharing — for example, selling each of 52 buyers one week a year in a unit for 20 years or so. That means the unit's vote is broken up into infinitesimal fractions and the place is treated like a motel room; nobody really cares how it's maintained as long as it's still there next year. Unless you're buying a unit strictly as an investment — to rent out by the week or month — avoid like yellow fever any development that allows time-sharing.

Are there limitations on your selling the unit? They're typical in co-ops, where the board generally has to approve any buyer you find and can reject virtually any deal without explanation. They can be downright picky, especially when demand is high. And while ethnic considerations have been known to play a part in such decisions, they usually focus on wealth more than anything else. The board may, for instance, want to look into a potential buyer's employment history, credit rating, debts, and education. It may demand to see a copy of last year's tax return as well as a financial statement. And it may insist that anyone who can't make a down payment of 50 percent just wouldn't fit in. What such demands mean, of course, is that only the wealthy need apply to certain co-ops and that many banks are wary of becoming involved, even where it's permitted, for fear they'll never be able to find an acceptable buyer for their collateral.

In general, condominiums are not so restrictive. But it's still well to be wary and ask some pointed questions. Many condominiums insist upon the right of first refusal — that is, once you've made a deal to sell, the association can match the price and take the unit. Be sure in such a case that the association will have to match your price, not just reject your buyer, and that it will have to do so within a reasonable time. In practice, though, condominiums rarely exercise that right, at least in part because to do so they would have to borrow money or assess all the other members to raise cash to purchase your unit. In publicly assisted projects — condominium or cooperative — there may be a limit on the profit you can realize from a resale; you may have to sell the unit for what you paid for it or for that sum plus some factor of what you've invested in it since you bought it. And some co-ops levy a "flip tax," a transfer fee based on the size of your profit. That's not necessarily wrong, but it's something you should know about before you buy.

What routine services will not be included in the monthly maintenance charges? Trash removal? The use of the master TV antenna or cable television? Utilities? Parking? Who made the estimates of maintenance charges in a new development? On what basis were they made? Has an independent managing agent certified them as reasonable? Does the local tax assessor's estimate of real estate taxes agree with the estimate in the projected maintenance charges? Does your insurance agent think that the provision for insurance premiums is adequate? When will you have to begin paying maintenance charges in a new development? When you sign a contract to buy, which is likely to be long before you start getting any services in return? At the closing, when you take possession of the unit? That's not unreasonable, but some early buyers in large condominium projects have been able to negotiate a delay in maintenance charges until a specified number of units have been sold. Will the developer warrant the maintenance charges — that is, guarantee that they will not rise for a specified period? Many developers warrant them — and indeed subsidize them — as long as new units are being sold. When the sales period ends and the developer walks away, the owners suffer cardiac arrest because their monthly fees suddenly double or triple. Is the developer required to pay full maintenance charges for any completed but unsold units? If not, and if sales are slow, the association or corporation may find itself sorely short of cash.

And how high are the monthly charges, anyway? They may be called maintenance fees, carrying charges, association dues, or even assessments, and the last term should not be confused with special assessments — extra charges levied from time to time when the place gets into a financial bind. Whatever they're called, the monthly charges should be within your budget, naturally, and they should be within the budgets of other folks who live in the development. So it's good to find out how many units are in arrears on their payments. If the total is more than 10 percent of all the units, there's trouble ahead; be careful.

In general, monthly charges for a condominium unit are a bit higher than the rent for a comparable apartment before taxes but lower than the comparable rent after taxes. So don't get your dander up before you figure the tax impact of this move. Also in general, fees are a tad more lofty in high-rise complexes than in comparable townhouse projects. In a high-rise, after all, the fee will have to cover elevator maintenance, probably central heating and air conditioning for every unit, and all exterior maintenance, perhaps including window washing, which doesn't come cheap 36 stories up. Each townhouse, on the other hand, may have its own heating and air conditioning plant, and each owner may be responsible for some outside maintenance. Only the most churlish of them will demand an elevator or refuse to wash his own windows.

How long has the project been on the market and what proportion of the units are sold? Do those sales represent closed deals or merely reservations? If the thing is moving too slowly, it may collapse of its own financial weight before there are enough unit owners to take over its management and make it pay for itself. If it's been hanging around for a year, say, and is only half sold — especially if the "sales" are not really sales but reservations — there's good cause for worry. Dropping prices are also an indication of potential danger. The situation to look for is brisk sales in a cross section of unit types, not just in one model or one part of the development, and stable or slightly rising prices. If you're shopping for a resale unit in an older development, try to find out how many sales there were in the last year and calculate the percentage of the total. A condominium or co-op in which fewer than 10 percent of the units turn over in a year is probably stable. If the rate is higher than 10 percent, it's worth some further checking. The problem may have nothing to do with the complex where you're thinking of buying — maybe the largest local employer has transferred his entire gum-wrapping operation to Segal's Notch, Nevada — but you'd better find out.

How long is the management contract? Can the unit owners vote to fire the managing agent and hire a new one on fairly short notice — say, 60 to 90 days? Even a year? Long-term, unbreakable management agreements represented one of the greatest abuses of the Florida condominium boom. Under what conditions can the owners cancel the management contract if they're not satisfied?

If the project has been around a while, how often have assessments beyond the regular maintenance charges been levied? In some places, special assessments are about as regular as the maintenance fees. How large is the contingency fund, the money set aside for major repairs? If it's inadequate, big assessments can be expected sooner or later, and if the owners can't agree on an assessment for a while, the repairs will be delayed and the value of the property will drop. The reserve should probably be the equivalent of 20 or 25 percent of the annual budget. In a new project, has the developer endowed a small contingency fund to get the thing off the ground?

Who is the managing agent? Are his employees who handle cash bonded? What other projects does he manage? Are residents there happy with him? Does his contract specify that there will always be a management representative on hand — 24 hours a day, even on Christmas — to take care of emergencies? Get bank references from the management company, and check them. In an existing project, does the association or corporation operate efficiently? Ask some residents. Who are the directors? Do they have some professional qualifications in such areas as law, accounting, management? How often does the board membership turn over? If there's a new board every year, the place must be a rat's nest of infighting and jealousy, not a pleasant home. Is there a regular bulletin or newsletter on co-op or condominium affairs? Is there an orientation program for new owners? Are there regular owners' meetings? Are there many absentee owners — people who use the place only for vacations or business trips or to hide their lovers? Absentee owners tend to ignore the rules and are often late payers. Those are qualities frowned upon by your better condominiums and co-ops. If the ads extol the rental potential of the place, be wary. And be sure the complex is run by experienced, professional managers.

In a resale transaction, find out something about the seller, too, or at least about his financial standing with the condominium or co-op. It's possible that if you buy his unit and he hasn't paid his bills, you will be held responsible for the unit's debts. It's just as your mother said: Always do business with nice people.

No matter how many questions you ask yourself, the seller, the developer, or the neighbors, what ultimately counts — in this kind of sale as in no other — is what's in the fine print. How well you fare in this venture will really be determined by the contents of a series of extremely detailed documents that you and your lawyer must study and understand before you commit yourself. In many instances, the seller may refuse to show you the basic documents until you've signed some form of binder or contract. That's a fairly good sign that you should take your business elsewhere, even if it means buying a cottage in the mountains instead of an apartment at the beach. To ask you to commit yourself before you've read the basic documents for a condominium or co-op is to ask you to buy before you know exactly what you're buying. That's just as stupid as it sounds.

It is absolutely essential that you and your lawyer have the basic documents before you sign anything at all. And not just 20 minutes before you sign.

These things can run to hundreds of pages — sometimes three or four thick volumes — and you have to have them early enough that your lawyer can read and digest them, advise you of their import, and answer your questions before you sign anything more binding than a postcard to your Uncle Walter. Make it clear to the seller that you simply will not do business until you have examined the documents, and if he refuses to budge, simply do not do business. Easy, ain't it?

CONDOMINIUM DOCUMENTS

Not so easy will be the task of deciphering all that verbiage once it's forthcoming. If it's a condominium you're after, the basic papers will include the declaration, the bylaws, the rules and regulations, the budget, the management agreement, the purchase agreement, and the unit deed.

At the root of it all is the "declaration," the instrument that creates the condominium and is recorded, probably at the county courthouse, so that all the world may know. It can be called the enabling declaration, the master deed, covenant, charter, plan of condominium ownership, deed restrictions, or declaration of conditions, covenants, and restrictions. Whatever it's called, once it's recorded the condominium is established and its provisions are, in effect, the law.

The declaration should provide for an association to run the condominium and for the assessment and collection of fees from unit owners. It should describe management procedures and insurance requirements and provide for the maintenance of the "common elements" — the areas owned by all the residents in common, also known as the common area, common property, or common estate — and the establishment of a reserve fund. The declaration should describe the common elements in painstaking detail and establish the percentage of ownership for each unit, probably on the basis of value, size, or some combination of the two. The percentage of ownership will control the taxes and fees levied on each unit. If the development is a large one that will include more than one condominium — each high-rise building, for example, may be a condominium unto itself — and two or more of them will share one common element like a big swimming pool, things get much more complicated. In that case, the declaration should set out each unit's percentage of ownership at each stage of development — when only the first condominium exists, after the second is finished, when the third is complete, and so forth. Since the ownership percentages are sometimes given in thousandths of one percent, you'll need at least a calculator to keep from hurting your head.

The declaration should give the exact size and location of each unit, right down to a plot or map of the site and describe the mechanical equipment in each. It should specify the precise scope of the project, giving the total number of units and an approximate schedule for their completion, and describe any easements and all allowable uses. If there are long-term commercial leases for parts of the development, they should be described in detail. Finally, the declaration should provide for its own amendment — perhaps by a vote of two-thirds of the owners — and for its own termination — most often only by unanimous vote.

The bylaws are the fundamental rules under which the unit owners in a condominium govern themselves. They should provide for the owners' association and its operations, describing the composition and duties of the board, the scheduling of meetings, voting powers, and so forth. The bylaws should also deal with finances — the composition of the annual budget and its allocation to the maintenance of the common elements and to a reserve fund, the adoption of the budget by the board and its submission to the membership, and how assessments are decided upon and prorated. The bylaws should stipulate the insurance coverage the association will provide for itself, its directors, and the common elements, and describe the restrictions on sales, transfers, profits, leasing, use, and occupancy. They should set out what happens if an owner fails to pay his fees on schedule and what remedies the association has for failure to pay. Those remedies may include fines, the forfeiture of membership privileges, liens, injunctions, actions to seize personal property, the foreclosure of the mortgage, or even the seizure of the unit itself. Finally, the bylaws, which have virtually the force of law, should provide for their own amendment. That's usually possible with a vote of two-thirds of the owners, but such a vote is mighty hard to get in most condominiums, so you'd better be fairly sure at the outset that you can live with the bylaws. (Nonetheless, the bylaws are usually easier to change than the declaration. So if you can buy in a place where the onerous rules are in the bylaws rather than the declaration, do so.)

The same sort of difficulty applies to the rules and regulations, the day-to-day laws of the condominium, which may govern such things as pets, loud parties late at night, storing household goods on your balcony, or consuming alcohol in the recreation room. The rules and regulations will probably be easier to change than the bylaws or the declaration — perhaps a majority vote will suffice — but that can be a hassle, too, and the rules can make life fairly miserable if they fly in the face of your bad habits.

The budget should set out all of the sources of association income and all projected spending for the year. Its estimates should be reasonable. If they look like incredible bargains now, they will probably have to be padded out with special assessments later. The budget should be detailed but as clear as possible; it should not be necessary for the average unit owner to hire an accountant every year to read the budget. Be sure there is provision for a sinking fund or reserve — the kitty the association is saving for the rainy day when the roof leaks.

What all of this legal mumbo jumbo produces is a condominium association composed of all the unit owners. Each has a vote weighted in proportion to his interest in the common areas, and that interest is usually a function of the size or value of his unit. Because your percentage interest in the condominium is so important (it governs not only your vote but the relative size of your payment each month), it should not be subject to change without your approval. If it is, buy someplace else. The condominium association usually elects a board of directors. The board enacts and enforces day-to-day rules, adopts a budget, and assigns to each unit owner a share of the operating costs. The board can also hire a managing agent or a staff.

The management agreement or contract is the document through which the association — or, in a new project for which no association yet exists, the developer — hires a professional managing agent to run the condominium under the board's direction. The agreement should be clear and very specific, providing for such services as these: The maintenance and upkeep of all common elements; the hiring and supervision of all employees; the preparation of a budget; accounting and record-keeping; the collection of fees and assessments; and control over a limited operating fund. Usually the managing agent is empowered to sign checks up to a given size, beyond which he must obtain board approval. It is most important, especially in a new project in which the developer has negotiated the management contract, that the association be able to cancel the agreement and hire a new managing agent if the incumbent proves unsatisfactory.

The purchase agreement is the contract you'll be asked to sign promising to buy your unit. In a new development, it's likely to be a standard document that the builder will not consider altering. In a resale, you may have more freedom to negotiate. It is no less important than the sale contract for any other form of housing and is a good deal more dangerous because it's more complicated. It's likely to be the first thing you're shown and asked to sign. But of course you will not under any circumstances sign it until you've read it with your lawyer and understood it and all the other basic documents in the sale. Of course.

The contract should, like the declaration, specify the percentage interest in the common elements that accrues to the unit you are buying, and you would do well to compare the contract and the declaration to insure that they are the same in this respect. The contract should further provide that the percentage cannot be changed without your consent. Not just the board's consent, yours.

It should give the exact location and dimensions of your unit. The dimensions are especially important if you're buying from a floor plan, where dimensions are frequently sketchy at best and are often accompanied by a warning that they're approximate or that the finished unit will be "substantially similar" to the plan. You want precision, not similarity. Know exactly what every dimension will be. Know what is a wall and what is a divider, what is a window and what is a door. Know how high the ceilings will be. Know whether the floor plan is likely to be reversed in your unit. The contract should also include exact details on the mechanical equipment, appliances, fixtures, and furnishings that will come with the unit.

The contract should provide that all liens on the unit will be removed at or before the closing (and that assertion should be confirmed by a title search). It should include a mortgage contingency clause if you need a mortgage, providing for the return of your deposit if the deal falls through. You can try to write in other contingencies, but it's unlikely that you'll get very far in a new development. One thing worth attempting is a provision for warranties from the builder and the manufacturers of various components and appliances, with the stipulation that the warranties will begin when you occupy your unit, not when you sign the contract or when construction begins or ends. You might also try to get the developer's personal warranty as well as that of the shell corporation that is building the project, but good luck. The purchase agreement in a brand new development that is not yet occupied should provide for the return of your deposit if a specified number of units have not been sold by some given date. The developer may not object; if he can't sell enough units in advance he may want to drop the whole project. In a new development, the contract should also stipulate that the unit will be delivered with a permanent, not a temporary, certificate of occupancy. Temporary certificates are often issued to unfinished units in a civic effort to help buyers who have nowhere else to go. Those buyers then sometimes wait a generation or so to have the final touches put on their homes.

Finally, the unit deed, the document you'll get at the closing signifying ownership of your home, should describe the unit and its location exactly and should jibe in all respects with the contract and the declaration. It will be recorded after the closing just like any other deed. This is one document that you can probably live without seeing in advance. If you've studied everything else before you commit yourself, it's a relatively simple matter to have your lawyer insure at the closing that the deed conforms to the deal as you know it.

In some states, virtually all of this written material may be gathered together into one document known as a prospectus or offering statement, and it may be given to you fairly early in your discussions with the developer. If everything's there, the prospectus may run to several hundred pages and require several volumes. But that happens only in states where the law requires it. A prospectus can also be the most cursory of documents. Judge it by its contents, not its cover. If it does not contain all of the basic documents, insist upon seeing them before you sign anything. In many cases, especially if there is a prospectus, salesmen insist that their developments have been "approved" by some government agency. That is almost certainly a misrepresentation. It may be true in the sense that some agency has ruled that the prospectus contains the information required by law. But it is virtually a sure thing that no arm of government has given its endorsement to the terms you are being offered or to the project as planned. Unless you see the governor's signature under a statement that this is no rip-off, don't believe it for a minute. And if you do see that signature, vote for a different governor next time.

If you're buying a resale condominium unit in an older development, the documents you want to examine before deciding to buy should be up-to-date versions. What the original declaration said is of little interest if it's been revised 111 times. In the same connection, an operating condominium can provide you with a certification of the common charges for the unit in question rather than merely an estimate of what they will be, and it can give you an official tax deduction statement showing what proportion of your maintenance charges you can pass along to Uncle Sam.

And if the project in which you're looking for your piece of the action has recently been converted or is in the process of being converted from a rental development into a condominium, every caution you've read heretofore goes double. Converted developments tend to be cheaper than new ones built as ownership housing — especially if you're already a tenant — but the amenities tend to be much fewer and the maintenance charges markedly higher. In part, the charges are higher because many older buildings are constructed in such a way that utility bills have to be included in the monthly maintenance fees, but the major reasons for the higher outlays are that older buildings need more fixing and replacing and that landlords contemplating conversion have a habit of deferring maintenance. Given those facts, an engineer's report on the condition of the building is doubly important in a conversion, and so are a detailed statement of past expenses and a proposed budget. Read all of them skeptically. Be aware that taxes may rise fairly sharply because tax rates are generally higher on ownership property than they are on rental property. If in the process of converting the building the owner is switching from one master electric meter to individual meters for each unit, you can anticipate a swift increase in utility bills, for the complex will probably be changing from a wholesale electric rate to a retail one. And think hard about the reserve fund, the money set aside for the inevitable repairs and replacements. It should be very generous.

Get the seller's written warranty that the place conforms to all applicable codes and is free of violations. It is also wise to take some pains to be sure that the owner is including in the condominium everything that's necessary to make the thing viable — all the privately owned utilities, recreation facilities, parking areas, and commercial space. If the landlord sells you the apartment but retains the water supply, he has you over a barrel. He can charge you whatever he pleases for water. If the landlord has relied upon commercial rentals to make the place pay for itself as a rental project, the chances are that it won't work as a condominium unless the association has that income, too. Be sure it does. Be sure as well that, if you're not a tenant, your contract in a converted building stipulates that your unit will be delivered vacant. The thing is of no use to you if it still contains a tenant protected by rent control laws who has no intention of moving for 15 years or so. Tenants in that frame of mind often wage bitter fights against conversion, so be prepared to hunker down.

Finally, remember your insurance, and see that it's tailored to your ownership of a condominium rather than some other form of housing. Your title insurance, for example, should protect you not only against the failure of title to the underlying land but also against a finding that the condominium was not properly established and is therefore invalid. The title to your unit depends upon both factors, so you should be protected against both. If you're unable to find a standard policy protecting you against both risks, try to persuade your insurance carrier to give you a written statement saying that the policy has been construed as covering both of them. It's unlikely that the insurer will be pleasurably overwhelmed at that suggestion, but you can always ask.

Homeowner's insurance is perhaps the one area where the condominium buyer has it easier than his fee-simple counterpart. There's one form of policy tailored specifically for the condominium unit owner, the Homeowner's 6, or HO-6, form. In general, it protects the personal property in your unit and the unit realty — whatever is not part of the common elements, including any alterations or additions made at your expense. It also gives you personal liability protection in case some clodhopper hurts himself swinging on your chandelier and decides to sue you. And it covers some extra living expenses you might incur if you have to vacate your unit for a while because of damage from a fire or storm. Like other forms of homeowner's insurance, HO-6 has available at extra cost endorsements that will raise the limits of coverage, reduce the number of risks excluded, and even provide protection against special assessments to cover uninsured losses by the association.

But perhaps the best arrangement for insurance in a condominium is one in which the association insures the entire project, including the units, and the individual owners buy liability protection and coverage for the contents of their units. The big advantage of this approach is that if fire or some other catastrophe damages several units there will be no hassle over who's responsible for what — the same policy covers everything — and no risk that one or more unit owners will be uninsured or underinsured.

COOPERATIVE DOCUMENTS

If you're looking at a cooperative unit rather than a condominium — that is, buying shares in a corporation rather than a physical unit — it's almost sure to be a resale since condominiums have pretty well supplanted cooperatives in new construction. The popularity of the co-op has always been geographically narrow, and even in the places where it has traditionally held sway — big cities, for the most part — new construction, when there is any, seems to be in condominiums rather than co-ops. In a sense, that makes life easier for the co-op buyer, since there are relatively fewer charlatans among people trying to sell their homes than there are among promoters trying to unload hundreds of units in a hurry.

Nonetheless, before you commit yourself to a purchase, you'll want to go over with your lawyer all the basic documents to be sure that you know what's afoot here. The major papers in a co-op are: The corporate charter or certificate of incorporation, the document that formed the corporation that is the basis for the whole thing; the bylaws, the rules under which it operates; the year-end financial statement, which tells you where it stood when it last closed its books; the current budget, which tells you how it expected to fare this year; the proprietary lease, the paper that gives you the right to use your unit and tells you where you stand in relation to the corporation; the minutes of meetings for the last couple of years, which tell you how harmonious and carefree life has been around here; and if it's a new development, the prospectus or offering statement, which may gather together under one cover many of these documents. All of the cautions that apply to reading condominium documents apply to those for co-ops as well.

The most informative of the co-op papers are likely to be the bylaws, financial statement, budget, minutes, and lease. The bylaws will probably tell you something about the social and financial limitations on tenancy and the restrictions on resales, renting, and interior alterations. The most important disclosure in the financial statement will probably be the amount of working capital — the difference between current assets and current liabilities. There are co-ops that keep a lot of working capital on hand and those that do not. Those that do not have to turn to special assessments to pay large and unexpected bills, a possibility of which you should be aware before you jump in. The financial statement should also tell you the size of all the outstanding mortgages, whether they are self-liquidating, when they mature, and what the interest rates are. A large mortgage means an inability to raise extra money without turning to assessments. A small one can mean a shortage of working capital. A mortgage with a low interest rate that is not self-liquidating and that matures soon will probably mean skyrocketing maintenance charges when the refinancing comes. There should also be in the financial statement details of the ground lease if the co-op does not own its land, the terms of any mortgages on the land or the leasehold, and details on any option to buy the land. Obviously, this is an area in which expert advice is in order. Consult your lawyer.

The budget should be examined with an eye to whether its projections are reasonable. It is not unknown for co-ops to use regular assessments in an effort to keep carrying charges down on the theory that high carrying charges make apartments harder to sell. The theory is undoubtedly sound, and you're its potential victim. Think about what's involved in running this place and the estimate you've been given of your maintenance charges. Does the budget make sense in those terms? Have you been reading newspaper stories about building employees negotiating a new contract? Is that going to upset the entire budget? Does some disinterested managing agent see these estimates as reasonable?

The minutes of past meetings may suggest that huge expenses lie ahead if, for example, the owners recently voted to wait a year before replacing the elevator or installing the new wiring required by the electrical code.

By all means the most interesting of all the co-op papers you come across should be the lease, the document that sets out your relationship with the co-op corporation and your neighbors. Be sure, first of all, that it is indeed a proprietary lease — that it lasts as long as your ownership of the stock it represents. Some co-op leases, especially in government-assisted projects, are not proprietary. They have terms of two or three years with no automatic right of renewal. They are designed to allow the public agency sponsoring the development to enforce its income limitations and to get rid of troublemakers. If you stand a chance of being booted out after a few years, be aware of it. Try to get as much detail as possible on the term of the lease, the conditions for renewal, and the continuation of co-op status in the project. It's possible that the whole thing was set up with the understanding that the leases would expire on some specified date and that when they do the corporation would be dissolved. That would be some surprise if you weren't expecting it.

The lease should stipulate that it is inseparable from the stock assigned to your unit, and it should specify how many shares it represents. It should say that the unit will be delivered vacant and that necessary painting and repairs will be completed before delivery. It should require that the corporation obtain insurance against hazards and liability to or on its property and that the corporation provide each shareholder with an annual financial statement, including necessary tax-deduction information. Notice what the lease requires of you as well as what it requires of the corporation. It may, for instance, say that before you can vote you must be a full-time resident and up-to-date on all your payments. It may empower the corporation to obtain a lien for unpaid carrying charges. It should specify whether you have the right to sublet your unit and if so under what conditions.

There may be some questions that the papers, complete as they are, will not answer but that need asking all the same. For example, is there a professional managing agent? What specifically are his duties? What other projects does he manage? Are the residents there happy with him? What is the policy on pets? If the board will allow you to finance part of the purchase of your unit, what lenders have made loans to shareholders here? Some lenders may have in their standard loan agreements terms that offend this board, and there's no sense in your fighting an uphill battle if you don't have to. Besides, a lender who is familiar with the place is more likely to give you a loan.

Once you and the seller have finished all your niggling and agreed upon a deal, his lawyer will probably draw up a contract for you and your lawyer to approve. It should contain an agreement to sell all the stock related to the unit in question and to transfer to you the seller's lease to that unit. The contract should be contingent upon the board's approval of the transfer and should set forth the steps both you and the seller may be called upon to take in an effort to secure that approval — such things as furnishing data and references, submitting to interviews, and so forth. It should require the seller to grant to the corporation permission to confirm for you any figures the seller has given you. It should list all personal property included in the transaction, specifying precisely what belongs to the seller rather than the corporation. It should provide that you will be given a copy of any notice of increased charges issued by the corporation between the signing of the contract and the closing and a copy of any announcement of a meeting to discuss such increases. If you have not received them before, you should receive with the contract copies of the current budget, the last annual financial report, and the most recent tax-deduction statement for the unit.

All the extra risks of buying in a building converted from rental status apply to a cooperative as well as a condominium. But the insurance question is even simpler. You own nothing in the way of real estate, you own shares in a corporation. So what you need is a tenant's insurance policy, one that provides personal liability coverage in your unit and protects you against the loss of your personal property. Everything else is the corporation's property and its worry.

When the lawyers, lenders, and board members have finished their harrumphing and given you the nod, you'll probably attend a closing much like that for a fee-simple purchase. At it, you should receive: a certificate of board approval for the transfer; the seller's stock certificate, endorsed to you; an assignment of the lease and the seller's copy of the lease; the managing agent's statement that the seller is not in arrears; the title documents; a bill of sale for the personal property; and, lo and behold, the keys.

29
What Should You Look for in a Mobile Home?

In virtually every respect, you're skating on thinner ice in attempting to purchase a mobile home than you would be in buying any other type of housing. The structure itself is likely to have been built with cheaper materials and by less skilled labor than other forms of housing. It was probably thrown together in seven or eight hours under only minimal supervision. While its initial price may be its largest attraction, the terms on which you're able to finance it will make the standard mortgage look like a gift from a doting relative. Mobile homes are usually financed as personal property — the same way cars are — and sold on conditional sales contracts that have relatively short terms and outrageously high interest rates. Beyond that, the price of the thing is likely to rise 15 or 20 percent by the time you pay for such extras — some of them essential — as anchors, skirting, piers, jacks, patios, awnings, and stairs. And the financing agreement may require you to buy insurance at rates two-and-a-half or three times those that apply to conventional homes.

The warranty on a mobile home is likely to be short — 90 days has been an industry favorite, though some states require a year — and virtually worthless. Some warranties require that you return the thing to the factory at your expense for repairs and, of course, find someplace else to live while the manufacturer is tinkering with it. Even if the warranty has some teeth in it, though, you may find it almost impossible to get reliable service. Few dealers maintain service departments, and public officials have not been anxious to regulate the independent entrepreneurs in the field.

Once you own a mobile home, moreover, you may have great difficulty finding a place to put it. Mobile homes are anathema to many zoning boards;

allowing their intrusion is seen — rightly or wrongly — as tantamount to inviting Hitler to join the P.T.A. That makes it difficult to buy a site, and renting one may mean that you'll be at the mercy of a greedy or arbitrary park owner or manager who's free to charge you what he pleases, to impose upon you any rules he likes, and to evict you whenever he chooses. In most places, the law does not offer much protection to the tenant, and the mobile home tenant usually enjoys even less protection than his apartment-house counterpart.

Your mobile home is likely to be cramped, poorly designed, and extremely dangerous in a fire or in high winds. Its appearance will probably be boxy and, to put it mildly, uninspiring. The chances are its outer skin will be metal and its roof flat or of shallow pitch. Its windows and doors will be small, its ceilings low, its hallways narrow. Most mobile homes are designed to sell on the basis of "flash" — gaudy decoration — rather than taste, longevity, or solidity. They have certainly not been designed to sell on the basis of safety. A 1975 study by the National Fire Protection Association concluded that the proportion of fires caused by construction, design, or installation deficiencies was twice as high in mobile homes as in conventional housing — 6.4 percent versus 3.2 percent — and that mechanical failure or malfunction started 44.1 percent of the fires in mobile homes as opposed to 27 percent of those in conventional homes. Federal construction and safety standards that became effective in 1976 should help to limit that gap, but if peace of mind is what you're after, a mobile home is not the place to find it.

Even if the thing doesn't burn down or blow away, however, it may depreciate at an alarming rate and ultimately be impossible to sell and prohibitively expensive to move. Its life expectancy is much shorter than that of a conventional structure — probably less than 20 years, as opposed to 50 years or more — and some experts say that a mobile home loses 25 percent of its wholesale value in the first year and 10 percent a year thereafter. Though its placement in a top-rated, well-maintained mobile home park may tend to reduce depreciation, it's unlikely that a mobile home will ever grow in value the way other homes quite regularly do.

Most of the problems with mobile homes stem from the fact that they're not designed to be permanent structures. They're built in factories on steel chassis, designed to be towed to sites where they're mounted on piers, pads or foundations. Highway restrictions generally limit their width to 12 or 14 feet, though there are some units 16 feet wide, and they run anywhere from 40 to 80 feet long. A growing share of the market has been taken in recent years by "double-wides," homes that consist of two units towed individually, then bolted together at the site to form a structure 24 or 28 feet wide. There are also expansion sections known as tip-outs, roll-outs, slide-outs, or pull-outs that collapse into the main unit during transportation, then are tipped, rolled, slid, or pulled out at the site to form a larger interior space. And there are tag-alongs, separate units designed to be fastened to mobile homes to enlarge them.

The dimensions given for all of these things by dealers and manufacturers can be deceptive because the standard length usually includes a towing hitch that's about three feet long; what's generally described as a 60-foot unit, in other words, is more likely to be 57 feet long. More important than the outside dimensions is the area, the living space in the home. The average for single-wide units is around 900 square feet and for double-wides about 1,300 square feet. The average area of new conventional houses is a bit more than 1,500 square feet. In general, the same area will provide a more livable home if it's in a wider unit. The shape of the single-wide tends to limit its floor plan to that of the railroad flat — one room wide and as long as the lot.

Mobile homes are usually offered fully furnished — containing everything except linens and dishes — but the quality of the furnishings and decorations tends to be lower than low. Furniture, draperies, and other such doodads are often not included in the warranty, and they are usually designed to last months, rather than years. Better furnishings are often available as options. Though the credit you'll get for buying the home without furnishings may be almost negligible, you may be better off to find your furniture and decorations elsewhere.

Because they're not considered permanent structures, mobile homes are usually not required to conform to the local building code. Until fairly recent years, in fact, they didn't have to conform to much of anything except the manufacturer's idea of what would sell. Since June 15, 1976, however, mobile homes have been built under federal regulations that set minimum standards for light, ventilation, ceiling height, room dimensions, emergency exits, safety glazing, flammability, firestopping, snow load capacity, wind resistance, condensation, air infiltration, insulation, heating, air-conditioning, and plumbing and electrical systems. The standards also require smoke detectors and now provide that the manufacturer supply the buyer with a manual giving operating and maintenance instructions, describing the warranties and the set-up procedure, the process of installing the home on its foundation and leveling it, and outlining the method for filing complaints. The mobile home is also supposed to bear a label indicating compliance with federal standards. That label does not guarantee you a good buy or a home that will deliver years of safety and comfort. It merely guarantees that the thing is not as flimsy as some of its older counterparts.

In most cases, the dealer from whom you buy a mobile home will deliver it to your site and set it up — put it on its piers, pad, or foundation, and see that it's level, which is critical to its proper functioning. In the process, he may remove the wheels and the hitch; some mobile home parks require that. He will probably leave the axles, though, and perhaps the wheels as well so that the home will not become a permanent structure legally and therefore subject to real estate taxes. You'll probably have to pay a sales tax on the home, and you may have to buy license plates for it, even though it will never move again. In a few jurisdictions, mobile homes are treated as real property for tax purposes, but they're usually treated as personal property — just like automobiles — and taxed accordingly.

FINDING A PARKING PLACE

Since a place to put the home is a critical problem in many areas, you should probably look for that even before you worry about buying the mobile home itself. Generally, there are two kinds of sites: individual lots purchased outright like any other land, and lots in mobile home parks, which may be bought or rented.

An individual lot of your own will probably be in a rural area because most incorporated municipalities would rather zone for rendering plants than for mobile homes. If that's what you're after, investigate the neighborhood as you would for any other sort of housing. Pay attention to potential zoning restrictions, to the feasibility of installing sewers or a septic system and other utilities, to the need for health department approval for the waste and water systems.

You can't just park the home in any empty lot, so you'll have to be prepared for all the extra expenses. There will be the land purchase costs, of course, including not just the purchase price but legal fees and other closing costs as well. There will be site preparation costs: clearing, grading, construction of piers, pad or foundation, a driveway, and provisions for electrical, telephone, sewer or septic and water service. There may be fees for inspections and a certificate of occupancy, you'll have to pay for the transportation, set-up, and anchoring of the thing, and you may want some landscaping or other extras such as stairs, skirting, carport, storage shed, and so forth.

On your own lot you'll lack the amenities on which mobile home parks pride themselves (swimming pools, tennis courts, playgrounds, and community halls), you won't be surrounded by friendly neighbors who share your interest in this kind of living, and you will not have the protection provided by minimum standards for upkeep that are enforced in most parks. On the other hand, you'll be spared the hassle of having to live the way your nosy neighbors and the park management think you should live. Keeping your home on a lot you own will in that sense be much like owning a conventional house.

Moving into a park is something like buying a condominium or a co-op: for better or worse, you'll have other people living very close at hand and influencing the way you live. The parallel is closest in parks that sell you a lot, rather than renting it to you. Such places may in fact be condominiums, which

WHAT SHOULD YOU LOOK FOR IN A MOBILE HOME?

means that they should be investigated in the same way any other condominium would be. They should also be subject to most of the questions you'd ask about a rental park.

Rental parks fall into two categories, open and closed. Open parks don't care where you get your mobile home; they just rent parking space. Closed parks won't let you in unless you buy your home from the park management or an affiliated dealer. The closed parks have a tendency to be huge rip-offs from a purely financial point of view, but they also tend to be the best maintained and most attractive parks, a fact that can help reduce the depreciation your home will suffer while you live there. Many parks, whether technically open or closed, are closed in the sense that they use legal or other means to restrict their tenancy. Mobile homes in parks may be the most segregated housing in the nation, and there are probably as many that bar children or young adults as admit them. And whatever their other characteristics, good rental parks tend to have waiting lists.

Perhaps the best way to begin the search for a place to put a mobile home is to visit some parks, look around, and ask questions. Does the place look attractive? Are the lawns trimmed, the roads paved, the lots neat and free of debris? Are there homes here like the one you have in mind? Some parks don't have room for double-wides or other large units, and smaller homes will tend to cheapen the larger, newer ones nearby. Is some effort made in this park to hide the monotonous, identical appearance of mobile homes?

Are there community facilities or recreation facilities? Are they things you would use and enjoy? Do they seem to be popular among the residents? Are they well maintained? Are the dressing rooms and rest rooms clean? Is the laundry room clean and neat? Do the machines work? How much does it cost to use them? How large are the individual sites? The average is 30 or 40 feet by 75 or 100 feet. Are they arranged to provide adequate privacy for each home? Are there natural or other wind barriers — trees, walls, or buildings? This is especially important in hurricane, tornado, or other high-wind areas. Are all of the units anchored — that is, fastened by cables, straps, or chains to anchors driven into the earth? If not, an errant home may blow into yours during a windstorm. Are there fire hydrants?

Having looked around, talk to some residents other than the manager or a staff member. Are the residents satisfied with the park and the way it's run? Do they think the management is arbitrary? Are the rules unreasonable? The fees excessive? Do the residents obey the rules? How long has the average owner been there? Is there an active tenants' association? Can the residents use any tradesmen, repair people, or vendors they choose, or are they restricted to people approved by the management? Do they have to buy fuel, milk, or any other goods or services from the management, or are they free to shop around?

If, after all that, the park still seems like a place you'd like to live, talk to the manager. Are there any vacancies? If not, how long is the waiting list?

What are the rental fees and what do they cover? Maintenance? Utilities? Trash removal? If utilities are included, how are they metered, by the utility company or by the park? Exactly what exterior maintenance does the management supply and what is the unit owner's responsibility? Are there rental surcharges for children or other family members? Are there charges for pets? What are they? One park is said to have charged for dogs by the pound. Is there an entrance fee? Transfer or departure fee? Is the transfer fee charged even if the park management does not act as broker in the sale of the home? Are there extra fees for the recreation facilities? Do you have to pay them whether or not you use those facilities? What other charges are there? There are reports of a park that charges a monthly tree rental.

Is a written lease available? For how long? What protection does it provide against rent increases? What restrictions are there on eviction? How much notice will you be given before you're evicted? In some places it's 24 hours. What are the rules and regulations? Get a copy and read them carefully. They can be extremely arbitrary. Some parks prohibit children, pets, motorcycles, clotheslines, boats, garbage compactors or disposals, scanty attire, and the washing of cars. Some of them limit the number of guests a tenant may have and the duration of the guests' stay. One is said to have banned all "improper conduct." And you know who decides what is "scanty" or "improper." Not you.

What special accessories are required? Among the possibilities are skirting, planters, porches, patios, decks, carports, garages, storage sheds, awnings, and special appliances. While one park may ban garbage disposals, another may require them. Is there always a management representative on the premises to deal with emergencies? Are there any restrictions on resale? Does the park management have the right to approve the buyer or does the home have to be sold to the park? Is it possible to rent both a home and a site to see how you like this sort of thing before you buy?

Be aware that whatever you don't have in writing you simply don't have. That goes for the space in the park and for protection against arbitrary rent increases and eviction. You may have great difficulty finding a park that will give you a written lease, but without one you're at the mercy of the management. If you get a lease, be sure to have your lawyer read it before you sign. And ask questions until you understand it, all of it. Don't underestimate your charges, either. Beyond the rent and other fees of the park, you may face charges for legal services, the transportation of the home to the park, set-up, leveling and anchoring, accessories, utilities, and perhaps deposits with utility companies.

After you've looked over and compared the available parks, you may want to see how they're rated by the bible of the industry, Woodall's Mobile Home and Park Directory. That directory, published by the Woodall Publishing Company, Highland Park, Illinois, 60035, lists all manner of mobile home manufacturers and movers and rates parks all over the country. Though it's the most widely used publication of its kind, its critics contend that it leans too heavily on retirement communities and that it concerns itself almost entirely with appearance and physical features while ignoring the human factors in mobile home living — the quality of management, the reasonableness of rules and fees. In that sense, Woodall's tells you more or less what you can see for yourself — what the place looks like — but if you want a second opinion, there it is.

FINDING A DEALER

Since there's an acute shortage of park space in some areas, you may be reduced to approaching your problem from the other end — through a dealer who may have the connections to get you in someplace once you've signed up for a home. It stands to reason that if a dealer hopes to sell any mobile homes, he must know of places to put them. But it also stands to reason that his interests are not the same as yours. Anyplace where the thing can be dropped and connected to utilities will probably suit the dealer. Kickbacks and other undisclosed financial arrangements are not unknown, so treat a dealer's suggestions with some skepticism and examine his favorite park just as closely as you would any other.

Finding a reputable and reliable dealer is a critical matter, for the mobile home industry is organized along stone-age lines and in many cases — though not in all cases by any means — its ethics are those of cavemen: Anything you can drag off by the hair is yours. A few states require the bonding and licensing of dealers, but most of them operate virtually without regulation or oversight. The majority of dealers — maybe 75 percent of them — are small local operations unconnected to anything else. Some of the others are part of regional chains, and a few may be owned by big mobile home manufacturers. Almost all of them — even those owned by a manufacturer — will sell several lines or brands of homes. In many cases, there's not so much as a written agreement between the manufacturer and the dealers who represent him. That means neither one has much control over the other, and your complaints about problems with your home may be shuffled back and forth with little in the way of results. Given that situation, the dealer is the fellow you'll have to rely on because he's more likely to be available. Check him out carefully. Ask for a list of his previous customers. Call a few and see if they're happy with the treatment they've received. Ask about his service department and try to figure out whether he seems proud of it. The service department shouldn't be a toolbox in the corner; if an automobile dealer needs a big, well-equipped shop, a mobile home dealer needs no less. Ask to see the service department and the parts department. If you can't find either one, you probably need a different dealer.

Find out whether the dealer is a member of the Chamber of Commerce and the Better Business Bureau. Ask about him at both, for whatever good that will do, and at the local consumer affairs office or district attorney's office. Call his bank, explain why you're interested, and ask about his standing with them. Ask if he's a member of the Mobile Home Dealers National Association or some local trade group and check with them. Obviously, you're better off with a dealer who's licensed and bonded, but that may be too much to expect.

FINDING A HOME

If you have some time available, you might ask the dealer to arrange a visit to the nearest factory of the manufacturer whose products interest you most. That could prove to be a very interesting trip, an opportunity to see just what goes into these things and how it's put in. It may also provide your only chance to see in the flesh the model you're thinking of buying. Your dealer will be able to stock relatively few models and will probably rely on the manufacturer's literature for descriptions of the rest. Like all advertising, however, that literature can leave a distorted impression of just how big and how luxurious the model in question really is. By all means, try to see the precise model you're considering, even if that means traveling some distance to the factory.

For most manufacturers, the materials and specifications will be the same for the whole line. The more expensive models will differ mainly in that they will provide more space and more "flash," more decoration in doubtful taste. You can therefore get a good idea of the quality and strength if not the size and layout of the model that interests you by examining any of the same manufacturer's homes. Approach that job as you would the inspection of any other home. Start outside, at a distance, and work your way in, looking for any indication of bad design, poor workmanship, or cheap materials. Look for all the things you'd look for on the interior of a conventional home, and look for other signs of stability as well. For example, slam the door — really slam it hard, as though it had just made a foul remark about your ancestry — and see if the whole joint rattles. Find a spot in about the middle of the home and jump up and down. Do the chandeliers sway? Do things fall off shelves two rooms away? Look at the backs and bottoms of pieces of furniture. This is likely to be the flimsiest element in the whole package. Sit in the chairs. Lie on the beds. The bedroom furniture will probably be the sleaziest of all.

Are there shutoff valves at all the plumbing fixtures? What's the size of the water heater? Are there any bulges or other signs of misalignment in the interior walls or in the skin on the outside of the home? The screws that hold it together should be aligned neatly and properly seated. Needless to say, none of them should be missing. They should not show any signs of rust. If the exterior covering is mounted in grooves rather than with screws, all of it should be properly seated. What's the roof made of? Plywood and shingles are generally considered better than metal. In models with tip-outs, pull-outs, tag-alongs, and other expansion units, inspect the joints carefully, looking for signs of leaks or gaps.

Hunker down and look under the thing. Can you see any indication of a sag? Mobile homes are usually built with a camber, a reverse sag, that is supposed to disappear in the course of transportation. If it has not only lost its camber but developed a sag even before it's sold and delivered, the future is not bright. Sight along the I-beams, the main structural members under the home. Are they straight? Do the outriggers, the braces mounted at right angles to the I-beams, extend out to the edges of the body? If there's any exposed plumbing under there, is it insulated?

Construction problems seem to be more common in mobile homes than in any other type of housing, and the most frequent complaints appear to concern doors, plumbing, waterproofing, furniture, heating, appliances, and wiring. You would be well advised, therefore, to pay close attention in those areas. And even closer attention when it comes to wiring. Aluminum wiring was in fairly widespread use in all types of housing between 1965 and 1972, but nowhere was it more popular than in mobile homes. The rules were changed in 1972, but with some special connections and other modifications aluminum wiring may have found its way into many models built later. Do not buy any home that you suspect may contain aluminum wiring. Not under any circumstances. Period.

One way to find out just what your mobile home contains is to get a copy of the blueprints and specifications. When your dealer refuses to give them to you, offer to pay for them. When he refuses again, write to the factory and request them, offering to pay. When they refuse, say that you want at least to look at and read them if you can't have a copy of them. If you get a copy, show them to an engineer and the local building inspector and ask for their opinions. If you merely get to look at them, read them very carefully and make notes on materials and sizes that you can later discuss with an engineer. Whether you get the plans or not, hire a building inspection engineer to go through the model with you and give you a report on its structural and mechanical soundness.

NEGOTIATING THE PURCHASE

Find out about the warranties before you sign anything. Exactly what is covered by warranty and what is not? How long is each warranty? Who stands behind each one? The dealer? The manufacturer? A manufacturer's supplier? Which of them provides the service under each warranty? Negotiate — preferably with the manufacturer rather than the dealer — for better warranties, especially on things like the insulation, storm windows, heating and air-conditioning, which you may not have an opportunity to use within the 90-day term of many warranties. Try to get the dealer or manufacturer to agree in writing that he'll repair specific structural or mechanical systems if they fail within a given period — that's what a warranty is all about — but try to get it stated as plainly as possible and try to get a personal rather than a corporate guarantee. Try to get a guarantee that transportation costs will be paid if you have to return the home to the factory for repairs under the warranty — and that your extra living expenses will be paid, too, while you're without your home. Try to get an agreement that part of your down payment will be put into escrow until the warranty expires so that you'll be sure of getting the necessary service. Good luck on that one.

The document in which all this should be written down is most often known as the dealer contract and purchase order, a cross between a home contract and a purchase order for a car. You will no doubt be presented with a "standard" form and told that it can't be changed. It can't be changed only because the dealer doesn't want to change it. It's all negotiable to one extent or another and can indeed be changed. If you don't change some of it after you have your lawyer read it to advise you on its implications, you're inviting trouble.

Be sure, first of all, that everything you expect to get is written down. Verbal promises don't count; only the contract does. Then assume that you'll negotiate every provision. Do not be told that this is the only model available and someone else is interested in it. By definition, mobile homes are built on production lines, and somewhere this model has a sister just as beautiful. Do not be told, either, that the price is fixed. The dealer has marked the home up by something like 30 percent, so he can afford to be somewhat flexible, even though he does have to pay expenses. Knocking off 10 percent is not unusual.

In addition to having some of your down payment put into escrow during the warranty period, insist that the deposit you pay when you sign the contract be held in escrow until the home is delivered. Your dealer wouldn't be the first one to disappear into the night with a deposit. The plans and specifications should be made a part of the contract and you should fight to the death the inclusion of any clause that allows the manufacturer to substitute materials or components or to change the dimensions or other specifications.

Write in a stipulation that the dealer will obtain all permits and certificates required for moving the unit and setting it up, including a certificate of occupancy if you need one. Specify that the dealer will deliver the unit to your site, set it up, level it, and connect it to the utilities, and that he will be responsible for all damage to it until it is fully set up and connected, even if the damage is not discovered until later. The contract should provide that the set-up will include anchoring the unit. Few states require anchoring and those that do tend to enforce the law spottily at best, but it's absolutely essential for safety in high winds — not just in hurricanes and tornadoes, for which anchors are hardly a match, but for any brisk windstorm. Anchoring may cost extra and you may have to hire a separate contractor to do it, but it's worth the trouble and expense.

Try to get the dealer to agree to return six months after delivery to level the home again after it's had a chance to do whatever intial settling it's going to do. And if you know you'll want to install or hang something, especially something large, when you move in, ask the dealer to do the work when he sets the home up. The walls in this place are likely to be different from any walls you've ever seen before, and working on them can be frustrating if you don't know what to expect.

The contract should, of course, give the exact model you're buying and the year of manufacture, the size, the name of the manufacturer, and the base price. It should list the options you've chosen. Some of the possibilities are: Better insulation, electrical service, appliances, furniture, carpeting, or mechanical systems; larger windows; bay windows; a removable hitch; and door chimes. The contract should list what each will cost. It should also specify the financing terms, the insurance charges if insurance is included in the deal, and the delivery date.

If the transaction involves accessories — some dealers don't sell them — the contract should list each one and its price. Some accessories are essential — for example, stairs for each door, piers, jacks, and anchors. Others are required by some mobile home parks — most often skirting (the metal or masonry walls that hide the undercarriage of the home and make it look more permanent). And still others are simply nice to have — such things as planters, awnings, porches, and patios. The dealer who does not handle all accessories will no doubt be willing to suggest someone who does, but your best bet is to shop around and get a couple of prices before you make a decision.

Your problems will be even more complex if you're shopping for a used mobile home than if you're after a new one. You can find used homes through classified newspaper ads, through dealers who accept trade-ins, through park managers, mobile home servicemen, and, in some areas, through brokers who do for mobile homes what real estate brokers do for conventional real estate. The generally accepted guide to prices for used homes is a mobile home Blue Book published by the Judy Berner Publishing Company, Westchester, Illinois 60153. Virtually any dealer or broker will have a copy, though he may not be crazy about the idea of showing it to you.

The major difficulty with buying a used home is that the federal regulations governing their construction did not become effective until 1976, so anything built earlier was not required to meet even these minimal standards. Beginning in 1969, the industry set some rules for itself, but they were not as strict as the federal regulations. If you're looking at used homes, you may find labels saying that they were built in accordance with ANSI A119.1 or with NFPA 501B, standards set by the American National Standards Institute and the National Fire Protection Association. Those standards, covering the body, frame, and heating, plumbing, and electrical systems, were followed by the members of the two big trade groups — the Mobile Homes Manufacturers Association and the Trailer Coach Association — before the federal rules took over. Before 1969, when those industry standards were adopted, it was every man for himself and the undertaker gets the last guy out. Given the hazards involved and the fact that the life expectancy of a mobile home is only about 20 years anyway, you probably should not buy at any price a home built before 1969. And given the widespread use of aluminum wiring until 1972, any home built until then would seem to represent a substantial risk, however reasonable its price.

FINANCING

Whether you're buying a used home or a new one, you'll have to pay for it, and unless you have a pocketful of cash you're likely to be bled pale in the process. Mobile homes are usually sold not with mortgages but on conditional sales contracts. That means the lender normally holds the title until you've made all the payments. It may also mean that he can repossess the thing if you're a few weeks late with one payment. He needn't go through the complex process of foreclosure, which can take a couple of years, as he would with a mortgage on a conventional home. A mobile home loan is usually backed by a chattel mortgage, which gives the lender the right to repossess if you don't pay up, and by a promissory note, which makes you personally liable for the debt. And since mobile homes sometimes depreciate fairly quickly, it's possible that you'll lose your home and still owe the lender thousands of dollars — the difference between the balance on your loan and the amount the lender realized from selling the unit.

The terms on mobile home loans — the time you have to pay them off — tend to be less than 10 years. Five to seven years is common. The Federal Housing Administration and the Veterans Administration allow much longer terms on loans they back, but many lenders refuse to make such loans.

And the going interest rates may be enough to make mortgage lenders look like philanthropists. The favorite device of dealers who offer financing is add-on interest — interest charged throughout the term on the entire principal, not the declining balance. An add-on interest rate that sounds quite reasonable translates into a simple interest rate — interest charged only on the balance due — that is sharply higher. The result of all this financial fast talk is that a mobile home loan may carry an interest rate 10 percentage points higher than that for mortgages in the area. Federal law requires that you be told the simple annual interest rate; mention that to the dealer when he starts to bandy about interest rates that seem strangely attractive.

Lending institutions generally offer better terms on mobile home loans than dealers do. Indeed, in some states the interest ceiling is lower for direct loans from institutions to borrowers than it is for loans that pass from institutions through dealers to borrowers. That makes it more attractive for the lender to get the dealer into the transaction. Moreover, the lender can often get some protection for himself by requiring the dealer to maintain an account that will compensate the lender for at least part of any losses suffered as a result of loans made through the dealer. That adds to the attraction of getting the dealer in.

Beyond that, once the dealer has built up a satisfactory balance in his account, he can take a commission on all the loans he makes. And under certain circumstances, the fees he gets for financing and the insurance that goes with it can far exceed the profit on a mobile home. The bottom line — as they say in big money circles while they fondle their watch fobs — is that you may have trouble finding a bank willing to make a mobile home loan directly. Everybody except you makes out better when it's passed through the dealer, so that's the way it's likely to be.

Even if you swallow the dealer's financing terms, though, he'll keep trying. If he can sell you some options and add their cost to the purchase price, he can probably increase the loan — and his commission. Then there's insurance. It's hard to find insurance more expensive than that on mobile homes unless perhaps your hobby is making bombs in the cellar. And nowhere is mobile home insurance likely to be more expensive than through a dealer. The deal may require that you buy physical damage insurance — protection against fire, wind, and so forth — and coverage to protect the lender in case you bury the home or run off with it in the night. And, of course, the dealer will extol the virtues of life insurance that will pay off the loan in case you're crushed by a giant turnip or eaten alive by a berserk gerbil. If the deal requires that you pay for several years' insurance in advance, you'll have to add that amount to your loan, right? Right. And that won't do any damage to the dealer's commission, right? Right.

Try to get your financing anywhere except through the dealer. The down payment may be higher — 20 or 30 percent is common, while dealers are talking about 10 percent — but the interest rate will probably be much more reasonable and you may have more time to pay. Even if you can't get a loan elsewhere, though, you probably can get insurance elsewhere. Shop around for it, and be sure that what you buy protects you as well as the lender.

THE TITLE

Ultimately, once you've picked your way through that minefield, you'll get a certificate of title, just like the document you got when you bought a car. It will describe the home and give the serial number, the manufacturer's name, and the year of manufacture. It will be recorded with the bureau of motor vehicles or the secretary of state or whoever handles such things in your state. If you pay cash for the home, you'll get the certificate when you take possession of it. If you have a loan, the lender will probably get the original certificate and you'll get a copy, perhaps known as a memorandum of title or registration. It will probably bear your name and that of the lender.

MOVING YOUR HOME

Finally, remember that whatever your home is called, it isn't all that mobile. You can't just throw a couple of cans of beans in the cupboard, hitch 'er up to the old LaSalle and head for Californy with the chickens on the roof and the goat tied behind. It takes special equipment and special skill to handle these things, and that means it's expensive. Moving one can cost you several dollars a mile, and beyond that you may have to pay for tolls, special permits, and even escort cars, which are required in some places. You'll need special travel insurance on the home itself and extra coverage on the personal property inside. You'll have to pay for some packing of the contents, the masking of mirrors and windows, the rearrangement of the furniture to improve weight distribution, the removal of stairs, skirting, awnings, and so forth. The home will have to be unblocked at the old site and set up again at the new one. If the old hitch has been removed, you may have to buy a new one, and you may have to buy or rent wheels if the old ones are gone. Moreover, you may have to leave behind many of your expensive accessories — things like awnings and stairs — because they're too bulky to move.

And after all that, you may discover that climatic conditions requiring special insulation, snow-load capacity, wind resistance, heating capacity, or some other quality mean that you can't live in the thing where you're going anyway. Despite federal efforts to devise what amounts to a national building code for mobile homes, they're still designed for regional weather conditions — just as all other homes are. A mobile home sold for use in Florida will be no match for a Minnesota winter.

What all this means is that, in the majority of cases, it's cheaper and easier to sell the home and buy a new one than to try to move it. There are nonetheless situations when moving is practical, in which case you want to be sure that the company doing your moving is licensed by the Interstate Commerce Commission as well as the states involved, and that it's bonded and insured.

You could, of course, just save up and buy some other type of housing. But it's your money and your life.

Index

abstracts of title, 200, 201, 256
accountants, advice from, 173-174, 299
adjustable-rate loans, 232-233
advertising:
   for development homes, 101-102
   for older homes, 117
advice, professional:
   from accountants, 173-174, 299
   from architects, 75, 77, 87, 94, 99, 176-177, 212
   from engineers, 174-178, 207-208, 212, 287
   from lawyers, 169-173
   from other experts, 178-180
agreements to convey, 239-240
air conditioning, 131, 140, 146, 154, 211, 264
aluminum wiring, 134
American Institute of Architects, 82, 86
American Institute of Real Estate Appraisers, 179
American Land Title Association, 252
American National Standards Institute, 289
antique homes, 60-61
apartments:
   new and old, 63
   pros and cons of, 31-32
   resale, 11
   single-story, 38-39
   two- and three-story, 40-41
appliances, 95, 121, 133, 142, 149, 264, 287
applications, mortgage, 249-250
appraisals, 75-76, 179, 207
appreciation of home value, 4, 60
appreciation participation, 234-235

architects:
   advice from, 75, 77, 87, 94, 99, 176-177, 212
   custom homes and, 81-86
   dealing with, 83-86
   fees for, 85-86
assessments:
   cost, of cooperatives and condominiums, 262, 268-269
   value, of real estate, 52-53, 149, 156-157, 198, 199, 200, 230
assumption fees, 253
attached single-family homes, 25, 26, 27, 29, 40
attachments, 198
attics, 39-40, 121, 144-147

balance of purchase price, 203, 222, 254
balloon mortgages, 5, 29, 234, 236
bargain and sale deeds, 199
baseboards, 139
basements, 121, 131-138, 153
bathrooms, 36, 121, 141, 143, 151
bedrooms, 36, 121, 142, 151-152
Better Business Bureau, 88, 110, 286
bids, 93-95
bi-level houses, 41
binders, 184, 186, 190-195, 196
   escape clauses for, 191-192
   litigation over, 194
   pros and cons of, 191, 195
Blue Book, mobile home, 289
bonds:
   mortgage, 230
   performance, 94, 212-213

bridging, 132
broad form insurance policies, 158
broker cooperatives, 113
brokers, mortgage, 219-220, 248
brokers, real estate, 75-76, 88, 180, 183-184, 185, 191, 192-193, 219, 248, 253, 256
   dealing with, 115-116
   and finding new development homes, 103
   and finding older homes, 112-116
brownstones, 31, 40, 160
building codes, 70-71, 74, 281
building inspection services, 98, 123, 174-178, 261, 287
building loans, 237-238
building moratoriums, 74
bungalows, 39
buyers' brokers, 114
buying real estate:
   economic considerations in, 121
   extra expenses in, 17-18, 162-163
   general considerations in, 119-122
   matters of opinion in, 152-155
   timing in, 9-12
   see also real estate

Cape Cod houses, 39
capital gains taxes, 5
ceilings, 121, 138, 265
cesspools, 149
Chamber of Commerce, 88, 110, 285-286
chimneys, 129, 130, 141, 142, 146
closets, 121, 139, 141, 144
closing costs, 18, 212, 244, 252-254
closing dates, 181, 182, 205-206
closings, 251-258, 278
   inspections at, 203, 255
   preparing for, 255
code violations, 201-202
colonial-style houses, 40, 60
commercial banks, 219
commuting, 7, 16, 43-44, 161-162
company mortgages, 224-225
comprehensive form insurance policies, 158
condominium insurance policies, 159
condominiums, 6, 63, 261-275
   documents for, 270-275
   financial considerations in, 262, 265, 268
   inspections of, 261, 263-270
   legal complexities of, 262
   maintenance charges for, 262, 267
   management of, 262, 268-269, 272
   monthly charges for, 267-268

   mortgages for, 265
   pros and cons of, 27-28
   renting rights and, 266
   selling rights and, 267
   social complexities of, 262-263
   types of, 26-27
   zoning and, 265
conservatism, 14
constant-payment loans, 231
construction, owner's supervision of, 97-98, 108-109
construction manager systems, 85
construction mortgages, 237-238
contingency clauses, 206-209
contractors, 65, 77, 81, 84-85, 87-93, 95-100
   contracts with, 95-97
   deciding on, 87-91
   fees for, 93
   interviewing, 90-91
   limited role of, 92-93
   negotiating with, 93-95
   settling disputes with, 98-99
   special arrangements with, 99-100
   supervising, 97-98
   see also subcontractors
contracts, 196-216
   closing and occupancy dates set by, 205-206
   for condominiums, 272-273
   contingency clauses in, 206-209, 210, 213
   with contractors, 95-97
   for cooperatives, 277-278
   deadlines for, 196-197
   as descriptions of property purchased, 197-203
   with developers, 210-213
   extra provisions in, 201-203
   for land, 209-210
   legal niceties and, 213-214
   for mobile homes, 288-289
   mortgages and, 203-204
   restrictions in, 198, 208
   specifications of, 95-97
   as statements of amount and method of payment, 203-205
   titles and, 199-201, 214-216
contracts for deed, 239-240
conventional mortgages, 230-231
convertible adjustable mortgages, 233-234
cooperatives, 4, 63, 261-270, 275-278
   balloon mortgages and, 5
   documents for, 275-278
   financial considerations and, 262, 265, 268

inspections of, 261, 263-270
legal complexities of, 262
maintenance charges for, 262, 267
management of, 268-269, 277
monthly charges for, 267-268
mortgages for, 265
pros and cons of, 28-29
renting rights and, 266
selling rights and, 266-267
social complexities of, 262-263
zoning and, 265
counteroffers, 194
covenants, 198, 208
crawl spaces, 137-138, 153
custom homes, 73-100
  designing, 79-86
  finding contractors for, 87-91
  finding land for, 73-78
  pros and cons of, 64-65

deadlines, 10, 189, 196-197
  closing dates, 181, 182, 205-206
dealers, mobile home, 285-286, 290-291
deeds, 198-199, 273
deeds of trust, 240
deferred-interest loans, 232
Department of Housing and Urban
    Development (HUD), U.S., 111, 225,
    252, 257, 266
designers, building, 81-83
designs:
  home, types of, 38-42
  style vs., 38
developers:
  checking on, 109-111
  contracts with, 210-213
development homes:
  choosing lots for, 105-109
  contracts for, 210-213
  new, search for, 101-111
  pros and cons of, 66-68
dining rooms, 36, 121, 141-142, 150
disputes with contractors, 98-99
documents:
  for condominiums, 270-275
  for cooperatives, 275-278
  preparation fees for, 253
doors, 120, 121, 127, 128, 137, 139, 141,
    287
down payments, 4, 7, 203, 212, 223, 235,
    288, 291
  equity and, 17

financing, 17-18
mortgages and, 16-19, 241
size of, 16-17, 203, 218
driveways, 120, 126
ducts, 136, 138
Dun & Bradstreet reports, 110
duplexes, 40

earnest money, 190, 192, 203
earthquake insurance, 159
easements, 198, 199-200
ecological regulations, 74-75
electrical entrance panels, 133
electrical outlets, 127, 128-129, 133,
    140-141, 142, 143
electrical wiring, 130, 134-135, 211, 287
elevators, 264
encumbrances, 198, 199, 200, 256
endowments, 219
engineers:
  advice from, 174-178, 207-208, 212, 287
  searching for, 174-175
environmental impact statements, 75
equity:
  down payments and, 17
  monthly payments and, 5
equity participation, 234-235
escrow, 192-193, 203, 212, 253, 256, 265,
    288
escrow agents, 251, 256
estoppel letters, 222
exhaust fans, 146
expansion, home, 37, 137, 150, 152, 209
  of one-and-a-half-story houses, 39-40
  in one-story houses, 39
expansion attics, 39
exteriors, 120, 126-131, 151, 286-287

factory-built homes, *see* industrialized homes
family rooms, 36, 143-144, 151
Farmers Home Administration (FmHA), 225
federal crime insurance, 160
Federal Housing Administration (FHA), 80,
    89, 111, 178
  mortgages from, 203-204, 220, 227-230,
    290
federal taxes, 5, 45
fee-simple homes, 25-26
finances, personal, 13-19
financing:
  advantages of, 217-218

Financing (cont'd)
  from developers, 212
  of down payments, 17-18
  see also mortgages
fire doors, 264
fireplaces, 141
firewalls, 264
flashing, 128, 129-130
flexible-rate loans, 232-233
flood insurance, 159
floors, 121, 132, 139
foundations, 129, 131
full covenant and warranty deeds, 198-199
fuse boxes, 133

garages, 120, 127, 152
garden apartments, 31
gas pipes, 135
general warranty deeds, 198-199
GI loans, 204, 220, 226-227, 229, 290
girders, 132
government mortgages, 62-63, 203-204, 220, 225, 226-230
grading, 108-109
graduated-payment adjustable mortgages, 232, 242
graduated-payment mortgages, 232
growth-equity mortgages, 232
gutters, 120, 129, 130

haggling, 19, 183-184, 189
heating systems, 121, 136-137, 139-140, 149, 153-155, 211, 287
high-rise ranches, 41
high-risk mortgage pools, 246-247
home inspection services, 98, 123, 174-178
homeowners' associations, 26, 263
homeownership, 3-8, 156-165
  comfort and efficiency of, 6
  commuting costs and, 7, 16, 43-44, 161-162
  expenses in, 5, 15, 156-165
  federal taxes and, 5, 45, 163-164
  financial advantages of, 4-5
  as investment, 4, 8, 16
  leverage and, 4, 217
  maintenance costs of, 7, 16, 163
  pros and cons of, 3-6
  psychological barriers to, 8
  social values and, 8
  types of, 25-29

Homeowners' Warranty programs (HOW), 89, 110
homes, 60-72, 101-119
  antique, 60-61
  custom, 64-65, 73-100
  development, 66-68, 101-111
  industrialized, 68-72
  new, 4, 59-60, 66-68, 101-111, 156, 157, 182, 194-195
  older, 4, 60-63, 112-119
  resale, 11, 112-119, 156, 157, 161, 182, 189, 195
  rundown, 61-63
  speculative, 68
home site, inspection of, 108-109
homesteading programs, 62-63, 225
hose connections, 128
houses, 38-42
  one-and-a-half-story, 39-40
  one-story, 38-39
  split-entry, 41-42
  split-level, 41
  two- and three-story, 40-41

improvements, home, tax breaks on, 5
income taxes, 5, 45, 163-164, 217
industrialized homes:
  pros and cons of, 68-72, 81
  types of, 69-70
inflation, 4, 13, 14, 65, 179, 201
inspections, 126-147
  of attics, 144-147
  of basements, 131-138
  on closing day, 203
  of condominiums, 261, 263-270
  of cooperatives, 261, 263-270
  evaluations after, 148-155
  of exteriors, 120, 126-131
  of home sites, 108-109
  of interiors, 120-121
  of living areas, 138-144
  of mobile homes, 286-287
  preparing for, 124-125
  by professionals, 98, 123, 174-178
installment sales contracts, 239-240
institutional owners, private owners vs., 187-188
insulation, 121, 135, 136, 137, 138, 140, 145-146, 211
insurance, homeowners', 14, 94, 157-161, 208, 230, 244, 254, 267, 274-275, 279, 291

kinds of, 158-161
   mortgages with, 161
insurance companies, 219
interest payments, federal tax laws and, 5
interest rates, 4, 13, 14, 221, 222, 229,
      232-234, 235, 241-242, 243, 290, 291
interiors, 120-121
interior zoning, 149-152
   in one-story homes, 39
   in two- and three-story homes, 40-41
Interstate Commerce Commission, 292

joints, 128, 138, 139, 145
joists, 121, 132

kitchens, 121, 141, 142, 150-151

land, 73-78
   contracts for, 209-210
   environmental restrictions on, 74-75
   financial advice on, 75-76
   growth restrictions on, 73-74
   looking at, 77-78
   negotiating for, 194
   for new development homes, 105-107
   technical advice on, 77
   see also lots
land contracts, 239-240
land leases, 223
landscaping, 66, 68, 104, 211
laundry rooms, 144, 151
lawyers, 169-174
   advice from, 169-173
   dealing with, 172-173
   fees for, 172-173
   searching for, 169-172
layouts, 141, 151-152
lease-options, 223-224
lease-purchases, 223-224
leases, for mobile home parks, 284
lenders:
   advice from, 76, 87-88
   closing date and, 255-257
   discrimination by, 246, 250
   income evaluation by, 13-14, 245
   increase of property value and, 4-5
   insurance policies for, 161
   mobile homes and, 290-291
   mortgages offered by, 18-19, 218-221,
      222, 226-250
   persuading, 247-248
   profits of, 4-5, 8
level-payment loans, 231, 242
leverage, 4, 217
liens, 96-97, 99, 198, 199, 200, 238
lightning rod systems, 130
lights, 127, 128, 140
listing services, 114
living rooms, 141, 150
loans, *see* mortgages
local government, 51-52
local taxes, 45, 52-53, 156-157, 164
location, 9-10, 30
   choosing, general rules for, 46
   commuting costs and, 43-44
   future expectations of, 45-46, 57-58
   living habits and, 44
   for mobile homes, 282-285
   neighborhoods and, 55-58
   for new development homes, 105-107
   public services and, 45, 52, 56, 149
   school systems in, 49-50, 56, 107-108
   social chic in, 45
   taxes and, 44-45, 52-53
   towns, 48-54
lots, 105-109, 152, 211-212
   minimum sizes of, 73-74
   for mobile homes, 282

maintenance:
   of cooperatives and condominiums, 266,
      267
   of homes, 7, 16, 163
market values, 179-180
Martindale-Hubbell Law Directory, 171-172
masonry, 153
medical services, 50-51
membership fees, 253
minimum construction prices, 74
Mobile Home Dealers National Association,
   286
mobile home parks, 282-285
mobile homes, 25, 26, 27, 279-292
   buying, 287-291
   contracts for, 288-289
   dealers for, 285-286, 290-291
   financing for, 290-291
   finding, 286-287
   finding locations for, 282-285
   inspections of, 286-287
   moving, 292
   pros and cons of, 32, 279-280, 287

Mobile homes (cont'd)
  regulations for, 281, 289
  setting up, 281
  titles for, 291-292
  used, 289-290
  warranties for, 287-288
Mobile Homes Manufacturers Association, 290
model homes, 103-105
modular homes, 70
monthly payments, 218, 223, 231-233, 236-237, 241-242, 245, 249
  and affordability of homes, 15-16
  equity and, 5
  gross weekly income and, 14
  mortgages and, 5, 16, 19-22
  taxes and, 5
monthly payments chart, 20-22
mortgage brokers, 219-220, 248
mortgage cancellation insurance, 243
mortgage life insurance, 161, 219, 234, 254
mortgage pools, high-risk, 246-247
mortgages, 4-5, 8, 157, 178-179, 198, 199, 208, 209, 217-250, 257, 290-291
  applying for, 249-250
  balloon, 5, 29, 234, 236
  ceilings on, 18-19, 241
  company, 224-225
  comparing, 248-249
  for condominiums, 265
  construction, 237-238
  contracts and, 203-204
  conventional, 230-231
  convertible adjustable, 233-234
  for cooperatives, 265
  down payments and, 16-19, 241
  Farmers Home Administration, 225
  Federal Housing Administration, 203-204, 220, 227-230
  government, 62-63, 203-204, 220, 225, 226-230
  graduated payment, 232
  graduated-payment adjustable, 232, 242
  growth equity, 232
  insurance policies with, 161
  interest rates on, 18-19
  limits on, 5, 18-19, 241
  maximum terms on, 18-19
  monthly payments and, 5, 16, 19-22
  new types of, 5, 232-236
  package, 239
  prepayment penalties on, 243-244
  purchase-money, 204, 209, 221-223
  renegotiable rate, 234
  second, 204, 222-223, 236-237
  seller's, 200, 204, 208, 221-223
  shared appreciation, 234-235
  shopping for, 241-247
  sources of, 218-221
  straight principal reduction, 231
  term, 234
  trust deed, 240
  variable rate, 232-233, 241-242
  varieties of, 231-236
  Veterans Administration, 204, 220, 226-227, 229, 290
  wraparound, 223
mouldings, 139
moving expenses, 18
multi-level houses, 41
multiple-family housing, 26-27, 29, 31-32, 160, 202
multiple listing services, 114

National Association of Real Estate Brokers, 114
National Association of Realtors, 14, 114
National Fire Protection Association, 289
negative amortization, 232-233
negotiations, 181-195
  anticipating seller's position in, 187-189
  basic rules for, 182-183
  binders and, 184, 186, 190-195
  first price offered in, 189-190
  haggling over price in, 19, 183-184, 189
  for land, 194
  making offers in, 187-190, 193
  pressures to sign in, 185-187
  stand-in negotiators and, 184-185
neighborhoods, 55-58, 119-120
  convenience of, 56
  of cooperatives or condominiums, 261
  environments of, 55
  future expectations of, 57-58, 107
  local schools in, 56
  neighbors in, 57
  public services in, 56
  rehabilitation of, 62-63
new apartments, 63
new houses, 4, 66-68, 156, 157
  negotiating over, 182, 194-195
  pros and cons of, 59-60
  see also specific types of houses
newspaper advertising, 101-102, 117
new towns, see planned unit developments

occupancy:
   certificates of, 96, 288
   dates of, 206
offers, 187-190, 193
   first, 189-190
   guidelines for, 189-190
   see also negotiations
older apartments, 63
older houses:
   finding, 112-119
   pros and cons of, 4, 60-63
one-and-a-half-story houses, 39-40
one-story houses, 38-39
origination fees, 204, 229, 243, 244, 253
owner-builder schools, 62

package mortgages, 238-239
paint, exterior, 120, 128, 149
panelized homes, 69-70
parking, at cooperatives and condominiums, 264, 265
patios, 120, 126, 152, 266
pension funds, 219
percolation tests, 77
performance bonds, 94, 212-213
personal income, 13-19
personal liability insurance, 159
personal property, contracts and, 202-203
pipes, 135, 138, 153, 263-264
planned residential developments (PRDs), 32
planned unit developments (PUDs), 32-34
pledged-account loans, 235-236
plot plans, 124-125, 151-152
plumbing, 135-136, 143, 149, 286, 287
points, 204, 229, 237, 243, 253
"pool" insurance, 160
pre-cut homes, 69
prefabricated homes, 69-70
prepayment penalties, 244-245
prices:
   buyer's advantage and, 182
   first offer, 189-190
   haggling over, 19, 183-184, 189
   institutional vs. individual owners and, 187-188
   of new homes, 194, 211, 212
   reasonable goals for, 182
   for resale apartments, 11
   for resale houses, 11, 189, 195
   seasonal variations in, 11
   zoning and, 74
privacy, in cooperatives and condominiums, 264

private mortgage insurance, 231
production units, 108
property taxes, 5, 52-53, 156-157, 217-218, 244, 267, 282
prospectus, for condominiums, 273
public services, 45, 52, 56, 149
purchase-money mortgages, 204, 209, 221-223, 254

quadruplexes, 31
quitclaim deeds, 199

rafters, 121, 145
raised-entry houses, 41
ranches, 39
   high-rise, 41
   raised, 41
real estate:
   haggling over, 19, 183-184, 189
   investment value of, 4, 8, 16
   reassessments of, 52-53, 149, 156-157, 198, 199, 200, 230
   trading, 220-221
   see also buying real estate
real estate advertising, 101-102, 117
real estate brokers, *see* brokers, real estate
Real Estate Settlement Procedures Act, 253
real estate taxes, 5, 52-53, 156-157, 217-218, 244, 267, 282
realtists, realtors, 114
   see also brokers, real estate
reassessments, 52-53, 149, 198, 199, 200, 230
recreation facilities, 264
redecorating, 18, 121
redlining, 246
relocation companies, 113-114
renegotiable rate mortgages, 234
renting, 5, 15
resale apartments, 11
resale homes, 156, 157, 161
   finding, 112-119
   negotiating for, 182, 189, 195
   price of, 11, 189, 195
reserve account loans, 235-236
restrictions in contracts, 198, 208
review fees, 253
roofs, 120, 127, 129-130, 149, 211, 263, 287
rowhouses, 31, 40, 160
rundown homes, 61-63
   sweat-equity and urban homesteading programs for, 62-63, 225, 228

sale expenses, 204-205
salesmen, development, 107-108, 111
savings and loan associations, 219, 220, 244
school systems, 49-50, 56, 107-108
screens, 128
search process, 9-12, 101-119
   for new development homes, 101-111
   for older homes, 112-119
   timing in, 9-12
   touring as part of, 118
   useful sources for, 101-102, 116-118
seasons, and availability of homes for sale, 10-11
second mortgages, 204, 222-223, 236-237
sellers:
   mortgages of, 200, 204, 208, 221-223
   questions for, 148-149
selling homes, 187-189
   best seasons for, 11
   tax breaks in, 5
septic tanks, 56, 77, 149
settlement charges, 243
settlements, see closings
sewers, 52, 56-57, 77, 149, 265
shakedown period, 58, 66-67
shakes, 128, 153
shared-appreciation mortgages, 234-235
shingles, 129, 130
sidewalks, 126
siding material, 128, 153
sills, 133
single-family homes, 25, 26, 27, 29-31, 40
single-story apartments, 38-39
size of homes, priorities for, 35-37
slabs, 153
social chic, 45
Society of Real Estate Appraisers, 179
soundproofing, 263
special form insurance policies, 158
special warranty deeds, 199
speculative homes, 68
splashblocks, 129
split-entry houses, 41-42
split-level houses, 41
sprinklers, 264
stairways, 120, 121, 128, 137, 139, 141, 142, 144-145
standard form insurance policies, 158
stand-in negotiators, 184-185
stock plans, 80-81
straight principal reduction mortgages, 231
stucco, 128, 153
style, design vs., 38

subcontractors, 65, 96-97, 100
   advice from, 88, 109-110
subflooring, 133
suburbia, 3, 8
sump pumps, 131
surveys of property, 78, 197-198, 243, 252
survivorship, rights of, 215
sweat-equity programs, 62, 225, 228
swimming pools, 152

tax breaks, 5, 224
taxes, 7, 14, 121, 149, 157, 173, 205, 212, 230, 254, 282
   capital gains, 5
   income, 5, 45, 163-164, 217
   local, 45, 52-53, 156-157, 164
   location and, 44-45, 52-53
   real estate, 5, 52-53, 156-157, 217-218, 244, 267
tenancies by the entirety, 214
tenancies in common, 215
tenants' insurance policies, 158, 278
termites, 127, 129, 132, 133, 148-149, 153, 211
term mortgages, 234
terraces, 120
three-story apartments, 40-41
three-story houses, 40-41
timed development plans, 74
time-sharing, 266
title, certificates of, 200, 201, 256, 291
title insurance policies, 200-201, 221, 244, 252, 254-255, 257
title reports, 200, 201
titles, 199-201, 291
   defects in, 199-200
   taking, 214-216
title searches, 78, 200, 221, 244, 252, 254
topography, 120, 126
townhouses, 31, 40
towns, 48-54
   local government in, 51-52
   local taxes in, 52-53
   medical services in, 50-51
   school systems in, 49-50, 56, 107-108
traffic considerations, 106, 264
Trailer Coach Association, 290
trash collection, 149
trees, 126
tri-level houses, 41
triplexes, 40
trusses, 145

trust deeds, 240
two-story apartments, 40-41
two-story houses, 40-41

Uniform Settlement Statements, 255, 257
upset dates, 206
urban homesteading programs, 62-63, 225
urea-formaldehyde insulation, 146
utility costs, 7, 121, 149, 156, 205, 212, 265
   in one-story houses, 39
utility meters, 129
utility rooms, 144, 151

variable rate mortgages, 232-233, 241-242
ventilation, 145, 146
vents, 121, 138, 145
Veterans Administration, 178, 252
   mortgages from, 204, 220, 226-227, 229, 290

walls, 120, 121, 127-128, 138, 265, 286, 289
warehouse fees, 253
warranties:
   broker's, 176
   for condominiums, 274
   developer's, 212
   inspector's, 176
   for mobile homes, 287-288
warranty deeds, 199
waste pipes, 135
water heaters, 136, 149, 211, 286
water supply pipes, 135
wells, 149
Western houses, 39
windows, 107, 120, 121, 127, 128, 139, 141, 143, 211
window wells, 129
wiring, exterior, 130, 211
wiring, interior, 134-135, 211, 287
Woodall's Mobile Home and Park Directory, 284-285
wraparound mortgages, 223

zoning:
   condominiums or cooperatives and, 265
   contracts and, 198
   expansion and, 152, 209
   maps of, 58, 106
   mobile homes and, 279-280
   new houses and, 65, 73-74, 106
   prices and, 74
   title policies and, 200